Meeting Jimmie Rodgers

How America's Original
Roots Music Hero Changed
the Pop Sounds of a Century

Meeting
Jimmie
Rodgers

Barry Mazor

OXFORD
UNIVERSITY PRESS

2009

Oxford University Press, Inc., publishes works that further
Oxford University's objective of excellence
in research, scholarship, and education.

Oxford   New York
Auckland   Cape Town   Dar es Salaam   Hong Kong   Karachi
Kuala Lumpur   Madrid   Melbourne   Mexico City   Nairobi
New Delhi   Shanghai   Taipei   Toronto

With offices in
Argentina   Austria   Brazil   Chile   Czech Republic   France   Greece
Guatemala   Hungary   Italy   Japan   Poland   Portugal   Singapore
South Korea   Switzerland   Thailand   Turkey   Ukraine   Vietnam

Copyright © 2009 by Barry Mazor

Published by Oxford University Press, Inc.
198 Madison Avenue, New York, NY 10016

www.oup.com

Library of Congress Cataloging-in-Publication Data
Mazor, Barry.
Meeting Jimmie Rodgers : how America's original roots music hero
changed the pop sounds of a century / Barry Mazor.
p. cm.
Includes bibliographical references and index.
ISBN 978-0-19-532762-5
1. Rodgers, Jimmie, 1897–1933.
2. Country musicians—United States—Biography. I. Title.
ML420.R753M39   2009
782.421642092—dc22
[B]   2008041924

1 2 3 4 5 6 7 8 9

Printed in the United States of America
on acid free paper

This book is dedicated to the musical heirs of Jimmie Rodgers,
the exponents and chroniclers who also have forwarded
his legacy—and to the evidence of your own ears

contents

Contents

Meeting Jimmie Rodgers

Louis Armstrong and Johnny Cash summon the spirit.

Introduction
Meeting Jimmie Rodgers Halfway

Nashville, October 5, 1970

The most influential, original performer in American music history pushes his way through the swinging doors of the flimsy saloon set, shedding, fast as he can manage — and that is still *fast* — the too-cute fourteen-gallon hat that someone has thought appropriate for this occasion. He grips it in one hand as he waves to the welcoming crowd at the Ryman Auditorium.

Rather dilapidated now, the "Mother Church of Country Music" will still be, for just a few more years, the home of the Grand Ole Opry. The Ryman is home also for these regular tapings of *The Johnny Cash Show* — a fresh prime-time, national TV series whose very existence is evidence of how broadly country music has spread, how far it has come, and how enwrapped with the rest of American pop music it has become by this night.

The guest is Louis Armstrong, the legendary Satchmo, in the last year of his life. He has just cut a country album, working in New York City with Johnny Cash's long-time friend, sometime record producer, and occasional songwriter, the irrepressible Cowboy Jack Clement. Jack recalls phoning the TV show's producer, suggesting that Armstrong might be a perfect, surprising fit for them — then arranging for a brass band to meet the jazz legend at the Nashville airport as he arrived in town.

From the varied numbers that appeared on that *Louis "Country and Western" Armstrong* LP, and a handful of those rehearsed for the show, Satchmo has chosen two to sing that had been introduced by African-Americans — "Crystal

Chandeliers" from the anomalous honky tonk star Charley Pride, and "Ram-blin' Rose," early '60s countrified pop from Nat King Cole. Race, it is clear enough in retrospect, is on Louis Armstrong's mind tonight. He has his reasons.

The man was not being perceived in 1970 quite the way he is known today, institutionalized for twenty-first century adults as a universal treasure, the "man who fused the sound of the blues with American popular song and taught the world to swing," as Wynton Marsalis put it in Ken Burns' widely seen 2001 documentary series *Jazz*. Louis is nevertheless often recalled by younger twenty-first century audiences merely as a gravelly-voiced guy who sang "What a Wonderful World" in movies and commercials.

In 1970, Armstrong is an utterly familiar pop star, everywhere, but intel-lectuals and some blatantly political latter-day jazz practitioners are regu-larly accusing him of being a clowning, mugging Uncle Tom who kowtows to white audiences too much to win their favor—as if he did not behave exactly the same way with black audiences; as if this powerful desire and aptitude for pleasing whatever audience was in front of him was not the very basis of success in the variety shows and honky tonk dives in which he had started; as if, for all of the art, this were not still show business.

"I never did fit in too well, with the folks you know," he sings to the over-whelmingly white Cash show audience, more pointedly, more sternly than Charley Pride has ever dared sing that opening of "Crystal Chandeliers." "It was plain to see, that the likes of me didn't fit with you." No one in the auditorium—a place in which Armstrong had given a concert in 1957 with enforced racially segregated seating—is noticeably offended.

And so, yes, race is on Mr. Armstrong's mind in this time and place: 1970 in Nashville, Tennessee.

The program's producer and writer, Stan Jacobson, had had doubts about having Louis on the show at all. Today, almost forty years after the broadcast, he recalls that doing so felt like more of the "sore point" booking that ABC and Columbia Pictures TV was forcing on him—jazzier, more swinging art-ists like Ray Charles, and even Liza Minnelli, whom he saw as all wrong for the Cash show. Among those Jacobson found right for the show at the time were the Monkees, Lorne Greene of *Bonanza*, Neil Diamond, and Burl Ives. But as for jazz and Broadway, *those* sounds were too foreign, too lacking in roots credibility to relate to 1970 country music. Bringing them in, he believes to this day, would have "caused the audience to lose faith in Johnny."

What changed Jacobson's mind in the case of Louis Armstrong was the surprising "discovery" that in Hollywood, California, in the summer of 1930, Armstrong had done a session with the country pioneer Jimmie Rod-gers. Over the course of two weeks, Jimmie had recorded everything from minstrel blackface sketches to Hawaiian-inflected pop, Bing Crosby–style ballads, vaudeville shuffles, hard blues, a gun-toting, macho, sex-laden Prohibition-era gangster boast—and more than a few songs about trains. On the next to last day of those sessions, he collaborated with Armstrong on "Blue Yodel No. 9," which, forty years later, became Louie's safe passage ticket to the *Johnny Cash Show*.

"We did a little research on some of your recordings," Johnny Cash says, on screen, after bringing Louis over to the ersatz "country living room" set. "We find that on July sixteenth, 1930, you played trumpet on a session with the late Jimmie Rodgers, the father of country music. What I would love to do is kind of recreate that recording session; I'll try to sing Jimmie Rodgers' lyrics, and you wail like you did on the record. Can we do that?"

And Louis responds: "We'll see. Let's give it to them—in black and white." Which they proceed to do.

Famous for dying young, still fighting to record with his last tubercular breaths, their subject, take note, is still referred to as "the *late* Jimmie Rodgers," thirty-seven years after his death. Not even a basic, one-line identifying bio is deemed necessary by the show's producer and writers at this point. There had already been *Johnny Cash Show* episodes in which Johnny related Jimmie's history, and Merle Haggard had sung duets with Johnny on Rodgers songs that were appearing on his brand-new Jimmie salute album, *Same Train, A Different Time*. Merle had also performed "Nobody Knows But Me" with a full arm-garter-sporting Dixieland band the previous May, the "too jazzy" rule apparently not applying there. Honky tonk hero Hank Snow had sung "Jimmie's Texas Blues" on the show and would return later with "Train Whistle Blues." John Hartford had raced through Jimmie's "Mule Skinner Blues" in a salute to the 1940 Bill Monroe version—the one that had propelled the birth of bluegrass—even as Dolly Parton's new version of the number was climbing the 1970 country charts. Folksinger Ramblin' Jack Elliott, who some years earlier had recorded an LP mixing a half-dozen Rodgers songs with others by Woody Guthrie, had appeared on the show too—his first prime-time network appearance in decades of performing. While Elliott's one-time folk protégé Bob Dylan did not feature Rodgers songs on his series-opening appearance, he had traded Rodgers blue yodel verses with Cash at the Nashville recording session that was the prelude to the TV appearance. For that matter, Johnny had already celebrated Jimmie in the regular "Come and Ride This Train" segment of the program and would add another salute the following year, as part of a special episode on country music history.

Johnny Cash does not feel the need to spell out who exactly this Jimmie Rodgers was to the general national audience he is reaching, this night in 1970, but not so long before it had been a very different story. In 1962, despite being in one of the dips in his up-and-down career, Cash had a minor hit with a version of Jimmie's "In the Jailhouse Now" and filled New York's Carnegie Hall with Cash-loving country fans. By his own account, Johnny Cash was then "obsessed" with Jimmie Rodgers' music and image and was collecting a considerable array of related memorabilia. A letter he had written to Jimmie's daughter, Anita, inviting her to the Carnegie Hall show, detailed his efforts to complete the redecoration of the Cash family's California den in a style that might be described as Late Rodgers Renaissance — complete with framed photos, handbills, Jimmie's personal effects, a couple of "tapestries," and one of his hero's own brakeman's lamps hanging from the ceiling. (He had been, he reported, "giving train signals to the neighbors, down in the little town below. No kidding, it really works great, just like new. Caused a lot of train crashes.")

Johnny was also attempting to produce a movie in which he would play Jimmie, to show the world beyond country music his story and to inhabit his persona on screen. The letter is filled with almost frantic pleas for more scrapbook material, clippings, and personal correspondence, more photos, any old interviews. He had been collecting Rodgers stories from Maybelle Carter, Gene Autry, and Ernest Tubb, and he had come up with what seemed a clever idea — to wear Jimmie's actual Singing Brakeman stage outfit onstage at Carnegie Hall, with only that original lantern for lighting, presenting a program exclusively of Jimmie Rodgers songs, in character. The suit had been a gift from Anita's mom, Carrie, Mrs. Jimmie Rodgers herself, as had a satchel in which Cash was then keeping all of his newly written songs, a sample of the kind of bequests with which Carrie had been giving her stamp of approval to selected country singers for years.

But in 1962 that New York audience of Cash fans had not gotten the visual references to Jimmie, or their connection to Johnny, at all. The Carnegie Hall crowd's devastating silence, Johnny would recall much later, was broken only by shouts for his own hits.

The way people viewed Johnny Cash at the time of the 1970 TV duet with Armstrong is not quite how he is most often depicted and understood today. He was decidedly not the singularly cool man of country, the supposed dark and dangerous first cousin to Nine Inch Nails, Soundgarden, and gangsta rappers, not quite the iconic, long-suffering, "man in black" then, either. Cash was at a peak of general popular success, especially with settled adults. He was about to make the on-air testament of personal faith and salvation that would lead to much time working with Billy Graham, the LP *In the Holy Land* (with its 3-D cover), and a reformed, evangelizing sort of public face that would lead the hipster rock critic Nick Tosches to ridicule him as "offensively pious" and "particularly tedious."

Meeting Jimmie Rodgers

But tonight's Ryman and TV audience is quite ready for the duet by *that* Johnny and this Louis Armstrong. Jazz historians had been suggesting that Louis did not even remember the Rodgers session, and had no reason to since it only involved that low hillbilly music anyway. For them, his on-air comments should have been revealing, but his off-air remarks were even more so.

"I'd been knowing Jimmie for a *long* time," Armstrong tells Cash on screen. "We met one morning, and he said 'Man, would you like to sing some blues with me?' And I said, 'Okay, daddy; sing some blues, and I'm gonna play behind you'—and that's the way the record started, you know."

Among the effects discovered in Johnny Cash's vast private audio collection since his death, unheard by the public, is a backstage rehearsal tape in which Johnny and Louis work out this very TV performance. Much of the talk is about when the trumpet starts, when Johnny should come in—about timing. Louis tells Cash precisely when to come in. "That's the way it was written; that's the way *Jimmie* did it," he tosses in, thereby answering any questions about his memory of what had happened in 1930.

In rehearsal, that unmistakable voicelike, beacon-in-the-dark tone of Armstrong's trumpet at first fills the space between Cash's lines, but Louis keeps loosening the rhythm further, pushing Johnny to a place far from the patented, locked-in Tennessee Two beat.

By the time they are making their third try at the opening, after a sobbing Armstrong solo, Cash starts to reach for surprising one-time-only blues notes and finds them, plays with the music, plays in ways he's never been heard doing on record at all. Johnny Cash may rock, swagger, and shuffle, and he always gets his stories told; but right here, uplifted, he *swings*, as if he were Merle or Lefty Frizzell—or Jimmie Rodgers.

Now Johnny invites Armstrong to do something he never did on the original record—to join him on Rodgers' end-of-verse yodels, at first, in this rehearsal, even using Jimmie's original "yodel-AY-dee-o" style.

On air, Cash is not quite as loose as he had been in that moment, but he is certainly looser than usual. The lyrics of the song underscore the special connection to Jimmie Rodgers, the song maker: "Standing on the corner," Cash belts, "I didn't mean no harm; along comes a PO-lice—and takes me by the arm."

In 1970, that might have been taken for a line Jimmie Rodgers wrote, or one more fragment lifted from floating blues verses of unknown origin, from some anonymous wandering minstrel, reaching Jimmie by that famously mysterious "folk process" of oral transmission. By now, however, diligent research into African-American music history by Lynn Abbott and Doug Serroff has uncovered the author of that line, one George Evans. It is from his 1894 song "Standing on the Corner, Didn't Mean No Harm," which was picked up by professional blackface minstrel outfits, then ragtime piano players. It had even worked its way, no doubt by simple theft, into the structure and melody of "You've Been a Good Old Wagon, But You've Done Broke Down," a song eventually recorded by Bessie Smith. In fact, when recording the number "The Bridwell Blues" with the dimly recalled barrelhouse singer Nolan Welsh in Chicago in 1926, Armstrong, Bessie's sometime accompanist, had used essentially the same "Standing on the Corner" first verse. All of these were out in circulation before Jimmie used the line in this song they were recording.

Jimmie also reused narrative ideas he had recorded in his own lasting version of "Frankie and Johnny," in the verse about the woman showing up with a .44 pistol, raging for revenge. Cash now sings that verse, too; he had already had a hit himself with an updated reading of Jimmie's version of the much-traveled nineteenth-century ballad.

But it is not, in the long run, the words that matter most on the Johnny Cash–Louis Armstrong recreation of the 1930 duet; it is that broadcast moment when they get to the yodel. Cash brings all of the ego and pugnacity and sheer energy Jimmie had to the "yodel-ay-dee, yodel-ay-hee hee"; and Armstrong joins him, not with a matching yodel, but with his own joyous, gravelly, patented "Oh, yeah-ahzzzz." We are privileged to witness these two hyperarticulate nonverbal moans blending into the sound of American music calling across time, out from the Ryman, from TV Land to our house.

In that moment, in that sound, there came Jimmie Rodgers—the transcendent entertainer who understood his audience, understood them not by what he learned or heard *about* them, but by what he shared with them, elementally. Armstrong and Cash had, together, summoned up the innovator who had injected his own wit, rhythm, sexuality, ego, aggression, and love of performing itself into the bloodstream of most every sort of popular American music that might be called "rooted." Whether that music would, over time, come to be labeled country, rock and roll, bluegrass, blues, western, jazz, or American pop, wherever there was space for music of the body and heart, not just of the spirit and the head, Jimmie Rodgers would be there.

If we put on a Jimmie Rodgers record today—and they are all in circulation—experiencing his music directly, without baggage, can seem difficult; we have to make that connection despite time, despite changing fashion, despite countless interpretations since his day exerting their force on how we understand it. Time can be estranging, things can be missed, and the very power of the musical variations Jimmie Rodgers' music has spawned

Meeting Jimmie Rodgers

has, by now, changed our notions of what's "hot" or "cool" or "cheesy" or "edgy" or "smart."

The elements Jimmie Rodgers and his many disciples introduced into the popular music we hear in the twenty-first century are so embedded in our cultural DNA that Jimmie's musical proximity can be obscured. Tracking and reuniting eighty years' worth of the scattered, mutant sequences of that cultural DNA may serve to reconstruct Jimmie Rodgers as the contemporary he is, live and whole and ready simply to be heard. It would be a summoning not unlike that accomplished by the Man in Black and Satchmo on that night in 1970, now as many years distant from us as they were from Jimmie's day—halfway back to Jimmie, halfway home.

Select Soundtrack

- **Jimmie Rodgers, with Louis Armstrong and Lil Hardin:** "Blue Yodel No. 9" (Victor, July 16, 1930).

- **Louis Armstrong:** *Louis "Country and Western" Armstrong* (Avco-Embassy Records LP, 1970; out of print).

- **Louis Armstrong and Johnny Cash:** "Blue Yodel No. 9," video as broadcast October 1970, ABC TV. The video duet itself became commercially available on the DVD compilation *The Best of the Johnny Cash TV Show* (Columbia Music Video, 2007).

Florida, 1925: Above, Jimmie, in his natural habitat, a pool hall/barber shop—and with his mandolin, at lower right, in a traveling show hawking DyanShine boot polish.

one

The Man Who Walked into Southern Show Business

We are dealing with a mystery, a mystery about continuing, transforming power. How could a man who performed so briefly, more than seventy-five years ago, have produced tones, tunes, and themes that have attracted and moved so many people for so long? How did he happen, in that short span, to originate the path for "up from down home" American roots music stardom? How did he become the very model for the way American roots music stars could rise to the level of popular heroes ever since—for Hank Williams, for Johnny Cash, for Elvis Presley and, very likely, for somebody new showing up on your music playlist of choice today?

How could an unwealthy, unhealthy, untrained man seemingly from nowhere create a musical legacy so sturdy and broadly understandable that, as we will see, it has worked its way across the globe? What is it in what he did and the music he made that has caused him to be claimed as "one of us" by schools of American popular music that seem to inhabit different worlds, speaking different languages to mutually exclusive audiences? Jimmie Rodgers is acknowledged as a defining, essential artist by the Country Music Hall of Fame, the Rock and Roll Hall of Fame, the American Songwriters Hall of Fame, the Blues Hall of Fame, and by the musical shrines, museums, and governors of several American states. He has been a source for both '30s showband tunes by the Jack Hylton Orchestra and Lonnie Donegan's '50s skiffle in central London—and for pop cowboy tunes from Sammy Ngako in central Africa. Seventy-five years after his passing, you can find Jimmie

Rodgers claimed as a source of personal inspiration by anyone from a shy, buttoned-down, upright bluegrass picker to a leather-clad psychobilly shock rocker—and both would have their reasons.

With this abundance of acceptance, Jimmie has been identified from his day to ours by a string of avatar-style nicknames as varied as those of the Greek gods—or, somewhat more recently, of that "Hardest-Working Man in Show Business/Soul Brother Number One/Mr. Dynamite," James Brown. He was regularly tagged, if not exactly identified, as the "Singing Brakeman," but you are not alone if you can not say precisely what a brakeman did for a living, or what it meant to his audiences that this singer had been one. He is "America's Blue Yodeler," but, almost from the instant in 1927 that his music first got onto records, appreciation for him was never much hampered by national borders. The "blue" references his connection to Mississippi blues and to hot, syncopated African-American sounds in general—daring and thrillingly new for much of his audience. It also hints at the suggestive, sexual aspect of what his audiences took to be "blue," as in "blue humor," and better still, to be, in that ever-so-loaded American term, "racy." Yet "yodeler" evokes a vocal gargling art that does not suggest a sexy matinee idol to most audiences today, or anything even remotely hep, hip, or hip-hop.

This man Rodgers is also quite often, perhaps most often now, referred to as the "Father of Country Music." Yet there is no evidence that he ever thought of himself as merely some sort of niche genre singer, and he died unaware that he would be deemed pivotal for something called "country music."

So who was this performer who could be so many things for so many?

For decades after his death in 1933, even the most basic facts about Jimmie Rodgers' life before stardom were obscured by many misleading tales about his background, his intentions, and his habits. The truth as we know it today was first seriously researched and brought together in clarifying detail in the late '70s.

James Charles Rodgers was born on September 8, 1897, in Pine Springs, Mississippi, not far from the rising railroad town of Meridian, an increasingly commercial, middle-class hub. His mother died before he was six years old, and his father, Aaron, was often away from home working as a railroad track maintenance and repair "section foreman." Without parents to restrict him, Jimmie led a sort of Huck Finn life in derby-hatted, pre–World War I Meridian, free to explore the young man's playground of barber shops, pool halls, and theaters, and to hobnob with the fast-talking salesmen, politicos, sportsmen, and gamblers that frequented them. He relished the silent cowboy movies of the Bronco Billy Anderson era, the trashy new magazines and newspapers, the wax cylinder recordings of ragtime songs, the passing medicine shows, and the "tent rep" traveling theatrical productions.

Under circus-style canvas tents, these theater companies journeyed all across the country and were now bringing, even into culturally conservative southern towns, sentimental melodramas of life's misfortunes and perilously sexual enticements, especially as seen in the interplay between rural and city folks. Tent rep shows had only lately begun to combine those dramas on their playbills with the pizzazz of up-to-date vaudeville specialty acts. Live southern shows were clearly broadening their scope beyond the strictly uplifting and purportedly educational lectures about mother, home, and heaven, which had for so many years been staples of the pious and popular Chautauqua circuit.

This thrillingly varied pre–World War I popular culture, imported from the big cities via the early mass media, was central to the forming of Jimmie Rodgers' sensibility and the music he made. In the words of a Tin Pan Alley number he would perform from early in his career, and eventually persuade the famously domesticated Carter Family to join him in singing on a 1931 recording, there could be, and probably often was, "A Hot Time in the Old Town Tonight."

By the age of twelve, Jimmie had attempted to stage a tent carnival of his own, and even took it on the road locally. He won first prize in an amateur contest for singing "Steamboat Bill" and "Bill Bailey, Won't You Please Come Home," commercial Tin Pan Alley songs. Both had been on hit records, and they concerned — somewhat prophetically, given what was to come — a hero of transportation and a footloose entertainer, respectively. Soon after, he ran away from home with a medicine show, having convinced the management, based on his amateur "experience," that he was a professional performer. He was already busy picking up ample numbers of girlfriends as a traveling showman, but also found time to pick up several stringed instruments: strumming mandolin and banjo in particular and, only secondarily, guitar. At that point, with the attractions of the show business life so clear to him, his father announced that Jimmie would be coming along with him to learn a legitimate, less frivolous trade, the rail-tending section crew work that he supervised. Jimmie's show business efforts were mostly put aside for the time being.

And so, for those track workers — who especially in the South were almost exclusively black — he would sometimes be that "little water boy" of his "Mule Skinner Blues." The novice, legend has it, would learn a range of songs from those African-American railroad men, the rail-adjusting "gandy dancers," though it is far from clear exactly which songs those might have been. To his first cousin Virginia Shine Harvey, a professional songwriter herself, Jimmie did describe learning instrumental skills from those coworkers, but examples researchers have had of gandy dancers' work chants seem to be predecessors of the U.S. Army's "I don't know, but I've been told" marching drill shouts rather than any sort of popular song of the era.

As we will see, as Jimmie came to work on the trains, as a brakeman and in other capacities, and traveled between railroad jobs, hobo-style, himself, he inevitably encountered black hoboes along the way, as well as in the so-called hobo jungle encampments near the stations where hoboes of all races slept, ate, talked — and traded blues verses. But beyond these generalities, which he repeatedly discussed with interviewers in his own day, we can only speculate about what tunes Jimmie might have learned working on the railroad, whether they were blues, jug band–style folk jazz, ragtime, lowdown story song, or any other style. The very romance of the song-trading scenario may well have led to some exaggeration over the years about how many songs he learned in that place and from those amateur, some would say "folk," sources.

For the next few years he was employed in increasingly tough and challenging rail work, filling mainly short-term jobs as a flagman, a mechanic, a baggage man, and sometimes, indeed, as a brakeman, often on the run between Mississippi and New Orleans. On that musically rich run he also met and married his first wife, the eye-catching humdinger and alleged femme fatale Stella Kelley, when he was nineteen. The marriage would be short-lived, however, as Jimmie showed no signs of being able to support her in the manner in which she plainly intended to become accustomed. The couple did produce a daughter, Kathryn. For years, Jimmie would not even know of her existence, but Stella made sure to introduce father and long-lost daughter once he had achieved stardom, considerable income, and a new family.

During one of his stays back home in Meridian in 1920, Rodgers met and wed Carrie Williamson. She was the relatively innocuous daughter of a highly respectable, music-loving couple; her father was a fairly liberal, light-hearted local preacher. Carrie would alternately support Jimmie's pursuits and harangue him for his indulgences for the thirteen remaining years of his life. She was by his side from the very lean, even desperate years immediately following their marriage to the time of his recognition on the world stage and relative, if rapidly consumed, wealth. Carrie and Jimmie had two daughters: Anita, born in 1921, was a considerable focus of Jimmie's attention, heart, and, occasionally, his songs, particularly after the devastating sudden death of their second child, June Rebecca, only six months after her birth in 1923.

The Roaring Twenties, it should be recalled, hardly roared ahead with equal financial vigor everywhere; in the rural and small-town South, there were unmistakable signs of the oncoming Depression well before the 1929 stock market crash. Jimmie had a hard time finding railroad work, or any sort of work at all. In infrequent tent show appearances during this time, he would strum a banjo and feature Tin Pan Alley chestnuts like "The Man on the Flying Trapeze." To keep cash trickling in, he would often ride a train, hoboing to the end of the line, perhaps as far away as Texas, where temporary train work might be found again.

He lived in such unhealthy, unstable conditions for years, exacerbating a history of pulmonary illnesses that went back to age fifteen. In 1924, a weakened Jimmie was diagnosed with tuberculosis, a disease that was then quite common, widespread, and often fatal. Since his family members were fearful of infection, there were times Jimmie resided in a sanitarium, even when back in Meridian.

He never stayed in any sanitarium for long. To the characteristic wanderlust he had always demonstrated and to that constant search for work were added frequent trips made in hopes of aiding his own recuperation. Jimmie would take off to places, with or without the family, following the accepted (but, in fact, mistaken) medical wisdom that dry or high places were best for recovering—first west to Arizona, then northeast to the resort town of Asheville, North Carolina.

As time went on, he increasingly sought work as an entertainer, the work he had always favored, and which was his only real alternative to the train jobs so detrimental to his health. Out West, his railway bosses had started to complain about the time off he was taking to perform here and there, and yet he didn't really know how to turn show business into a full-time career. For a spell, he led a jazzy, pop-oriented working act that included horns in the band and Carrie's sister, Elsie McWilliams, at the piano. At dances just outside of Meridian, the group would play Charleston numbers like Gene Austin's "Why Do You Do Me Like You Do Do Do?" Rest, the one treatment likely to extend the life of a T.B. sufferer at the time, Jimmie would neither find nor pursue. His musical career was about to take hold.

Early in 1927, while working odd jobs in Asheville and performing briefly with some local musical acts, he met the Grant Brothers, the hard-driving core of an Eastern mountain-style string band, the Tenneva Ramblers. Jimmie talked his way into becoming their lead singer, and newly dubbed the Jimmie Rodgers Entertainers, the group performed at dances and made some well-received radio appearances over the ensuing months. They heard of a call from a Victor Records executive who was recording new talent in the Tennessee/Virginia border town of Bristol, the Grants' home territory, and headed there. At Bristol, that record executive, Ralph Peer, separated Jimmie and his Entertainers, recognizing them as two very different sorts of acts.

At those now-famed Bristol sessions, the once-again solo Jimmie recorded two songs with guitar for Peer on August 4, 1927. This recording of an old lullaby and a freshly concocted, vaguely antiwar song about a young woman's loss of her soldier sweetheart did not have the instant life-changing effect Jimmie had hoped for. It did not even elicit the excited response from Victor that he had expected. So, in November, Jimmie took Carrie to New York City, checked into a fine hotel, went to the label's offices, and announced that he was ready for his next big session. Peer was so impressed with the sheer boldness of the demand that he set up a session for just a few days later, down at Victor's studios in Camden, New Jersey. It was there, on the last day of the month, that Jimmie Rodgers of Meridian, Mississippi, recorded the tough, suggestive, even murderous twelve-bar blues he had been saving up for this moment. "T for Texas" featured infectious, propulsive guitar runs and surprising, audience-pleasing line-ending "oh-de-lay" yodels; Peer duly retitled the song "Blue Yodel." It was an immediate smash. In that day, sales figures were tightly guarded, and those that were announced were often exaggerated for effect but, by some informed estimates, "Blue Yodel" sold a million copies—indisputably many hundreds of thousands. Jimmie Rodgers was suddenly, in an instant, among the top recording stars of his day.

According to Carrie's memoir, she had begged him, and begged producer Ralph Peer, too, to record that breakthrough blue yodel at the first session at Bristol, but Jimmie had held the song back. Thinking strategically, he had figured that some decision-makers would find the lyric about "poor Thelma," whom the singer casually informs us he has shot "just to see her jump and crawl," a bit too rough—distracting attention from his singing qualities and solo instrumental fills, the talents he wanted to make sure they noticed.

Vocally, Jimmie could hardly have been mistaken for any of the acts that were under contract at Victor Records, or other important record labels, in 1927. Yet, from the first, he showed himself to be a performer of his time, absorbing into his singing, whether consciously or not, elements from a wide range of sources. Jimmie had a substantial record collection, Carrie later told us in her memoir, no doubt including popular hits and jazzy blues that he had studied and analyzed in detail. She reported specifically that he had not been very fond of much material then being put out for the fledgling hillbilly market.

His own singing on-mike was loose and comfortable, closely akin to the way he spoke. At times it was nearly conversational, and he would take it further, breaking in with spoken asides of the "Play it, boy!" variety. His style contrasted sharply with the old school, declamatory style of vocalizing that was still holding on in pop operetta, early Broadway shows, and revues but was rapidly being washed away in popular recordings. A growing number of record buyers, and, at the same time, of radio and sound film audiences, too, looked for something that seemed to stem more directly from the American vernacular—and that sounded more intimate, not designed to be boomed across a concert hall.

A technology-driven vocal revolution was taking place, and Jimmie was not alone in offering this new lower-key style. The better of the contemporary white crooners were singing "relaxed American" as well, singers like Nick Lucas, "Ukulele Ike" (Cliff Edwards, later known as the voice of Jiminy Cricket), and Rodgers' friend-to-be Gene Austin. Those hit-makers, too, knew how to sing into the microphone with intimacy in their phrasing. They knew, to some degree, the musical traditions and "heart songs" left over from the minstrel show and early parlor song publishing days. And, like Jimmie, they could add distinctive, vaudeville-derived idiosyncrasies and gimmicks to their vocal lines. None of those pop singers, though, happened to use yodels, or train whistle noises, or, more importantly, had digested as well as Jimmie had the sounds and attitudes from the growing professional and amateur blues world.

Jimmie differed crucially from those other raccoon-coat-era pop stars in that vocally, you always knew literally where he was coming from. The speech from which his singing extended was Mississippi speech, not just in references, but also in sound. On record, his accent is particularly light, sweet, and most of all present—not diluted or eradicated. In popular music, a legitimate, place-derived accent would be basic to the very notion of "rootedness"; and a rooted pop star Jimmie would be. When in "T for Texas" he rather charmingly loses a few middle-of-the-word r's to rhyme a very liquid *barrel* with *gal*, you can no more miss that Jimmie Rodgers is from the humid, small-town Deep South than you could miss that Paul Simon was a guy from urban New York when he dropped a final r to rhyme "naked light I saw" with a jagged "maybe more" on a hit of forty years later.

The contents of Jimmie's lyrics, tied to his own history, his home region, and his working-class experiences, were also fundamentally different from those of his competitors in the middle-class-oriented pop market. His chosen references were important in that they spoke directly to the traditional, downhome, downscale segment of his audience, even as he sought broad popular appeal. You will not find his less-rooted competitors fitting mentions of *lard* into their songs. From that starting point, defined as much by who he was as what he was aiming to be, began the making of a pop roots music performer.

Perhaps most important, Rodgers' performing style was about emotional immediacy. He sang the lyrics of a song—whether tough or sentimental, comic or sad, narrative or mood evoking—according to the meanings of the lines and verses, communicating the drama of the story as it unfolded, word by word. This set him apart from most all pre-Bristol southern rural singers, and from most of the acts recorded at those celebrated sessions themselves.

Southern rural singers generally came out of church, ballad-singing, and fiddle band traditions in which singing the set meter of a song was preferred to any dramatic interpretation of the lyrics. In these stylistic traditions, a singer virtually never "broke" a line just to emphasize some point or moment in the narrative. In addition, those same early hillbilly acts were often uncomfortable in the newfangled recording situation, which resulted, in many cases, in the sort of stiff, affectless singing that Greil Marcus would famously describe as the sound of an "old, weird America." It was that lack of narrative drama and emotional clarity that Jimmie would tell his wife he so disliked about many of those early hillbilly records, not their regional references. His own records would sound very different.

In his 1974 overview of great, innovative American popular singers, the classically-trained jazz enthusiast and musicologist Henry Pleasants considered Jimmie Rodgers in the same terms as Bing Crosby and Ella Fitzgerald, Frank Sinatra and Nat King Cole, and compared his ability to sing "wistfully" to that of Billie Holiday, Judy Garland, Édith Piaf, and Hank Williams. Pleasants also singled out Rodgers' speech-derived singing for special comment. Jimmie's "range is short," he elaborated, "hardly more than an octave and a third," but he praised Jimmie's ability to swoop beyond that range with his falsetto yodels, staying on pitch through the leaps. "What grew on me was not so much the voice as what was being done with it—the phrasing, the coloring, the gentle slurring, the lightest and briefest of grace notes. Jimmie wanted the listener to get not only the words in the story they told, but also the feel of the story, [and to do so he would take] rhythmic liberties that are the very essence of *jazz*."

More recently, in contrasting Jimmie's vocals to those of others captured in the Bristol sessions, music analyst and theorist Thomas Townsend found that in his approach to "The Soldier's Sweetheart" and "Sleep Baby Sleep," "in addition to employing an ornamented singing style, Rodgers incorporated drama by altering the melody slightly as the song unfolded, overriding the predictable repetitions typical to the traditional old-time style. In fact, Rodgers never sang any two verses with exactly the same melodic line." In general, Townsend added, "Rodgers frustrates expectations of a cyclic pattern, upsetting listener expectations," generating real drama and, he concluded, beginning the altering of what would be the country music vocabulary, right there, on his very first sides.

Roy Acuff, the "King of Country," who expressed decidedly mixed feelings about Jimmie Rodgers and his music throughout his own storied career, commented succinctly on Jimmie's vocal impact in country music: "I think Jimmie was the first one on record that ever really went *commercial* with voice." In this 1972 conversation with the historian (and latter-day singing cowboy) Doug Green, Roy was addressing two of Jimmie's innovations: his refocusing of what is important when you sing—bringing the emotional heart of the song home to the audience, not just relating the words of the story—and his putting the solitary singer up in front of the group. It would take some time for the Grand Ole Opry, with singing stars such as Acuff himself, to feature acts that would do both.

From Jimmie's day to this, you can encounter listeners and players who take him to task for some of these very musical attributes—going "off rhythm," adding a syllable, or inserting an instrumental phrase—often with the suggestion that he did not know how to sing and play the song straight ahead. These sorts of critiques tend to emanate from journeyman dance band, ensemble-oriented players—sidemen in Texas swing bands, or pyrotechnic-picking-oriented bluegrass bands, for example. Of course, you could find precisely the same sort of griping about Jimi Hendrix and Charlie Parker as instrumentalists, or about unpredictable singers from Mac Wiseman to Bob Dylan, in interviews with backup band members who did not understand what the groove-breakers were up to.

Nobody puts Jimmie Rodgers' guitar playing, his instrumental focus once he turned to recording, in the class of the instrumental innovation of Hendrix or Parker. He did, however, introduce surprisingly bold flat-picking chords and runs in both his occasional longer breaks—see the original recording of "Blue Yodel No. 8 (Mule Skinner Blues)," for instance—and, most characteristically, between lines, verses, and phrases, inserted and used for emphasis, much like his yodels.

Doc Watson, one of the most subtle and most envied of acoustic flat-picking guitar players, responds today to such critiques of Jimmie's sense of time: "Jim played the best he could, because he hadn't studied music and timing . . . but I'll put it this way: some of the first guitar licks I learned were what he was doing. I may have added a few more notes in the runs, but I loved what he was doing with the guitar. He wasn't a Chet [Atkins], or somebody like that, but he played *what* he played and he played it well. His funny way of putting a bunch of chords in, in certain songs, even between the lines sometimes, which he'd then get back on, to sing and pick—I kind of liked that. He was one of the fellahs who laid down some groundwork in guitar playing; most people never realize that—those basic runs and things, and also some of the things he did later in his career—because he got better, you know, on the guitar."

And there are some telling 2007 comments on Rodgers' sense of time from Hoyt "Slim" Bryant, too. Back in the day, Slim himself added sophisticated, jazz-influenced, Eddie Lang–like single note guitar runs to some of Jimmie's best records, including the lush "Miss the Mississippi and You," the vaudeville-like "Peach Pickin' Time Down in Georgia," and the proto-country "No Hard Times." Slim also served as a sort of translator between Jimmie and chart-bound, trained orchestral players during a 1932 session in New York. At age one hundred as these words are written, he still plays, the last one known to be with us who played with Jimmie Rodgers.

"As a guitar player," Slim says, Jimmie did well what he did. If you heard him strum just a few bars before he started to sing, you'd know it was *him*, and when he started to sing, he did it in his own way. If you had played with him a little bit, you would look out for that. I wouldn't say it was a disadvantage to him [his timing], because it was his style. If he wanted to stick in an extra bar or something—which he did—then you had to be conscious of that, and play along with him. I've backed up some of the better musicians and singers—and what you do is, you go with *them*. If he sticks in an extra two beats or something, you'd just better be in there with him."

So Jimmie Rodgers showed up at recording studios, plucked from obscurity, with considerable, identifiable, usefully idiosyncratic performing talents. But an inventory of his skills no more explains the breadth of his impact than do the details of his early life. What we need to explore is how Jimmie Rodgers came to be understood as he was by both his listeners and his many admiring interpreters. What chords did he strike that kept on striking? What did he seem to them to be and say? What, in short, did they see in him that would make him a prototypical pop roots music star and, for many, even a hero?

The modern concept of popular stardom was just taking hold at the time Rodgers reached his public. Systems of mass communication were swiftly developing that would enable a Charles Lindbergh, a Babe Ruth, a Rudolph Valentino, or an Albert Einstein to become famous in ways in which nobody had ever been famous before; they could become household names. For one thing, with newsreels, newspaper and magazine photos, movie appearances, and faster travel that made possible more, better-publicized live shows, you could *see* them.

Almost every description of Jimmie Rodgers given by those who knew him or simply saw him perform mentions his star-quality, how people's attention inevitably went right to him. Rodgers' personal electricity and even sex appeal may puzzle some as they encounter his old photos, here in another

Meeting Jimmie Rodgers

century. Clearly, a good deal of that power was based on his winning, grinning, backslapping charm, but he was sharp and even-featured enough to be considered attractive in his day. Especially when photographed with the right hat, he seemed just the sort of laid-back, smirking type that was considered rakish and sexy through the early '30s. Think Fred Astaire or even Bing Crosby—and Jimmie was a southern variation, at that.

Scarce photos of Jimmie in his natural state—small and frail, balding and with studious-looking glasses—such as the early shots taken with the Entertainers, show that his more familiar hail-fellow-well-met photos, let alone any that suggest a rougher and rowdier side, required some preparation. Jimmie paired the instincts of a showman with an understanding of the newfound importance of public image and the benefits of being able to take on and adjust to a variety of roles. He would deliberately add to the array of nicknames he was given still more popular images with which to face the public: a bowler-hatted, man-about-town rounder; a decked-out cowboy; a working stiff; a wealthy, successful recording star; and more. As both Frosty the Snowman and the actor–film director and country star Dwight Yoakam found out, there can be some very useful mojo in donning the right hat.

Jimmie Rodgers showed remarkable ease and interest in moving through an array of public images and sounds. This protean, shape shifting quality, and the ways it could be put to work, would be marks of pop superstars decades later. For Johnny Cash, there would be a series of themed "working man" or "cowboy" or "prison-bound" albums. For Elvis Presley, there would be movies that placed him in the very settings created in Rodgers records—from the jailhouse, to the army, to New Orleans, Hawaii, and beyond. Eventually, there would be the virtually album-by-album visual and aural makeover of Bob Dylan—or even, if you will, David Bowie. But these transformations for novelty and appeal were working for and tested by Jimmie Rodgers *then*.

The multiple hats he donned were precisely right for the time, and surely deliberately so. There is a telling scene in a popular, classic comedy shot in fledgling Hollywood just as Jimmie arrived at Bristol to record—Buster Keaton's *Steamboat Bill, Junior.* In fact, the entire film works as an excellent introduction to the transitional, volatile world in which Jimmie Rodgers succeeded. The hero's girlfriend is a flapper in a fast new roadster, but his dad is still a working steamboat captain—named, of course, for "Steamboat Bill," the hero of the very song Jimmie first sang in public.

In a sequence of particular interest to us, Keaton, as the ukulele-playing, duded-up, overurbanized, northern-educated Junior, has been taken to find a replacement for the beret his dad will not abide; he looks for headgear that will be more fitting back home down here in Mississippi. So Junior checks out a series of alternatives—a cap with a big visor, a straw boater, a derby, a cowboy hat, a rakish Panama—a collection that might accurately be labeled "image-building headgear of Jimmie Rodgers in review."

The culturally estranged father and son in the film find common ground when Dad lands in the jailhouse (now) and the son attempts to spring him—while singing the most well-known part of the early country music hit "The Prisoner Song," the part that goes "If I had the wings of an angel." (The lyrics have been conveniently posted on the wall outside the cell so we can watch Keaton sing along with them in silence!) Steamboat Bill and Junior will soon be brought back together by a natural disaster, a tornado in which no sports car or steamboat is spared. Jimmie Rodgers' career takes hold in that starkly transitional time and place, where the distance between rural subsistence and living securely, in style, and with full modern conveniences is not great—and new middle-class security flimsy enough that a single act of nature can blow it away.

Keaton, like Rodgers, a vaudevillian with a great fondness for trains, as was well demonstrated in several famed feature films, built his basic world-beloved character on two attributes—stoic resilience and surprising reserves of inventiveness in the face of real trouble. Keaton had his own whistling past the graveyard sensibility. One dark comedy short ended with him dead, his most celebrated, characteristic hat, the flattened porkpie, left on his grave-stone, a cold-blooded image that always evokes a final laugh. It certainly invites comparison with such startling, vivid, wisecracking descriptions of death by tuberculosis in Rodgers' songs as "they plant you in the ground" and "put you on your back and throw that mud down in your face."

It would be oversimplifying matters—and underestimating Jimmie Rodgers' potential impact with audiences—simply to note that he could be Keaton-like. His music and image were just as readily comparable to the other two great silent clowns of that time, Charlie Chaplin and Harold Lloyd.

There are certainly enough songs about hoboes and lonesome wanderers in Jimmie Rodgers' repertoire (and derived from experience, at that), to evoke Chaplin's "Little Tramp," the down-and-out, often homeless, yet resilient outsider. There is the undiluted sentiment in Rodgers' story songs to evoke a sentimental Chaplin masterpiece such as *The Kid* as well.

And yet, as stardom struck, Jimmie would show himself to be, in image and song, *also* an ambitious, sometimes cocky, small city up-and-comer, a man who went for big cars and big houses—and let you know he owned them. That was precisely the screen persona of the young American go-getter, and eventual real-life multimillionaire and Shriner potentate, Harold Lloyd. Rodgers, too, would happily be made an honorary Shriner and Texas Ranger in real life, and in those photos where he has his glasses on, he even looks like the very comfortable Lloyd.

These were three differentiated, competing personas with which three world-class movie comics competed against each other, each winning affection and acclaim and building a celebrated career. It says much about the potential universality of Jimmie Rodgers that in him we can easily detect the themes and attributes of all three at once. Casual, natural-seeming inclusiveness, even of traits that can seem outright contradictory, is a special and unusual capability, but Jimmie Rodgers had it. The way he made use of it would have consequences for his acceptance by audiences and by other performers, both in his day and in ours. Yet a musical performer's sheer range, inclusiveness, and adaptability did not—and do not—automatically make for lasting impact and broad acceptance.

Consider Jimmie's contemporary Carson Robison, a singer of considerable talent and charm, who knew how to genre-hop but never achieved Jimmie's level of traction. Robison recorded "old southern favorite plantation ballads," then moved on to pop, blues, and jazz, adapted himself to '40s cowboy harmonies in the style of the Sons of the Pioneers, and lived long enough to take stabs at rock 'n' roll. But he never was closely associated, in fact or in the public imagination, with the lifestyles and history implied by any of those genres and never discovered a strongly identifiable vocal or instrumental style to bring to them. No one would say of any later singer, "Boy, he reminds me of Carson Robison."

Jimmie Rodgers was a man who tended to say "yes" to opportunities, and he had an unmistakable style to imprint on everything he sang. But he was not working to become a pop everyman for everybody. There were places his sensibility, his style, and his song content could not appropriately go, and he was more effective with his audiences for knowing it. This trainman knew where to get off.

Crooner Gene Austin was southern-raised like Jimmie and had been, by all measures, poorer to begin with. Then, from the mid-'20s through the early '30s, he had enormous popular success with his records of "My Blue Heaven" and the self-penned "(Look Down That) Lonesome Road." By all reports, Austin certainly drank as much as and probably substantially more than Jimmie did and appears to have had more fleeting amorous adventures than Jimmie ever did. When Jimmie was away from home without explanation, as would often be the case, "I was out with Gene Austin" was, according to a bemused Gene himself, a regular cover story that he offered to Mrs. Rodgers.

Parts of each man's repertoire were interchangeable: Austin's hit "Carolina Moon" and Jimmie's "Mississippi Moon," or Austin's "Yes Sir, That's My Baby" and Jimmie's "My Blue-Eyed Jane" bore easy comparison, as did, thematically at least, Austin's suburban smash "My Blue Heaven" and

Jimmie's atypically domestic "Home Call." All of these songs were contemporary pop, but their makers' careers and audiences were tellingly different.

Though quite often explicitly southern, Austin's songs consistently referenced the modern world of the New South, tending to target a more urban, increasingly upscale audience. Once Gene Austin hit it big with those golf sweater audiences across the country and had opportunities to work in the movies singing and appearing with Mae West and to explore other enticing mainstream endeavors, he virtually never looked back. He had headed uptown as fast as he could and stayed there, performing from the early '20s until his death in 1969, most familiarly in top hat and tails.

Jimmie was by no means antimodern or antiurban, as many in country music would eventually be, but his own sounds and lyrics remained varied enough and determinedly rooted enough that they never cut him off from where he had come from, or from whom he had been. The folks back home were not forgotten, never became "them" to him, no matter how high he would rise. As adventurous as it would get, Jimmie's music would always be about and for this original "us."

He would also carefully avoid appearing to be so backwoods that it limited him. For contrast, there is the case of Charlie Poole. A hit on his own terms, Charlie and his hot, talented, jazz-influenced stringband, the North Carolina Ramblers, always sounded rural and always assumed and found a rural audience. Charlie got hold of old Tin Pan Alley songs and shaped them for contemporary country folk, driving the songs harder and faster. He would modernize old minstrel and "coon" songs and old rural fiddle and banjo tunes and, in doing so, sold a lot of records in the 1925–30 period. He came up with such songs as "Don't Let Your Deal Go Down," "White House Blues," and "If I Lose, I Don't Care" that would last, picked up by bluegrassers in the '40s and a few countrified rockers later on. In Poole's modernization of roots material in ways that gave them staying power, there are certainly grounds for comparison with Jimmie Rodgers.

But Charlie Poole's musical attack and sound only scored with the southern rural segment of the '20s musical audience. He was confined to a niche in his time, and his music has survived primarily in the old-time music field, which came into its own during the '60s folk revival, taking hold among a limited, specialized audience looking for stringband music older and simpler than modernized bluegrass. Charlie was not exactly born to reach out beyond where he started—and he sounded that way.

Volatile and even violent, Poole may have made as many enemies as Jimmie Rodgers made friends, allies, and advocates. He may well have had the talent and originality to become a sort of darker foil to the superstar Jimmie—a Jerry Lee to Jimmie's Elvis, a Rolling Stones to his Beatles—but Charlie's response to the broader world his music had tentatively begun to reach was disastrously in character for him.

Faced with a motion picture contract, Jimmie Rodgers' style would no doubt have been to offer a few suggestions for incorporating songs into the script, to check out his costume options, and to cooperate with producers' plans for the picture. He would, in fact, go on to star in an unusual, widely distributed musical short of his own in 1929.

In 1931, Charlie Poole, digesting the news that he, too, had been offered a chance to be in a film, responded characteristically—drinking himself to death in a binge that went on, as Hank Sapoznik has detailed, for thirteen weeks. Prodigious, yes, and a dramatic ending for a sort of country outlaw model, no doubt, but probably a poor move for extending and broadening a musical legacy.

If Jimmie was not the ultimate self-destructive outlaw, there are also important, defining ways Jimmie's music and career differed from those of the domesticated and nearly as famed original Carter Family. The two acts recorded together a little, and both, reasonably enough, would eventually be deemed progenitors of commercial country music. The sentiment in their songs, as in Jimmie's, was directly expressed, without reservation, and the lives of rural people were reflected in their lyrics. With A. P. Carter leading the way in developing their material, the Carters, like Jimmie, introduced new songs and updated and reshaped older ones from varied sources for their own time. And in the rhythmic, elegant, and highly adaptable guitar accompaniments of Maybelle Carter, the act found its most important, most influential element of musical modernization. Her driving accompaniment made their records not just slight variants on traditional folk sounds, but also a basis and starting point of a whole strain of guitar-driven commercial roots music ever since.

There were crucial differences between the Carters' music and Jimmie's, however—and between the two acts. The Carters were not the act Roy Acuff would deem "the first to go commercial" with *their* singing. There remained in their rural harmonies much of the old-style tone, derived from the church and the front porch. The Carters offered the striking lead vocals of Sara Carter and Maybelle's instrumental inventiveness, but their records would not feature the more urbane stress on by-the-lyric vocal phrasing and varied instrumentation that Jimmie's would. Their music would eventually, quite understandably, be claimed by the preservationist folk world as much as by commercial country music.

The Carters' material did evolve and respond to market trends; their records would include blues, a share of far-from-domesticated outlaw and hobo songs, and even new, popular country hits such as "You Are My Sunshine" on their mass-audience-seeking Border Radio broadcasts. Yet the central attraction of their music was its familiar, particularly domestic, and domesticated sound, perfectly reflective of the family's own impulse to stay close to home.

While Jimmie Rodgers hit the road to play shows and extend his fame in commercial venues of notable size and impact, with press accounts covering his moves along the way, the Carters, as their biographers Mark Zwonitzer and Charles Hirshberg have recounted, rarely ventured far from their home except to record. Their hit records notwithstanding, they were still playing in church socials and school auditoriums. Later in the '30s, virtually national Border Radio broadcasts would establish them more widely, but those were still live, on-the-radio rather than in-person performances, which kept the Carters at more than an arm's length from their audience.

What particularly distinguished the Carters' music from Jimmie's was the substantial and unremitting presence of downhome religion in their sound and attitude. Their appearances at those small, local venues were preceded by a celebrated announcement that their program would be "morally good." Jimmie Rodgers made no such promise, and the songs he performed almost entirely avoided moralizing themes. He eschewed hymns and religious material almost entirely and regularly ventured into material that spoke frankly of sex, violence, crime, divorce, and other facts of the listeners' lives, pushing well past the period's limits of church-defined propriety.

With Sara and A. P.'s separation and their divorce in 1936, the Carters were living a much more complicated and modern life than their public recognized, but the central public identity of the family, like their sound itself, remained fixed, domesticated, and self-constrained. Jimmie Rodgers and the Carters were both commercial acts, and wildly successful with the audience for what was later termed "hillbilly" and then "country" music, but Jimmie was fundamentally freer, and fundamentally different. You could decide to cut a risqué vaudeville number like "Everybody Does It in Hawaii" with Jimmie, and it would be funny and sly and terrific — but that was as far outside the Carters' range as hymn singing was outside of his. By comparison, Jimmie looked, sounded, and behaved like a hellion.

Asked once to sing before a Bible study group in Florida, Jimmie offered even that assemblage not a hymn, but one of the songs he performed most regularly, the then often-censored, disreputable, cold-blooded murder ballad "Frankie and Johnny." Jimmie's lasting version of the storied "gutter song," as the genre was known, concluded with the comment "this story has no moral; this story has no end," borrowed from the recording by vaudevillian Frank Crumit, but all the more provocative in such a context. It was daring to be singing the thing in front of polite mixed company down South at all, let alone before that audience.

Only recently, Mae West had tried to resurrect the old song up North on Broadway in her musical show *Diamond Lil* and been arrested multiple times for performing it. Ms. West's regular portrayals and personifications of the retro-sexy Gay Nineties and Jimmie's regular use of musical allusions to that same era were not, finally, such different strategies. The nostalgic package was supposed to make the daring less threatening—and, at least sometimes, it did.

"Frankie and Johnny," sung by Jimmie Rodgers throughout the South, was also being employed as a provocation on the more experimental end of the New York stage, as adapted by celebrated writer-critic Edmund Wilson in a surreal, freak show of an avant-garde musical, *Him*. The show's book was by poet e. e. cummings, and the song was functioning for its more-or-less bohemian audience as an example of unleashed and, unsurprisingly, specifically African-American passion—interrupted and shut down on cue every night by representatives of the Society for the Contraception of Vice. This is some indication of the transgressive, undomesticated musical company Jimmie was keeping circa 1928, knowingly or not, and it was not company the Carter Family could or wanted to share.

Jimmie Rodgers could venture successfully at will into the strikingly varied territories of Gene Austin, Charlie Poole, and the Carter Family—as drastically different as those acts were from each other and as distinct as he was from all three. He broke through boundaries, working both sides of fences the marketplace worked to raise, but he also tempered his rule-breaking tendencies with a natural inclination toward moderation. He seemed neither too hot and threatening nor too remote and cold, but just right for the growing, modernizing audience still based down home—and from that well-placed, distinguishing home base he could reach out to charm broader audiences.

In one engaging performing package, Jimmie, in effect, split the difference between two archetypal, if seemingly contradictory, sorts of frisky southern boys. He could seem by his very nature a rambling rounder-to-be, a genuine outsider and antihero in the Huck Finn mold; "a stranger in your town," as one of his songs had it, radically estranged from the polite, middle-class society around him in real ways and ready to "take off for the territories" out West rather than be forcibly civilized. But there was Tom Sawyer in him, too; the essentially harmless town rascal destined to grow up to be the local auto dealer, civic booster, and vice president of the Junior Chamber of Commerce, well married to the judge's daughter with, perhaps, an eye for the ladies—naughty, but no outlaw.

Representing himself as both of these at once was to propose a brand-new public model, a new synthesis. Jimmie Rodgers showed up, in his day, as the sort of popular roots music hero Kris Kristofferson described so many years later in his song "The Prophet," "a walking contradiction, partly truth, partly fiction"—at once an edgy outsider antihero and an ambitious success-ful star, an insider mastering show business. And so, too, did Johnny Cash, and Elvis Presley, and Hank Williams, and Bob Dylan.

Jimmie Rodgers sang convincingly of both poor little orphan children and vamps; from the standpoint of drifting hoboes and of the enforcers who would generally toss them from the trains; of sexual conquests and personal defeats; of the shackled and of the freewheeling; of women who were tough, rough mistreaters and others who were the sweetest girls in the world; of lonesome strangers riding the blinds (or horses) and of happy dads return-ing to a happy nuclear family; of the possibilities of life and of impending, looming death.

Sometimes he did so with sounds that titillated yet scared some of his audience, sometimes with the sentimental sounds of old parlor sheet music. He found a new way to evoke the freedom in the blues while still deploying the safe, old "Hot Town" sounds that had been daring a generation before— employing anything from his guitar to fiddles and horns. And he would be accepted doing all of that.

Through him, vicariously, you could identify things you wanted in your own life, perhaps furtively, things that somebody was finally singing about. You could go places you could never quite dare or afford to go, hear of worldly things (with a grin attached) with which you would like to appear to be familiar—and all without leaving the safety of your own home. As the monument erected in his home town of Meridian would eventually say so eloquently, "We listened. We understood."

He walked into southern show business not only as one man stepping out from among his own audience to make good, "one of us" writ large, but as an amiable, available magnet for his audience's hopes, fears, and fanta-sies. Rodgers was equipped to spotlight personality elements as varied as the hats he donned, as catchy as the musical phrases, lyric lines, and riffs he provided. Seemingly from out of nowhere, he had scored an enormous early hit with "Blue Yodel," in an explosive meeting of audience desires and what this unknown performer had brought to the show. Jimmie Rodgers was on his way to becoming a roots music pop star.

Select Soundtrack

(Note: throughout these soundtracks, all albums/compilations are CDs unless otherwise noted.)

Original and Fundamental Jimmie Rodgers Recordings

The recordings of Jimmie Rodgers, both the original releases and the often important alterative takes, are heard at their cleanest and most complete in the six-CD box set *Jimmie Rodgers: The Singing Brakeman* (Bear Family, 1992), accompanied by a book with bio-essay and detailed discography by Nolan Porterfield.

The 1991 career-spanning Rodgers set on Rounder Records, sold as eight individual, chronological CDs, is of slightly inferior sonic quality, though derived from the same sources; it is no longer officially in print but can readily be found on the used CD market, and offers the possibility of picking and choosing which CDs interest you. The five-CD set *Jimmie Rodgers: Recordings 1927–1933* (JSP, 2005), is a reasonable lower-cost, near-completist alternative. There are numerous shorter Jimmie Rodgers hits compilations, and many of his most familiar sides are also available individually online.

The Bristol Sessions (Country Music Foundation, 1991) remains the best way to hear the first Rodgers recordings in context, alongside the Carter Family, Ernest Stoneman, the Tenneva Ramblers, and others recorded in that summer of '27 and fall of '28 by Ralph Peer. The Rodgers cuts are also included in the shorter *RCA Country Legends: The Bristol Sessions*.

Let Me Be Your Sidetrack: The Influence of Jimmie Rodgers, a unique six-CD set (Bear Family Records, 2008), traces Rodgers' musical influences from his day to ours by bringing together versions of his songs as performed by others from a variety of genres and nationalities.

Tenneva Ramblers: "The Longest Train I Ever Saw" is on *The Bristol Sessions* CD; "If I Die a Railroad Man" is on the Juneberry Web site.

The Grant Brothers: "Tell It to Me" is on *Good for What Ails You: Music of the Medicine Shows* (Old Hat, 2005). All three are among a dozen Tenneva Ramblers/Grant Brothers sides on the box set *Worried Blues* (JSP, 2005).

Key Contemporary Alternatives to the Jimmie Rodgers Style

- **Charlie Poole:** The box set *You Ain't Talkin' to Me: Charlie Poole and the Roots of Country Music* (Columbia/Legacy, 2005) includes Poole's songs as interpreted by earlier artists and comprehensive history and commentary by the knowledgeable annotator Hank Sapoznik.

- **Gene Austin:** Three more or less available collections of crooner Austin's southern-identified pop are *Gene Austin: Singer and Songwriter* (Collector's Choice Music, 2002), *The Voice of the Southland* (ASV/Living Era, a now deleted 1996 UK issue), and *A Time to Relax* (Take Two Records, 1995). Two of Austin's 1924–25 country recordings with Blind George Reneau, "Railroad Blues" and "Lonesome Road Blues," have surfaced on *Country Pioneers on Edison* (Document, 2006). Someone ought to release more of Austin's several dozen early country sides.

- **The Carter Family:** As with Jimmie Rodgers, the cleanest-sounding, most deeply annotated complete Carter Family set is on Bear Family records, *In the Shadow of Clinch Mountain* (2000). There is a less elaborate version of the complete works, broken into two sets, *The Carter Family 1927–1934* (JSP, 2001) and *The Carter Family 1935–41* (JSP, 2003). And there are many compilations and online downloads available of their hits.

- **Carson Robison:** Far more of his recordings are out of print than in, but there is a cross-era sampling of his music on the CD *Blue River Train and Other Cowboy and Country Songs* (Jasmine, 2007).

two

Close to the Ground
The Singing Brakeman

"The Singing Brakeman" was both the first of the potent public identities that Jimmie Rodgers embodied and a moniker that would never leave him. Even after he had become uncomfortable with its implication that he was a part-time amateur performer, venue operators would continue to use the phrase in newspaper ads and handbills. It would be the title of his one motion picture, shot in the fall of 1929. Almost half a century later, Jimmie Rodgers giving the "thumbs up" signal would be the image chosen for a commemorative U.S. postage stamp in 1978.

By then, however, the railroads and railway lore of Jimmie's day were encrusted with the peculiar attractions of quaintness. A strong sense of the loss of the great steam trains from our daily lives was the emotional touchstone as Merle Haggard sang "I Won't Give Up My Train" and "My Love Affair with Trains" and as Steve Goodman, Arlo Guthrie, and then Willie Nelson all lamented the "disappearing railroad blues" in the '70s hit "City of New Orleans." Country star and Rodgers acolyte Hank Snow had been feeding the appetite for train nostalgia since the '50s. Doing so no doubt struck a chord—but one virtually the opposite of that which had made the Singing Brakeman identity powerful in the first place.

When the emerging recording star Jimmie Rodgers arrived in one of the small southern towns where he most often played, or even in the larger cities—occasionally donning his brakeman's suit on stage—working trainmen were still seen by the relatively homebound residents as larger than life. They were literally men of the world, utterly up-to-date, possessing both real and imagined access to tantalizing outside experiences. They had been places, knew things, brought back the news. In addition to the trainmen you might be lucky enough to encounter firsthand, there were plenty of train songs in circulation, songs of mystery and tragedy and suggestive personal drama that added to the allure of the railroad and the railroaders.

This was a time when townsfolk seeking life advice reportedly headed down to the local station to talk to the station agent. That tendency to look up to uniformed railway men, to find them worldly and exciting, transcended race. African-American Pullman porters often did some side business by bringing unavailable recordings—and blues in particular—south with them from the northern cities, supplying outlets and customers the record companies themselves did not. They were truly connected communicators. President Jimmy Carter, in his memoir of his boyhood in rural Georgia in the Depression years, recalls how the black section crews that were regularly working on the nearby Seaboard Airline Railroad tracks were, for him, musically fascinating. For local African-Americans whom he knew well, they were men "with the most cherished jobs in the community," who "wore their work clothes with pride."

The very positive image a "singing brakeman" projected in the late '20s is comparable to that aura of modern, connected coolness popularly attached to passenger jet pilots in the '50s, or to the romance and mythology attached to long-haul truck drivers and then NASCAR stock car racers in later country music culture—thrilling, *ongoing* fantasies, not nostalgia. Trainmen were hotshots who came from a class and region that you, out in the audience, shared, and you could imagine being one of them yourself, if only you could get the job. The very word *hotshot*, in the sense of "a cocky man of action," entered American speech precisely in Jimmie Rodgers' day and was sometimes used to describe Jimmie himself. Before then, the "hot shot" signified the fastest direct run of an express mail train.

Brakeman was only one of a number of railroad jobs that Jimmie Rodgers had held, but it was the one with the most sonorous and suggestive title, certainly more potent than, say, the Singing Baggage Master. The on again/off again "boomer brakey" work of Jimmie's era centered on coupling and uncoupling cars to make up and break up a train, doing some switching, and assisting the conductor. It was still physically challenging work, but much of the romance perceived in the job was left over from the days before air brakes were introduced in 1888, the time when brakemen generally rode atop train cars to operate the brakes manually, car by car—particularly grueling, dangerous work that had cost many their fingers, or their lives.

That's why brakies, nearly as frequently as brave engineers, had long been appearing as folk heroes in songs that portrayed the dangers they had faced and the heroics they had demonstrated. "A True and Trembling Brakeman," "The Unfortunate Brakeman," and "The Dying Mine Brakeman" were all sympathetic ballads of that type. In songs concerning hoboes and in early blues, on the other hand, brakemen were generally presented quite differently—because, except in situations where violent "railroad bulls" were put on the payroll, brakemen were the railway employees most likely to be tasked with rousting hoboes from trains.

Provocatively, if somewhat ironically, Jimmie Rodgers sang about that negative side of the brakeman's reputation, seeing it from the hobo's point of view, just as often as he sang of being a brakeman himself. In "Hobo's Meditation," he worries whether "there will be any tough cops or brakemen" to hassle hoboes in heaven, while in "Anniversary Blue Yodel" he begs a brakeman not to "put me off your train." Most famously, in "Waiting for a Train," he gives a brakeman "a line of talk" hoping to get on board, only to be told "Get off, get off, you railroad bum" and tossed aside. Playing—and embodying for audiences—both the brakeman and the hobo at the same time, Jimmie Rodgers manages to have things both ways, to switch between personalities but leave the listener recalling only the positive aspects of each. At just this time there also happened to be specific reasons why the brakeman and the hobo were less far apart than they had ever been.

Hoboing had become so common as the Depression took hold that even the relatively well-off Jimmy Carter would recall: "The most frequent travelers we saw in front of our house were tramps, some looking out of open boxcar doors as the trains passed." That term *tramps* is a sign of how some things had changed. There had been certain long-established distinctions among men and women of the road; terms such as *hoboes, tramps,* and *vagrants* all had specific shades of meaning, understood by others in transit and in many cases defined by the law, as well.

You could be an illegal vagrant, a bum subject to arrest, in some jurisdictions if you had just arrived in town answering a call for migratory workers and turned out to be one more applicant than the temporary employer actually chose to hire. But a hobo, in common parlance, was not precisely the same sort of person as an aimless, endlessly wandering tramp, let alone a bum. A tramp, before the Depression, was someone who had, at least supposedly, chosen an unencumbered, home-free alternative lifestyle. A hobo, on the other hand, when grabbing a ride, was headed somewhere in particular—especially toward a job or a new place to stay at the other end. A hobo possessed a degree of workingman's dignity.

In this sense, Jimmie Rodgers had been a hobo himself—grabbing rides to reach other temporary train jobs, mingling with other hoboes with stories of their own along the way. In times as hard as these were becoming, however, the distinction between having and not having an end in sight while traveling was becoming increasingly meaningless. Often there were no jobs to be had at the end of the line, and many thousands of individuals and even families were on the road, not so much job-hunting as randomly, desperately searching for a more welcoming place to settle.

Albert Fullam, a longtime railroad engineer, first ran into Jimmie Rodgers in early 1927 as Jimmie sat singing his then unknown "Brakeman's Blues" on the depot platform at Meridian. They struck up a lasting friendship on the spot, and Fullam later recalled the situation they shared: "'Boomers' they called [people] like me and him, and a whole multitude of other men who just followed the railroad industry . . . In those days, you didn't ask [personal] questions . . . The biggest thing was how much money you had right *then*, where you were going to spend the night . . . [Jimmie] said any old place he hung his hat was home sweet home to him; that was his saying! I said I was going to the Florida East Coast; they were hiring men right now, and he said, 'Well, I'll just mark off and go with you.'" When the Florida climate proved too humid for Jimmie's health, it was Fullam who set Jimmie up to stay with relatives and friends he had in Asheville, North Carolina—a destination that proved to be a key stop on the road to Bristol and the musical destiny of the Singing Brakeman.

Audiences who saw Jimmie Rodgers at the first big-time venues he played once "T for Texas" became a hit saw a performer who had forgotten none of his past and shed only the poverty. By September 1928, Jimmie was playing substantial theaters in Jacksonville, Bradenton, and Miami, Florida. There was a Gainesville auditorium show, too, where already half the profit could go to the University of Florida Athletic Fund. Not long before, he could have nearly starved looking for work in the same territory.

On November 6, the *Norfolk (VA) Ledger-Dispatch* reported: "Jimmie Rodgers made his formal vaudeville debut in the South at Lowe's State yesterday. Rodgers appears on the stage as a railway brakeman with his guitar, which has won him fame and much cash. He sings five songs in a soft southern voice and yodles [sic] parts of three of them. His Mississippi dialect, which is genuine, charms the audience. Before his third number, a request, the capacity matinee crowd joined in an ovation for the singer, whose real ability was undisputed."

Observant *Ledger-Dispatch* reporter E. M. Holmes captured a number of key elements of a Jimmie Rodgers performance: the surprisingly uncompromised Mississippi drawl, the success story of the self-acknowledged ex-brakeman who has earned fame and cash success, and the strong audience response to this downhome attraction. News accounts of this early big-time tour reported the earthy songs Jimmie was performing at similar shows all through that autumn—"Never No Mo' Blues," "In the Jailhouse Now," "Brakeman's Blues," "Frankie and Johnny," and "Waiting for a Train" among them. The ad for the Tuesday night show of the Norfolk stand promised that incoming national election returns would be read from the stage between Jimmie's brakeman-style performance and the evening's harrowing feature film. Herbert Hoover won; Lillian Gish was harshly buffeted in *The Wind*.

Jimmie's loose and audience-responsive performance style, which included snappy patter and comic stories between songs whenever time permitted, assured that those who saw him were left with strong, lasting impressions of the ties between the man, the songs he sang, and the world he had experienced. During a March 1929 tour in Texas, the *Abilene Daily Reporter* would describe how he had charmed audiences there with comic tales of "incidents in connection with the songs, to add spice to the program." The *Midland Reporter-Telegram* described a show where he decided spontaneously to introduce an unnamed song he had written just days before but not yet recorded, and how "a momentary silence" was followed by a "detonation of applause—wave after wave for almost two minutes."

News reports and newspaper ads for those large theater shows reveal something else. Jimmie was visiting local record dealers—usually general music or furniture stores—all along his route, signing records and photos for fans. He was also stopping by local radio stations or hanging with newsmen after shows for quick promotional interviews. The *Abilene Daily Reporter* noted that an astounding two thousand "admirers" showed up to shake Jimmie's hand at the "in-store" there. All of this was happening at a time when the Carter Family, who had reached prominence as recording artists more or less simultaneously, were rarely traveling much farther than to school auditoriums near their Virginia home.

From very early on, and despite bouts of respiratory trouble that made the schedule all the more challenging, Jimmie Rodgers would leave that big-bucks vaudeville circuit to appear in smaller towns and tiny hamlets, in venues that drew the sorts of people who came from his world. He deliberately chose to stage these sometimes nearly continuous strings of engagements in places where not many acts, let alone stars of his magnitude, bothered to appear.

As the Depression deepened, money for a ticket was hard for his fans to come by, and yet they kept on coming. Ernest Tubb, the future cornerstone of honky tonk country, was then just a Brownwood, Texas, kid willing to go hungry to buy the latest Jimmie Rodgers record. He would later recall how locals lined up for blocks to see Jimmie Rodgers in person at a full dollar ticket price, even for a passing twenty-minute appearance on a vaudeville bill, when the same movie theater was finding it difficult to fill half the house showing a movie for a dime.

Jimmie Rodgers' often-repeated appearances in these out-of-the-way towns and his close-to-the-ground performances for these hard-hit, hard-working audiences were full of personal encounters with locals. Such appearances actually account for much of his time and effort entertaining, but they have been only slowly uncovered and documented because the reporting on them, where there was any, was so local.

A case in point would be a previously unchronicled set of small-town shows Rodgers did in Texas in late January to early February of 1930. Notations in his handwriting on the back of a handbill for the final shows of that run at the Burntex Theatre in Burnet, Texas, list sixteen little towns he played in succession heading southwest from Ft. Worth. Fans saw and heard Jimmie Rodgers that winter in Weatherford, Mineral Wells, Jacksboro, Graham, Breckinridge, Cisco, Eastland, Ranger, Tomball, Stephensville, Granbury, Glen Rose, Dublin, Comanche, and, yes, in Ernest Tubb's Brownwood, too. Notes suggest a follow-up February tour may have stopped in as many towns again heading southeast from Dallas to Benton, Tyler, and Waco.

It has been established that just a few weeks later, with the Swain's Hollywood Follies company, he would be doing forty-three one-night stands from the Texas panhandle up into Oklahoma and Kansas. When people say Jimmie Rodgers never stayed still for long and went out to let the people see him up close as much as was humanly possible, this is the sort of schedule they are talking about.

The songs Jimmie performed in such towns not only conveyed his recognition of the day-to-day facts and concerns of the audience, but also appealed to their individual fantasies of unencumbered travel, experience, good times, and lives of gutsy chance-taking. He would sing about how Portland, Maine, and sunny Tennessee were "just the same" to him, but how many at one of those shows had been to either place or had any way to compare them? The point was to suggest that he knew both towns well — and a thousand others, too — to have the crowd nodding along in imaginary shared sophistication. A song like "Jimmie's Texas Blues," with its multiple place-name-dropping and the title reference in particular, would have extra appeal to anyone from those places, as would the geographically broader "My Dear Old Sunny South." Jimmie also sang them songs of mom and dad and the baby, of soldier and sailor veterans, of the lonely and blue, of the need to get by somehow, anyhow, in tough times.

Jimmie Skinner, born in Kentucky into a not very well-off family and raised in nearby rural Ohio where, as he put it, "there really wasn't any

Jimmie's forty-three Swain's Hollywood Follies shows followed weeks on the road in out-of-the-way Texas towns.

money for anybody to make, either," would eventually be a successful folk and country singer, record sales entrepreneur, songwriter, and knowledgeable interpreter of Jimmie Rodgers' songs. Around 1927–29, he was a fascinated young kid listening to a lot of Jimmie Rodgers records, connecting with them instantly. He would note, "When I heard [Jimmie], I knew that *that* was the man that I liked better than anyone else in particular." Skinner would stress the strong pull Rodgers had, regionally and beyond, on people like himself of the Depression era: "I don't call them hillbillies . . . You could find one in Ohio, or anywhere. [They were] my kind of people."

In reality, there had always been — besides the hard-case brakemen featured in so many songs — some who exchanged jokes, empathized with, and even liked the passing hoboes, who would wink and let them ride those rails in exchange for something as simple as a song. Jimmie Rodgers was one of those. The Singing Brakeman image, smiling on you, thumbs up, in that famous publicity photo seen in newspapers and autographed in stores said, unequivocally, "Look at me. I know you; I'm one of you — and here I am. Things are changing crazily fast, sure, but they could be looking up — and they might just include you, too. As far as I'm concerned, you are *not dismissed*."

That message was all the more potent as his own fame and wealth grew, as the big, fast cars he bought in succession became trademarks, along with the flashy clothes. The Rodgers' big house in Kerrville, "The Blue Yodeler's Paradise," was as publicized as his buddy Gene Austin's yacht, the *Blue Heaven*, named for Austin's hit "My Blue Heaven," had been earlier. (The yacht's naming had probably inspired the house's.) Here was a star with all of that going for him and his picture in the papers, with—you would imagine—all the women he would ever want to know beckoning as well. Amazingly, despite all of that newfound success, he was not severing his ties to the likes of us or lessening his interest in us. He was singing for us.

This was potentially potent stuff. Within just a few years, Texas's W. Lee O'Daniel and Louisiana's Jimmie Davis, performers who were both acquaintances of Jimmie with constituencies similar to his, would ride such connections right into the governorships of their respective states.

It was not in Jimmie Rodgers' temperament even to consider such a career route. In none of his songs is there any explicit political wrong to fight, any cause identified, any opponent other than some maker of purely personal difficulties. He did not go in for preaching or overt messages, rarely pointed a finger at anybody. Beyond jokes about how his subject "should have known better" found in "In the Jailhouse Now," or the point that "I would have been better off living straight, as mama suggested" in "Mother, the Queen of My Heart," Rodgers rarely suggests what people "ought" to do at all. An attempt to tack a lesson on the end of his train ballad "The Mystery of Number Five," in which it is discovered that suddenly, inexplicably a fireman friend is dead, produces the rather pallid "Take warning . . . play this game fair, so when the Master calls on us, we'll meet my fireman up there." There's no attempt in the story to attribute the fireman's fate to any previous behavior; the man just dies.

Indeed, there's very little of a church-developed vocabulary of sin or retribution anywhere in the songs of Jimmie Rodgers. True, a child is orphaned when his mother dies of a broken heart after the gambling, drunkard dad has been "stolen away by Hell"—the story of "A Drunkard's Child" written for Jimmie by Atlanta preacher Andrew Jenkins. But then, a mother dies of a broken heart when her son is falsely imprisoned in "I'm Free from the Chain Gang Now." The emphasis is the same in both cases—what the aftermath of actions feels like, not the sin or lack thereof that preceded the heartbreak. Jimmie is perfectly content in "Moonlight and Skies" to have a pal named Blackie, a "lad with a true heart" who is shot dead while trying to pull off an armed robbery, go on to meet a sweetheart in *heaven*. That may or may not be a statement of easygoing theology; perhaps we can take it as a sort of theological corollary to the story Jimmie sings in "Gambling Barroom Blues," where the drunken singer kills a pal ("smokes" him) and then essentially gets away with it scot-free by sharing lots of liquor with police who are generally "just as drunk as me." You can easily imagine the audience laughing in recognition when they first heard that one.

Jimmie's songs and style built a strong sense of "us" all along the way, but with little corresponding sense of an excluded or repellent "them" to fight. He rarely got involved with politics, one known exception being his support for the mid-1920s Texas gubernatorial campaigns of Ma and Pa Ferguson, who were populist and fast and loose in ethics, but tellingly anti–Ku Klux Klan at a time when that organization was at the height of its racist influence.

Perhaps a man who knew he had such a limited life expectancy was simply not particularly concerned about big, long-term issues. You would have no clue from the Singing Brakeman's songs of hoboes and trainmen that the radical Wobblies, the Industrial Workers of the World, were then having considerable success in organizing and recruiting hoboes—perhaps a third of those in transit by some estimates—in part by fighting for their protection from hobo-robbing hoodlums and violent railroad bulls alike. The always musically attuned radical union had worked up dozens of recruiting songs, some penned by the legendary Joe Hill, many of them hobo-targeting parodies of the numbers Salvation Army bands were using to draw residents of the hobo jungles to their missions. Enough pointed Wobbly-sponsored songs were in wide circulation to fill a chapter in *The Hobo's Hornbook*, a volume of hobo songs and poetic narratives assembled by professor and sometime tramp-by-choice George Milburn in 1930, in the middle of Jimmie's career.

Jimmie Rodgers was not singing any of those. He no more aspired to be an organizer of his audience than to be their state's chief executive—or their preacher. Indeed, it is difficult to imagine Jimmie filling any of those roles. His songs and his relationship to his often down and suffering fans were both essentially rooted in empathy and understanding, in conveying his connection to their lives as he entertained them.

"The undercrest dog is just as good as I am, and I'm just as good as the toppest dog," his wife would quote Jimmie as saying frequently. The sentiment was reflected in everything he sang and did—and thousands upon thousands of fans responded to it. In their eyes, Jimmie Rodgers would stand as their unelected representative; he offered a vision of what people from his world might have it in them to be. Almost from the first, he would be the sort of legendary popular hero people would brag about having crossed paths with and tell stories about, whether truthful or not.

Commonplace anecdotes say much about who Jimmie was in his admirers' eyes. Somebody has some bootleg liquor with Jimmie on the porch after he drives up in that big Cadillac of his. A music store proprietor offers to play

Jimmie, with somebody else's dogs.

a stranger the hot new Jimmie Rodgers record and the stranger turns out to *be* Jimmie Rodgers. Jimmie empties his pockets to help a fan in need. Jimmie replies, when someone unaware that it is him standing there is praising him to the skies, "Oh, that guy Rodgers is just overrated." One story in particular, the often-reprinted one where the hard-up farmer goes into a store and asks for "a quart of milk, a dozen eggs, and the new Jimmie Rodgers record" no doubt started out in just that way—despite the fact that it has never made much sense. At the time records were almost never sold where eggs and milk were, and the latter items are among the least likely a hard up farmer would need to buy at a store in any case.

Jimmie's growing status as "people's hero" was further boosted across the South Central states by an action he took in the face of the Great Drought of 1930–31, an early stage of the Dust Bowl ecological disaster. A year and a half without rain had compounded the effects of the South's catastrophic dependence on a single over-produced crop, cotton, which had left the land subject to the ravages of extreme weather. Conditions were dire, outright famine resulted, and local rationing was instituted. When ration forms ran out in the town of England, Arkansas, on January 3, 1931, some 550 local residents and farmers from the surrounding area staged an angry, though nonviolent, march demanding food. The event was widely reported in the national media as a food "riot," even a "rebellion," which only led to investigations in Washington of alleged subversives, not serious relief.

Will Rogers, the extraordinarily popular cowboy trick roper turned movie star and dispenser of cracker-barrel political wisdom in syndicated newspaper columns, surveyed the area by plane. He then flew to Washington to persuade President Hoover of the drastic need for a federal response in the form of a massive immediate contribution to the Red Cross. Rebuffed by Hoover, Rogers noted in his January 16 column, "He feels that once the government relieves the people, they will always expect it . . . If we want to see somebody helped, we better go ahead . . . [before] it will be too late to save the fellow who is hungry now . . . No matter what the politicians do, whether it's called a 'dole' or a 'gift,' you can't live on . . . speeches." In a radio address out of Little Rock a few days later, Will Rogers announced that he would headline a three-week relief tour across the region. Jimmie Rodgers heard the address and responded immediately with a telegram to Will suggesting that he go along on the tour, though he was uncertain whether Rogers—who was perhaps the leading nonmusical downhome star and hero of the day—would even know who he was. Will knew, and responded that he loved Jimmie's music and welcomed his help.

On January 25, the *San Antonio Light* reported, "Along with Will Rogers' dry wit . . . the familiar yodel and guitar accompaniment of Jimmie Rodgers, recording artist of Kerrville, will be heard. Jimmie Rodgers has 'come down out of the mountains' to join Will in his campaign for funds." The geographically fictional mountain reference was a sign of Jimmie's increasing association with hillbilly music. The report was otherwise accurate.

Rogers, Rodgers, and crew flew from town to town across Texas and up into Oklahoma, pulling in unprecedented amounts of cash for relief—$9,100 in Depression-era money at Wichita Falls, $18,000 at Ft. Worth, $6,500 at Abilene, $30,000 in Tulsa, every dime going to the Red Cross for food and basics like vegetable seeds, so families could stay fed. The organization fed some eight thousand families in the area around England, Arkansas, alone. At stop after stop on the relief tour, Will would describe Jimmie as "the Yodler De Lux" and sometimes jokingly introduce him as "my distant son." At one point, they got to a drought relief show in time by using a car of Carrie's, because, ironically enough, their plane had bogged down in mud. Will and Jimmie hit it off extraordinarily well, a relationship cemented as they brought both renewed hope and specific aid to thousands—including some $300,000 from the tour. There was talk of continuing their monologuist and singer act more formally, even of Jimmie appearing with Will in his downhome-oriented Hollywood movies "once Jimmie was healthier" and "wouldn't look so wan on screen." That the Singing Brakeman had appeared in as many relief shows as was physically possible, even while his health deteriorated, was never to be forgotten in the areas directly affected, especially by the very class of people to whom his music spoke so directly.

If Wobbly-style political train songs were not in Jimmie's repertoire, neither did he offer his audience overromanticized ballads about the freedom of happy wandering "princes of the road." In songs like "Hobo Bill's Last Ride" and "Hobo's Meditation," however, he did deliver the sort of material George Milburn decried in his *Hornbook* as "the sentimental tramp ballad, known to the barroom and the vaudeville stage [but] not heard in the jungles."

There is an irony here. Milburn portrayed tramps and hoboes as "gutter jongleurs," the last of the medieval-style troubadours, while laughing at contemporary folklorists who couldn't "differentiate between genuine hobo ballads and the pseudo ballads offered by co-ed ukulele virtuosos and catarrhal phonograph yodelers." Yet apparently the tramp academic did not notice — or chose not to, because the song is so strong — that "Waiting for a Train," the most often-recorded hobo ballad concoction of the most famous catarrhal phonograph yodeler of them all, was indeed included in his book, virtually unchanged, under the title "The Railroad Bum." Milburn recalled that he first heard this "genuine" hobo ballad sung "by a beachcomber in a New Orleans riverfront saloon." Perhaps so — but that beachcomber had a record collection.

The sorts of hobo lyrics actually given the slightest attention in Milburn's tome were the varied, memorable, widely shared, and modified lines that traveling African-Americans had put in the blues. Lines from that musical arena, which Rodgers would have learned along the way or from records, were among the nonoriginal ones he was most likely to adopt. It may surprise many to this day, if they are unfamiliar with the blues repertoire of Jimmie's era, that such iconic Rodgers lines as "When a man gets the blues, he grabs a train and rides," "Hey little water boy, bring your water round," and "I can get more women than a passenger train can haul" were all in circulation, and even on record, before Jimmie made them his own, too. Making them your own, *too*, was a blues singer's job. And there was no musical fact more shaping of Jimmie Rodgers' music and his lasting image than the fact that he was a blues singer.

Select Soundtrack

Train Life Song Recordings of Jimmie Rodgers (chronologically)

"Ben Dewberry's Final Run," "The Brakeman's Blues," "Waiting for a Train," "Train Whistle Blues," "Hobo Bill's Last Ride," "The Mystery of Number Five," "Travellin' Blues," "Jimmie the Kid," "Southern Cannonball," "Hobo's Meditation."

Studio portrait, Washington, D.C., just as "Blue Yodel" was making Jimmie a recording star.

three

America's Blue Yodeler No. 1
This White Guy Sings Blues, Too

In 1928, it was highly unusual to see any reviews of American roots music records at all, but one pioneer, the lawyer and critic Abbe Niles, was regularly commenting on new releases in jazz, blues, "hill-billy," jug band, and folk balladry in a column in the upscale literary magazine *The Bookman*. On July 28 that year, he noted, with a few slight errors, that we really ought to "Meet . . . Jimmy Rodgers singing 'Down on the Mountain' and his engaging, melodious and bloodthirsty 'Blue Yodel.'" Niles then goes on to quote in full the verse about shooting poor Thelma. In subsequent columns, he would follow up with reviews of "Blue Yodel No. 2," "Blue Yodel No. 3," and "Never No Mo' Blues" as they were released—under the subheading, in one case, "White man gone black."

In the '20s, that word choice, "bloodthirsty," was being used in ads placed by record companies in newspapers read by African-Americans as a selling point, applied more than once to jazzy, so-called classic women's blues in the "I'm gonna kill my triflin' man" vein. Victoria Spivey's "Blood Thirsty Blues" was only the most obvious occasion for putting the description to use. Niles' use of it in praising "T for Texas" suggested to his transparently art-conscious and upscale white readership, as that "gone black" subheading said outright, that Jimmie Rodgers had gotten well inside the blues—across color lines. It was the equivalent of a much later generation's common praise description, "He's *bad*."

It was not only an intellectual columnist who saw Rodgers as somehow "like a black man." Jimmie's downhome friend, sometime accompanist, and blues-singing competitor Cliff Carlisle would later note of him, "His leg didn't do like mine does; my leg won't hang down . . . he put one leg over the other, and it was hangin' right down . . . And he opened that mouth, and he had a long face, you know, long jaw like, anyhow. It just flopped! Jimmie, he reminded me more of a colored person, a Negro . . . than anybody I ever saw. He had that old . . . long, southern drawl, you know."

However much inaccurate racial innuendo the comment may or may not have been intended to carry, there was a point of consequence behind it. No Caucasian singer before Jimmie Rodgers had so successfully digested the basic, inherent ethos of the blues, had inhabited the music so convincingly and, it seemed, effortlessly. From his very first hit, this was a central attraction of his act and style for audiences and performers, white and black alike.

It was not that there weren't other white, Southern singers of some sort of "mountain" or "hillbilly" blues. Dock Boggs, Frank Hutchison, Dick Justice, Charlie Poole, and Jimmie Tarlton all must be reckoned with, to varying degrees, in any history of early country music or of the "white man's blues," as some call this genre. But much of the music they sang was blues by song title only, not by structure or depth of connection to the performance style. Such artificial blues titling was a common, commercially driven effect of the blues genre's yielding so many hits. More important, these hillbilly blues-makers only occasionally showed that they had direct access to the thick, duality-encompassing sensibility behind black blues. Jimmie Rodgers had that and demonstrated it—the humor and joy in the blues mingled with the loss, grief, and occasional anger, the "we" of implied community balancing the "I" of signifying, boasting, and self-expression.

Understandably, virtually every commentator looking for the origin of that mysterious difference in Jimmie Rodgers goes to his biography—the upbringing in Mississippi where blues were often, it is said, "deeper," the lack of money, the early interchange with music-making African-American railroad workers and hoboes, his exposure to vaudeville and professional performers' repertoires as well as the more rural blues styles, and especially to the resigned-but-alive view of life that can result when you know, from early adulthood, that you have a serious, probably terminal case of tuberculosis.

All of that makes sense, and all of it probably contributed to who Jimmie Rodgers was, but how much the backstory explains the temperament and character of the man is a matter of speculation and even of mystery. There were plenty of people who shared a number of those experiences— and they did not become "America's Blue Yodeler."

Perhaps it is relevant here to recall how Jimmie Rodgers' sensibility embodies qualities of the great silent screen clowns—Chaplin's chosen outsiderhood, Lloyd's energy, Keaton's seemingly nonresistant entanglement with nature's puzzles—because taken all together, these tendencies add up to something very much like the great critic Albert Murray's famous description of the blues sensibility: "elegantly playful, and heroic in its nonchalance." Murray has also noted, in discussing the heroic aspect of the blues sensibility, "Perhaps the 'happy ending' that is commonly associated with the story pattern of comedy does not so much suggest that death has been conquered but that *life* has been mastered, at least for the moment." While Murray would not be a fan of the sentimental side of Jimmie's music, he nevertheless provides there a serious clue to what makes Jimmie Rodgers genuinely *of* the blues—his liveliness within what life he had.

That Jimmie Rodgers attracted and influenced African-American blues singers in a way few white blues performers ever have is not incidental; it is particularly revealing about his relation to the blues and the nature of his music, and is, no doubt, one factor behind his widespread fame.

B. B. King, Mississippi born and raised, arguably the most world-renowned, financially successful blues performer since the day of the blues queens of the '20s, believes the reasons for Jimmie's acceptance across racial lines are clear enough: "Mississippians, black and white weren't getting the best end of the stick, so we all kind of understood everybody's trouble. There was a lot of white people who felt like some of us do—and *some* of 'em weren't ashamed to talk about it, or sing about it. Jimmie Rodgers was one of those people. We knew he was white; he sounded like a white person, but that white person sounded good to me, singing blues. Jimmie Rodgers, in my opinion, was one of the great, great singers. He sang a lot of blues, a *lot* of blues, and he was very, very good at it."

Born in 1925, B. B. King—the seminal guitarist; smooth, winning singer; and blues ambassador—had first heard Jimmie Rodgers singing during his boyhood. It was on a record at his great-aunt Mima's house in the tiny Mississippi hill town of Kilmichael, and, from the sound of it, very possibly one of Rodgers last singles, "Gambling Barroom Blues" backed with "Long Tall Mamma Blues."

"My aunt was kind of a collector of music of her time," King recalls now, looking back some seventy-five years, "but she only collected the music she wanted to hear, and Jimmie Rodgers was one of the artists she had. In the record of his I heard, he seemed to be having trouble with the law; he was not necessarily angry, but he was a little disgusted with the police! She had his blues records right along with ones by Lonnie Johnson, Blind Lemon [Jefferson], and [later] my cousin Bukka White's. But of the many she had, Jimmie Rodgers was one of my own favorites, along with Lonnie Johnson. I never tried to yodel—though *he* was good at that."

If B. B. King's musical tastes proved expansive and his own celebrated style relatively sophisticated and urban, another Mississippi blues man, Chester Burnett—better known as Howlin' Wolf—with his steel-wool-and-blood voice as fierce, warm, and astringent as American music would ever know, was obviously made of rougher-hewn, more rural stuff. Wolf would regularly bring up Jimmie Rodgers as a key influence, even to perplexed interviewers who didn't suspect the connection and certainly had not asked about it. For example, in a 1970 backstage interview with filmmaker Topper Carew, after talking about the first record he ever heard as a boy, one by "Mother of the Blues" Ma Rainey, and praising the guitar playing of Blind Lemon Jefferson for its clarity, the Wolf gleefully volunteered, "And then, *my* man that I dug, that I really *dug*, that I got my yodel from, was Jimmie Rodgers. See, he yodeled, and I turned it into something more of a howl."

When a kid in the Mississippi Delta, who has already been personally tutored on guitar by rural blues master Charlie Patton and seen the driving Mississippi Sheiks stringband live, gets hold of his first records and they are by Ma Rainey and Jimmie Rodgers, this indicates several things of note. One is simply that Rainey, like Jefferson and Rodgers, was selling a lot of records; she had a hit-maker's reach like theirs. But there is more: If you were looking for any examples before the arrival of Jimmie Rodgers on the national stage of American musical performers who seemed to their audiences to be "like us, writ large," they were probably such heroines as Ma Rainey, Bessie Smith, and Clara Smith—the "queens" and "empresses" and other grande dames of the vaudeville blues era, the years just before Jimmie recorded. When these formidable stars blew into town with their cars and jewels and furs, singing with such ebullient assertiveness about living with and beyond the hard facts of the audience's lives, they must certainly have been tantalizing visions of what somebody black, southern, and female might be.

Were they in some sense models for Jimmie Rodgers? There is not the slightest doubt that he would have heard stories about them from fellow vaudevillians, seen trade press coverage of their comings and goings, or known their records. He also would have known that his manager, Ralph Peer, had signed many of the classic blues singers to Okeh Records, including Mamie Smith, whose hit "Crazy Blues" sparked the commercial blues craze. He had signed some of the key jug bands as well. Whether Peer ever simply handed Jimmie Rodgers some of the earlier records he had been involved with was a question nobody ever asked either one of them. So were Ma Rainey and Bessie Smith the prototypes for the roots music pop hero model that he presented? Only to a degree.

Meeting Jimmie Rodgers

The position in society and in show business of these select stars was so special, even unique for their time, that they must have seemed to their core audience almost like magical visions. In her analysis of the music and careers of Ma, Bessie, and Billie Holiday, Angela Davis makes a credible and convincing case that the first two, even in the '20s, embodied both social protest and their audience's aspirations in the awe-inspiring ways that they were who they were. She also acknowledges, however, that in that highly racially segregated and gender-role-defined place and time, there were limits to what that embodiment could mean. It is difficult to argue that many black women could see these stars as representatives of the kind of people they themselves could become, or even resemble. There were also limits to how wide an impact the divas' profound music could make—as there were for black-made blues in general.

The record companies were not trying in any concerted way to take either Ma or Bessie into the pop mainstream. A little of that was attempted with Bessie at the end of her life, but too late. The blues divas' records and shows were marketed primarily to African-American audiences. That Ma Rainey and Bessie Smith also reached white audiences in the '20s and into the early '30s, which they did to a degree, is testimony purely to their own extraordinary performing power. Relatively attentive roots music critic Abbe Niles would even explain in print to his white readers how they might request records "made for colored consumers" from their neighborhood record dealers in order to avoid getting so close as to, as he put it, "bother the Negroes." In general, Ma and Bessie were not admired heroines by many white Americans or many men in the '20s. Additionally, they were markedly sophisticated in their musical presentations and abilities, professionally tied to the agendas of big-time vaudeville booking agencies, and they generally appeared in big-cast touring variety shows in major cities— situational factors that limited the degree to which they could function as downhome heroines, a role they do not seem to have particularly wanted to fill, in any case.

For all of the hardships he endured, there were, of course, obvious distinctions between Jimmie Rodgers' life and role in the world and theirs. He did not have to deal with hotels or theatrical rooming houses that would not let him sleep there because of his race; he did not have to enter theaters through back doors; he did not, as Bessie Smith's biographer Chris Albertson has pointed out, have to deal with Ku Klux Klansmen trying to pull down the tent in which he sang. (She managed to scare them off with swearing, fist-shaking audacity.) Nor was he a woman on the road singing about that special experience of being out there at a time when so few were—black or white.

While there were connections between what Jimmie was doing and what they had done, the many differences between them limited the potential for his direct reuse of the vaudeville blues queens' themes and verses.

Indeed, how this particular young white man adapted existing blues ideas from African-American blues singers, male and female, cannot be reduced to the cliché of simple white-from-black appropriation. It was more a case of *complex* appropriation, of the sort that is at the very heart of the blues-making phenomenon. As David Evans amply demonstrated in his seminal 1982 study of the relation of the individual blues singer to blues traditions, creative blues performers enter a living blues community that is defined by the marriage of shared notions and musical tools with individual contributions. To become a blues singer — and, as B. B. King puts it, Jimmie Rodgers was a good one — is to take part in a performance in which there is a constant conversation between the "I" and that broader, existing "we."

Between Jimmie's tough but vulnerable sensibility and the '20s blues divas' assertive adventurousness, there was some common ground in themes and material. Lines show up in his songs that had been recorded by Ma Rainey; the unrelated Smiths: Trixie, Clara, and Bessie; and the somewhat less well-known Maggie Jones, recording stars in the years when Jimmie was still more or less unknown. There is generally no need for gender-jumping translation, although when Jimmie sings, "When a woman gets the blues, she hangs her head and cries; when a man gets blue, he grabs a train and rides," he inevitably introduces different emotional and narrative implications than when Trixie and Clara Smith told us about that disparity. Prominent among verses he appears to have gotten directly from African-American sources are ones in which the vaudeville divas — and also a few lesser-known male blues performers of the era — are singing about trains or using railway imagery. No surprise there — in several senses.

The influence of train work life, railroad metaphors, and chugging locomotive rhythms on the blues is axiomatic and has even been the subject of a worthy, detailed, book-length examination: Max Haymes' *Railroadin' Some*. The title of one of its chapters expresses well today's blues researchers' understanding of the meeting of trains, folk blues, and professional acts: "Cross-fertilization of Rural and Vaudeville Blues Via the Railroad." The dated assumption that all blues were derived from amateur, rural male singers (preferably from the Mississippi Delta) and were then adapted by vaudevillians and jazz singers is replaced there by a more dynamic, and clearly more accurate, picture of give-and-take between the professionals and the so-called folk. Plenty of verses in songs by the professionals originated with them, if sometimes composed for them by songwriters, and made their way to the country—which gets us back to the Jimmie Rodgers records heard by Howlin' Wolf and B. B. King along with those of other blues singers.

The Mississippi Delta region and African-Americans who resided there were hardly as isolated from general musical trends and commercial trends as blues aficionados of years past—whether following the outdated assumptions of academic folklorists or moved by rock 'n' roll romanticism—tended and wanted to imagine. Howlin' Wolf loved Jimmie Rodgers. Muddy Waters told researchers Alan Lomax and John W. Work about his great fondness for Gene Autry songs, and "(I've Got Spurs That) Jingle Jangle Jingle" in particular; he had been playing that one at dances attended by white folks. It will still surprise some, but as bluesman Johnny Shines recalled of his traveling musical partner, Robert Johnson, "The country singer Jimmie Rodgers—me and Robert used to play a hell of a lot of his tunes, man, and I liked him. Robert played *all* that stuff." Other "stuff" Shines recalled Johnson playing included Gene Austin's "My Blue Heaven" and the Autry/Sons of the Pioneers' "Tumbling Tumbleweeds," all accompanied by slide guitar.

Jimmie Rodgers, like other blues singers, made use of existing blues themes: sexual boasting; drinking; bouts of violence; going to jail; leaving a lover or being left or betrayed by one; being alone, lonely, and worried; or being jubilant at getting past all that. Before Johnny Cash sang of shooting a man in Reno just to watch him die, Jimmie sang of shooting poor Thelma just to see her jump and fall, with that great long gun. But even before that, Bessie Smith had been singing about how she was going to "get me a gun long as my right arm, shoot that man because he done me wrong" and, elsewhere, how she had "stood there laughin' over him while he wallowed round and died."

There was nothing unusual about taking up common blues themes or verses; avoiding it would have made you less of a blues singer. Nor did it make you less of a blues "writer" to remake earlier verses, either; indeed, how you pulled verses together and attached them to yourself was a crucial part of the art. An art it was, with feelings given form. As Albert Murray has noted of African-American blues artists, contrary to the common romantic—and condescending—view of them as "raw" and unfiltering emotional performers, "Blues musicians do *not* derive directly from the personal, social and political . . . They derive most directly from styles of other musicians who [played] the blues, and who were infinitely more interested in evoking or simulating raw emotion than in releasing it."

That means of creating blues is no less true of Jimmie Rodgers than of the black blues musicians—but it was arguably no more true either. At least thirty-five songs that bear his name as a songwriter are blues, and you would not go too far wrong in assuming that a combination of hoary "traveling verses" and new lines and turns are brought into play in all of them.

Jimmie joined the community of the blues-making art, and the credibility his audience found in the dozens of blues songs he sang is evidence of how well he could do it. As for the sharing of verses and notions, in Jimmie's case, that was a two-way street. Given the nature of the blues community, it will never be possible, with precision and certainty, to say in all cases, "Jimmie got this from others here; they got that from him there," but in many instances, the situation is clear enough to be revealing. Those with whom he shared song ideas, his extended blues family, had overlapping sensibilities with somewhat related repertoires, and generally worked in his original home region—roughly, between New Orleans and Memphis.

Rodgers especially shared much with the performers who were known as songsters, as opposed to instrumentalists. Their emphasis was on playing a variety of song styles, including but not limited to blues, mainly solo, and they worked in tents, at parties, in vaudeville when they could, or on the streets. The songsters' audience might be racially mixed, when they were going after tips on the street or playing white parties, and they needed to know a wide range of songs that might be requested. Papa Charlie Jackson from New Orleans, for instance, was on the short list of men who made a good living performing and recording during the heyday of the blueswomen—he even recorded duets with several of them—and he moved easily between bawdy hokum songs of the "Shake That Thing" variety and blues. His background was working tent shows and vaudeville, and his singing had some of that generations-old minstrel show tone. His instrument was the banjo-guitar—a six-string banjo tuned and played guitar-style, but with the plunking banjo sound. It is worth recalling that banjo was one of Jimmie's instruments of choice, along with mandolin, before he began recording. Papa Charlie's banjo runs on songs like "Texas Blues," recorded in 1925, may give some idea what Jimmie's banjo style would have been like. That they ran into each other along the way seems likely, but in any case, Jackson's records were ubiquitous—and he was the one who first sang, on "The Faking Blues," about "getting more women than a passenger train can haul."

Mississippi John Hurt was a pure songster, one of the most winning of them all, with a light style that could sound more Southeast Coast/Piedmont than Mississippi; that is, if you are expecting everyone from Mississippi to sound like Robert Johnson. It seems he never ran into Rodgers, but he knew the "Waiting for a Train" record when it was new, kept Jimmie's tune in one he wrote himself, and later recorded the original lyric when asked to.

It is not unusual, it should be noted, to find bluesmen of that era mentioning that they liked Jimmie's ballads, and that best-known one, "Waiting

Meeting Jimmie Rodgers

for a Train," in particular. It is another important, not obvious indication of a very significant respect in which Jimmie Rodgers' sensibility brought him closer than most white blues performers to the mind-set of the blues-makers.

Folk song researchers, contrasting narrative ballads authored and sung by African-Americans and those authored and sung by southern whites, have frequently noted the tendency among the white narratives to find a moral, a lesson to be culled—or dragged—from the flood or train wreck or holdup story. Jimmie Rodgers' way, however, was precisely to avoid doing that; he would relate the drama of what occurred, lay in the details, shine a light on them, make them real and memorable in and of themselves, and then leave them alone, no lesson implied. That happens to be how African-Americans in the South usually composed ballads, as well. No one told Jimmie Rodgers to fashion story songs that way; it is unlikely he was even aware of the distinction, since it is not widely known even now. That was just Jimmie. Quite simply, in his attitude toward the stories he told, he was more in the African-American mold than were most other writers or performers of country music ballads.

The tradition of blues world songsters comfortably assimilating Jimmie Rodgers pieces has continued through the decades. Perhaps the most celebrated to do so was Huddie Ledbetter Lead Belly. Reporting on meeting and then promoting the formerly imprisoned Texas songster, folklorist John A. Lomax detailed how he, Lomax, had systematically chosen to preserve songs that seemed most "folky" (his word) to keep in Lead Belly's repertoire and ruled out material that he—and the left-wing intellectual audience he planned to bring Huddie to—found less "appropriate" for their notion of what an outspoken ex-convict African-American "should" care about. They wanted, for instance, protest songs about the Scottsboro Boys. "Prime examples" of Lead Belly's favorite but "inappropriate" material, according to Lomax, included Gene Autry songs and "the yodeling blues and ballads of Jimmy Rogers [sic] of recent fame, whose ardent admirer Lead Belly still remains . . . He could never understand 'why we did not care for them.'" Lead Belly understood Rodgers songs well enough to record, when free to, committed versions of Jimmie's "Daddy and Home," "My Rough and Rowdy Ways," and pieces of "Mule Skinner Blues."

Incidentally, some of the key lines in "Mule Skinner" concerning the little water boy and the captain had appeared on records by the relatively obscure blues singer Tom Dickson, who apparently played around Memphis, and by the quite well-known pairing of Lonnie Johnson and Texas Alexander, in both cases before Jimmie made the material his own. But if you actually had been a water boy, had actually worked on the railroad, and built a persona as the Singing Brakeman, all of those train verses would naturally become better-known in your hands and be attached to you. There is no evidence that the blues singers whose train imagery he borrowed had worked those railroads. Jimmie was attracted to the verses because they described his natural territory.

One more songster with a wide Rodgers repertoire to mention was John Jackson out of Virginia, born in 1924, who became a familiar figure on the folk and blues festival circuit around Washington, D.C., from the time of the '60s folk revival through the '90s. He had learned numerous Rodgers songs from a trove of 78s sold to his family at ten cents apiece, and over the years, he recorded a half-dozen of them.

It was not only the lighthearted songsters of the black musical community who encountered Jimmie Rodgers directly. The fertile blues area around Jackson, Mississippi, and Crystal Springs to the south appears to have been a nexus for interaction between Jimmie and black bluesmen—hardly surprising since neither place is far from Meridian, and Jackson was the next big town nearby, with musical opportunities to match its size. One connection that has long been a subject of speculation is that between Jimmie Rodgers and his contemporary Tommy Johnson, whose seminal songs recorded for Victor in 1928 range from "Cool Drink of Water Blues" with a haunting falsetto moan that has a certain yodel-like quality, to the woman-saluting "Big Fat Mama Blues," with its very skillful interchange of guitar and vocal parts.

Jimmie Rodgers undoubtedly spent plenty of time around Jackson during the very period when Tommy Johnson was a local celebrity. It is even possible to coordinate their appearance calendars to find some known weeks when they were both in town. What seems to have finally nailed the connection, however, is a recording Tommy Johnson made for Paramount in 1929, which was not issued at the time but surfaced in 2001 on a test pressing (an initial quality check version of a recording of which only a few copies would exist) at an antique dealer's near the company's Grafton, Wisconsin, location. Finally released the following year, "I Want Someone to Love Me" proves to be an outright Jimmie Rodgers-style ballad with 1890s sentimental overtones—and Johnson's moan, in this case, does turn into an outright yodel. Musically at least, we have contact.

The highly popular black stringband the Mississippi Sheiks, from the same general area, who were themselves clearly influenced by Tommy Johnson, recorded several tunes, including "Jail Bird Love Song," patterned directly after Jimmie's blues records in themes and runs—in a style that probably influenced western swing bands later. Sam Chatmon, the last survivor of the Chatmon brothers who made up most of the band, claimed, in the '70s, to have played bass for Jimmie Rodgers at dances on several

Meeting Jimmie Rodgers

occasions. Sam was not above making boastful claims that could not stand much inspection, but this one may have been true.

While researching blues traditions in that region, David Evans encountered enough volunteered references among his African-American informants to having known Jimmie Rodgers and his music to collect them in a paper. He was struck by the fact that Jimmie was virtually the only white, country music–associated musician to have been recalled that way. Musicians with claimed firsthand memories of Jimmie performing in his early Mississippi days included recorded ones such as Rubin Lacy and Ishmon Bracey and unknowns such as seventy-six-year-old Herb Quinn, who assured Evans that Jimmie had been a working farmer right there in Tylertown, Mississippi, and had a wife named "Lady" to whom he called out on every record—as in "Oh, My Lady!"

Generally accepted as accurate—and tending to buttress Sam Chatmon's recollection of playing with him—is the story told by Houston Stackhouse, a bluesman encountered by David Evans in 1967 as he was researching the music of Tommy Johnson. Stackhouse only then started to record, when he was near sixty. He had been taught violin by the Mississippi Sheiks' fiddler Lonnie Chatmon and guitar by Johnson himself. Apparently Jimmie Rodgers had heard Stackhouse and his cousin Robert Lee McCoy (better known later as Robert Nighthawk) playing live on WJDX radio in Jackson in 1931.

As Stackhouse told *Living Blues* magazine's Jim O'Neal, "We was on the streets there in Jackson, playin' . . . and he came along that evenin' . . . [We'd] sound so good to him he'd come by lookin'. 'What about gettin' you boys to play with me tonight? I'm playin' at the hotel here . . . Where y'all gon' be at about seven o'clock?' . . . So we got ready and we come on down there. He come down, dressed up, 'Come on boys, y'all ready?' . . . Went up there and *jumped* with him; yeah—we had a time. I was playin' behind him . . . Jimmie Rodgers was playin' his numbers and Robert blowin' that harp pretty good, right along with that. Make the harp kind of yodel, too. We clownin'. Yeah, we had a good time *that* night."

Colorful and detailed, but less reconcilable with personal timelines or any other evidence, is the story Hammie Nixon, the harmonica-playing sidekick of Memphis-area bluesman Sleepy John Estes, told the same magazine's Kip Lornell. Nixon reported knowing Jimmie well from time spent living in the hobo jungle near the Memphis train station: "Old Jimmie Rodgers was with us; he was out there too. He was out there drinking that alcohol . . . denatured . . . I see him take that . . . cut it with sugar . . . I seen him take that old shoe polish and do the same thing. He'd strain it through that white bread . . . He was a good cook, too. I know we did a lot of playing together." Nixon then sang "Waiting for a Train" for the interviewer and added, "He was around Memphis, all along the road . . . He had a good old guitar, too. Jimmie Rodgers was a terrible guy, could beg his ass off for food . . . Big old wide-ass hat, and he was crazy about those boots." Perhaps there is some element of truth in that story, too; admittedly, by the time Estes and Nixon were established in Memphis, Jimmie was a recording star and unlikely to be hanging in hobo haunts as he once had. Still, Nixon's vagueness about the circumstances and timing did not necessarily mean he was mistaken or dissembling about the encounter itself.

About one set of blues musicians' involvement with Jimmie Rodgers there is no doubt whatsoever—those who, unusually enough in the days of segregated recordings, accompanied him on his records. The most celebrated of these cases was, of course, the "Blue Yodel No. 9" session with Louis and Lil Armstrong—and Armstrong was, among much else, a great blues singer if there ever was one. A coda to his knowing Jimmie Rodgers and recording with him out in Hollywood in 1930 was a number Louis recorded in 1932 with his New York orchestra, which begins with the chug of a locomotive and Louis saying, "Listen to that rhythm train, boy; I bet all them hoboes are all set under them rods." It was a hit pop novelty, not much loved by jazz critics, a bit of jive titled "Hobo, You Can't Ride This Train." "All aboard for Pittsburgh . . . Harrisburg . . . all them burgs!" Louis calls, setting off his brass section. "I'm the brakeman; I'm a tough man!" he announces later. He had played with the blues queens, Bessie included, played on that "Bridwell Blues" record that had bits of lyric that would show up on his record with Jimmie, recorded with the famous hobo brakeman— and now this may have been a sly salute to the whole chain of events. In any case, it's an infectious memento.

In June of 1931, Jimmie was in Louisville, Kentucky, for the recording sessions that included his sketches with the Carter Family. It was during one of those that he volunteered a relevant comment to Sara Carter: "I've had the blues all day; I guess you've got no business with the blues unless you can *sing* 'em." Then they duet on "T for Texas." It was also at those sessions that Jimmie cut records with both the Louisville Jug Band (otherwise known as Earl McDonald's Original Louisville Jug Band or The Dixieland Jug Blowers) and with skilled blues guitarist Clifford Gibson.

The practiced jug ensemble, led by jug blower and vocalist Earl McDonald and the reputedly obnoxious but effective fiddle player Clifford Hayes, had been around for years. A 1915 postcard has surfaced showing them already at work, and smart and set-up enough to have a fitting Kentucky sponsor; they were "The Old Grand-Dad [bourbon] Jug Band" back then. Jug bands were, in effect, folk jazz outfits, the sort that had once been known in New Orleans as "spasm bands" or "skiffle bands," using improvised instruments to play hot dance and novelty tunes, often of scurrilous sorts, for party occasions. By 1931, Louisville and Memphis were the two main homes of this raucous style. The Louisville Jug Band's skills were far from rudimentary, and their instrumentation now included a clarinet. Their 1927 version of—get this—"In the Jailhouse Now," sung as "In the Graveyard Now," is one of the hottest recorded. It is also one of the funnier sets of lyrics applied to that vaudeville song of nineteenth-century origin, for which the whole point is to introduce your own best verses to the story. (Jimmie's sets have lasted better than anyone else's.) We do not know how this band came to record with Jimmie; presumably he knew their records or had heard their broadcasts and asked them to join him. They backed him on one of his most successfully jazzy numbers, "My Good Gal's Gone Blues." Surviving lyric sheets from the session show verses from several hands coming together to form the song. It is fascinating that "Try and Treat Her Right" by black vocalist Ben Ferguson, cut the very same day at the same place and with the same Louisville backup musicians as Jimmie's cut, was provided a tune and arrangement virtually identical to "My Good Gal's Gone."

There is ample reason to suppose that Jimmie was familiar with the better known Memphis jug band players, as well. The city was within his known stomping grounds, and he probably heard the more stripped-down but amusing version of "He's in the Jailhouse Now" that Gus Cannon and Blind Blake recorded in 1927, as well as the particularly loose, raucous version recorded by Will Shade's Memphis Jug Band (another act Ralph Peer recorded for Victor) in 1930. It should be noted, too, that the "T for Texas, T for Tennessee" line appeared in Memphis bluesman Frank Stokes' "Nehi Mamma Blues" recorded for Victor, again by Peer, the same month Jimmie cut it. That could set off endless speculation—except that the line had already appeared in Lonnie Johnson's "Kansas City Blues" in 1927.

Clifford Gibson was a Lonnie Johnson disciple from St. Louis and a worthy, fine-picking guitarist. He backed Jimmie on the best take of the terrific "Let Me Be Your Side Track," but that version would not be released until years later. An interesting sidelight is that among the handful of tracks Gibson recorded for records of his own during the Louisville sessions was "Railroad Man Blues," laid down two days before the Rodgers song. The melodic and rhythm patterns are essentially the same, while the theme is "you can't keep your woman and be no railroad man." Gibson happens to receive first-class piano backing, evidently by Roosevelt Sykes. Too bad Sykes did not stick around to back Jimmie, too. Gibson also sings on that track, "I'm not telling you what I heard; I'm just telling you what I know," which might be taken for a precursor of Jimmie's stronger "I'm not singing the blues, I'm telling you the hard luck I've had" on "Jimmie's Texas Blues," except that Jimmie had recorded that two years earlier. The "let me be your side track" verse itself, on the other hand, had already been recorded in 1926, to no great stir, by the relatively obscure New Orleans Willie Jackson, who had sung with King Oliver's jazz band. We are looking at a community with shared interests.

Jimmie's "Side Track" would reappear in 1947 in the able hands of John Sellers, a one-time gospel singer out of Chicago, in a unique version that is pure postwar jump blues, has Willie Dixon on bass, and updates the lyric slightly to refer to "hep cats!" It is probably no accident that this singular jump blues Rodgers adaptation comes from a former Mississippian. Sellers had started out in the Delta and had no doubt heard Rodgers records there.

Jimmie Rodgers, unlike most black blues singers, who had access only to black listeners, could take this music out into a much larger pop arena and to broader audiences. He was allowed—and he was able. We should not let the injustice in the discrimination that made it easier for him to profit from blues music blind us to what he did for the idiom, if from his privileged position. Offering no imitation of African-Americans in his diction, accents, or word choices, Jimmie Rodgers found ways to further the spread and acceptance of the blues without an ounce of condescension to the musical material he loved, and without a trace of minstrelsy in his blues performances. And, as white musicians have repeatedly commented over the years, Jimmie provided them a route to the blues that avoided minstrelsy or, at the very least, avoided musical theft without love.

The country singer Jimmie Skinner, as noted in chapter 2, grew up a poor white farm kid, not so far from Louisville. His parents were fans of the blues and had a collection of African-American originals, the so-called race records, but the young Jimmie, with dreams of performing, had found the musical style of those performers out of reach to him, intimidating. What's more, his father had told him what so many people said—that a white man could not sing the blues.

"I was partial to the blues as a kid, "he would recall, "and my daddy was, and my mother was. So I came by that honest. I don't know why I like the blues so well, but they did and I did, too. But we hadn't heard the blues sung like Jimmie Rodgers did them, you know . . . Jimmie was the first white artist I ever heard sing the blues. I admired and loved the Carter Family, too, but I could kind of *go along* with Jimmie . . . I got me a cheap guitar and I tried to yodel and strum like [him] . . . This man was a great man." Skinner then relates how the mere playing of Rodgers' new "T for Texas" in a Hamilton, Ohio, saloon circa 1928 could set off altercations. It was rough, it was tough, and it led to things. "It could definitely set off fights." For whites, that macho aspect would have implications that would reverberate right into the era of rock 'n' roll.

The Blues Hall of Fame first recognized Jimmie Rodgers' contribution to that central American musical form in 1984, in a special W. C. Handy Award that cited his "perpetuation of the blues in country music." In 2007, the state of Mississippi made the park by the Meridian, Mississippi, railway station, now known as "Singing Brakeman Park," the site of the first Mississippi Blues Trail marker honoring a white artist. The state marker reads, in part, "Jimmie Rodgers introduced the blues to a far wider audience than any other artist of the time, black or white . . . The influence of his famous 'blue yodels' can be heard in the music of . . . blues artists including Howlin' Wolf, Mississippi John Hurt, Tommy Johnson, and the Mississippi Sheiks."

Blues music is often discussed and delineated much as Jimmie Rodgers is—as a sort of inkblot test of American culture. Jazz fans and critics speak of blues and mean someone like Jimmy Witherspoon; folk critics, an act like Sonny Terry and Brownie McGhee; rockers, a Muddy Waters. They find what they look for. What remains consistent, though, is how often blues reasserts itself in new commercial pop trends—as it once was itself. Here comes swing as a commercial fad, and it's blues. Here come jump bands, and they play blues. Here comes Elvis, or the Rolling Stones, and here we are again. The other part of the Jimmie Rodgers blues story is this: he started one of those pop fads himself.

Select Soundtrack

Playlist: Key Rodgers or Rodgers-like blues verses and references on record before Jimmie Rodgers recorded them

(Available from the completist blues label Document Records or online public domain music sites except where noted.)

- **Ma Rainey:** "Southern Blues," 1923 ("If your house catches fire . . ." and "Let me be your rag doll, until . . ."), and "Travelin' Blues," 1928 ("I went to the depot and looked up on the board . . .").
- **Trixie Smith:** "Railroad Blues," May 1924 ("When a man gets the blues, he grabs a freight train and rides . . ." and "I asked

the brakeman to let me ride the blinds . . ."). Also in **Clara Smith:** "Freight Train Blues," September 1924. (See also **Lee Morse,** chapter 4.)

- **Bessie Smith:** "Louisiana Low-Down Blues," 1924 ("Mississippi River, I know it's deep and wide . . ."); "Sinful Blues," 1924 ("Get me a gun long . . ."); and "Send Me to the 'Lectric Chair," 1927 ("stood there laughin' over him . . .").
- **Papa Charlie Jackson:** "The Faking Blues," 1925 ("I can get more women than a passenger train can haul . . .").
- **Maggie Jones (a.k.a. Fae Barnes):** "Undertaker's Blues," 1925 ("Cemetery sure is one more lonesome place; when you're dead, they throw dirt in your face . . .").
- **New Orleans Willie Jackson:** "Railroad Man Blues," 1926 ("Let me be your sidetrack . . ." and "I'm a section hand, workin' on the L&N . . .").
- **Blind Lemon Jefferson:** "Wartime Blues," 1926 ("I'm going to drink muddy water, sleep in a hollow log . . ."). Also, there is a "Texas/Tennessee" pairing in "Long, Lonesome Blues," 1926; and "I had a dream last night . . ." in "Lonesome Home Blues," 1927.
- **Mike Jackson:** "Kissing Mule Blues," 1926 ("Hey, hey, hey! . . ." and "she grabbed hold that train . . .").
- **Wylie Barner:** "My Gal Treats Me Mean," 1927 ("See that spider climbing . . . to get his ashes hauled").
- **Texas Alexander and Lonnie Johnson:** "Section Gang Blues," 1927 ("Water boy, bring your water round . . . set your bucket down").
- **Blind Blake and Gus Cannon:** "He's in the Jailhouse Now," 1927. See also: **Earl McDonald's Original Louisville Jug Band:** "She's in the Graveyard Now," 1927, and **Memphis Jug Band:** "He's in the Jailhouse Now," 1930.
- **Lonnie Johnson:** "Kansas City Blues Part 1," 1927 ("T for Texas; T for Tennessee"). See also: **Frank Stokes:** "Nehi Mama," 1928, which also includes the verse "When a man takes the blues. . . ." See also: **Willie Brown:** "Future Blues," 1930.
- **Tom Dickson:** "Labor Blues," 1928 ("Good mornin' captain; good mornin' shine . . .").

- **Willard (Ramblin') Thomas:** "Back Gnawing Blues," 1928 ("I ain't ever loved but three women in my life . . ."), and "Ground Hog Blues," 1932 ("Some ground hog is rootin' round my back door . . .").

- **Willie Baker:** "No No Blues," 1929 ("I'm a stranger, just blowed in your town . . .").

- **Ben Ferguson:** "Try and Treat Her Right," the 1931 "My Good Gal's Gone" clone, is on the CD *Ruckus Juice and Chitlins: The Great Jug Bands Volume 1* (Yazoo/Shanachie, 1998).

- **Jimmie Rodgers accompanied by African-American blues musicians:** "Blue Yodel No. 9" with Louis and Lil Armstrong, 1930; "Let Me Be Your Side Track," with Clifford Gibson; "My Good Gal's Gone Blues" with the Louisville Jug Band (Clifford Hayes, Earl McDonald, et al.), 1931.

Blues and Songster Recordings Markedly Influenced by Jimmie Rodgers or Using Verses He Had Previously Recorded

- **Tommy Johnson:** "I Want Someone to Love Me," 1929, is available on the *bluesimages.com* Web site, and on *Times Ain't Like They Used to Be, Volume 8* (Yazoo, 2003).

- **Peg Leg Howell:** "Broke and Hungry Blues" and "Away from Home," 1929 ("Waiting for a Train" references).

- **Furry Lewis:** "Old Hobo" (1967 "Waiting for a Train" version); "Furry's Blues," 1928 ("I'm going to get my pistol . . . I'm going to shoot my woman, just to see her fall").

- **Mississippi John Hurt:** His 1963 versions of "Waiting for a Train" and his adaptation of it, "Mermaids Flirt with Me," are both on the CD *D.C. Blues* (Fuel, 2000).

- **The Mississippi Sheiks:** "Jail Bird Love Song," "Yodeling Fiddling Blues" (both 1930).

- **Clifford Gibson:** "Railroad Man Blues" (same 1931 session as "Side Track," with Jimmie).

- **Louis Armstrong:** "Hobo, You Can't Ride This Train," 1932, on *Complete RCA Victor Recordings*, 1997, and online.

- **Tampa Red:** "Worried Devil Blues" (1934, with Rodgers-style yodel).

- **Lead Belly:** "Daddy I'm Coming Home" (version of "Daddy and Home") and "Honey I'm All Down and Out" (with "mule's behind" reference, etc.), originally 1935, are recorded by the BBC on *Bridging Lead Belly* (Rounder, 1999); "Cowboy Song," 1940, with "My Rough and Rowdy Ways" lyric and "In the Jailhouse" patterns, is on *Bourgeois Blues: Lead Belly Legacy, Vol. 2* (Smithsonian Folkways, 1997).

- **John Sellers:** His 1947 jump version of "Let Me Be Your Side Track" is on the Bear Family *Let Me Be Your Sidetrack* Rodgers' influence box set (2008).

- **Snooks Eaglin:** "Helping Hand/A Thousand Miles Away from Home" ("Waiting for a Train" via Fats Domino, 1959) is on *Snooks Eaglin: New Orleans Street Singer* (Smithsonian Folkways, 2005); "Give Me the Good Old Boxcar," 1958, is on *Country Boy in New Orleans* (Arhoolie, 1993).

- **John Jackson:** "T.B. Blues," "Waiting for a Train," and "He's in the Jailhouse Now" are on *Country Blues and Ditties*; "Mule Skinner Blues" is on *Don't Let Your Deal Go Down* (both Arhoolie). "Mississippi River Blues" is on *Deep in the Bottom* (Rounder). His version of Jimmie's "Frankie and Johnny" is on *The Harry Smith Connection* (Smithsonian Folkways).

- **Scott Dunbar:** "Blue Yodel," 1970, is on *From Lake Mary* (Fat Possum, 2000).

- **James Cotton:** "Muleskinner Blues" (with Peter Rowan) is on *Baby Don't You Tear My Clothes* (Telarc, 2004).

four

America's Blue Yodeler No. 2
Instigator of Blue Yodelmania

There are moans in the blues, shouts and whispers, laughs, titters, and cries, with many variations, often meaningful, often musically functional, sometimes both. When you hear Jimmie Rodgers' blues, you know that you are going to hear one variation, his own blue yodel. As a matter of fact, you will hear some version of that most distinctive part of his vocalizing in just about every recording he made. From the first, there were many listeners enthralled by the expectation of hearing that yodel—and some who were not.

Eddy Arnold, who became hugely successful by straddling country music and pop, was happy, all through his life, to sing "Waiting for a Train" at the drop of a Rodgers hat, and his "Cattle Call" was a yodeling country classic. Yet in recalling his own plowboy youth when Jimmie's records were hitting (and supplying the old hick accent of his Tennessee neighbor to tell the tale), he said, "I remember, as a boy, to everybody in the rural area where I lived, Jimmie Rodgers was like *God*. Yodel-Layee-Oh! But there was an old farmer, I'll never forget it, out there, who said, 'I hu-wish that Jimmie Rodgers was *daid*.' And they asked him why. 'Well, 'cause he learned every boy in the country how to yodel!' Yodel-ay-eee!"

W. E. Myers, a phonograph dealer, record producer, and wannabe poet from Richlands, Virginia, who asked Mississippi John Hurt to put his "Let the Mermaids Flirt with Me" lyric to music—a request Hurt answered by marrying it to Jimmie's tune for "Waiting for a Train"—printed a guarantee on every last record put out by his little Lonesome Ace label: "Without

Young Gene Autry demonstrates the way a Blue Yodeler sits.

a Yodel." Buy one of Lonesome Ace's new Dock Boggs records, circa 1929, and the phrase would jump out at you, emblazoned below the image of a biplane in flight—ace aviators, good; blue yodelers, bad. A guarantee, just so you would be safe from the yodel blight.

Such reactions show how crazy both record buyers and producers had become for blues with yodeling touches, from the moment of the release of Jimmie's first smash hit, "Blue Yodel," in early 1928. Eighty years later, there can be no doubt that the blue yodelmania of the following years was set off by that record's success.

In the waning years of the twentieth century, however, the question of how far Jimmie was responsible for creating the "blues with yodel" sound, genre, tactic, or, if you insist, gimmick, in the first place came to be raised, particularly by crafty advocates for an alternative blue yodel inventor; no, not the Earl of Oxford, but the idiosyncratic, sometimes brilliant, in some ways groundbreaking latter-day blackface minstrel Emmett Miller.

Miller had had no advocates until Merle Haggard, privately introduced to the man's music by Bob Wills in the early '70s, began recording "I Ain't Got Nobody," "Right or Wrong," "Big Bad Bill," and "Lovesick Blues," explicitly linking them to the then forgotten Miller. The open questions about this mysterious figure first intrigued, then obsessed the writer Nick Tosches, a flamboyant literary stylist and—generally—quite careful researcher. Tosches would eventually gather virtually everything knowable, unknowable, and tangentially relevant about "the minstrel man from Georgia" in his far-ranging, often enthralling, and occasionally misleading 2001 book, *Where Dead Voices Gather*.

The proposition that Tosches first hints at cautiously, then argues for outright in those pages (employing some agile sleight-of-hand to get there) is that Miller, not Rodgers, introduced the application of yodeling to the blues and bluish singing. That argument can immediately be dismissed for one simple reason: Demonstrably, neither of them did, for both had well-documented predecessors, as well as contemporaries toying with similar ideas who clearly were not influenced by either of them. *Similar* is the key word here, for similar does not mean alike. The plain fact is you will not find a blue yodel that is identical to Jimmie Rodgers' at any time before he started recording—though there would be many who would imitate what he did or extend his sort of yodel into new territory once he had shown the way.

The yodeling background is altogether less mysterious than it once seemed. The entry of yodeling of any sort into American popular music (and into many other global idioms), has been explored in detail by the resourceful Bart Plantenga in his 2004 book *Yodel-Ay-Ee-Oooo: The Secret History of Yodeling Around the World*. What emerges from his extensive research is that whether the yodel came into American song and show business by way of German-speaking Swiss settlers in Central Pennsylvania who migrated South, or evolved from African voice-shifting tricks, or from rural southern field hollers gone tuneful and rhythmic, or was adapted by arriving Americans (black and white alike) from Native American falsetto chants, or was fueled mostly by touring nineteenth-century Alpine yodeling acts playing split weeks in Toledo in short pants—whatever its origin—yodeling was already very well established as a performance technique in the nineteenth century; and some variety of yodeling could be found everywhere in the world.

Yodeling is essentially a simple physical act that some people can do, and once they find that they can do it, they tend to toy with it. Others try for years to do it and simply cannot. Looking for an ultimate inventor of vocalizing that cracks and leaps into falsetto is like looking for the inventor of whistling, snapping your fingers, wiggling your ears, or curling your lip. (No, that was *not* Elvis.)

Some have jumped to the unfounded conclusion that Jimmie yodeled the way he did because he could not handle the "real" Swiss style, but Jimmie appears not to have cared very much for that athletic, showy style of yodeling, with its emotional disconnection from the lyric. In the spring of 1930, when one of his periodic bouts with illness sidelined him from performances with Swain's Hollywood Follies, he telegraphed Gene Autry asking if Gene could hurry and audition to sub for him, specifically because "I understand they are going to run a friek [sic] yodeler in my place." *Freak* in 1930 was not a compliment.

As for the notion of adding a yodel to a bluesy number, that had already been tried in the 1923 song "Yodeling Blues," recorded both by Bessie Smith and as a duet by Sara Martin with Eva Taylor. Taylor, incidentally, is an artist Jimmie reportedly crossed paths with on the vaudeville circuit. She was also the wife of the song's author, Clarence Williams.

In his September 1928 *Bookman* magazine column, reviewing Jimmie's "My Loving Gal Lucille"—under the subheading "White man singing black songs," no less—Abbe Niles had already made this connection, while underscoring Rodgers' singular role in the unfolding story: "[It's] Part II of Jimmie Rodgers's 'Blue Yodel,' Part I of which started the whole epidemic of yodelling blues that now rages," Niles wrote, adding "though Clarence Williams wrote a good one five years ago." In fact, no one would confuse the sounds on the "Yodeling Blues" records of 1923 with the ones Jimmie was making; the so-called yodeling in the earlier recordings is limited to the rhythmic repetition of the word *yodel*. (As we will see, at this stage even the spelling of this term, whether in noun, verb, or gerund form, was unfixed.)

Meeting Jimmie Rodgers

The immensely clarifying research of Lynn Abbott and Doug Seroff into nineteenth-century and early-twentieth-century African-American show business includes an extensive history of yodeling as it was applied to increasingly "hot" ragtime and bluesy material. They have retrieved information on the careers of such utterly forgotten vaudeville acts as Monroe Tabor, "the Yodelling Bell Boy," who was singing and making florid yodel noises around 1907; the Jolly Hendersons: Beulah ("America's Only Colored Lady Yodeler") and husband Billy, who were performing "Sleep Baby Sleep" a full generation before Jimmie (or Riley Puckett) did; and one artist we can at least hear on record for comparison, Charles Anderson, who was known as the "Yodeler Blues Singer."

Anderson, who sang with Bessie Smith for a spell and went on to record such numbers as "Yodle Song Coo-Coo," "Laughing Yodle," and "Sing 'Em Blues" in 1923–24, reportedly sang "Sleep Baby Sleep" onstage in nurse-mammy drag, a presentation format he used also for "St. Louis Blues." By 1915, he was being hailed not only as an especially convincing female impersonator (and as an arresting singer out of drag, too) but also as a great note-holding yodeler, "like a bird poised on its wing, flying without a flutter," and a singer of this brand-new "phase of ragtime," as it was described, called "the blues." On record, you can hear Anderson's ladylike (and, in retrospect, maybe somewhat cowgirl-like) falsetto yodel swoops on "Roll On Silver Moon," with its Jimmie-like song title, though with a tune closer to "Who's Afraid of the Big Bad Wolf?" than to anything from the Rodgers discography. On his numbers with "Yodle" titles, the singing has a musty whiff, left over from the minstrel era (as would also be true of Emmett Miller), while the yodeling has a flavor of Gilbert and Sullivan burlesque gone Swiss, the showy note-holding having nothing much to do with the blue yodeling fostered by Jimmie Rodgers.

Anderson's turn on "Sing 'Em Blues," one of the more creditable of older blues numbers, is a mind-blowing bit of vocal cross-dressing in itself. (Did Bessie Smith learn from this guy, you wonder—or is he burlesquing her?) But the "blue yodel" is far from the kind we are looking for; it is ornamentation, stage bravura—having nothing discernibly to do with the lyric or even the song structure. Nonetheless, he was advertised as a "Yodeler Blues Singer," and was—of a sort. Similar to a degree, but not alike.

A performer of the '20s did not have to be a female impersonator, or African-American, or to have heard either Jimmie Rodgers or Emmett Miller to bring yodel-like leaps into jazz and bluesy torch songs. Take, for instance, the extraordinary, sexy, hard-living, yet now rarely recalled vaudeville and Broadway singer Lee Morse, who was billed as the "Southern Aristocrat of Song," despite having come from a family of entertainers and preachers from Idaho.

The quite Caucasian Ms. Morse regularly "doot-doot-dooted" and "whoa-hoed" at the end of lines for effect, bent notes, and broke words in ways that often explicitly imitated black singers; there is minstrelsy there in that sense, but no mockery. Most Rodgers fans would be stunned to hear her use of the traveling blues verse "when a man gets blue, he grabs a train and rides," right along with a line-ending yodel, of a sort, on her record "Mail Man Blues." She can be seen singing it, with guitar, in two short 1930 Vitaphone sound films, *A Million Me's* and *The Music Racket*—in the latter case, complete with black urchins dancing to her yodeling scat. Gene Austin knew her; there is no evidence that Jimmie Rodgers did—though he would have certainly read about her (as she would of him) in the trade papers.

More entries of note from the vaudeville yodelsphere, white people's division: As early as 1898 to 1902, in the Edison cylinder recording era, vaudevillian George P. Watson had recorded both "Sleep Baby Sleep" and "Roll Along Silver Moon," presaging Charles Anderson's set list, though in a style more remindful of a concert singer like John McCormack. Watson also recorded medleys of "Emmett's Yodles," which included the fairly well-remembered old voice-cracking phrase "Go to sleep my bay-*hay*-bee"; the title referred to Dan Emmett, the original nineteenth-century minstrel man, not Emmett Miller. In the early '20s, Frank Kamplain, a popular recording artist, both alone and teamed with the even more prolifically recorded Al Bernard as the Record Boys, was recording dated, genteel but conceptually suggestive "coon songs" and "mammy ditties" with yodels such as "Oleo-lady," "Broken-Hearted Blues," and the minstrelsy-laden story song "Yodelin' Bill." ("He's doggone pretty," they inform us and "works down by the flour mill." The piano is asked to "yodel for us" too, and the player simply picks up the yodel melody—a sign of musical things to come.)

One last entry in this catalog: The obscure vaudevillian Roy Evans was reintroduced in the company of Jimmie Rodgers and Emmett Miller in a 1999 CD featuring "Blue Yodelers" as they recorded with jazz greats, however fleetingly. Evans, the "Eccentric Voice," made records for some years for Columbia, almost immediately after Jimmie started recording for Victor; sides such as "Weary Yodelin' Blues" and his jazzy song "Syncopated Yodelin' Man," which features lyrics that seem to be *about* Jimmie. But since Evans was evidently singing similar stuff before "T for Texas" hit the streets, we cannot simply dismiss him as a bandwagon hopper. Nor does he exactly sound like one; he had the benefit of the premier stride piano man James P. Johnson on some sides and the great guitarist Eddie Lang, and even young Benny Goodman on clarinet. With that musical aid, Evans lets his syllables shudder and vibrates his "yodel-ay-ee-oo"-type yodels, which function as breaks between verses but, nevertheless, do not finally *mean* a thing (or have much swing)—except that somebody wants to make a bluesy record with yodels. Virtually nobody since has much cared about the results.

Which brings us back to Emmett Miller, the "Famous Yodeling Blues Singer," as he was sometimes billed. The secondary allegation in Nick Tosches' book (raised with the caveat that it might not hold water, but made, for all that) is that Jimmie Rodgers did not record "T for Texas" during his first session with Ralph Peer at Bristol, on August 4, 1927—rather than four months later, at Camden, New Jersey—because he couldn't. The reason: he had only just picked up the blue yodel idea, perhaps while encountering Miller in Ashville, so he would not have had a handle on the style yet. Tosches had suggested the possibility of a Jimmie-Emmett meeting back in 1925 earlier in the narrative, but the evidence was not convincing, so the theory requires this later date to back up the claim of direct imitation. Necessarily for his case, Tosches brushes off Carrie Rodgers' firsthand report of Jimmie's explanation—that he had held back on the song till later for strategic career reasons—by calling it a lie. The word used is "doubtful," and the suggested explanation is that she is abetting her husband in stealing a credit that belonged to Miller. There is then a lot of breathless, D. W. Griffith–style crosscutting between what Emmett's doing through the fall of '27 and what Jimmie is doing somewhere else, apparently implying that Miller was out there taking the lead in the (one and only) blue yodeler sweepstakes while Jimmie dawdled—though it is not entirely clear how any of that detail of diverging itineraries is supposed to have affected what Jimmie actually knew how to sing, or what Emmett did either.

Let's get a grip on some facts. First, the old-time tent rep showman Billy Terrell, in the Spring 1954 issue of the Jimmie Rodgers Society fan journal, the *Blue Yodeler*, offered a perfectly credible, detailed portrait of the young Jimmie auditioning for his show and then performing fresh, crowd-riveting blue yodels in it—in 1923. This is what Terrell reports, beginning at the point when Rodgers has just informed Billy that he is a blue yodeler ("something I'd never heard of") and then stunned him at the audition by proving it: "I told the performers and musicians I had discovered a boy that was a blue yodeler and plenty good to my way of thinking. Jimmie and I had to listen to the wise cracks by some of the wise-guys that run [*sic*] like this: 'I expect his number will be plenty *blue* alright.' 'What is a blue yodeler, a farmer?' 'Oh, I bet he's going to wear a Swiss outfit.'"

That mockery certainly suggests that Jimmie's sort of blues with yodels was something the boys in the band had not actually seen or heard before. Terrell continues: "The big tent was packed that night   out came Jimmie with that big smile on his face; he walked to the center of the stage and started whipping that old guitar—then he pulled his train whistle and he

had them in the palm of his hand . . . three numbers and two big encores."
At that point, the impressed, formerly wisecracking musicians proceed to
apologize to the blue yodeler.

Returning to that supposedly crucial period four years later, around the
middle of 1927, Tosches also suggests that the Jimmie Rodgers Entertainers—
Jimmie and the Grant Brothers—had left Ashville by the end of June for
points north, with no time to work on blue yodels in their haste, immediately after (just possibly) having seen Emmett Miller perform. That simply is
not true. The Jimmie Rodgers Entertainers' show at the nearby Henderson-
ville, North Carolina, high school auditorium, described by Claude Grant
to Nolan Porterfield as a fiasco where hardly anybody showed up, can now
be precisely dated—by a previously unreported handbill for the show, preserved in Carrie and Jimmie Rodgers' personal vaudeville scrapbook. The
date was actually July 16, 1927, which means that the band stayed around
Asheville for weeks longer than Tosches suggests, and until much closer to
the Bristol date, the one at which Jimmie had supposedly been too busy traveling and too unpracticed in blue yodeling to record anything of the kind.
The handbill promised the North Carolina audience "good popular singing, blue singing," and "yodeling." Evidently Jimmie already had something
good enough to show—but then, he had had that for at least four years.

If Jimmie Rodgers had any reason for holding off on recording a blue
yodel at Bristol, beyond those he suggested to his wife—that he thought the
deciders at Victor might find the blue yodel too risky; that if he could get
signed for a familiar number like "Sleep Baby Sleep," he would have something big ready for them next—it was almost certainly a single, new, and
entirely practical factor.

For years before Bristol, by all reports, he had been putting blues verses
together at will, just as other blues singers did—winging it from familiar
verses interspersed with others he had made up, incorporating yodels that
seemed to fit. With the sudden interest in recording blues numbers, many
blues performers were suddenly confronting the need to have a set of more
or less narrative, or at the least thematically coherent verses for recording—
enough to provide a novel, distinguishable turn for each of what were now
discrete songs. That was something nobody had much bothered about when
they were only thinking in terms of live performance.

Jimmie had never had to provide the sort of finished, specific, thematic
"song for a new record" Ralph Peer was now looking for—indeed, demanding. In those weeks between Bristol and Camden, what he probably did was
fix up and polish blues songs for recording and in the process decided to
concentrate on one in particular, about this wreck-making woman named
Thelma who is going to get herself shot by the singer.

Reports of Jimmie's shows in the months that follow suggest that, "T for Texas" aside, Jimmie was still tending to put together verses and add relevant yodels that worked for what he sang. Over the course of a year, some of those works-in-progress would become good enough to record, once Jimmie had done the work that turns a casual blues sung on a porch, or in a caboose or juke joint, into a finished piece of popular music called "Blue Yodel No. 4" or "Brakeman's Blues."

It takes nothing away from Emmett Miller's real contribution to American popular music to point out that there is simply no significant evidence that he was a particular model for Jimmie Rodgers, or vice versa. Indeed, the first thing that will strike anybody listening for the basis of Jimmie Rodgers' blue yodel in Miller's recordings is that, although Emmett's singing is often extraordinary, with a modern and effective way of varying his phrasing and breaking up or extending syllables for melismatic effect, there is very little that can be called a discrete yodel at all.

You cannot be sure what someone meant by "yodeling" in these old reports without having heard the sounds, or at least getting some really good detailed description; the definition of the term is as slippery as the sounds identified by it.

Jimmie Rodgers does exhibit some of the elements Miller exploited so well in his singing of a line like "I've got the Tee-hee, Bee-hee . . . Blue-hoo-hoo-hooze," where we are not far at all from Emmett's "I've got a feeling for the blue-oo-hoo, uh-hoo-Hooze since my mama said goodbye." And, yes, Jimmie may have been aware of that, given the show business roads they were both traveling and may have even picked that up from Miller. Alternatively, Miller may have been influenced by Rodgers. But whether either was influenced by the other is probably quite beside the point anyway because Bert Williams, the singular, heartbreaking African-American burnt-cork vaudeville star, had been recording that sort of expressive word extension and voice break since his record of "Nobody" in 1906—and there can be no doubt that both Rodgers and Miller would have known that. In their world, that was unavoidable music, and information.

But was, say, Emmett Miller's 1924 or 1928 recording of "Anytime," the Happy Lawson song that would be a hit for both Eddy Arnold and Eddie Fisher decades later, in Rodgers' personal record collection or somewhere vaguely in the back of his head as he set down his "Any Old Time" as recorded in February 1929? For all anybody knows, it could have been. The two men's records and songs have some similarities in concept and sound: proving love is true, coming back home, any (old) time, and all enunciated more or less jazzily. But there are dissimilarities as well and the additional complication that "Any Old Time" has always had a cowriting credit assigned to Elsie

McWilliams' niece Lula Belle White, who is said to have supplied the initial idea for the song. The contents of Lula Belle's record collection are lost to history.

What is probably more to the point is that Rodgers and Miller were two vaudevillians springing from overlapping though not identical performing backgrounds, working similar territory between pop and black-derived blues—often, no doubt, with similar audiences. The brother- and sisterhood of traveling vaudeville, late minstrel, burlesque, and medicine show performers was as much a community in its own way as the blues community, with which it intersected here and there.

Vaudevillians, like blues musicians, caught each other's bits of business and shared them knowingly, sometimes gladly, or at least realizing that they would inevitably show up elsewhere anyhow. They might try to be protective of their special "bits of business," but generally speaking, as here in the Internet age, exclusivity was just a matter of time. That more than one touring performer might be using a yodel, a bird whistle, a train whistle, or a falsetto leap in the manner of Gene Austin to make sure you remember them till they rolled into your town again a year or more later—that is perfectly understandable, and it happened. (In the backwaters where Jimmie Rodgers sometimes traveled, for the audiences of somewhere like Stephensville, Texas, the performers might never be coming back at all.)

Let's step beyond musical examples to illustrate the point. Charlie Chaplin's "Oceana Roll" bit in *The Gold Rush*, where forks and rolls become his head's dancing legs, is among his best-known and most rightfully lauded routines. Yet it had been done on film by Fatty Arbuckle years earlier, and Arbuckle's protégé Buster Keaton apparently knew it, too. The crucial difference was how Charlie did it, and in what context, and to what end. It was not really about the novel idea of combining high kicking tableware and baked goods. So, too, for combining blues and yodelish sounds. What mattered was how and when you did it.

Make no mistake; while singers of his time and before his time had shown off plenty of variations on the yodel, Jimmie Rodgers' blue yodel had its own specific nature. As Cliff Carlisle, the steel guitarist who had accompanied Rodgers and found him so "blacklike" and who would go on to become a key Jimmie-style blue yodeler himself, explained, "I don't think there's *anything* like a blue yodel . . . I'm not talking against the Swiss yodel or any other yodel that anybody does, but to me, all this other stuff is done by the *tongue.* The blue yodel is done from down in *here . . . From* where, I don't know, but I don't think everybody can do [it]." Carlisle evidently means his lower throat by that "down here," though he might just as easily have been referring to his heart, gut, or gonads.

Meeting Jimmie Rodgers

The blue yodel was Jimmie Rodgers' own in every sense that could possibly have mattered to anyone—a forceful, varied outpouring of his own nature; sometimes heartbroken, haunted, lonesome, or doomed, at other times gleeful, mocking, or boastful. Whatever the intended effect, it would show up in the song in precisely the form and at the moment the song required. The yodel was not a sideshow breath-holding contest (as if he could have competed in one of those), not a demonstration of high note scaling or a display of stringing together nonsense syllables.

Jimmie's musical uses of his blue yodel were many. Frequently, the tune applied to the yodel mirrors or finishes off the guitar run that introduces the song. Take "No Hard Times," for instance, where the yodel following the verse subtly but precisely matches the halting guitar intro, picks up on it. Often, too, the yodel drives the song forward or into the next line or verse; as in "My Good Gal's Gone Blues," for instance, where Jimmie's yodel modulates gently up to kick off the clarinet solo by the Louisville Jug Band's George Allen. As put to work in Jimmie's more driving sides, this practice would be of continuing interest to singers and instrumentalists in later propulsive genres such as bluegrass and rock 'n' roll. We could compare, for example, the celebrated live and recorded performances of the 1970 number "Stage Fright," by The Band. Rick Danko trills the line "sings just like a bird" till it breaks into almost yodel-like bird tones, which are immediately and seamlessly picked up and mimicked by the keyboards. This may be a good time for a long overdue salute to the all but anonymous Ruth Ann Moore, who picks up on Jimmie's yodel on "Gambling Polka Dot Blues" and runs with it on the ivories. Somebody had to be first.

Ernest Tubb initially felt a tremendous loss when a tonsillectomy robbed him of his ability to yodel Jimmie-style but came to realize that this limitation forced him to find his own inimitable vocal approach. When asked about Rodgers matters, he would always stress, with his usual perceptiveness, how different the impetus behind Jimmie's yodeling was from that of showboating yodelers, not least in his inventive, virtually song-by-song variations that added to the song's mood and tone, whether that be lonesome, light, or blue.

Such dexterity in capturing varied emotional precision is a rare performing gift, but Jimmie Rodgers had it. His mercurial tendencies—and skills—would become all the clearer as his records deployed an arresting variety of backings, themes, and sounds, in addition to the stylistically and functionally varied yodels and jumps between different musical genres.

That he could demonstrate all of this diversity without losing anything of his individuality is a measure of the force and solidity of the man everyone was meeting, someone very appealing who knew who he was and could translate it stylistically. This was a *somebody* who was wending his way through those variations. The audience that heard him, the musicians who played with him, and the performers of his music who have followed have always known that.

So when we consider why Jimmie Rodgers has had a musical after-life powerfully different from that of the forgotten Miller, it is worth noting that even the musicians who recorded with Emmett did not really seem to be able to remember him. He left no strong personal impression; whereas anyone who ever met Jimmie seems to recall all of the moments in detail and is often willing to ornament the memory further. Does this not tell us something?

Miller spent his entire career hiding behind that burnt-cork minstrel blackface, practically addicted to it, it is said. Putting aside everything else that is repugnant about the whole minstrelsy enterprise, blackface is not a good way to leave audiences with strong impressions of your essential self, of an evocative individual personality.

Miller seems to have had a small number of friends, only a few lasting fans, and virtually no advocates until so many years later when interest in what he had accomplished would amount to curiosity about something old, lost, and intriguing. It would remain a specialized interest, too, shared only by clued-up insiders; Miller's recordings, having come back into circulation, quickly disappeared again (not that this matters so much in the digital age).

Jimmie Rodgers' music, too, as we will see, went through a period when interest ebbed; after so much exposure, that was inevitable. But it was never obliterated, and interest in Jimmie and his music was revived under very different circumstances, involving both memory and commercial interest; because the pop potency, the potential energy in what Rodgers had created has never died.

Jimmie Rodgers had, as it happens, briefly donned blackface in a medicine show in his teens but scrapped it instantly and never went back. He was a man utterly uninterested in overt disguise; he favored instead a varied line of eye-catching clothes in which he clearly felt at home, being expressively, flamboyantly Jimmie, and in doing so, he could project some notions of what "being Jimmie" could mean. But for the unfortunate anomaly of his rarely mentioned "Pullman Porters" recording, an all-talking minstrel sketch, you will not find a note of racial mockery in the recorded works of Jimmie Rodgers. Whereas on Miller's records, you have to get past a good deal of dated, often distasteful material like that before you get to some music.

Rodgers' blue yodels, like his singing and almost everything else about his public face, were projections of the very stuff that would make him a roots music hero. Along with the drifting train-catcher and the rowdy, even dangerous woman-chasing (or woman-victimized) rounder, typical themes of the songs they were most often attached to, the yodels would be the first element Rodgers' imitators would jump on. After the unmistakable success of the first blue yodel, "T for Texas," brazen imitators immediately started to appear, matching the blue yodeling on their records as closely as possible to the original. A similar flood of imitators followed the mambo, the Twist, the British (pop) Invasion, disco, and indeed the arrival of blues records in the first place.

The body of blue yodelmania recordings produced during Jimmie's working lifetime and the few years afterward has been gauged and analyzed scientifically by engineers in a clean room at the National Institute for the Study of Record Industry Redundancy, and yes, there was a ton of them. Many were utterly inconsequential; many only good enough to be recalled in their context, in collections such as the CD box set *Sounds Like Jimmie Rodgers*.

But Jimmie was also quite lucky, because especially prominent and pro-lific among the many imitators he had were three slick young men whom he knew personally. Many of their early records were either pastiche exten-sions of his ideas, covering the same territory but differing slightly in detail, or outright covers of his songs—in the original meaning of the term *cover*, a recording specifically devised to exploit the success of the original. Yet, so far as we know, Rodgers never uttered a word of complaint. All three were substantial, evolving talents in their own right, beginning their careers by working through an imitative, commercially expedient phase of Rodgers emulation. They were Cliff Carlisle, the steel guitarist we have already met, Louisiana's future governor Jimmie Davis, and a rough-raised Oklahoma kid born with the unsonorous given name Orvon Grover Autry, now, with Jimmie's buddy Gene Austin's blessing, calling himself the more appealing sounding Gene Autry.

Carlisle, son of an impoverished Kentucky sharecropper dad who had taught the old church-based shape-note singing, had learned to play on a cheap Sears Roebuck guitar and had been performing in Masonic Lodges, amateur shows, and school auditoriums. With his Hawaiian-influenced Dobro playing and often quite noticeably *country* singing, he made the leap to radio and the B. F. Keith vaudeville circuit—sometimes alone, sometimes in bands with names like the Buckeye Boys, the Buckle Busters, and the Carlisle Brothers. The bands included guitar-picking tenor singer Wilbur Ball, Fred Kirby, or Cliff's younger brother Bill—later the Opry star Jumpin' Bill Carlisle. And Cliff's initial model was Jimmie Rodgers.

"Although I started about a couple years after he did," Cliff recalled, "he was still my idol, because I loved that blue yodeling; that was what I worked on for a long, long time . . . I learned to yodel from his recordings . . . Of course, [then] I met Jimmie; I recorded with him in Louisville, Kentucky . . . I thought a lot of him, and I think he thought a lot of me. I *hope* he did."

Carlisle and Ball would add their forward-looking steel sound to Jimmie's "When the Cactus Is in Bloom" and "Looking for a New Mama" during the same week of sessions in June 1931 in which Jimmie would do the sketch records with the Carter Family and be backed by the Louisville Jug Band and the bluesman Clifford Gibson. Cliff Carlisle was on hand for some of those events.

"A. P. [Carter] made that big mistake on that record, that [one] take," he recalled, laughing. "Recorded half a day and then cussed on it; he thought they had it turned off, and they didn't. Peer liked to died, man! . . . When we got through recording with [Jimmie], he wanted us to go with him. He had two or three big old black Cadillacs with those tops, you know? You remember the gangsters' pictures that used to have them? He called that his boxcar. 'I got mah box cah . . . I'd like for you and Ball to go with me, put on some shows.'" Which they did.

Cliff Carlisle's own prolific recording career, for half a dozen major labels and under a variety of names, had already begun the year before with a very notable preponderance of Jimmie Rodgers covers and clones. By the time he and Jimmie worked together, Cliff had about a dozen covers or very close approximations of Rodgers records in circulation, but Jimmie clearly did not mind. Like all of the most talented Rodgers-style blue yodelers, Cliff found ways to extend the form and contribute to it. There were some obviously Jimmie-derived "new" songs like "Waiting for a Ride," "Boxcar Yodel," and "High Steppin' Mama," but Cliff's special lyric contribution was in an area all of the "big three" followers pursued successfully and with some relish: pushing Jimmie's sexually suggestive material from the mode of "Let Me Be Your Side Track," "Rootin' Ground Hog," and "What's It" into the explicit. The likes of "Sal Got a Meat Skin," "That Nasty Swing," and "A Wild Cat Woman and a Tom Cat Man" are little gems of horny boasting, while "Shanghai Rooster," by some accounts, was a song Jimmie had actually half-written, figured he could not really record for Victor, and gave to Cliff to finish off.

But Carlisle's writing skills are not to be taken lightly; a truly original song of his like "I'm Savin' Saturday Night for You" will stand up against Jimmie's blue yodel numbers in this same vein. He introduced the ancient ballad "Black Jack Davy" into the realm of the driving American song, and "Footprints in the Snow" years before bluegrass. Unconstrained by respiratory problems (though poor health would somewhat limit his career in later years), he was an especially effective blue yodeler, able to hit the top of a yodel with a sting while really throwing himself into the rhythm of the thing. He was an expressive singer, able to handle heartbreaking story songs and gifted with a thoroughly hillbilly voice that grows on you, and he answered that singing with his own innovative steel guitar lines.

Jimmie Davis was, like Cliff, the son of an impoverished sharecropper, but unique among early blue yodelers in having gone to college and graduated, singing his way through. His is a singular story in many ways; none of the other blue yodelers was going to be governor of Louisiana. Davis seems to have been born with particular gifts for positioning himself, remaking himself, and applying original rhetorical flourishes that would be notable in his lyrics long before they were put to use in self-serving stump speeches. His singing would be influenced almost as much by the crooning of Gene Austin (he would pick "Ramona" and "My Blue Heaven" out of Austin's song bag) as by Jimmie Rodgers' more earthy approach, and he would always say so. Davis knew Jimmie firsthand, running into him in recording studios and elsewhere.

"I wasn't around him too much," he told researcher Tony Russell. "A few times. I saw him in Kilgore, Texas, one time, in a tent out there, singing in a tent. Just jammed to the rafters. He'd sing about forty-five minutes, maybe, . . . just take his time, just sitting on a chair. Just himself . . . He influenced me, yes. Most of us were influenced by him, because we'd kinda take . . . uh, copy him as much as we could."

Jimmie Davis emphasized a point about Rodgers' singing that few mention but that he, inclined as he was to straddle the line between rural sounds and themes and more urbane crooning, could not help but notice: "Jimmie Rodgers," he said, "had the best *diction* of anyone I ever knew." His own singing could be as smooth as Austin and Bing Crosby, yet he has assimilated enough of Louisiana blues that his accent and phrasing occasionally combine to approximate the vocal attack of Shreveport songster Lead Belly. Like Jimmie Rodgers, Davis would record with a number of black performers, and he would work with Rodgers-influenced western swing bands and Rodgers acolytes such as Patsy Montana, Buddy Jones, Lani McIntyre, Johnny Bond, and Vaughn Horton.

The performer of "Nobody's Darling But Mine" and the huge hit "You Are My Sunshine" evidently thought of his blue yodels as work in a separate genre of its own: "I used to do a lot of those, all that kind of stuff, but then I quit yodeling and was doing just straight *country* . . . then I finally got into all gospel music for a long time."

Davis recorded only a few Rodgers covers ("Peach Pickin' Time in Georgia" and "Moonlight and Skies Number 2," for instance), but his recordings between 1928 and the mid-1930s are loaded with fresh songs in that mode, often self-penned and showing a sophisticated grasp of the themes and subjects that Jimmie scored with, not just the yodeling surface. Such titles as "Deep Mississippi Blues," "Gambler's Return," "Hobo's Warning," and "Penitentiary Blues" speak for themselves, and when Davis got around to material more explicit than Rodgers', in songs like the highly imaginative, incendiary "Tom Cat and Pussy Blues," "High Behind Blues," and "Red Nightgown Blues," he created a body of party song yodels that became semilegendary—stuff he went out of his way to forget or even suppress when his political career took hold. "I used to sing some that were a little suggestive," he admitted when pressed in 1976. "What do you call it, these *rock* tunes, you see—that just didn't start here in the last year or two . . . They don't beat around the bush now; they just go ahead and say it . . . [but] they were doing it way back then."

It still surprises some listeners to learn that young Gene Autry, who later promoted the ostentatiously wholesome "Cowboy Code" for kids, produced about as much single-entendre, blue-indeed blue yodel material as Carlisle and Davis did. But that hardly sums up the Autry-Rodgers connection, which probably begins before Gene started recording, with his own railroad work—though it was the relatively cushy, indoor job of railway telegraph operator, not brakeman. Autry would meet Rodgers on several occasions, initially when their mutual friend Gene Austin introduced them in New York.

Recording dozens of outright Jimmie Rodgers covers on multiple low-priced labels under several names, Gene may have understood as well as anyone ever has how Jimmie Rodgers' singing and blue yodeling appealed to audiences. His covers and Rodgers-like pastiche songs can be startlingly close to the originals when he wants them to be. They are often rendered with somewhat different backing, thickened up or stripped down, but sung with similar charm and conviction. It is one more bit of proof that, as the old saying goes, the second rate can only imitate, but the first rate steal. Photos of blue yodeler Gene sitting with his legs crossed "just so," Jimmie Rodgers style, or with his foot up on a box, as Jimmie often performed on stage, say boxcar-loads about the attention to detail in Autry's study of his model.

Autry can capture the Rodgers sound, right down to an assumed Mississippi accent on certain vowels, as in recordings such as "Anniversary Blue Yodel" or his numerous versions of the Rodgers-like "Jailhouse Blues." (RCA Victor would embarrass themselves years later by mistakenly including one of Autry's records on an LP of hits by "Legendary Performer" Jimmie Rodgers.) Gene could also, and generally did, add or subtract a beat here, shift the emphasis there, hold notes and yodels, leaning toward a more swinging yet still utterly simple style—hotter at times than Rodgers, at times more languid—that was going to help make him a huge roots music pop star, too. Autry's "Texas Blues," "Any Old Time," a slowed-down "Travelin' Blues," and "Blue Yodel No. 8" (one of the very few covers of "Mule Skinner Blues" before Bill Monroe's), for example, are masterful vocal performances in their own right. He would add an expansive recitation to "Waiting for a Train" that presaged the better side of his screen acting style to come, while reminding you how well he was doing on radio.

Autry would be among those who memorialized Jimmie Rodgers in song when he died, but soon afterward he left his own blue yodeler stage behind, and from that point on, he generally tended to minimize the Rodgers influence, when he could be persuaded to discuss music at all. But, as we will see, Rodgers themes and a few relevant Rodgers songs would still linger in his singing cowboy repertoire.

Adaptations and extensions of Jimmie's Rodgers' yodeling style did not end with the initial blue yodel craze. Rodgers-style yodels would be features of significant country music and western music careers, as well as of the music of other countries (Australia, for example), for years to come. The performer often rated the best singing yodeler of them all, Ozark-bred Elton Britt (born James Britt Baker), is said to have auditioned for Jimmie Rodgers while still a teenager, during one of Jimmie's appearances at the Oklahoma base of Buffalo Bill's partner Pawnee Bill's "Round-Up" show.

The star performer, the story goes, encouraged Elton to look for work in California. They would encounter each other again out in Hollywood, and Jimmie would write to Ralph Peer, "You'd better come out here and sign up this kid. I think he's going to make bums out of all of us." Britt was set to make his first records in New York in 1933 when news came of Jimmie's death. He told a Grand Ole Opry audience in the '60s during one of his periodic comebacks, "I was so heartbroken that I cried for weeks; I worshipped the man."

What Jimmie had apparently noted was how Britt managed to stretch blue yodeling to pyrotechnic yodel heights beyond anything he had tried (or seemingly wanted) to do himself, applying some of that Swiss/vaudeville showboat approach to Rodgers-style songs, to the point where he was sometimes billed as "the world's highest yodeler," even while singing in a suede pop style that would make him a star by World War II. Britt could leap to the top of a yodel in the middle of a single, quick syllable and get safely back in rhythm. He rarely let the yodeling display bring things to a halt or interfere with the meaning of the song—a legacy of Rodgers' influence.

In his early days, Elton would record the occasional, appropriately pop-oriented Rodgers number, such as a rather syrupy "The One Rose."

However, it was his album-length tribute LP *The Jimmie Rodgers Blues* and the single of the same name, an extended piece rather cleverly made up out of Rodgers song titles turned biographical, that marked Britt's last stand on the country charts. His most expansive comment on his music's relation to Jimmie's, it came out in 1969. By that point, Elton could exploit his stunning vocal range with finesse, stretch his "odelays" in a singularly smooth style, tackle the pop of "Roll Along, Kentucky Moon," then transform the vaudeville of "Peach Pickin' Time" and "My Carolina Sunshine Girl" into post-Sinatra after-hours saloon singing, his tone somewhere between that of Ray Price a la "The Night Life" and the later retro crooning of Tompall Glaser.

Britt's LP included "My Little Lady," which had long been a standard test for athletic yodelers with an interest in Rodgers songs. The rambunctious, old-timey, yet near-rockabilly Grandpa Jones, star of the Opry and *Hee-Haw,* had included the song in his 1962 tribute LP *Grandpa Jones Yodeling Hits*—a set of quite varied, yodel-friendly Rodgers tunes that played a role in fuzzying later generations' notions of Jimmie's relationship to Swiss yodeling. Grandpa appears on the LP jacket in lederhosen and a Tyrolean hat, apparently yodeling across an Alpine ravine. Featuring his punchy, growling country hit version of "T for Texas," the album tacks on the pure Swissery of "Tritzem Yodel," so listeners will be forgiven if they imagine that it has something close in common with all those partially Swissified Rodgers songs it accompanies.

Significantly, it is not Grandpa's old-time banjo frailing that is featured on the album, but the flat-top guitar mastery of Nashville "A-team" session man Ray Edenton. Jones was not the first or last musician to feel that banjo sounds clashed with Rodgers music. Today, his widow and long-time musical partner Ramona Jones barely recalls backing her husband on guitar on Rodgers songs "because I played behind him when he was on banjo"—and when Grandpa sang Rodgers songs, he generally was not.

Louis "Grandpa" Jones, in real life one of the more sophisticated and articulate country music stars, however much he played someone more rustic on TV and stage, had passed his first performance test thirty-three years before, at an amateur night in Akron, Ohio, in 1929 run by the "red-haired music maker" Wendell Hall of "It Ain't Gonna Rain No More" fame. He had done it by imitating Jimmie, singing his "Dear Old Sunny South by the Sea."

Jones would recall, "My brother Gordon bought every Jimmie Rodgers record that came out back then, and when he got one, for the first few days he wouldn't let me play it because he was afraid we would get our hands on the grooves and make them greasy . . . Gordon and I were really stuck on Jimmie Rodgers; I used to listen for hours to how Jimmie did his yodels, and before long I'd learned the words to a lot of his songs." When Grandpa Jones performed Rodgers tunes, they were—lesson understood—energetic projections of his own warm but aggressive personality as a performer. They would remain part of his repertoire all through the ensuing decades, a link between the age of vaudeville in which he began and the age of network TV in which he finished up.

"My Little Lady" also makes an appearance on another 1969 salute LP, *Wilf Carter Sings Jimmie Rodgers* (Merle Haggard's Rodgers salute seemingly having started a small salute LP trend around this time). On the American side of the U.S.-Canadian border, Wilf had been known primarily as a yodeling cowboy singer billed as "Montana Slim" ever since a New York radio show cast him that way in 1935. In fact, he had begun his yodeling ways in traveling shows after seeing vaudevillians do the same in his native Nova Scotia, before World War I. From his first recordings in 1933, there had been a Rodgers blue yodel influence as well as that of the Swiss athletic sort, and he had mixed in varied country and pop material, contemporary songs and nostalgic cowboy material, much like his fellow eastern Canadian Hank Snow would. The *Wilf Carter Sings Jimmie Rodgers* LP was a reminder that there was more to Carter's repertoire than cowboy songs, and his lean, nearly spoken vocals backed by simple guitar and fiddle are charming for that very simplicity—even as his yodeling style expands the "Jimmie plus Alpine" mutation.

Knowing as we now do that vaudeville yodeling had been around for quite a while before 1928 and that adding yodeling to blues or bluesy songs was not entirely unheard of, we have to tackle another question: Besides the fact that Jimmie Rodgers was simply quite good at it, why did the blue yodelmania craze take hold so strongly? And why then?

Part of the answer may lie in the effects of changing technology. Jimmie Rodgers' recordings are all products of the electric microphone era. In retrospect, it seems no coincidence that a range of emotions expressed wordlessly, by means of various bodily created noises, should show up on record at just the moment when it became possible for the singer's very breath to be audible. Whether it was a Mississippi Delta "deep blues" singer breaking into a high falsetto moan, the early scat singing of Ukulele Ike, or Bing Crosby's crooning "bubba-buh-dohs" and whistles, the record-buying audience was not hearing those sounds exactly as they might have heard them earlier in one of their annual visits to a vaudeville hall. These emotional murmurs and cries were becoming downright intimate and, for many, downright sexy, too. What could be recorded, what was recorded, and how strongly audiences might respond to it were in no small measure consequences of new technological capabilities. Anyone who has lived through the movement of pop, country, and other music into the video arena and of the once seemingly everlasting album format to downloadable singles will get the point. The method of delivery not only altered the music, it also determined what music was likely to elicit a response.

A final point about Jimmie as the instigator of a fad: The phenomenon of the hit record was relatively new. Jimmie Rodgers' blue yodels were copied so often not just because they were so riveting, but also because they were the ones heard most often, in a variety of ways, in the most places. The pop reach of roots music heroes, like that of other pop stars, feeds on itself; pop, famously, eats its own tail to grow. Because a lot of people had latched on to Jimmie Rodgers, many more were going to. The man who had walked into southern show business hoping for success in vaudeville had in fact arrived at the gates of the global, multimedia marketplace. Jimmie Rodgers' music, his image, and his legend were going to go to places he never could.

Select Soundtrack

The Blue-ish Vaudeville Yodelsphere

- **George P. Watson:** His Edison cylinder recordings "Medley of Emmet's Yodles" (1898), "Sleep Baby Sleep" (1902), and "Roll Along, Silver Moon" (1902) have been made available online via the Cylinder Preservation and Digitization project of the University of California, Santa Barbara: http://cylinders.library. ucsb.edu/.
- **Bert Williams:** "Nobody" (1906), "Never Mo'" (1915), etc., are on *The Complete Bert Williams* (Archeophone).
- **Sara Martin, Eva Taylor, and Thomas Martin:** "Yodeling Blues" (1923) is on *Sara Martin—Complete Recorded Works Volume 1* (Document, 1996) and the Red Hot Jazz website: www.redhotjazz.com.
- **Bessie Smith:** "Yodeling Blues" (1923) is on *The Complete Recordings, Volume One* (Sony, 1991).
- **Charles Anderson:** "Comic Yodle Song," "Sing 'Em Blues," "Yodle-Song—Coo Coo," and "Sleep Baby Sleep" (1923) are all on *Eddie Heywood and the Blues Singers 1923–1926*

(Document, 1995); "Laughing Yodle" and "Roll On Silver Moon" (1924) are on *Male Blues Singers of the Twenties* (Document, 1997).

- **Frank Kamplain:** "Broken-Hearted Blues" (1922), "Oleolady" (1923), and "Yodelin' Bill" (1926), the latter two with Al Bernard, are posted on a number of early recording public domain websites.

- **Lee Morse:** "Mail Man Blues" (1924), "Tentin' Down in Tennessee" (1926), "Main Street" (1928), etc., are on *Lee Morse: Echoes of a Songbird* (Jasmine, 2005); her 1930 films *The Music Racket* and *A Million Me's*, with the Rodgers-like "Mail Man" number, are available for viewing at www. leemorse.com.

- **Roy Evans:** "Syncopated Yodelin' Man" (1928). "Weary Yodelin' Blues" (1929), and "Jazzbo Dan and His Yodelin' Band" (1928) are all on *Blue Yodelers 1928–1936: Jimmie Rodgers, Emmet* [sic] *Miller, Roy Evans* (Retrieval, 2005).

- **Emmett Miller:** *The Minstrel Man from Georgia* (Columbia Legacy CD 1996) and the *Blue Yodelers* compilation, above.

The Blue Yodeler Craze

- **Cliff Carlisle:** *Cliff Carlisle: A Country Legacy 1930–1939* (JSP box set, 2004) and *Cliff Carlisle Volume 2: When I Feel Froggie I'm Gonna Hop 1930–1941* (JSP box set, 2006).

- **Early Gene Autry:** *That Silver-Haired Daddy of Mine* (Bear Family box set, 2006), one disc of the *Sounds Like Jimmie Rodgers* box set (JSP), and *Gene Autry: Blues Singer 1929–1931* (Sony, 1996).

- **Early Jimmie Davis:** *Governor Jimmie Davis: Nobody's Darlin' But Mine* (Bear Family box set, 1998).

- **Blue Yodel Craze:** See the box set *Sounds Like Jimmie Rodgers* (JSP, 2005) for other early blue yodeling imitators and extenders, including Daddy John Love, Riley Puckett, Frankie Marvin, Buddy Jones, and Goebel Reeves.

Rodgers-Based Athletic Yodeling

- **Elton Britt:** *The Jimmie Rodgers Blues* (RCA Camden LP, 1969).
- **Grandpa Jones:** *Grandpa Jones Yodeling Hits* (Monument LP, 1962)
- **Wilf Carter:** *Wilf Carter Sings Jimmie Rodgers* (RCA Camden LP, 1969).

five

International Multimedia Star

By 1931, the liner notes on a now nearly forgotten Victor album of Rodgers records titled, unsurprisingly, *Jimmie Rodgers, America's Blue Yodeler*, could boast: "'Blue Yodel' was sold to more people than almost any other selection ever made! Jimmie Rodgers' voice and strumming guitar were heard in every corner of America, from the palace in New York, to the little cabin in the hill country of the South. You will be interested to know, also, that Jimmie Rodgers' records are in demand in almost every country in Europe and South America, and even in Australia, South Africa, and the Orient."

The Mississippi adolescent who loved the traveling tent rep and medicine shows, who watched the silent cowboy movies and dreamed of show business, could never have foreseen that the world in which he would emerge as a successful entertainer would be such an astonishingly different place. Jimmie Rodgers' career began just as revolutionary new technologies were changing the entire show business landscape with new media developments and associated pop marketing tactics as fast-breaking and scene altering as those we are experiencing in the early twenty-first century. These were central, practical facts of Rodgers' working career, and they would have a huge impact on how the world would come to know him and his music.

As Jimmie made his first visits to a recording studio in the summer and fall of 1927, portable 35-millimeter still cameras and flash bulbs were coming into photojournalists' hands, boosting the use of all kinds of photography in newspaper reports and ads. The breakthrough talking picture *The Jazz*

Contemplative, successful—and posed with one of many fancy cars he purchased.

Singer with Al Jolson opened on October 6—just eight weeks before Jimmie recorded "Blue Yodel." One year earlier, in November 1926, a new firm, the National Broadcasting Company, had gone on the air, linking a chain of radio stations with New York's WEAF as its home base—a network. Radio would now expand its reach rapidly, so much so that some would soon see it as a threat to record sales. American record companies, some with histories that went back over thirty years, were reaching out for new audiences both within the borders of the United States and, through marketing ties to labels or subsidiaries around the world, well beyond them.

It was not an accident that Ralph Peer was busy just then signing acts with potential, in the language of a later day, to target new demographics. As he explained to writer Lillian Borgeson in 1958, the temporary spike in the incomes of poorer southern whites and blacks as both moved toward new factory work in the '20s had provided them with fresh disposable income to spend on entertainment. Marketing records to these groups, following the models of the foreign-language recording series the major labels had already created, was now recognized as a strategy worth pursuing.

Given their moderately updated, yet sufficiently commercial "country folks" sound, Ralph Peer could take the Carter Family further than they could imagine. Given his ability to handle a very broad range of material and to sound credible and personable doing it, Peer would help take Jimmie Rodgers places nobody would have imagined. As Peer analyzed the difference, "Jimmie Rodgers appealed to a much wider audience, because he had what was a *popular* version of hillbilly; he used hillbilly, but he also used Negro . . . [and also] many of the songs he recorded were popular [i.e., pop]. They had a verse and chorus. He got them from many sources . . . He could record *anything.*"

There would be Peer-produced Jimmie Rodgers recordings featuring Hawaiian bands, jazz bands, country stringbands, pop orchestras, protocowboy and Texas swing contingents, and also those groundbreaking sessions with African-American musicians from Louis Armstrong to the Louisville Jug Band. Critics have sometimes complained that, single appearances by Louis and Lil Armstrong or bluesman Clifford Gibson aside, Jimmie Rodgers was not supplied with a stream of crack instrumentalists to accompany him—names like the Dorsey Brothers, Benny Goodman, James P. Johnson, and Eddie Lang, whom you find backing more obscure acts such as Emmett Miller and Roy Evans. There were, however, indisputably capable musicians behind Jimmie Rodgers, players as varied as the Hawaiian steel player Joe Kaipo and guitarist Lani McIntyre, the modern-minded fiddler Clayton McMichen, and the inventive lead guitarist Slim Bryant. No doubt there could have been better-known and, indeed, better bands playing on the likes of "Any Old Time" or "California Blues," but for all that, those recordings have worked their particular magic for eighty years. Some of Jimmie's most effective orchestrated numbers are backed by spirited no-name bands; you will not find "Bob Sawyer's Jazz Band," for example, which played on the striking "Jimmie's Mean Mama Blues," in any list of major jazz acts.

In retrospect, Ralph Peer came to believe that the solidity and variety of the songs Jimmie Rodgers recorded had more to do with their acceptance than the backings did. Those songs, after all, ranged from sentimental mother ballads and rural reminders of "buckets of lard" to hard blues numbers and the near scatology of "What's It?" and on to the Bing Crosby–like lush contemporary pop of "The One Rose" and "Roll Along, Kentucky Moon." This was extraordinarily unusual pop breadth.

Apparently, the only songs proposed by Jimmie for recording that were rejected by Peer were old, already established pieces with no potential for new copyright credits. A steady supply of novel, copyrighted songs, as Peer prophetically saw, was the very basis of a pop music industry. Jimmie was tasked with having dozens and dozens of them ready—fast. Rodgers' potential for broad appeal was such that the pace of recording was breakneck; few recording artists today have had the experience of laying down 111 sides in less than six years as Jimmie did, let alone with sounds as varied as he would handle.

"My policy," Peer explained, "was always to try to expand each artist, by adding accompaniment, or adding a vocalist, or what-have-you. Finding new stuff month after month was not easy! . . . I kept taking [Jimmie] from one place to another so people wouldn't get tired of him. With many of these things, I was trying to change the flavor, so I'd get some outside accompaniment for him . . . but he'd pick his own selections. He didn't need *anybody* to decide what was good for him."

Jimmie would run his proposed selections by Peer in advance of the recording sessions, to check for any overchallenging matches of tune and lyrics, and took typed-out lyric sheets to the sessions, with spots marked for yodels and not-so-spontaneous spoken interjections. Since all the known outtakes of the recordings have long been available to listeners, we have come to know that takes were sometimes quite different from each other, in rhythm and sometimes even in instrumentation. We commonly hear today that extraordinary alternate version of "Let Me Be Your Side Track" with Clifford Gibson joining Jimmie on guitar; nobody outside the recording studio heard that one at the time.

Hoyt "Slim" Bryant, describing the Camden and New York recording sessions he worked on with Jimmie in 1932, recalls that the music was "scoped out in advance" enough that things went very easily in the studio.

"Ralph Peer was right there in the room," he recalls, "waiting for everything to go on, one thing right after another, and if you hit on something
he didn't like, he would say so. But I never saw him get rowed up about
anything . . . Everything we did, we just rehearsed it and did it. Jimmie never
made any suggestions in the studio; if he had any ideas, he would express
them in the rehearsals. It was very, very low key. Jimmie was very easy to
work with. We did it, and that was it!"

Byrant recalls a flighty music copyist being there in the recording studio, taking down what was recorded: "Yeah; he was settin' at the piano, taking these tunes down, and writing down the music to them. He had a shelf
with booze setting on the piano, too, and right in the middle of one of the
recordings, the booze fell off on the floor and ruined the record. Peer just
laughed! We did the record over again."

The songs taken down on the spot would rapidly be published in sheet
music form; and in some cases, quietly shown to potential cover artists such
as Gene Autry even before publication. One early extension of Jimmie
Rodgers' (and Elsie McWilliams') tunes into the world of pop and jazz saw
a two-sided single, "Everybody Does It in Hawaii" backed with "Frankie
and Johnny," recorded by King Oliver and His Orchestra in the winter of
1929–30—with Roy Smeck joining on steel guitar, a sound which, along
with the prominent banjo, has flummoxed some jazz critics. It was surely
no coincidence that Oliver had been recorded by Ralph Peer in his earlier
heyday; or that he was now on Victor.

The published sheet music, as was common in that era, featured colorful graphics suggestive of the song's mood and often Jimmie's image, too,
which put his picture on pianos in a great many parlors. Less commonplace,
and a sign of how worthwhile it seemed to take Jimmie's music in novel
directions, were the specialty record formats in which some of his songs
were released, even after his passing. After appearing on Victor or Bluebird
labels, Rodgers records would swiftly be licensed to the giant mail-order
firm Montgomery Ward so that fans with no local record dealer could order
them from the Ward catalog. International Victor subsidiaries and such
overseas labels as Regal-Zonophone and HMV took Jimmie's music across
the English-speaking world and beyond. A "Jimmie Rodgers Medley" record
containing edited sections of three of Jimmie's hits on each side was issued
in the United Kingdom and subsequently in Australia, Ireland, and India.
There was "Rodgers' Puzzle Record" which put extracts from three songs
("Blue Yodel," "Everybody Does It in Hawaii," and "Train Whistle Blues")
on the same single, and depending on where the needle first fell, any one of
the three might play—sheer novelty. And there was one of the world's first
picture discs, a limited release with a casual photo of Jimmie pressed into

the record of "The Cow Hand's Last Ride" backed with "Blue Yodel No. 12." Copies sell for about $500 at auction today.

Least known and most surprising of all, unrecorded as it has been in any existing Jimmie Rodgers discography, is that 1931 album *Jimmie Rodgers: America's Blue Yodeler*, certainly one of the earliest pop record albums to be released. The liner notes suggest that Jimmie wants, in this album, to present the records "he thinks are his best." Yet, unusually, there is no lineup of specific songs. The release appears to have been a customizable album cover, able to hold whichever five of Jimmie's singles the buyer or record dealer chose to include. It may also have worked as a sales tool, enticing the buyer to fill it with singles one by one. Accordingly, no discs with different, album-specific catalog numbers needed to be manufactured, the absence of such records being one reason why the album was forgotten and unknown by collectors. A copy survives in the archives of the Country Music Hall of Fame and Museum; its purple cover was an image in the 2004 *Encyclopedia of Country Music* edited by Paul Kingsbury. The photo of Jimmie included inside the album was the same casual, legs-crossed shot used on the picture disc.

Extensive biographical liner notes, very likely to have been written or inspired by Ralph Peer, give a brief overview of Jimmie's life, describing in some detail his recent Red Cross tour with Will Rogers and how he has lately been made an honorary Texas Ranger. Unmistakably, the picture of Jimmie that emerges, aimed at his fans, is of a man who had come from out of nowhere, is rooted ("brought up to be familiar with the quaint tunes of his locality"), has known personal struggle, and has really made it now, big time.

The Horatio Alger theme is explicitly stated: "In his life's story, Jimmie fulfills all the requirements of the traditional rise from obscurity to fame, so dear to Americans' idea of romance and love of achievement." Outward signs of Jimmie's spectacular success are emphasized. We are told about his big and beautiful home in Kerrville, Texas, the Yodeler's Paradise, and simultaneously reminded that its purchase was "made possible by the profits of his many successful Victor records . . . He probably has more admirers than any young man in the country . . . [this] singer who knew the secret of appealing to all hearts with simple, straight-forward, unassuming songs and ballads, sung in a way in which nobody but Jimmie Rodgers could sing." Jimmie Rodgers not only had the attributes of "one of us, writ large;" his promoters also knew it and were saying so.

The hectic schedule of live, close-to-the-ground performances he maintained was inevitably affected by the changing face of the live venues a vaudevillian could play in those years. There were no more than a dozen

Meeting Jimmie Rodgers

big-time vaudeville houses left in the United States that were devoted to live acts alone. Whether playing in huge, lavish Loews theaters in the bigger southern cities or neighborhood theaters in the smallest of towns, Jimmie Rodgers was most likely to be seen live on the bill with a Hollywood movie. Even the handbill for his appearance at that out-of-the-way Burntex Theatre in Burnet, Texas, while heralding the coming to town of the famous Blue Yodeler "sweeping the country like a prairie fire," added "Don't miss this chance to See and Hear your Favorite Record Star. *Also, Good Picture in addition*. Prices 50 and 75 cents."

This booking practice was referred to in trade papers as "vaudefilm." Generally, four to seven live acts, often traveling as a unit, would appear on a bill along with the latest movie release. Begun as a ploy by theater owners to preserve live vaudeville, with all the variety and intimacy their customers had long loved, vaudefilm, as it proved in practice, would only turn more of those customers into regular moviegoers instead. That unintended consequence had even greater effect once the movies themselves began to talk, sing, and dance. In the end, as the Depression sapped movie attendance, vaudefilm would be used as one more, no-cost-added attraction, like the regular dishware giveaways or bingo games.

It would seem logical that vaudefilm's live entertainment would be coordinated with the movie content, and in a few cases, that was so. A young Jean Harlow or Dick Powell might appear before the picture they starred in, or on occasion, themes of the films would be taken up in the revue—a practice that lingered into the '60s at New York's Radio City and Roxy show palaces. But coordination of that kind was actually rare. While it may be easy to imagine Jimmie Rodgers singing before, say, *Beggars of Life*, the 1928 talkie hit with Wallace Beery and Louise Brooks concerning a tragic hobo love affair, or some forerunner of "Ma and Pa Kettle" country comedy or a hillbilly feud melodrama, that was not the context of his many vaudefilm appearances.

The reality was more interesting because it shows as clearly as anything how Jimmie's audience was being exposed, as regularly as anyone more citified or northern, to up-to-date fare from a changing world—and how closely Jimmie was associated with that new, incoming culture. Indeed, since he was the big attraction on the bill, he must at times have been the one who introduced his audience to the more "with it" movies he appeared alongside.

Whatever Jimmie's audiences made of them, they saw him sing on bills with the likes of *Why Be Good?* with flapper Colleen Moore or the gangster drama *Four Walls* with John Gilbert and Joan Crawford. He preceded an on-screen Ronald Colman, who played a sixteenth-century masked avenger dating Vilma Bánky in *Two Lovers*; comedy shorts by raconteur Robert

Benchley; *Are You There?* with the sophisticated transatlantic comedy star Beatrice Lillie; and features starring Clara Bow, the "It Girl." Any suggestion that when Jimmie was singing such numbers as "Everybody Does It in Hawaii" and "What's It?" the suggestiveness in the songs must have been lost on the simple folk who bought his records should be put to rest. When, backstage in Midland, Texas, Jimmie shared jokes with local reporters about his baby daughter, Anita, being "the living image of Greta Garbo," he was not making an unfamiliar or utterly incongruous comparison.

Fortunately for posterity, and for all since his day who have wanted the chance to see Jimmie Rodgers perform, he became a participant himself in the medium that would finally kill the dual live-and-film format. In November 1929, Jimmie was filmed in Victor's hometown of Camden, New Jersey, for *The Singing Brakeman*, a musical performance short in the ongoing "Columbia/Victor Gem" series. Despite the technical audiovisual crudities that stultified virtually all such early talkies, the nine-minute film is a fascinating portrayal of Rodgers the performer. Although we are not shown the easy patter and audience response that were essential parts of his live shows, he handles the lines he is given for the train station skit well enough and responds engagingly to the elderly women listening to him sing. His potential as a screen personality — perceived at the time but never realized — is evident. As Jimmie sings of longing for his daddy and home or of "the state he dearly loves," you can see him visualizing them. It is credible but unsubtle acting, a sort of mugging that generally works better live across large rooms than in screen close-ups, but there are few such close-ups here. He handles the medium close-ups that are included, adapting to that visual intimacy just as he had learned how to sing into a mike. At times he eyes his guitar intently, and there is ample chance to see the gusto with which he plays it, even at middle distance.

Jimmie no doubt captured many in the film audience from the moment he began to perform, as he pursed his lips and let loose with the famous, long train-whistle sound that sets off "Waiting for a Train." There is no mistaking the sound for a real whistle here; you can see the trick he is pulling off and admire it for what it is. It is possible to become so used to the solo performance in the film, just Jimmie alone with his guitar, that you forget that the original record was orchestrated. On film, he replaces the record's horn intro with a fairly athletic '20s pop "voh-doe-dee-oh-DOE," a modern bit of business fully in keeping with the sound of the anonymous jazz band that plays over the opening and closing credits.

Incidentally, one of the oddest, though not infrequently repeated examples of Rodgers misinformation is that the unidentified grannylike nonactresses who watch as Jimmie sings "Waiting for a Train," "Daddy and Home,"

Jimmie on the set of his film *The Singing Brakeman*, consulting, most likely, with director Jasper Ewing Brady.

and the "T for Texas" blue yodel are Maybelle and Sara Carter—whom they resemble in no way at all. For the record, the fellow who rushes through the scene early on wielding what appears to be a baseball bat, is not A. P. Carter, either. The hit song lineup offers a carefully chosen view of Jimmie's musical range, and happens also, with the frequent addition of "Frankie and Johnny," to be the set he often performed whenever allotted time was short.

There is a still unresolved and rarely noted mystery about the film, in that it exists in two substantially different versions. The original 1929 release, which opens with a "sparkling torch" version of Columbia Picture's "torch lady," credits the film's direction to Colonel Jasper Ewing Brady, a colorful army veteran who had been author of melodramatic novels and reports on railroad disasters; the aging gent photographed coaching Jimmie on the set is likely Colonel Brady himself, born in 1866. The original studio publicity for the short credited Brady as well, and Dal Clawson and Frank Zukor as the cameramen. That version of the film, which actually lists Charles Harten and Buddy Harris as the cameramen in the on-screen credits, circulated in collectors' hands and was used at the occasional screening of *The Singing Brakeman*, for years.

But there is a second, different version of the film released in 1930—the one most commonly seen and available today—and virtually every shot in the second version is a different take. Where Jimmie says "Well, by the looks of this board here, I've been called for an extra West at 10:15" on the 1929 edit, he says, "Yes, by the look of this board here, I'm going West at 10:15" in the 1930 release. He reverses the order of the words "woman" and "mama" in singing the two versions of "Blue Yodel," as well. These are alternate performances, if almost surely from the same day.

For reasons unknown, the second release credits Basil Smith as director; they might have included a crediting mistake in version two, there may have been a change in studio politics unpropitious for Colonel Brady, or perhaps even different directors were actually employed. Smith was Jimmie's age, much younger than Brady, came from Ottawa, and, in a brief directing career, managed to work with both a young Ginger Rogers (*A Day of a Man of Affairs*) and a set of marionettes. In the 1930 release, the cameramen are listed as Frank "Zucker" and "Chas. Harten" (no doubt the Zukor referred to in the publicity hand-out); Zukor also shot the well-known sound W. C. Fields short *The Golf Specialist* and some Yiddish language films. Charles Harten, credited onscreen in both versions, later filmed Kate Smith and was nominated for an Oscar as cameraman on *Butterfield 8*. Buddy Harris was still shooting B-movie and television Westerns in the 1950s. Perhaps correcting the clearly confused cameraman credits for the second version led to a mistaken recrediting of the director.

No documentation in Columbia Pictures' archives explains the existence of the two variants, and there is no evidence that any of the other dozen-plus "Columbia Victor Gem" shorts filmed in succession in the autumn of 1929 saw second printings — even though they had included acts as good and popular as Mamie Smith in *Jailhouse Blues* and Frank Crumit in *The Gay Caballero*. We are left, pending additional cinematic research, with the provocative possibility that, alone in the series, further distribution of Jimmie's film was needed because so many were demanded, and the producers turned to an alternate take negative as a source for new prints.

In any case, the medium where most people who never saw Jimmie live could hear him in his casual, offhanded glory was radio. Details of his radio performances have always been scanty, in part because they were almost all live and no recordings of them (such as airchecks or transcriptions) are known to survive. From his first taste of fame in Asheville, North Carolina, in 1927 until his last days in Texas, however, broadcasts were a regular part of the way Rodgers reached the public.

A reporter for the *Houston Chronicle*, in a profile published on Christmas Eve 1931 that was derived from interviews with Jimmie, looked back at his first broadcasts at WWNC in Asheville: "He sang for his first audience of the air crooning southern melodies, blues songs which trailed off into a yodel. And as he played, he plunked away on his guitar. The program went over big." In her memoir, Carrie relates how Jimmie, who first performed unspecified old-timey numbers at WWNC with the Helton Brothers, then yodeled "novelty numbers" that were "a treat" (as the local paper described them), was then replaced on their air by a more genteel program, though the station had received a mass of fan mail asking to hear more from him.

When stardom struck and the Rodgers family was living temporarily in Washington, D.C., Jimmie had a regular radio stint on WTTF there through the first half of 1928, sometimes accompanied by Julian Ninde on guitar and Ellsworth Cozzens on steel, the three appearing on-air as "Jimmie Rodgers' Southerners." These were the musicians who had backed him on classic records like "Brakeman's Blues," "In the Jailhouse Now," and "Treasures Untold" in February that year. On the radio, they provided backing to such early Rodgers hits as "Sleep Baby Sleep," "T for Texas," and "Away Out on the Mountain," and also, as a local report noted for the week of April 28, "a half hour of request numbers."

When Jimmie was living in Texas and staying closer to home, he made frequent radio appearances there, including a regular weekly show on KMAC in San Antonio in which his music, jokes, and patter were featured; when he was out of town, his records were played in his place. A typical one-shot live song and patter broadcast was recalled by Grant Turner, the country radio disc jockey, Grand Ole Opry announcer for forty-seven years, and Country Hall of Fame inductee: "In my earliest days in radio, back at KFYO in Abilene, Texas, before that station moved to Lubbock, Jimmie and Mrs. Rodgers came there to do a . . . show. Jimmie had come over from Breckinridge, where he had sung for a jeweler who'd had a 'Going Out of Business' sale; they'd paid Jimmie $750 to make several store appearances in one day! When he came over to Abilene, he autographed records at the local music store [and then] at 2:30, on that Sunday afternoon, in that tiny studio at the old Grace Hotel, Jimmie took up his old guitar, he put his foot up on a chair, braced his guitar over his leg, and played and sang 'T for Texas,' 'Looking for a New Mama,' and 'Daddy and Home.' I'll never forget that . . . The program lasted for an hour, and we received thousands of phone calls—and not just local calls. They came from miles around."

"Border radio"—the broadcasting of programs at megawatt levels well beyond the legal U.S. limits from transmitters just across the border in Mexico, blasting toward a large chunk of the United States—was just getting under way during Jimmie's last years in Texas. While the border blaster stations did not play the central role in connecting Jimmie to listeners that they eventually would for the relatively homebound Carter Family, Jimmie did make some border radio appearances. When the pioneering "Voice of the Two Republics," XED, first went on the air from the border town of Reynosa, Tamaulipas, Mexico, in the fall of 1930, Jimmie starred on the opening-night program from a studio in McAllen, Texas, on the U. S. side of the Rio Grande. The station would before long reach 150,000-watt, teeth-rattling strength and be co-owned by W. Lee O'Daniel, the manager of the Light Crust Doughboys Texas swing band. Thanks in part to the enormous radio reach of his persuasive speaking voice, O'Daniel would go on to be elected governor of Texas.

Many of Jimmie's border radio appearances were ramshackle affairs, not the stuff to build a career on. He befriended a Houston movie theater owner, the stunt-loving showman and sometime philanthropist Will Horwitz, a local legend who'd brought air conditioning to Texas theaters and let people pay to see movies with canned food—which he used to feed as many as nine hundred of the local unemployed a day. When Horwitz purchased XED and renamed it XEAW, he would occasionally meet Jimmie, have a few while out on the town in Houston, then somehow drive or be driven to the station, where they would go on the air with nicely oiled conversations, jokes, and songs.

Jimmie's most serious radio opportunity was a proposed regularly sched-uled national show of his own on NBC out of its WEAF home base in New York City. A pilot program was aired within days of the late-August 1932 New York recording session that produced "Miss the Mississippi and You." Relocating to the big city for a national broadcast requiring no regular travel might well have worked for him, as stints in New York did for the careers of Will Rogers, Tex Ritter, and others with irrepressible rural or cowboy roots.

Important, too, might have been a planned tour of England by Jimmie with Slim Bryant and Clayton McMichen accompanying him. By the time these propositions arose, Jimmie Rodgers was certainly much more than a southern regional artist, but his declining health forced him to cancel tours in northern and western states. And even when he recorded in Hollywood, Camden (just across a bridge from Philadelphia), or New York, in order to conserve energy, he did not play unannounced shows or join local musicians in clubs. He had become a guy, Slim Bryant recalls, who just could not do that. These limits on his appearances elsewhere probably contributed, to a degree, to Jimmie's lasting identification as a southern act.

Neither the radio series nor the tour of England would happen, but as that comment on the *America's Blue Yodeler* album cover had noted, Jim-mie's music had not only gone well beyond the South, it also had traveled far outside North America by means of record sales alone. There was strong interest in Jimmie Rodgers' music all across the English-speaking world.

His records have always done well in the U.K. At times, the understand-ing of Jimmie's music there has actually benefited, as would much American popular music, from a certain fuzziness or even ignorance about audience distinctions and genre definitions in America. That Jimmie might be perceived as some sort of niche hillbilly singer, if a distinctive one who sang that "pop version of hillbilly," as Peer put it, or, on the other hand, was somehow "like Negroes," was a distinction often lost there. That he was a recording artist broad enough in appeal that his releases were being mentioned and reviewed in the new *Time* magazine along with those of other pop stars—if often in distinctly condescending tones reflecting antisouthern, antirural bias—was not something of which English fans at the time had any reason to be aware.

The invigorating result of being immune to all those implications can still be heard in a 1932 British recording of Jimmie's "In the Jailhouse Now," by the popular Jack Hylton Orchestra. It is a pure vaudeville jazz romp with wailing clarinets, wah-wahing muted trumpets, and male choruses that shout "He's in the jailhouse now!" en masse between verses more or less croaked by the comedy-song specialist Leslie Sarony. Hylton, son of a Lancashire mill worker, had risen to stardom with his "show band" orchestra—an outfit attuned to appearing on the variety stage rather than to working-class dance halls. His orchestra, accordingly, played everything from musical smutty limericks to Paul Whiteman–style jazz to variations on Rachmaninoff. His recording of Jimmie's original "I had a friend named Campbell" version of "Jailhouse" placed the song firmly in the pop vaudeville market. Hylton's band also played Gene Austin's "Yearning" and the not-quite-country downhome pop song "It Ain't Gonna Rain No More," launched by the singer and ukulele player Wendell Hall. The British tendency to look at regional roots music as one more example of music hall or variety fodder and the musicians as "acts" would never entirely fade. The British skiffle craze of the 1950s, in which, as we will see, Jimmie's "Mule Skinner Blues" would have a key role, was rooted in a similarly blithe concatenation of American idioms such as jug band, folk, pop, and jazz.

And yet Jimmie Rodgers' music, demonstrably, could also be more than novelty entertainment in the U.K. and could speak directly to the British heart. There is no more striking saga of Rodgers' effect on an individual than that of Shetland Islander Thomas Fraser. Born in 1927, a young Fraser was given his first American country music records by locals serving in the Merchant Marine who brought them back from overseas. He first heard Jimmie Rodgers records played on the regular country show broadcast to American Armed Forces across Europe during World War II via a battery-powered radio. The young fisherman was soon buying one of them after another, teaching himself guitar, fiddle, and how to sing and yodel the songs note by note.

Thomas Fraser's grandson Karl Simpson says, "He lived and breathed Jimmie Rodgers—his absolute idol. I think Thomas looked up to him as the ultimate in what could be achieved musically. He would spend hours listening to the records and analyzing the music, often with close musical friends. If it were not for Rodgers . . . Thomas would never have devoted the time to his own music that he did. The only reason he recorded all his music was for the sheer love of the songs and being able to try to emulate his hero in his own personal way."

When electricity first reached the remote Shetlands in 1953, the intensely shy Fraser purchased a good reel-to-reel tape recorder and began, simply for his own pleasure, to record songs he loved. His guitar playing was by this time immaculate, while his singing reflected deep understanding and absorption of Jimmie Rodgers' storytelling vocal attack. His diction was perfect, with traces of his own accent detectable rather than being a direct imitation of Jimmie's. His repertoire stretched across country music, jazz, and blues, but with Rodgers tunes always the core. Since he never intended anyone but a few close friends to hear them, Fraser's recordings were personal expressions, distinctive and touching. He never really attempted to develop a public performance style of his own; he recorded what he wanted, when he wanted, as he wanted—which, for over thirty years, was in the style of Jimmie Rodgers. Meticulous about the recording quality, Fraser would tape well over a thousand tunes before he died in 1978, after sustaining injuries in several boating accidents.

The tapes lay in the collections of family and friends, essentially unheard and unknown, until his grandson took them out of storage and assembled some favorite cuts into a collection at first intended only for family. In the day of the World Wide Web, however, the local family story attracted attention, the songs were heard, and they became a phenomenon. Today, there are four critically praised commercial CDs of Fraser's music, each featuring Rodgers songs. An annual Thomas Fraser Memorial Festival in his hometown of Burra attracts audiences from around the world. The acts that perform there, acts which have included Jimmie Rodgers' great-nephew (and Elsie McWilliams' grandson) Rick McWilliams, play the sorts of music Thomas Fraser loved. That is how far Rodgers' music could be taken to heart by an amateur performer far removed from Meridian, Mississippi, or San Antonio, Texas.

In Australia, the dissemination of Jimmie Rodgers' records would have wider impact, making him, in effect, a godfather of Australian country music. What began as a wholesale importing of Rodgers' style and its American content—his sentimental ballads almost exclusively—mutated before long into the local "bush ballad" tradition. A country singer named Norm Scott

Meeting Jimmie Rodgers

seems to have been featuring Rodgers songs in shows there as early as 1929, and a Rodgers Fan Club was operating in Tasmania by 1935. Tex Banes, a singer who would be associated with Rodgers music for decades and was still appearing in U.S. Rodgers memorial shows in the '70s and '80s, was fired from his farm job for letting practice on his Rodgers-style yodel distract him from his milking—in 1936.

The first popular Australian country singer, Tex Morton (born Robert Lane in New Zealand), would mix cowboy songs, as his adopted name and the western gear he wore suggested, a good deal of yodeling, and Rodgers-style balladry. Tex generally sang solo, accompanied only by his own guitar; and, quite often, with an adopted American accent far different from his Aussie speaking voice.

"I'd get up and sing one of my Jimmie Rodgers numbers," Morton would recall later. "I'd sing it as much as I could like Jimmie Rodgers." On the air in 1941, after being introduced as "that Balladeer of the Bush, your yodeling cowboy friend," Tex noted, "Jimmie Rodgers was a grand fellow; you'd have to go a long way to beat some of the stuff he wrote." When this "father of Australian country music" wrote songs, they would be squarely in the Rodgers mode in sound and theme. His celebrated "The Gundagai Line" is a Rodgers-like but specifically Australian hobo number, and he also performed nostalgic songs about his mother and his dear old pals that featured Rodgers guitar runs.

As Andrew Smith, an Australian historian of his nation's country music, has pointed out, Rodgers' strong influence there (and that of a few other American country artists such as Carson Robison) had everything to do with which American records were released Down Under. Stringbands and even groups such as the Carters and the Stonemans were not at first heard there, so a lone singer like Jimmie, accompanying himself on his own guitar, became the dominant image. It stayed that way for years; Australians were still singing in the sentimental, solo acoustic Jimmie Rodgers mode when American tastes had moved on toward western swing bands and electric small-group honky tonk. Although almost every Rodgers recording was released in Australia, local singers drawing on the Rodgers repertoire rarely took up his blues songs at all and made no attempt to replicate his band or orchestral accompaniments; decisions, Smith argues, that reflect the preferences of a handful of local record label executives and their sense that the harder-hitting "outlaw" blues numbers were stuff too tough and urban for rural audiences.

With this scaled-down, constricted repertoire, what saved the music from sheer monotony was the talent of the individuals who performed it. Morton was one of the most adept Rodgers interpreters anywhere, expert in phrasing, guitar accompaniment, and the integration of the two. A saddle-weary, wistful sense of experience permeates his singing, an inherent suggestion of the blues mentality akin somewhat to Ernest Tubb's, which comes through even though he does not sing blues. Rhythmically, however, Morton is never harder hitting than in his lightly jaunty takes on "My Little Lady" and "Frankie and Johnny." Ralph Peer produced Morton for a while, and he found some limited success in North America.

The slightly later and smoother Australian country star Buddy Williams could build on what Morton had started by accenting the local. When Buddy sang "Waiting for a Train," he changed the nickel he didn't have to an Aussie dollar and related how "they put me off in West Australia, a state I dearly love." When he recorded a rather celebrated LP of Rodgers songs in 1962, Williams, like Morton, more or less stuck to the wistful ballads, his polished style sometimes reminiscent of Hank Snow, who was particularly attuned to the same sorts of Rodgers songs.

The latter-day Australian country music hero, Slim Dusty, an exuberant entertainer who would eventually be referred to as "the man who *was* Australia," regularly sang Rodgers tunes as well. On several occasions, he recorded them as close duets with his wife Joy McKean or his daughter Anne Kirkpatrick, good examples of one approach to singing Jimmie Rodgers story songs that never caught on outside Australia: the male-female close harmony duet. Tex Morton had performed a few with his stage (but not actual) "sister" Dorrie, and the team of Rick and Thel Carey had some success along the same lines in the '50s.

Meanwhile, the Zonophone label, based in London, was manufacturing records for African colonial markets. In South Africa, there were quite early indications that the power of Jimmie Rodgers' music could reach across cultural lines. In Jimmie's own day, Zonophone ads appeared in the black press, for black audiences, in segregated South Africa, featuring both his records and Zulu language discs, side by side.

Demonstrably, you did not have to speak Jimmie Rodgers' language for him, in the deepest sense, to speak yours. The strongest early evidence for that was back in the United States in Cajun country. Geographically, this was not surprising, since the Acadian French-speaking "Third Coast" lies precisely between Rodgers' two homes—Mississippi and Texas. If there was still a somewhat isolating language barrier for many Cajun Americans in the late '20s, there was also an overlap between the music they were developing and American English-language country, blues, and swing. This Louisiana-based culture was, in comparison to that of many rural southerners of Jimmie's day, relatively free-spirited, emotionally direct, and

Meeting Jimmie Rodgers

unabashedly physical. For one thing, Cajuns downright loved to dance. Noting the appearance nearby of a rising performer who stressed the physical over the spiritual, the rough and rowdy as well as the rural, the heart-breaking and the sentimental—well, they were not going to try to resist him. Cajun musicians' love affair with Jimmie Rodgers' music began almost as soon as they encountered it.

Cajun music began to be recorded in order to target one more ethnic group—like the "race" and "hillbilly" markets—and Ralph Peer, predictably, was in the middle of it all. The very first Cajun music on record was a pair of accordion sides by Joseph Falcon on the Columbia label, issued in the summer of 1928. Victor rushed to respond, so what is considered the second Cajun music recording session took place in Atlanta that October when Maius LaFleur and Leo Soileau traveled there, under Peer's auspices, to record such tunes as "Mama, Where You At?" which in itself shows you within a couple of minutes what you need to know about both Cajun music's wild good-time flavor and its bluesy longing. This recording took place during precisely the same week of Atlanta recording sessions in which Jimmie Rodgers, with horns behind him, was laying down "My Carolina Sunshine Girl," "I'm Lonely and Blue," "California Blues," and "Waiting for a Train." In fact, Peer had the groundbreaking Cajun pair and Rodgers holed up in the same place.

"We stayed at the same hotel as the great Jimmie Rodgers, the old Blue Yodeler," fiddler Soileau would recall, "and it was really a thrill for us to meet him. He was there for a recording session, too." Other reports of the encounter describe how "Jimmie knew where to secure a supply of moonshine of such high quality and refinement" that the three of them "chatted and drank the night away." That may be true, or one of those after-the-fact Jimmie stories, but all three recorded classic sides in the days that followed. In a reminder that we are not in genteel territory here, nine days after the session, the feisty LaFleur was shot dead in an altercation over a truck. He was gone before the recordings were released.

Soileau's band, which absorbed some of the innovations of Texas swing as oil strikes in the area led to new jobs and increased ethnic interaction, would eventually record a driving, rambunctious version of Jimmie's "Frankie and Johnny." You can hear Leo shout "Yeah, man!" in the middle of it. One member of Soileau's band the Four Aces, drummer Tony Gonzales, had an accordion-playing brother who would take the Rodgers-Cajun interaction even further.

In July 1929, Roy Gonzales recorded a series of memorable, though mostly long unavailable sides for Paramount that translated Jimmie Rodgers songs into Acadian French—versions of "Lonely and Blue," "T for Texas," and "Waiting for a Train" among them—and they are nothing short of terrific. The plaintiveness of the vocals and the, well, *French* yodels require no understanding of the language to provoke emotional involvement—the way many French speakers, no doubt, responded to hearing Jimmie's original records. Blues with structures quite close to those of Rodgers' blue yodels worked their way into Cajun music quickly, the 1937 "Les Bleus de Bosco" by the Rayne-Bo Ramblers, led by Leroy "Happy Fats" LeBlanc, being a good example. One of the Rayne-Bo Ramblers' earliest records would be "Dor, Baby, Dor"—an American French version of Jimmie's "Sleep, Baby, Sleep." "My guitar style," LeBlanc would note, "was based on Jimmie Rodgers'; I taught myself . . . We were always poor people. My daddy was a rice farmer, and one rice season my mother gave me a sack of rice and I traded it for a guitar."

A pair of much-evolved versions of Happy Fats' "Bosco" blues number, created and recorded around 1950 by the man often referred to as the greatest of Cajun recording artists, accordionist and singer Iry LeJeune, drew the Rodgers connection closer. His "Grande Bosco" is enough like Jimmie's "Anniversary Blue Yodel (Blue Yodel No. 7)" in its basics that Rodgers is now sometimes listed as coauthor, and in his other "Bosco" variation, "It Happened to Me," the connection is unmistakable. The remarkable LeJeune retrieves much of Rodgers' lyric about walking the railroad track, as well as a Jimmie-like "house on fire" metaphor—in French, of course, despite the English title.

In an age of mass distribution of recordings across the world, even in places where English was not spoken, people heard Jimmie Rodgers music, and as the monument in Meridian puts it, "understood." The most often-noted instance of Rodgers music speaking viscerally to people who neither comprehended nor, perhaps, even cared about his words, just his sound, is that encounter between his records and the Kipsigi people of Kenya. As documented in each of three different field recordings made by folklorists visiting the district in 1950, the Kipsigis had already been evoking a spirit or sound they pronounce "Chemirocha." That's "Jimmie Rodgers" to you and me.

These recordings, now known by the blue yodel–like titles "Chemirocha 1," "Chemirocha 2," and "Chemirocha 3," have too often been portrayed (condescendingly, if with understandable astonishment), as naive cargo cult–like misunderstandings of who Rodgers was and what his records entailed. But the earliest descriptions of what the stringed-instrument-accompanied chants mean and what Rodgers suggested to their makers, reveal, in fact, a remarkably sophisticated, varied response. As the song collector Hugh Tracey reported, in "Chemirocha I," Rodgers' name, learned as his records became the first to penetrate into the non-English-speaking areas of Kenya, stands for all things strange and new and from out of town—and not necessarily in entirely positive terms. The same number asks why white men have taken over the country.

"Chemirocha 2," sung by a male chorus (as is "Chemirocha 1"), is more unabashedly enthralled. They have been taken by the sound of Jimmie's guitar playing, which strikes them as much like that of the local six-string bowl lyre, and it is mysterious and wonderful that it should be so similar, coming from this audio visitor from who-knows-where. (This happens to be almost precisely the response Westerners have to hearing about the Kipsigi record.) The singers suggested to Tracey that this song really belonged to their shy sisters, and the third version, sung by the young girls after a little persuasion, makes the full connection. This mysterious singer "Chemirocha," with his sexy, high falsetto singing and pounding rhythms, is transmuted, with due amusement, into a very Pan-like local god of the libido, with antelope's feet. The Kipsigi girls sing his name, with high tones noticeably like his yodel, with a power that is intended to make the "Chemirocha" visitor dance so hard he'll lose *his* clothes. Jimmie Rodgers' physicality and musical power, understood across oceans, cultures, languages, and decades, is summoned up, quite knowingly, for a female fertility dance. Elvis Presley and his fans, it might be noted, would not emerge for several more years.

The music's attraction in Africa also extended to places that were considerably more urbane and modern. There is the case of Sammy Ngako, a yodeling cowboy of the Kikuyu people from elsewhere in Kenya, a little later in the '50s. He made professional records of Rodgers-style singing, yodeling, and guitar runs—in his own tongue—and performed wearing a cowboy hat. In the '60s, there was the singing star S. E. (Soolimon) Rogic, billed as "the Jimmie Rodgers of Sierra Leone." He rose to fame doing straightforward Rodgers imitations and went on to have hit pop recordings in the "Palm Wine" African pop style. His "I Wish I Was a Cowboy" evokes at once the sound of Rodgers and the smooth vocals of Jim Reeves.

As that 1931 Victor album cover noted, Jimmie's music had reached "the Orient" as well, most notably, Japan. Ramblin' Sho Suzuki, a Jimmie Rodgers acolyte and chronicler, first heard Rodgers songs such as "Ben Dewberry's Final Run" and "Lullaby Yodel" on a 1958 Japanese radio show called *Western Town*. He recalls how some translation problems at Nippon Victor in prewar Japan had led to the release of the relatively obscure "Blue Yodel No. 10 (Ground Hog Rootin' in My Back Yard)" as "Blue Yodel" (by implication "No. 1"), when they had meant to release "T for Texas." Other early Japanese releases included the actual "Blue Yodel No. 2," "Roll Along, Kentucky Moon," and "Dear Old Sunny South by the Sea."

American country music has had a huge following in Japan since before World War II. In the postwar years, a homegrown country act of a new generation, Jimmie Tokita and his Mountain Playboys, starred on weekly Tokyo Opry broadcasts. Tokita could fill stadiums there, as an annual country music festival does to this day. Jimmie Rodgers' "Mississippi Delta Blues" was reportedly the Japanese star's favorite song, though he mainly recorded more contemporary fare. A memorial album for Tokita features latter-day versions of that Rodgers number and "Peach Pickin' Time Down in Georgia"—in *his* honor.

Extraordinary Rodgers fan Toshio Hirano today enjoys a loyal following as an engaging performer of Jimmie's songs in San Francisco clubs, singing with passion and finesse and playing the familiar Rodgers runs on his guitar. He first heard the music of Jimmie Rodgers in the late '60s, when he was a banjo-playing, bluegrass- and American-folk loving student at Waseda University in Tokyo. A college friend had brought in a new LP of Jimmie Rodgers hits and suggested that if Toshio did not know Jimmie Rodgers' music, he did not really know country music. Toshio borrowed the album.

"I didn't know even the name of Jimmie Rodgers," he recalls now. "But in the photo of him on the cover, leaning over his Cadillac, in his cowboy hat, he was looking *good*! Then I saw, from the liner notes, that this was very old—recorded in 1929. Wait a minute! He was before Bill Monroe, like the Carter Family—so what did this guy *do*?

"Well, the first tune on that album is 'Peach Pickin' Time in Georgia,' starting with that sweet fiddle intro, and that sounded good. Then the *moment* came along, my moment, to be honest—the moment of my life. When I heard that first line, his voice, everything—background music, the melody, every element in that recording—just blew my head into pieces. To me, that moment was almost beyond music—something coming from this man's voice. I'd been listening to country type music, but wow, what was going *on* there? And that was it."

Back then, Toshio, who today is married to a woman from Texas and teaches English in Silicon Valley when he is not performing, knew next to no English. "No; it was just the sound. Bit by bit I could pick out simple words; he was talking about 'picking' and going somewhere. But as for the whole song—I had no idea what he was talking about. The voice was carrying something to me anyhow. And then I put all the bluegrass tunes in my closet and just concentrated on 'Peach Pickin' Time' and 'Waiting for a Train.' For the next ten years, I *only* sang those two songs. They were enormous enough a challenge for me. Now I know a lot of them."

Hirano, who resettled in the United States to be closer to the music, remains amazed and amused that most Americans do not know much more about Jimmie Rodgers than many in his San Francisco audiences seem to: "One day I played about five or six of the songs and a man came up to me and said, 'Toshio, that song about the train was great! *When did you write it?*' And I just joked and said, 'Well, it was about 1928.'"

A snazzy cover photo, some sounds, and a life altered—a world away and forty years later.

There was one other piece of information (and we might also say disinformation) about Jimmie Rodgers brought up in the liner notes on that old forgotten 1931 album regarding his health, startling for raising a subject explicitly that you do not see even alluded to in contemporary print accounts. "All was not well with Jimmie Rodgers," fans were told outright, looking back at his earliest performing years. "The doctors told him that unless he could get to higher country, where the air would be easier upon his lungs, he could not expect a long and hearty life. But they couldn't frighten Jimmie, and he gaily swung his guitar over his shoulder and took to the road." By the time his hit records came along, bought by fans such as you, the notes assured fans, "his health greatly improved as a result of the wholesome and careful living which his better fortunes made possible." Fans were, it was over-optimistically suggested, keeping the man alive.

Jimmie Rodgers' music had gone to the ends of the earth. He would come up with some more great records and have some important appearances in his months after 1931, but the truth was that he was coming to the end of his life.

Select Soundtrack

The 1935 U.K. "Jimmie Rodgers Medley" record, Part I ("My Old Pal"/"Dear Old Sunny South"/"T for Texas") and Part II ("Daddy and Home"/"Away Out on the Mountain"/"California Blues") appears at the end of the *Sounds Like Jimmie Rodgers* set (JSP).

The Singing Brakeman: Columbia Pictures, a Columbia Victor Gem, 9 minutes; filmed 1929. The best quality copy of Jimmie Rodgers' only film generally available is on the DVD *Times Ain't Like They Used to Be* (Yazoo/Shanachie Video); the 1930 release version is used there. The full audio soundtrack of the film is included on the *Jimmie Rodgers: The Singing Brakeman* audio box set (Bear Family), but a noisy soundtrack copy of the original 1929 cut of the film was used for the transfer. VHS versions of the '29 film cut still circulate.

Jimmie Rodgers in the U.K.

- **Jack Hylton and His Orchestra:** "In the Jailhouse Now" (1932) is available on several Web sites.

- **Skiffle Recordings:** by Lonnie Donegan and others, see chapter 10.

- **Thomas Fraser:** volumes now available include *Long Gone Lonesome Blues* (with seven Rodgers songs), *You and My Old Guitar* (nine Rodgers songs), and *Treasure Untold* (eight Rodgers songs). A fourth, *That Far Away Land*, is slated to feature five more Rodgers songs. All are on Dada Records and at the www.thomasfraser.com Web site.

Jimmie Rodgers in Australia

- **Tex Morton:** "Yodelling Cowboy," "My Old Pal," "I've Only Loved Three Women," "Daddy and Home," and "Frankie and Johnny" from '40s radio broadcasts are on *Tex Morton Yodelling Cowboy* (Castle, 1994). "You and My Old Guitar," "My Little Lady," "Treasure Untold," and "Waiting for a Train" are on *You and My Old Guitar: The Original Tasman/Rodeo Recordings, New Zealand 1949* (Festival, 1981). "You and My Old Guitar" also appears on the eightieth anniversary Rodgers anthology of the same name (Jasmine) and "Treasures Untold" on the anthology *I Am Sad and Weary* (Bear Family, 2003).

- **Buddy Williams:** The 1962 LP *Buddy Williams Sings Jimmie Rodgers* includes a dozen Rodgers songs; one of which, "Gambling Polka Dot Blues," is on the *You and My Old Guitar* Rodgers collection (Jasmine, 2008).

- **Slim Dusty:** "Any Old Time" and "Frankie and Johnny" (with his wife Joy McKean), are on the EP *Any Old Time* (Columbia, 1954) and *Slim Dusty: Regal Zonophone Collection* (Pid, 1995). "Mother, the Queen of My Heart" is on the box set *The Man Who Is Australia* (EMI Australia, 2000); "You and My Old Guitar," with daughter Anne Kirkpatrick, is on *Travellin' Still—Always Will* (EMI Australia, 2002).

- **Rick and Thel Carey:** "She Was Happy Till She Met You" is on the *You and My Old Guitar* anthology (Jasmine). They also

Meeting Jimmie Rodgers

recorded "When Jimmie Rodgers Said Goodbye," which is on *Regal Zonephone and Beyond* (Gum Tree, 2000).

Jimmie Rodgers and Cajun Music

- **Roy Gonzales:** "Anuiant et Bleu" ("Lonely and Blue") and the blue yodel–like "Chocktaw Beer Blues" are on the box set *Paramount Old Time Recordings* (JSP, 2006). Among other 1929 Gonzales recordings of adapted Rodgers songs cut for Paramount, but not now in print, are "Attendre pour un Train" and "Un Fussi Qui Brille" ("A Great Big Shiny Barrel," based on "T for Texas").

- **Happy Fats and His Rayne-Bo Ramblers:** "Les Blues de Bosco" is on *Cajun Country, Volume 2* (JSP, 2005). "Dor, Baby, Dor" is on the Bear Family *Let Me Be Your Side Track* set (2008).

- **Leo Soileau's Four Aces:** "Frankie and Johnny" (1935) has been available on a number of public domain download Web sites.

- **Iry LeJeune:** "Grand Bosco" (1956) and "It Happened to Me" (1955) are on *Iry LeJeune, Cajun's Greatest: The Definitive Collection* (Ace, 2004).

Jimmie Rodgers in Africa

- **Sammy Ngako:** "Rosana: and "Gwitu Ni Ribai" appear on *Classic Kikuyu Music: Yodelers, Guitars, and Accordions*, available from author-performer Elijah Wald at www.elijahwald .com/kenyacds.html.

- **Kipsigis' "Chemirocha" recordings:** three of them are currently available on the Smithsonian Institution's Smithsonian Global Sound Web site (www.smithsonianglobalsound .org): Charondet Arap Ng'asura and Kipsigi men; Chemutoi Ketiienya with Kipsigi girls; and Bekyibei Arap Mosonoick with Cherwo Arap Korogem.

- **S. E. Rogie:** "I Wish I Was a Cowboy" is on *S. E. Rogie: Palm Wine Guitar Music* (Cooking Vinyl, 2002).

Jimmie Rodgers in Japan

- **Henry Yaitu and the Eiji Hanaoka Dixie Ramblers:** "Mississippi Delta Blues" and "Peach Pickin' Time in Georgia," with strings and horns, are on Henry's *Tribute to Jimmie Tokita: Mississippi Delta Blues* (Audio Park, 2003).

- **Toshio Hirano:** "Peach Pickin' Time in Georgia" and "Waiting for a Train" have been available via audio and video links at his Web site: www.toshiohirano.com.

SIX

Doomed Singer-Songwriter with Guitar

Jimmie Rodgers recorded "T.B. Blues" in January 1931 and "Whippin' That Old T.B." in August 1932, openly associating himself with tuberculosis and announcing—in songs, yet—that he seemed to be losing his fight with the disease, that he could foresee the graveyard as his destination. That was tantamount to a public confession. In his day, middle-class people did not talk about tuberculosis very much, and celebrities even less.

Tuberculosis had been commonly understood only a few decades before to be an indicator of noble character, a sign of aristocratic gentility and probable poetic genius, often attested to as such in artistic and even "scientific" paeans to the "spiritual glow" supposedly exuded by sufferers. Since 1882, though, when it was first discovered that the disease was the result of an infectious bacillus, it had, predictably, lost its romantic cachet. It was now associated, not without reason, with those who were too poor to be protected from exposure to it—people living lives marked by insufficient food, shelter, and medical attention. Sufferers were stigmatized as crude underclass reprobates who coughed up phlegm in public and might infect you. They were often subject to quarantine, ruled out for many jobs, and otherwise treated much as lepers had once been—though the disease, in fact, is not that easily transmitted.

In truth, tuberculosis, which had long been lumped together with emphysema, lung cancer, black lung, and other then indistinguishable respiratory diseases all labeled "consumption," was still descending upon people

of every social class. The '20s fad for building new houses with open-air "California" or "Florida" sunrooms, often on the second floor, hints at the many quietly anguished, ineffectual middle-class attempts to cure afflicted family members by having them "sleep out every night" in the supposedly refreshing open air, preferably on some attractive wicker furniture. So, no, you did not have to be a disadvantaged outsider to contract T.B., but people knew that if you were, you were more likely to contract it. And they probably exaggerated that aspect until many people thought it was shameful to have it, just as many thought it was shameful to be poor.

For most of its millions of victims, tuberculosis and its energy-sapping, severely painful symptoms passed within a couple of years. A substantial minority, however, were doomed to die from the disease as it continued to advance through a series of worsening attacks marked by violent lung hemorrhaging. Jimmie Rodgers proved to be in that unfortunate minority. In the '20s, tuberculosis was still a leading cause of death in the United States; elsewhere in the world, it still is. It has never been eliminated. It did not really begin to be tamed until antibiotics were developed in the '40s—too late for Jimmie Rodgers. The treatment options for T.B. when Rodgers was diagnosed with it in 1924 were basically two. You either submitted to a hideous, largely useless, and often deadly rib-removing operation, which was meant to help by draining the chest and alleviating pressure, or you tried to get a lot of rest to help the infection pass.

Sanitariums and spa towns dotted the national landscape, particularly out West with its allegedly advantageous desert or mountain air. The poor and afflicted, not always welcome even in their own families, had filled many such towns, only to learn when arriving that staying at the private sanitarium was prohibitively expensive. Worse, local authorities in such places had begun to restrict immigration of the ill and even to bar locals from supplying more beds. Partly as a result of those policies, some poorer T.B. victims could be found in makeshift "lunger" tent colonies, which provided little but a place to lie down. Ironically, Asheville, North Carolina, where Jimmie found early career success, had itself been a mountain sanatorium site before being modified into a general resort to stem the incoming tide of the tubercular.

When the recording star Jimmie Rodgers came to play your town, he had already traveled around the country, in vain, searching for a better climate—to Florida, to Arizona, to Texas. He had been in a charity ward situated near Meridian and later, when he was more financially solvent, a sanitarium near San Antonio, but in keeping with his restless nature, he had bolted from both at the earliest opportunity. He knew very well what it was to be destitute and afflicted; he had been there himself for most of the '20s.

No small percentage of the audiences he addressed would have had similar experiences, or at least been very familiar with them. Increasingly, as that open, if overly optimistic, discussion of his health on the 1931 album cover demonstrates, they knew that he was afflicted himself.

"Lungers" and their loved ones were another considerable group with whom Jimmie Rodgers had a special empathy, and whom he would come to represent. There would be many who had been in the same institutions as Jimmie at one time or another, such as Claude Townsend, a musician friend, and the father of Bob Wills' biographer Charles Townsend. Identification between those directly involved with tuberculosis was strong and virtually automatic. As the writer O. Henry put it in "A Fog in Santone," his nightmarish 1908 story concerning a desperate morphine purchase in San Antonio by a Memphis-raised T.B. sufferer, "there is a freemasonry . . . between the members of the not-so-small fraternity of the T.B.-afflicted . . . that does away with formalities and introductions. A cough is your card; a hemorrhage a letter of credit."

Jimmie was singing of these matters for all to hear, and the combination of that confessional, very personal content and the style in which he most often presented it—alone on stage with only his acoustic guitar for accompaniment, pouring it all out to you—established a model that would eventually reverberate through popular music. The prime reason he was out there singing solo, of course, was that then, as now, it was much less expensive for him to do that than to carry orchestras or even small bands with him everywhere he went, even if the performance did not match the orchestration on his hit records. You can search in vain for a convincing example of an American performing songwriter who would sing to you of his own real or apparent experiences in just this way before Jimmie came along.

"From where I stand," remarks contemporary singer-songwriter Steve Earle, "it's arguable that we just wouldn't *have* this consistent, lasting genre of music based on one guy singing and accompanying himself on a guitar, that's been pervasive in American pop music—country included—without him. I think he's the guy, the prototype, for a Woody Guthrie, a Hank Williams, *and* an Elvis. What's important with Jimmie Rodgers is that he accompanied himself on an instrument that could fill in all the gaps. A guitar has overtones; it will make you hear other instruments."

As a much-traveled, multigenre performer himself, Earle points to another reason Jimmie's choice to sing alone with a guitar was significant: that it enabled closeness to the audience, availability. "You can accompany yourself on a piano," Steve notes, "but you can't *hitchhike* with it. A guitar's portable; that's why I'm a guitar player. Anybody can learn how to play it, and that's why it's the most important instrument in modern human history. Jimmie Rodgers was the first guy to do this who got recorded consistently and reached such a large audience—the first general impression. I think he invented the *job*."

Twenty-first-century Grand Ole Opry star Marty Stuart adds, "Jimmie set the template for the troubadour who stands in the middle of the stage with his guitar. And he had an incredible ear for great guitars, too, by the way! I've played his guitars, and they're wonderful."

A few bluesmen and songsters had featured solo performances with guitar that brought it out of the genteel parlor or the hands of Spanish language balladeers, Blind Lemon Jefferson being a highly successful example. Jimmie Rodgers did more with his solo performance; he added the sense that while the material he was singing and playing was pop music meant for all in his expanding audience, sometimes he was also involved in deeply personal storytelling.

It was not until some forty years later, when the notion and image of the guitar-strumming singer of his own songs had been elevated in stature by the evolving, subsequent examples of Woody Guthrie, Hank Williams, and Bob Dylan, that Jimmie Rodgers would come to be singled out as the original model of the suffering singing songwriter with a Martin guitar in hand. That is an entirely understandable view, but it calls for an important caveat.

Jimmie's most personal songs, whether their subject was health, money, work, family, or women, were part of the repertoire of an extrovert not much given to brooding, let alone navel-gazing. In performance, those songs were likely to heighten the sense of engagement with his audience, of his sharing these experiences with them. They were signs not of someone with special sensitivity, alienated and tragically alone up there, but of solidarity. The familiar sort of latter-day singer-songwriter who specializes in regular introspection or the practitioner of "emo" rock is not particularly in Jimmie Rodgers' tradition.

How such personal songs as "T.B. Blues," the life-story narrative "Jimmie the Kid," or "Home Call," which mentions his immediate family members by name, came to be an element in Jimmie Rodgers' repertoire has been accounted for in more than one way. Author and critic Yuval Taylor makes a strong case that when Jimmie recorded "T.B. Blues" and "Jimmie the Kid" on the same day, it constituted nothing less than a milestone "in the development of personal authenticity in popular music." He sees Jimmie turning in this direction as a calculated strategy, the songs as much about self-promotion and market response as confession or testament.

"It was only after he became a celebrity," Taylor maintains, "that he started singing about his battle with tuberculosis, for it was only then that his audience knew enough about him to care about his personal problems . . .

His listeners all thought he was singing about his own life [anyway] . . . why not, then, actually do what they already thought he was doing? They were buying his records, after all, not just because they liked his music, but because they wanted to learn more about *him*."

Performing songwriter Steve Forbert, who was raised in Meridian, Mississippi, and has been a frequent performer of Rodgers songs since the '70s, sees Jimmie's move toward personalizing his material in less calculated, if perhaps more romantic terms. He focuses on the traumatic winter of 1923–24 when Jimmie and Carrie's baby daughter, June Rebecca, died. Jimmie took off for points West for months, then returned to Meridian and received the formal diagnosis of tuberculosis — which, by then, he had surely understood was coming. Rodgers' focus on being an entertainer full-time began to develop at that point, and so, as Forbert sees it, did crucial parts of his sensibility.

"After his child died," Forbert suggests, "he disappeared — out West; they think he got as far as Arizona. Well, I think this was a turning point where Jimmie went off into some personal soul-searching, off into the wilderness. Think about that loneliness. He's out on the plains, after riding on trains with hobos . . . all alone, under the stars at night. You could have a sort of personal epiphany in a situation like that, really get in touch with yourself.

"I think, right then, he made a sort of bargain with the realities of his life and fate — about the rest of the time he had left, and with *that* focus, he built up a certain inner energy that was unstoppable — the kind so intense that you can pretty well see the turning of events for the next few years. You know the future, and you're just going to play it out. He knows he has such limited time that everything is so of the essence . . . So he both has that new focus *and* he's resigned to fate; he knows things can be done, *and* he knows he's dying of tuberculosis. It's what lies behind his confidence, when he got that Victor recording contract but nothing happened, to go up to New York City on his own, find Ralph Peer and say 'I'm here — at your expense! Let's do something.' And they do."

In Forbert's view, Jimmie's emotional focus and intensity throughout his song-making, professional performing years added crucially to his listeners' sense that whatever he was singing was personal, his own story, one that mattered — right now. Taylor suggests that Jimmie was sufficiently aware of this to exploit it. There is no inherent clash between those apparently very different understandings of how Rodgers' personal experiences came to be reflected in his songs, though they do suggest different perceptions of his nature.

Personalizing song material, making it his, was by all accounts Jimmie Rodgers' habit from the very beginning of his career, whatever the source of the material, and it is reflected in his first-person adaptations of common-place blues verses, which account for dozens of the songs he is credited with. As we have seen, contributing your own turn on the familiar was part of the very nature of being a successful blues performer, all the more so if you were making a series of commercial records that needed to be both distinguishable from each other and identifiable as from the same source. The railroading, quick-to-ramble womanizer who may be worried, but not for long, emerges as a recurring character in Rodgers' blues material, whether the song carries a personalized title like "Jimmie's Texas Blues" or "Jimmie's Mean Mama Blues" or a blues with just a yodel number and not a name.

Personalization, however, played a similarly central part in the way Jimmie would prepare and present his ballads. Slim Bryant recalls how Jimmie changed precisely one line of "Mother, the Queen of My Heart," a song Slim had written and brought for him to record. It was already a story song told in the first person, but Jimmie wrote the line "I knew I was wrong from the start" near the end—the whole function of which is to make the storyteller's own reaction to the story the emotional punch line of the tale.

There is no Jimmie Rodgers ballad better known or more often revisited by country, folk, blues, and rock singers alike than "Waiting for a Train." It came to be the much-loved story song we know through a process that made it not only a powerful pop music attraction, but also a personalized Rodgers creation. The basic idea was no sudden, Promethean inspiration that overtook Jimmie and emerged from his pen and guitar. Norm Cohen, in his comprehensive study of the railroad in American song, *Long Steel Rail*, lists dozens and dozens of recorded variants of the "10,000 Miles Away from Home" ballad that had preceded Jimmie's song. These lyric ancestors went back as far as a mid-nineteenth-century London music hall number, "Standing on the Platform," and they are on record as having taken a hobo-related lyric turn as early as a version circulated in a 1909 railroaders' magazine. Versions that were not Jimmie's song but clearly shared that background and some of the old lyric fragments he absorbed were still being recorded in his day: the Stripling Brothers' "Railroad Bum," and the Carter Family's "Western Hobo," for two.

The first recorded version, Blind George Reneau's 1924 "Wild and Reckless Hoboes," has a tune quite different from Jimmie's and a narrative that, for all the now familiar lines in it ("My pocketbook is empty; my heart is filled of pain") is difficult to follow, let alone get close to, as it careens confusingly between first and third person. Ultimately, Reneau's version seems to be about the not-so–universally-pressing matter of finding girls who will agree to have dinner dates with hoboes. Simply put, no other version of the "10,000 Miles" ballad has ever had anything like the worldwide, lasting power and familiarity of Jimmie's continually rerecorded "Waiting for a Train."

The material first came up as something Jimmie Rodgers might tackle "over the transom," as Ralph Peer would recall: "It was some old song with a different tale . . . Somebody sent the words to Jimmie, a garbled version, and he looked at them and said 'I remember *that.*'" But the tune Jimmie recalled did not work with this particular set of words, Peer continued. "Jimmie couldn't fit the chords he knew to those words, and, anyway, he didn't like the words the way they were—so he changed those. We ended up with what has never been challenged as a completely new song, because both the music *and* the words were changed."

Remaking the material into the compact, tuneful, first-person, "brakeman and bum" standard did not come to Jimmie easily. "Waiting" is a song credited to Jimmie alone but may well have been one of a number of songs for which he turned to his sister-in-law Elsie McWilliams for some uncredited help. It is not a story she brought up publicly in the interviews she gave in her later years, in the '70s and '80s, but one she shared with her performing songwriter grandson Rick McWilliams.

"Right!" Rick recalls. "They used to get together on Sunday evenings sometimes and kick stuff around about what to write about—and then they'd write songs and work on them. She told me that Jimmie came in one Sunday with a little tablet, and the first thing he did was tear off a page, wad it up, and throw it on the floor. He laughed when she went over and got the paper and unfolded it—and it was the first part of 'Waitin' for a Train.' Grandma told me that Carrie and her helped him finish the song—that Carrie suggested 'He put me off in Texas' would be a good line for him to sing, to put that in there."

While it is likely that Grandma Elsie, who was generally (though not always) reluctant to take credit for her songwriting contributions to the Rodgers oeuvre, was just passing a little credit to her sister Carrie in that story—Carrie not being known to have even tried to write a word of any other song—the overall picture of harried collaboration has the ring of truth.

The image of Jimmie Rodgers as a solitary, confessional singer-songwriter is complicated by the undeniable fact that he wrote only a minority of his songs outright, alone. In fact, he wrote neither of the two songs that seem most intensely autobiographical, "T.B. Blues" and "Jimmie the Kid," however compellingly our contemporary singer-songwriter notions make us want to believe otherwise. In another irony, thanks to the aggressive marketing of Jimmie's material to other singers by the Peer organization and Victor Record's Eli Oberstein, blue yodeler Gene Autry actually had his own cover versions of both of those milestone "personal" songs out on records before Jimmie Rodgers did.

As for "T.B. Blues," there had been earlier songs on the topic by nonvictims—Ma Rainey's "Dirty T.B. Blues," for instance. Jimmie had not decided, in response, to sit down to compose a T.B. song that would be his own. He had taken the thought of having such a song directly to Elsie, who had seen him go in and out of tubercular crises, in and out of sanitariums, and he asked her to write it. She had said no; she could not bring herself to write any such thing, loving her sister and brother-in-law too much and finding the theme too upsetting. So Jimmie found a writer who would, another frequent collaborator, Ray Hall—a prisoner in the Texas State Penitentiary. Obligingly, Hall, as specifically requested, "tossed together" some T.B.-related twelve-bar blues verses and sent them to Jimmie. It was Jimmie himself, Hall told Nolan Porterfield, who raised the stakes, emotional temperature, and sense of doom of the song by adding, after the intended finale, "Ain't nobody ever whipped the T.B. blues," an offhand last stanza, chillingly vivid no matter who might have written it, but all the more so coming from the man who was doing the singing, the man who had envisioned the scene: "Gee, but the graveyard is a lonesome place. They put you on your back, throw that mud down in your face; I've got the Tee-ee, Bee-ee blues."

"Jimmie the Kid," with its utterly different tone, today seems to be a predecessor of story of my life songs like Loretta Lynn's "Coal Miner's Daughter." In a few snappy verses, it relates how Jimmie was a Mississippi-born brakeman who worked for a lot of railroads, rode the freight trains, yodeled his way to fame, and now goes "Cadillackin'" with his wife every night, from his beautiful home, that Yodeler's Paradise, all fixed up so nice. The song was not, however, written by Rodgers, but by his friend Jack Neville, author also of Jimmie's can't-fail vaudeville number "Sweet Mama, Hurry Home or I'll Be Gone."

Jimmie Rodgers did write some personal, confessional songs; "Whippin' that Old T.B." was one of them. As Elsie would note, "He had the nerve to go ahead and write [songs like that]; he wasn't a sissy about it." However, it may be more remarkable in retrospect that this songwriting performer whose vocal style and persona evidence a strong personality and ego, some of it of a rough, even macho variety, could so easily and unself-consciously turn to others for songwriting help, including his own sister-in-law.

Even a glance at the published credits for Jimmie's songs shows that most of the strongest ones he wrote himself, alone, besides the many personally-assembled blues numbers, were not searing autobiographical confessionals, but the stuff of vaudeville and variety—the likes of "My Carolina Sunshine Girl," "High Powered Mama," and "When the Cactus Is in

Doomed Singer-Songwriter with Guitar

Bloom." Alternatively, they exhibited the outwardly directed "life down here as it is" observational style of "No Hard Times," not self-examination.

In truth, Jimmie Rodgers was a solo songwriter only occasionally. He was required to come up with fresh material at an extraordinary rate, even as he was out performing so much, often exhausted by work and disease. Specifically authorized by Ralph Peer to find material and sign on writers to help him with new songs, he did just that, sometimes collaborating with them, sometimes simply recording their songs in his own interpretive performance style. He thus became not only a precursor of the self-expressing singer-songwriter, but also an early example of the collaborative popular songmaker-producer of the sort found later in the song assembly lines of New York's Brill Building and Nashville's Music Row.

Elsie McWilliams alone composed or significantly contributed to some 39 of the 111 of her brother-in-law's issued recordings, though she is credited officially with only half that many. She wrote many of the songs on demand, on themes Jimmie had asked for, or, as was the case with "Daddy and Home," "You and My Old Guitar," and even "Everybody Does It in Hawaii," based directly on—and sometimes written just minutes after—comments he had made concerning his own experiences. There were times where she was asked to provide words for existing tunes, as when she supplied the lyric for a tune the Hawaiian guitarist Joe Kaipo had come up with for Jimmie, making it "Tuck Away My Lonesome Blues." In the right mood, she would even admit to having had a hand in some lines in the more risqué blues numbers, lines she did not want to be associated with, some, apparently, even in Jimmie's image-shaping "Mule Skinner Blues" and "My Rough and Rowdy Ways."

Elsie had written popular verse and music for her children's school plays; she could read music and play piano. When Jimmie discovered he was going to need a lot more songs than he had imagined, he had turned to her first. She was doubtful that she could help but knew that success in music was his best and maybe only chance to support himself, her sister Carrie, and their daughter, now that his sickness was limiting his creative output.

As she told Steve Forbert in a detailed 1984 interview (during which they also sang some duets), "Jimmie said, 'Sis; I've got an opportunity, but I haven't got the time to write the songs. I've *got* to have some original ballads, so *you've* got to write 'em!' And I said 'Jimmie, you know good and well I can't write you songs for you to sing,' and he says, 'Well, I know good and well that you *can*; I've got to have the songs—so you just *do* it!'

"On the music part," she recalled, "he would change it anyway, so mostly I say I wrote words for him . . . I told him not to put my name on anything; I said 'You're the inspiration of all of it—so it's not telling a story to say that you're the composer. If you hadn't made me do it, I wouldn't have.'"

Jimmie would attempt to win parole for his collaborator Raymond Hall, a long-time prisoner, but Ray would not be pardoned and set free until 1976, after fifty-five years in prison. He would die forgotten, a footnote in the Rodgers saga, in 1983. A neighbor, touched by Hall's story, erected a monument over Hall's grave near Memphis with the names of the songs Ray had written on it—"Moonlight and Skies," "Southern Cannonball," "Gambling Polka Dot Blues," and "T.B. Blues" among them. "Moonlight and Skies" is actually a fairly detailed report on how Hall himself wound up in the jailhouse in the first place, with names named, but so powerful and personalizing is Jimmie's handling of the song that everyone thinks of it as his own. The ethics and ironies and happenstance related in the song attach themselves to Rodgers as closely as if he had written it. "Whether the songs are old, new, borrowed, or blue," singer-songwriter Forbert says succinctly, "they're *his.* That's the power of this guy."

There were many Rodgers collaborators. Waldo O'Neal wrote five songs for or with Jimmie, beginning when he was a very young man himself, including "Hobo Bill's Last Ride," "Pistol Packin' Papa," and "My Time Ain't Long." "My Time" has seemed to listeners, from the day Jimmie's recording was released in May 1932, to be as much about the existential condition of America's Blue Yodeler as about the unfortunate fellow facing the gallows in the lyric. O'Neal had supplied Jimmie one further self-explanatory lyric for a song that would have been called "I'm a One-Man Mama Now," but the time, truly not long, ran out before Jimmie found a tune for it that pleased him.

As he headed for New York by steamboat from Texas in May of 1933, Jimmie had in his satchel another nine songs to record, but only one of them was his own composition, a blues, and a good one, the song that would come to be known as "Jimmie Rodgers' Last Blue Yodel."

There are moments on these last records when you can hear that his breathing has become difficult. He was sipping whiskey just to clear his throat enough to get out a song, and as is often recalled in even the shortest of his biographical sketches, between songs he had to lie down and rest on a cot that had been brought into the East Side studio. But still he kept making music.

Back in 1924, in those life-changing months that may well have been crucial in making Jimmie Rodgers the man the world would know, at the time of his first, shocking tubercular hemorrhage, he was visiting his dad, Aaron, in Geiger, Alabama. Twenty-seven years old then, he had long since come to terms with having grown up without a mother at hand, but now, in his distress, he cried out, "Get me to Mama; get me to Mama; she'll know what to do," by which he had actually meant Carrie and Elsie's mother,

Kizzie Williamson. He just wanted to get home to Meridian, not so very far away.

Near midnight, on the night of May 25–26, 1933, at the renamed Taft Hotel near Times Square, New York City, the very hotel where he had checked in back in November 1927 to tell Ralph Peer that he was ready to make that big record now, a feverish Jimmie Rodgers was hemorrhaging again, badly.

The hotel management called for help, and a Peer employee named Castro, who was heading the new Latin America division of the firm, went up to see what could be done. Awake for the last time, Jimmie collapsed in the helpless man's arms, muttering about Carrie and Elsie's sister Annie's house in Washington, D.C. "Just get me to my sister in Washington. Can't you take me? They'll know what to do." Maybe, he must have been thinking, he could get there—halfway home. It was not to be. A great heart was broken.

Connecting with audiences as he did had made Jimmie Rodgers a star, a hero, and a legend in the making. Reaching out to collaborators for help had shaped the making of his music. His time was over. The music would need disciples now. And it was going to find them.

seven

Aftermath
The Late, Great Jimmie Rodgers

Over time, it would be clearer: The life and reach of Jimmie Rodgers' music had only just begun as his old friend, engineer Homer Jenkins, carefully, repeatedly set off the train's whistle. The sound was so heartbreakingly mournful that many who heard it would speak of it for years, how that whistle just kept crying as they carried Jimmie Rodgers' body home, heading south, more than seventy-five years ago. People lined the trackside watching the train steam by—much as they once had, on other tracks, for Lincoln.

The impact of who Jimmie Rodgers had been and of what he had managed to do in fewer than thirty-six years of life and just five of fame would far outlast the era of his personal contributions. What other people would make of him now, advocates for some version of him, for some offshoot of his music—musical interpreters, chroniclers, critics friendly or otherwise, and exploiters, too—would further the story. It was their time.

The mainstream media reports of Jimmie's death prefigured future attitudes toward him. The day after Jimmie died just blocks from its offices, the *New York Times* described him as "a singer of 'Hill-Billy' songs on the radio." The term *hillbilly*, virtually always dismissive at the time, was beginning to be tossed around a lot, however it was spelled.

A more extensive and knowing report in the Memphis *Commercial Appeal* pinned Jimmie as essentially a preradio performer and kicked back at northern dismissals, recalling "vocalists and critics in New York" who "smiled and shook their heads when they heard him . . . Before national networks spread their spider web all over creation and made music a knob-turning matter, Jimmie Rodgers was America's No. 1 melody man . . . Even now, Jimmie Rodgers tops Paul Whiteman in the record shop sales . . . Fame didn't bother him. Many afternoons he sat in Saul Bluestein's music shop on Main Street here, thrumming and singing anything requested of him." In this obituary prose, Jimmie was still connected to "us," still downhome, no matter how far he had traveled or how jazzy his music had become.

Time magazine proceeded to portray him as an outright hillbilly stereotype, shiftless and, inevitably, a drunk, who had, amazingly, nonetheless somehow sold "20 million records" and made some people a lot of money. The newfangled news weekly had taken an early national lead by reviewing some of Rodgers' singles alongside those of Enrico Caruso and torch singer Ruth Etting, if with a certain "for those who like that sort of droning" disdain, but only got around to a postmortem on Jimmie a year after he died, with some remarkably inaccurate reporting, including a reference to "Nashville, North Carolina."

This report's snide tones were fast becoming the norm for national coverage of the emerging country music field. *Time* informed readers that Rodgers had "yodeled his way around the North Carolina countryside, drinking all the corn whiskey he could get . . . Tired, unshaven, racked with tuberculosis, he twanged his guitar, sang, and yodeled 'Sleep Baby Sleep.' . . . It sold more than 1 million copies . . . [so] he could buy all the whiskey he wanted." They finished off with the news that "his widow still gets about $200 a month in royalties" and that a Panamanian firm had just named a line of rum for him.

Thus arrived the descriptions from "above." But there were quite different ones from supposedly less lofty places. Jimmie Rodgers' death set off a phenomenon to which we are accustomed today, but which was something fresh and telling then—the recording and release of memorial songs marking his passing, some eighteen of them. The most lasting of them, "When Jimmie Rodgers Said Goodbye," was written and first performed by Rodgers' friends and song providers Dwight Butcher and Lou Herscher, the same pair out of East Tennessee by way of Tin Pan Alley who had penned his "I'm Free (From the Chain Gang Now)" and "Old Love Letters."

There is something intrinsically touching about their breezy-as-Jimmie, almost flip description of his death as one last train ride to grab, angelically perhaps. ("He caught a fast one on the fly.") But where Butcher and Herscher were onto something, and early, was including in their lyric a list of the widely varied sorts of music Jimmie was leaving behind—blue songs for brakemen, lullabies for kids, love songs for sweethearts, yodels (for cowboys, especially), and southern music. This memorial song was still being recorded twenty years later, but the most effective early version was not Butcher and Herscher's, nor Bradley Kincaid's, nor the truly painful, note-scraping one by the radio team of Asher Sizemore and child singer Little Jimmie, but Gene Autry's.

Autry, who had realized the power of personalizing a song, not just providing an emotionally blank narrative, adds "And *I* lost my pal and true friend, when Jimmie Rodgers said goodbye." Gene was more personal still in one of the three other Rodgers memorial songs he recorded, the self-penned "Good Luck Old Pal," in which he recalls singing harmony with Jimmie in Texas on "My Little Old Home Down in New Orleans," a song Gene had never recorded himself. The memory rings true; they had crossed paths in Texas in 1928. The record itself might as well have been entitled "Gene Autry's Last Blue Yodel," because it was; Autry stuck to recording in his own style alone from that moment on.

As a recording artist, sometimes using the pseudonym "Slim Oakdale," songwriter Dwight Butcher had already covered seven Rodgers tunes himself—a pair of them, it is startling to note, on May 31, 1933, within days of Jimmie's burial. That rushed timing may not have meant that the tribute was any less sincere, but somebody also saw the circumstances as a show business opportunity to pounce on. There is a fairly consistent pattern in the posthumous tribute records of including unsubtle reminders that Jimmie himself can still be heard on record—especially, but not exclusively, if the tribute happened to be on Victor or Bluebird. W. Lee O'Daniel, leader of the Light Crust Doughboys, got that band's "Memories of Jimmy [*sic*] Rodgers" single out quickly, with a lavishly printed copy of the lyric available for those who wanted to hang it on the wall—and a reminder that "his records are so sweet, in the city and the country, folks say he can't be beat." Bradley Kincaid recorded a couple of tributes written by the topical songwriter Bob Miller (songs also covered, less dryly, by Autry), and also a one-off weeper, "Mrs. Jimmie Rodgers' Lament," written by a particularly notorious copyright grabber, Joe Davis, under the pseudonym Richard Kuster.

Mrs. Jimmie Rodgers herself had last heard from Jimmie in a postcard and a four-page letter mailed from the Taft Hotel, the scene of his death; by the time they reached her in San Antonio, he was gone. Though Carrie alludes to them in her memoir, their contents have not previously been detailed publicly. On inspection, they reveal a Jimmie Rodgers who was still joking. ("We've only recorded eight songs so far, but you know how slow Ralph is.") He offers his advice on what to tell her lung-cancer-ridden brother, Covert, whom she was home nursing at the time: he should keep right on smoking; it would make him feel better. They were taking a day or so off from recording now, he reported, to go to the beach—which they did.

And there were pressing practical matters. Jimmie tells Carrie that a new recording contract he is agreeing to sign with Victor's Bluebird label would be good for them; Ralph Peer has promised that he will be receiving the same royalty on those new 35-cent records as he had been on the 75-cent Victor label ones earlier, and they would no doubt sell more with the lower price tag. These last letters are affectionate, breezy, husband-to-wife affairs with nothing portentous about them at all.

This direct evidence may help clear up a few long-debated matters. Jimmie's typically cheerful tone obviously masks the fact that at the end there, he was managing to record only by resting on a cot between takes. But both the tone and content rebut the frequently suggested notion that Jimmie had somehow known that this, of his many recording sessions and bad bouts with T.B., would be the last of both. The correspondence also casts serious doubt on the view expressed by some who had known them that Jimmie and Carrie's marriage had effectively ended before Jimmie died. These were the words of a man content to go on living just as he had — the wandering entertainer away much of the time, doing as he pleased, yet with credible family affection on display when he got back home.

Putting aside all romanticizing of Jimmie's sad, untimely, but ultimately predictable end, the hard facts for Carrie Rodgers now were those that even that Memphis newspaper obituary had mentioned: "He made fortunes and spent them." Soft-touch Jimmie had made much money and given away plenty, and the two of them had spent even more. "The money was running out," Carrie told radio interviewer Ken Berryhill in 1958. "[Jimmie] was never out of debt to Southern Music or the Victor Company."

There were still well more than a dozen unreleased sides to come out in the years just ahead, some of them recorded at the last sessions, others previously rejected or held in reserve. The posthumous releases included such classics as "Mississippi Delta Blues," My Good Gal's Gone," "The One Rose," and "Jimmie Rodgers' Last Blue Yodel." Most of them, however, would come out at the height of the Depression and, obviously, without Jimmie to promote them in performance. Given the terms songwriters were getting years later, when the Jimmie Rodgers contract with Ralph Peer was renewed, it is certain that more royalties from Jimmie's songs were coming to Carrie in the '50s than could have been the case during Franklin D. Roosevelt's first term.

Though it is rarely mentioned, Carrie would remarry, very briefly, at the end of the '30s to a fellow named Powell, though she had begun her stand as the very public widow of the late, great Jimmie Rodgers by 1935. Historian Nolan Porterfield discovered that she went so far as to specify explicitly in her quick divorce decree that she be entitled to resume calling herself

"Mrs. Jimmie Rodgers." However retiring she had been before Jimmie's death, Carrie was going to be a public figure now.

That "Mrs. Jimmie Rodgers" appellation even appeared on a couple of records. It is still astonishing, given that her singing capability was less than that of even the notoriously limited Audrey (Mrs. Hank) Williams, but Carrie herself recorded two shrill Jimmie memorial songs for Victor, composed for her by her sister Elsie McWilliams. The first and better of the two was the Jimmie-like song "We Miss Him When the Evening Shadows Fall," which benefited from the simple, catchy title phrase. To her credit, Carrie hums at the point where the yodel she knows she cannot pull off is called for. Elsie lays the bathos on rather thick in the lyric, reprising the "Carrie, Anita, and me" line from "Home Call" as a song request heard "from the radio cabinet" and managing to get Jimmie's poor little dog, Mickey, in there, too.

Carrie's much more lasting media contribution from that time, however, would be her book-length memoir of her years with Jimmie, *My Husband, Jimmie Rodgers*, first published in 1935. There had been no precedent for such a remembrance of any American roots music performer. She had the help of a "poetic" actress friend, one Dorothy Hendricks, in writing the volume she says Jimmie had wanted her to write. Ms. Hendricks is sometimes credited with (or blamed for) the book's tone, but the tear-jerking style, heavy with purple passages, and its blatant efforts to portray Jimmie as Mrs. Rodgers would have us see him, are quite consistent with what Carrie would say and how she would say it in later bylined magazine pieces and occasional interviews.

Not even Carrie's greatest friends and admirers have ever suggested that she was particularly savvy musically, and she had, more often than not, been home when Rodgers was out performing. That makes it all the more likely that the quotes she attributes to her husband about musical choices and thoughts are genuine. Carrie gives us eyewitness descriptions of some key moments in Jimmie's career — recording at Bristol, getting career advice from Gene Austin — and she supplies small but charming, homely details only a wife would know or recall: that his favorite color was blue, that Wild West showman Pawnee Bill had given Jimmie Buffalo Bill's china mug.

Consistent throughout the book is Carrie's attempt by various means to skew her late husband's existing image, to make Jimmie Rodgers seem more innocuous in memory than he had ever made himself out to be. The tack is partly self-protecting; such matters as the existence of his previous wife and child or stories of his footloose ways on the road were shameful to her, as family and friends attest, and, she seems to have believed, damaging to his image. These were subjects she simply wanted to suppress. She also works hard to supply the audience she perceived for the book with the sentimentalized, Horatio Algerish, plucky, and pious Jimmie she believed they wanted to find. She furnishes him with a new and heartfelt interest in matters religious, but you sense her defensiveness about the reality since she actually raises his widely understood lack of piety to "correct" that accurate perception. She awards Jimmie a newfound and commercially convenient Irish sensibility, something never demonstrated or even mentioned during his lifetime. And she repeatedly employs a tactic of going all aghast and aflutter over small instances of Jimmie's behavior to show how he was, yes, a little rougher than she was maybe, but only in that nice, rascally, Tom Sawyer way, no harm done. She has Jimmie come by with friends to serenade the Williamson house at 2:30 in the morning as she is nursing her sick mother ("The idea was preposterous and I told him so!"), and then the late-night singing, it turns out, just soothes Mrs. Williamson to a pleasant sleep.

Carrie fosters a number of not particularly credible Jimmie stories that have been repeated and embroidered ever since, like the one where he is a poorer kid than he actually was and goes out begging for milk to pour on his cornflakes—an item a boy living in his Aunt Dora's country house would surely not have needed to look for, let alone beg for.

The widow Rodgers could not have foreseen, at first, that one of her most lasting, significant contributions would be her fostering of the career of a twenty-two-year-old Jimmie Rodgers worshiper and imitator, a local Texas singer who called her in 1936 looking for an autographed photo of his hero. He was already singing Jimmie's songs weekly on a San Antonio radio station. His name was Ernest Tubb. In short order she lent him, long-term, the most famous of Jimmie's guitars, the trusty Martin with "Thanks!" emblazoned on the back that he had used on most of the recordings; got Ernest a contract with Victor Records; lent him Jimmie's tuxedo and derby hat to use in publicity photos; and even performed with him, singing on a number of early live appearances.

Among Tubb's first, blatantly Rodgers-imitating Bluebird records would be "The Passing of Jimmie Rodgers." Written by Elsie McWilliams, the song has Ernest promising on record, literally and explicitly, that from here on he would not cease singing the songs of America's Blue Yodeler, unworthy but "happy to try to finish the task he'd begun . . . with his memory my inspiration." This appointed task is said to be "to banish your sighs and your frowns," but you can't help hearing it as involving something larger and more challenging than that—and you're meant to.

Ernest Tubb's own stardom would not come until the '40s, when he dropped the Rodgers imitations and found his own, charming, massively influential country singing style. He would, however, take that commitment to Jimmie Rodgers' legacy very seriously, as he would his gratitude to Carrie.

Newcomer Ernest
Tubb dressed in
the late Jimmie
Rodgers' own tux
and bowler, 1935.

Their friendship would last so long and be so public that visitors to Meridian's Jimmie Rodgers Museum would still ask, long after they both were
gone, whether their relationship had perhaps been intimate. There is, in
fact, no evidence or reason to believe that Tubb saw Carrie as other than a
generous mother figure. His promulgation of Jimmie's music was not only
pleasing to her, as she would often say publicly, but provided financial payback as well.

More than seventy years later, performers on "The Ernest Tubb Midnight Jamboree," the radio show that has followed the Grand Ole Opry on
the air since Tubb's time there, are still required to sing a Rodgers song at
the start of the show. A Rodgers record was played or a song sung live from the
first. But there would be a lot more to it than that; Tubb would be the single
most significant advocate for Jimmie Rodgers' music for a longer time than
Jimmie had been alive.

Ernest never met the man face-to-face, though he might have when Jimmie played his town, Brownwood, Texas, at the outset of the '30s. Jimmie loomed so large in his mind that young Ernest was intimidated and did not attend. As he told his biographer, Ronnie Pugh, "I was afraid to meet him . . . afraid he would do or say something that would upset the image I had of him . . . I was just afraid to go." The intensity of his Rodgers worship was easy to gauge.

"One time," Tubb recalled, "my parents were going away for a couple of days, and they left me one dollar to eat on . . . But a Jimmie Rodgers record came out, and I paid seventy-five cents for it. I used the quarter to eat for two days." He was soon buying Jimmie Rodgers records so frequently that he was able to strike a deal with a record store owner to buy samples of incoming Rodgers records intended for store use only, even before they were formally released.

Ernest had studied that growing collection of Rodgers records in great detail. The earliest, Rodgers-like Tubb records, with a yodel he would no longer be able to execute after having a tonsillectomy, did not fare that well. With so many of the blue yodel fad era Rodgers imitators still around, he was not the only one contending to be "Jimmie's successor"—although both Gene Autry and Jimmie Davis would be in the major phase of their careers before long, the blue yodeling style left behind.

For a short spell, Victor Records imagined they had found a "new Jimmie Rodgers" closer to home in Jimmie's singing first cousin Jesse Rodgers (later spelled Rogers), son of Jimmie's father's brother Eff. Jesse originally sported a dapper mustache and a derby that, as with so many singers of the day, soon switched to a clean-shaven cowboy image as he recorded more than forty sides for Bluebird from 1934 to 1937, many with quite Jimmie-like tone and subject matter. They were not particularly successful; Jesse's early records tend to be catchy only so far as they sound like Jimmie's. The yodels recapitulate his cousin's but are not so carefully attuned to the song's mood. Though he has a similar Mississippi-Alabama border accent, rhyming "linguhs" with "finguhs," Jesse's phrasing lacks Jimmie's flair. He consistently drags blues and ballads alike, and his guitar playing is often rudimentary. When Hawaiian or other backup patterned on Jimmie's records is added, it does not improve things much.

Jesse does offer some originality in content, such as "Auto Love Song," a number that moves transportation songs into the next era. More often, the level of imagination is that of "Hot Dog Blues": Jesse wishes he had one. The more he would try to establish a sound of his own, the duller and shriller the result seemed to be—not a formula for distinction. Nevertheless, he did have a long if limited career with interesting twists and turns, mainly as a western music king in the Philadelphia area—Philadelphia, Pennsylvania, not Philadelphia, Mississippi. He appeared as an early TV cowboy on the regional series *Ranger Joe*, married long-time Philly kiddy-show hostess and singer Sally Starr, and eventually won some recognition from Tubb, Hank Snow, and Eddy Arnold, among others. Jesse still had rockabilly-oriented discs coming out in the '50s—some on the same label as yodeling Bill Haley, before the Comets and "Rock Around the Clock." A replacement international roots music hero he would not be, however, nor would anybody else who would try to get there simply by imitating Jimmie.

Tributes to Jimmie Rodgers have never stopped, though there has naturally been an ebb and flow to them over time. Forty and fifty years after his death, when the ranks of people who had known the man personally were thinning and references to Jimmie had become more metaphors than memories, there would still be recorded tips of one style hat or another to him and his music. Songs such as Hank Locklin's "Country Hall of Fame," Shel Silverstein's "Me and Jimmie Rodgers" (as recorded by Bobby Bare), James Talley's "Are They Gonna Make Us Outlaws Again?" Mel Tillis's "Good Woman Blues," Waylon Jennings' "Waymore's Blues," Lynyrd Skynyrd's "Railroad Song," and Greg Brown's "The Train Carrying Jimmie Rodgers Home" all raised the name, imagery and legend of Jimmie Rodgers again, so many decades later.

Jimmie's life story was poignant enough that there has always been talk of making a Hollywood movie from it, talk that never quite pans out. Carrie Rodgers fostered the idea in the late '40s and '50s with her book as the proposed source, and Johnny Cash did so in the '60s, seeing himself in the role. In the '70s, Jimmie's grandson Jimmie Dale Court and singer-actor Billy Ray Reynolds did extensive research together for a screenplay they cowrote, with southern rocker Dickey Betts of the Allman Brothers band or actor Keith Carradine (who had a one-man Jimmie Rodgers salute show of his own) in mind for the lead. In 2007, an independent Hollywood team, Frank Antonelli and Caroline Zelder, were talking up a proposed film, perhaps starring the Australian actor Hugh Jackman, who sings and physically resembles Jimmie. So far, there has been no movie in the seventy-five years since Jimmie's death—perhaps because nobody has quite found a box-office way to portray this complex character.

In the time just after Jimmie's passing, the Hollywood-style cowboy gear that his cousin Jesse adopted and the halting rise to prominence of Texan Ernest Tubb both pointed toward the place where Jimmie Rodgers' music could next get a boost. It was to be pulled and mutated through the '30s and into the '40s in fresh, contemporary directions—directions to which Jimmie himself had, in fact, had time to point.

Maybe the evening shadows had fallen, as Carrie's record had it, but for Rodgers' music, the sun was rising in the West.

Select Soundtrack

Memories of Jimmie Rodgers (Bear Family, 1997) collects the key tribute records issued after Rodgers' death by Gene Autry, Dwight Butcher, W. Lee O'Daniel, Bradley Kincaid, Ernest Tubb, and Carrie Rodgers, among others. *When Evening Shadows Fall: A Tribute to the Legendary Jimmie Rodgers* (RCA Victor LP, 1968) assembled a few of the same '30s sides, along with later tracks from Elton Britt, Jim Reeves, and Hank Snow.

- **Early Ernest Tubb:** His tribute songs and early, heavily Rodgers-influenced '30s sides appear on the set *Walking the Floor Over You* (Bear Family, 1996). A number of them are also included in the previously described *Sounds Like Jimmie Rodgers* set (JSP).
- **Jesse Rodgers:** Jesse's dozens of mid-'30's sides on Bluebird and Montgomery Ward are out of print. Among the Jimmie-reminiscent titles: "Yodelling the Railroad Blues," "Roughneck Blues," "San Antonio Blues," "Back in Jail Again," "Give Me Your Love," and, "Leave Me Alone, Sweet Mama." Two of Jesse's later pre-rockabilly recordings (when he was known as Jesse Rogers), "Jukebox Cannonball" and "That's What She Wrote," appear on *Legendary Cowboy Recordings, Volume 2: Bill Haley and Friends*, along with a yodeling Haley and numbers from cowboy crooner Ray Whitley (Hydra, 2003).

eight

South by Southwest
An Easterner in a Cowboy Hat

When Jimmie Rodgers' body was carried away from New York on that "Train Carrying Jimmie Rodgers Home," it was headed back to Meridian, Mississippi, back to the Deep South, back to the town where the monument that was eventually raised to him would have to note—in all honesty, but rather ruefully, it seems, for letters etched in stone—"Moved to Texas in 1929."

A handsome blond leather briefcase that Jimmie had toted on that last trip north had been placed in his casket, then removed in Meridian and handed to Carrie Rodgers. A generation later she would present it to the Rodgers-obsessed Johnny Cash, who would eventually give it to singer Marty Stuart (a native of Philadelphia, Mississippi, the next town up from Meridian), who would put it on public display for the first time ever at the Tennessee State Museum in Nashville, in 2007. That briefcase was emblazoned "Jimmie Rodgers, San Antonio, Texas."

By the time he died, some were already referring to Jimmie as "a western singer." It was not a notion that he had discouraged.

On that famous (or is it infamous?) "Jimmie Rodgers Meets the Carter Family" sketch record recorded in Louisville, Kentucky, A. P. Carter had welcomed him to "Virginia" as "the first cowboy we've seen in a long time"—as if this were a document of the first tentative encounter of "country" and "western." That Jimmie was a putative cowpoke apparently needed no explanation—nor the visual aid of one of his cowboy suits.

A little buckaroo meets Jimmie Rodgers.

He had moved his family first to Kerrville, Texas, then on to San Antonio, partly for medical reasons, but also, it seems clear enough, because he had always been attracted to the territory. Texas was both the true and the dramatically fabled home of those cowboy heroes he had been enthralled by in the silent movies and seen lionized in Wild West shows and melodramatic dime novels; it was also a real place where he had learned that he felt right at home during his many journeys and stays there while working for the railroads.

He kept telling everybody about this pull toward the West, and Texas specifically, in his recorded songs from the beginning, well before he moved there—how it was the place he "dearly loved," how the "rails were leading west," how it was "those Texas women" who especially had his number and "thought the world" of him, too. After having moved there, he sang, at least partly autobiographically and certainly poignantly, "Let me rest out in Texas, the land of my boyhood dreams, for I'm getting so old and feeble; my days are nearly done."

Jimmie had publicly befriended Pawnee Bill, the sometime show business partner, sometime competitor of Buffalo Bill Cody, and taken a leap in imagination (and in creative marketing, as well) by donning some flashy western duds for a set of now well-known publicity photos. Reportedly, he even appeared once or twice wearing the big cowboy hat, chaps, and holster on stage. And he had begun, as early as 1929, to record new songs with lyrics that introduced a novel, potently attractive image of the lonesome roving cowboy, drifting along, lazy and free, amidst the prairie sunsets and blooming cactus, under noteworthy moons that had apparently just drifted west from Mississippi and Kentucky and were now hanging magically over the prairie and the plains.

Don Edwards, probably the best-known western balladeer of our own day, notes of more contemporary cowboys, "Most of us who are familiar with what Jimmie Rodgers did agree by now that he was the guy, even having been 'The Singing Brakeman' and 'The Blue Yodeler' from Mississippi, who really *created* this western genre. Because with his early recordings of 'When the Cactus Is in Bloom,' 'Cow Hand's Last Ride,' and all of those songs—*he* was the one that the others picked up on; *he* first went at it from a more romantic sense."

In the earliest outright cowboy song Jimmie recorded, "Yodeling Cowboy," written for him on demand by Elsie McWilliams in 1929, there is a line that already describes the lonesome trail as the place where "a friend is a friend," a phrase requiring only the slightest of altering to be reused by Rodgers fan and acolyte Ray Whitley in his song "Back in the Saddle Again," the wonderful number that would go on to become the ubiquitous theme song of former Rodgers imitator Gene Autry, Mr. Singing Cowboy himself.

More strikingly, Jimmie Rodgers' cowboy songs had a wistful, romantic, written-on-the-breeze sound running through them that, as Edwards suggests, was going to stick around for a long time, see a lot of use, and which had few precedents in the sort of old working-cowboy folk tunes already collected and anthologized by John Lomax. Airy, loss-laden songs like "Get Along Little Dogie" or Mexican favorites like "Cielito Lindo" may have indicated a general direction for the haunting sound of Jimmie's "Prairie Lullaby," "Moonlight and Skies," "The Land of My Boyhood Dreams," "The Cow Hand's Last Ride," "When the Cactus Is in Bloom," and "The Yodeling Ranger," but these songs were essentially new sorts of constructs. They would ride that boundary line between solitary despair and gleefully getting past it, one Jimmie had already so well explored and now imparted, sometimes subtly, to this new genre.

It was not difficult for other writers to grasp what Jimmie had in mind here and pitch more material of the sort to him. For instance, he had already been doing fathers' lullaby songs—untypical for any era—so the cowboy-oriented turn in "Prairie Lullaby" (written by a young Billy Hill, who would later compose the pop hits "The Last Round-Up," "Empty Saddles," and "Have You Ever Been Lonely?") required only working in western refer-ences for the new setting. This custom-made novelty sort of "Good night, sleepyheaded little buckaroo" song proved sturdy enough that it would still be around in the form of James Taylor's "Sweet Baby James" in the '70s and Steve Earle's "Go to Sleep, Little Rock and Roller" in the '80s; and no doubt someone, somewhere, is composing another right now, well beyond the boundaries and '30s heyday of the singing cowboy genre itself.

Rodgers was already singing about modern barroom gamblers, jailbirds facing the gallows, and pistol packin' train robbers (who drove cars) with no more regard for region than the gamblers and robbers had. But any singer who simply dons a cowboy hat and takes on the same material instantly seems "old western." That popular Rodgers yodeling test number "My Little Lady," in which the rounder singer cavalierly and easily shifts affection from one girl to the next in just a few verses—a song originated and largely written by Elsie McWilliams after she was amused by a neighbor's name, Hadie—was one of the first numbers to become a generic western song. Jimmie's notable yodel-ing made it a natural for a lot of cavalier cowboys to come, but there were no overt western references in the song itself. And while there is essentially no credible evidence that any actual cattle workers had ever yodeled in the moonlight, after Jimmie Rodgers developed this cowboy theme, legions of screen and recording cowboys were going to be doing it until people across the world thought yodeling cowboys were history, not fantasy.

"He left a yodel for the cowboy," Dwight Butcher's 1933 memorial song succinctly put it. But in fact, he had left them a lot more—the basic fantasy content, the room to roam, and the tone of the whole idiom. There is no clearer, cleaner example than this western music saga of how Jimmie Rodgers and his music have worked their way quietly into our musical DNA, providing blueprints and building blocks with which others would produce hundreds of songs and records. This southwestern chapter of the story is not just about a handful of songs and a yodel.

Likely because Rodgers had remained so close to his audience and to their circumstances in increasingly desperate Depression-era Texas and Oklahoma, and because the world of train-grabbing, shuddering travelers was not just some borrowed literary metaphor for him, early on he perceived a change in attitude toward the hobo theme he had done so much to establish. It was becoming unpalatable. Not just in early hillbilly music and blues, but also in popular culture of the '20s in general (in pop songs, movies, plays, and magazine pieces), there had been a barrage of good sport ladies hailed approvingly as tramps, scads of vagabond princes, of happy hobo wanderers, and of references to that gypsy in your free-spirited soul—all variations on a single Roaring Twenties conceit that was about to go completely out of fashion for at least a quarter of a century. It would not return in force until the generally safely housed and domesticated context in which Jack Kerouac and the Beats formed a new metaphor, and a sometime lifestyle, of being back out on the road, devil-may-care and unencumbered. But if somebody had asked a homeless, jobless drifter in 1932 Bob Dylan's inquiry of 1965, how exactly did it feel to be "on your own, no direction home, a complete unknown," the answer simply would have been "Terrible." Jimmie's hobo blues were now cutting too close to the bone to work as fantasy, or even to be borne.

But even the down-and-out—perhaps especially the down-and-out—can use a good metaphor and an attractive fantasy now and then, and the free, contented singing cowboy was now just the ticket: unencumbered, out in nature, dignified, with a self-defined and chosen identity, not disinherited, even holding down what seemed to be not too taxing a *job*. Jimmie was bringing his audience and followers not just a tramp, but a new, improved fantasy—a playful saddle tramp.

The seminal country music historian Bill C. Malone has shed considerable light on how Rodgers' audience was captivated by the widespread musical results of this innovation in what remains one of the best introductions to what makes commercial country music tick, his short 1994 book *Singing Cowboys and Musical Mountaineers*. But even while Jimmie was still alive and recording, it was possible to see the impact of his western move, beginning with the sincerest form of flattery.

All of his most significant, friendly competitors in the blue yodelmania sweepstakes—Cliff Carlisle, Jimmie Davis, and Gene Autry—as well as some lesser ones such as Goebel Reeves (the "Texas Drifter") and cousin Jesse Rodgers, were moseying toward yodeling cowboy material, in a few cases with outright covers (Carlisle would record "When the Cactus Is in Bloom" and "Desert Blues," for example). Quite often they did this with songs that were the most obvious sort of minimally changed Rodgers pastiches, with slight western-bending switcheroos applied to this Jimmie tune or that, just to follow the new trend. Charming as they are as performances, if records like Jimmie Davis's "Moonlight and Skies (No. 2)" or Cliff Carlisle's "Cowboy Song" (to the tune of "Waiting for a Train") and "Cowboy Johnnie's Last Ride" seem to ring a bell, or, for that matter, if Davis's "When It's Round-Up Time in Heaven" seems to come from the same mental production factory as Cliff's "When It's Roundup Time in Texas" (where a "friend is a friend," once again)—well, they should.

The case of Gene Autry is a singular one in this regard—as it would have to be, given the role he would go on to play on screen, record, radio, rodeo, and lunchboxes as America's favorite singing cowboy and formidable roots music pop star. With his actual and none too romantic Oklahoma background, Autry had shown no special interest in cowboy type material in his early, Rodgers-imitating years; he may even have been avoiding the theme, preferring hillbilly and mountain references to western ones. (For him, *those* were a sort of fantasy.)

The only specifically western tune of note in Autry's early Rodgers-like period is "Cowboy Yodel," which he recorded at least four times in 1929 and 1930 with varying arrangements. And it is a song that keeps the cowhand working at a corral while "paddling his own canoe," which is not only a muddy mixed metaphor, but also proved not much of an attraction. Cowboy songs start showing up in his work in earnest in 1933, the year of Jimmie's death. In records of that year, such as "Cowboy's Heaven," you can hear Gene moving away from the Rodgers manner, virtually take by take, as he invents his own, different, identifiable sort of cowboy crooning.

This supple voice, which would hold its own in popularity against Bing Crosby's, had more in common with the singing of those '20s southern pop crooners Gene Austin and Cliff Edwards (Ukulele Ike) than with Jimmie's.

After recording the Jimmie Rodgers farewell numbers "The Death of Jimmie Rodgers" and so forth, Gene would never be mistaken for Jimmie again, never sing blue yodels as such, never use the yodel as part of a line reading rather than occasional ornamentation. Sometimes, on the rare occasions when he discussed his musical career at all, he would deny that Rodgers' music had ever played much of a role in his own.

But there was no denying that the content of Autry's sagebrush songs, in references and tone, had been well established by Jimmie, or that when Gene yodeled, it had come from somewhere in particular. The union of pop crooning and cowboy content essentially began when Jimmie Rodgers did a little of both—and if anyone doubts that the sound of his "Prairie Lullaby," to take an obvious example, would be precisely the stuff Hollywood cowboy soundtracks were going to be made of, they should take a look at Gene's 1936 feature *Melody Trail*, in which he coos—along with a bevy of quite sightly cowgirls—"Go to bed, little sleepyhead," lifted right from "Prairie" into a "new" one called "Western Lullaby." With comic sidekick Smiley Burnette, Gene renders a duet version of Jimmie's "In the Jailhouse Now" in the 1938 Republic picture *Prairie Moon*, singing it to a trio of tough, hog-tied contemporary urban kids being taken west for rehabilitation. And in his more polished, bigger budget 1941 feature *Back in the Saddle*, he would go on to reprise that "cowboy" jailhouse song alone—during a scene full of nostalgic talk about the truly wild old West, and also sing a breakfast chow-time rendition of "When the Cactus Is in Bloom."

Most important, Autry, following the Jimmie Rodgers model of roots music pop stardom, would prove to be an unsurpassed master of associating his own public persona—that of a smart, successful guy up from the roots—to his wide-ranging music, which could encompass both "Mexicali Rose" and "Rudolph the Red-Nosed Reindeer." More than Jimmie Rodgers had ever dreamed, he would lasso that public image to multimedia marketing and worldwide fan reach. Musical feature films and TV would take Gene further than Rodgers would live to be able to go—and Autry, in addition, proved to be industrious, ambitious, and something of a born down-home genius when it came to business. At one point, Jimmie had owned an Orange Julius juice stand franchise; Autry would own a collection of broadcasting stations and the California Angels major league baseball team.

The truly fresh side of the singing cowboy sound in its '30s heyday, which began within a year of Jimmie's death, would be introduced by a harmony singing group, the fabled Sons of the Pioneers of "Tumblin' Tumbleweeds" and "One More Ride" fame. The group's most celebrated original members, writer Bob Nolan and singer Len Slye (who would soon be transmogrified into Roy Rogers, "King of the Cowboys"), would acknowledge the part Jimmie Rodgers' western music played as building blocks of the new sound they constructed. Indeed, their earliest radio repertoire, in 1934–35, would contain versions of "My Little Lady" (sung fast and established from this start as a Slye/Rogers yodeling showpiece), "T for Texas" (laid-back now, with room for jazzy guitar fills), and "Yodeling Cowboy" (with a fiddle lead).

"Jimmie Rodgers had some impact on my decision to make yodeling a strong part of my singing," Roy would tell Sons of the Pioneers chronicler Ken Griffis. "By taking these yodels, changing the rhythm and breaks, I created a style all of my own; we may have been the first to do *trio* yodeling."

The Sons' eerie, otherworldly harmonies are somehow soothing even when, in their "cool water" mode, they are describing desperation and death as pointedly as might the Delta bluesman Charley Patton. They can also be energizing when they choose to pick up the clip-clop tempos. These sounds are unmistakable and were widely imitated ever after. The poetic western émigré Bob Nolan, a Canadian whose compositions would give much of the distinctiveness to their repertoire in their most important years, detailed to Griffis in a radio interview how Jimmie Rodgers impacted the Sons' content as well as their sound—and, incidentally, how this reluctant introvert became a performer:

"My Daddy got a little of whatever that [poison] gas was they were using in World War I," he said, "so they sent him to Tucson, Arizona; that was my first introduction to the West . . . When I was going to . . . the University of Arizona, I wrote a column called 'Tumbleweed Trails' for the Arizona *Wildcat*; it was all in poetry; a lot of that stuff, I just took . . . and put music to it. [Then] I got a job as a lifeguard down at Venice [California], but I lost that when the stock market crash came in 1929; I was starving to death, and I would have done anything. At that time, there were a lot of Chautauquas— the old tent shows, you know—going through, and they'd have amateur nights, so I'd write my own songs, and I won quite a few of them. And I needed to—badly!"

The first western song Nolan wrote was "Way Out There," with a yodel at the end of each verse and a lyric featuring desert sands of the prairie, a moon that calls you "old pal," and a man who kicks the hobo narrator off a train for yodeling "a southern [not a western!] tune"—obvious Rodgers building blocks put to work. As Nolan told Griffis, "It was more of a hobo tune. Jimmie Rodgers, you remember, was America's Blue Yodeler, and he sang a lot of railroad songs—so I wrote 'Way Out There' and had a train whistle yodel. And I won, I'd say, at least one of those amateur Chautauqua nights a week with *that* song!" (Nolan's even better-known "One More Ride" is a deliberate sequel to "Way Out There," with more Rodgers-style imagery.)

Nonwestern Canadians seemed to have a marked proclivity for this emerging romantic western material; Nolan had been born Robert Clarence Noble in New Brunswick. Another former Clarence, who came to call himself Hank Snow, was out of maritime Nova Scotia and would begin his professional singing career at just this same time—with a transitional mixture of very

Meeting Jimmie Rodgers

markedly Jimmie Rodgers–derived material that was equally "blue yodeler hobo" and "Yodeling Ranger," as Snow was first known. With full fantasy cowboy regalia and all, the young Snow was singing "Blue Ranger," "The Texas Cowboy," "My San Antonio Mama," and "Goodnight Little Buckaroo."

"Jimmie Rodgers became my idol," he would write in his memoir, "the moment I first heard his [western] record 'Moonlight and Skies.'" Snow would later—considerably later—become one of the most significant interpreters of Jimmie Rodgers' music, but this cowboy image and material would not be the route; it would have to do with a new nostalgic take on train songs, near rockers, and sentimental story songs in the '50s.

Another Nova Scotia native, Wilf Carter (whose acrobatic yodeling approach applied to Rodgers' songs has already been noted), also began his long—if compared to Snow's, relatively obscure—career at this point, with Jimmie-style cowboy numbers very much to the fore. "Montana Slim" became his alternative recording name in the United States, as first heard on his CBS radio show, which emanated from a place that will sound unlikely to those unaware of the active and influential cowboy music scene there in the early '30s—New York City. Almost as much as Chicago, where the famed National Barn Dance broadcasts were home to Gene Autry, Patsy Montana, and the Girls of the Golden West (and we will get to those Rodgers-inspired cowgirls later), a group of cowboy singers had been finding airtime, club dates, and success in New York, including Tex Ritter, Rosalie Allen, and the Jimmie Rodgers emulators Dwight Butcher and Ray Whitley.

Raised in Georgia and Alabama and steeped in the blues, Whitley was hardheaded enough that the Sons of the Pioneers turned to him as their contract negotiator and tough enough that, in addition to a stint cracking whips on the rodeo circuit, he worked construction on the Empire State Building and the George Washington Bridge. In New York for the construction jobs, he also crooned on the WHN Barn Dance along with Ritter. With an introduction from Butcher, Whitley was all set to meet Jimmie Rodgers in person but was turned away at the last minute; it turned out to be the day before Jimmie's death, and he was already too sick for visitors.

Ray's early recordings would include excellent Rodgers pastiches such as "Blue Yodel Blues" and a sort of postyodel, post–Charleston era, much recorded comic novelty, "Wah Hoo"; then, most famously, he wrote "Back in the Saddle Again," with that "friend is a friend" line of Jimmie's somewhere in his head. Like his pal Ritter, he would soon be heading for Hollywood and roles, if secondary ones, in singing cowboy pictures. By the mid-'30s, there were a good many singers raised on Rodgers who would be cast in Hollywood A- and B-movie musical westerns—spreading the DNA of yodel, croon, and strum as they traveled.

Jimmy Wakely, raised poor in Oklahoma, as Autry had been, was an avowed admirer of both Jimmie Rodgers and the Milton Brown/Bing Crosby skillful crooning school—and it would always show, as he moved from cowboy backup singer to crossover pop star, singing duets with pop's Margaret Whiting, synthesizing the two idioms. He would have particular success in the late '40s with his own pop/hillbilly triangulation. He took the stunningly idiosyncratic phrasing of the jazzy Texas honky tonker Floyd Tillman and great songs of Tillman's such as "I Love You So Much It Hurts" and "Slippin' Around" and simultaneously smoothed them out, just enough, and attended more closely to the sense of the lyrics rather than the playful sound of the words (as Tillman had, Dylan-like), to give them mass-scale appeal.

Wakely would also make the case, as well as anyone, that once you were accepted as "a crooning cowboy" and wore the right outfit, you could widen the song material and it would still be considered western and acceptable for other western singers. The Rodgers songs he recorded came from Jimmie's most pop, mainstream side—"The One Rose," "Roll Along, Kentucky Moon" (not even modified to "Montana Moon" or some such), and "For the Sake of Days Gone By," all rendered with note-nailing, clean articulation, but also with rhythmic variation within lines and phrases and the strong emotional specificity that distinguishes only the strongest of pop crooners. The backing would be sweet, muted horns, accordions, or oozing steel. Listening to Wakely with his models in mind, you could begin to argue that Jimmie Rodgers had, in effect, been promulgating "country crossover" before genres were even defined or anybody was sure there was a commercial line to cross.

As Jimmy Wakely went on to star in his own series of singing cowboy pictures, his Hollywood-based trio would put two avowed long-time Rodgers-inspired performers beside him—Johnny Bond and Wesley Tuttle. Bond could be seen performing Jimmie's "Train Whistle Blues' on *Town Hall Party*, the honky tonk and rockabilly dance party show televised from Compton, California, in 1959, and he often referred to Jimmie in the on-air interviews he conducted on the show; he would still be performing Rodgers material in the '70s. Without assembling a slew of Rodgers covers himself, Johnny would nevertheless become so dedicated in his interest that he compiled a near-complete, annotated Rodgers discography, published by the John Edwards Memorial Foundation; it was a tool used by the interested for a good many years.

Another later "Town Haller," Wesley Tuttle, would tell various authors of liner notes that at age twelve, in the '20s, he had heard Jimmie Rodgers on the radio and loved the yodeling so much that he had begun doing some himself, accompanied by a ukulele. Wesley would contribute a brand-new "far end" for the journey of Jimmie Rodgers influence in 1937 when he supplied a Jimmie-ish yodel to the beloved Dopey character in Walt Disney's *Snow White and the Seven Dwarfs*.

By the early '50s, singing cowboys themselves would mostly be ghettoized, along with cartoons, as "kids' stuff," with Gene's and Roy's television series and cut-down feature films scheduled to target small-fry. Cowboy films themselves had gone adult and psychologically realistic in the *Bad Day at Black Rock* era, and there were new replacement fantasies in the air—often having to do with space cowboys on that fresher, interplanetary frontier. (*Star Wars'* Hans Solo can be seen as a latter-day embodiment of Jimmie Rodgers' cockier cowboy attitudes!)

There was one place where cowboy songs themselves persisted, however; on the folk scene—although they were mainly old cowhand work songs of the sort John Lomax gathered up, not the post-Jimmie pop variety, and were necessarily presented in a folk-friendly style. A teenaged Don Edwards, a New Englander who'd been born in New Jersey, headed to Texas and points west in the late '50s to perform in that somewhat limiting urban cow-folk corral, but he sometimes performed early Gene Autry and Jimmie Rodgers songs along with the folk bag sort—though for many years not many people noticed. Unusually, Edwards had first heard Gene Autry not through his better-known cowboy songs, but through the pre-1933 Autry blue yodeler records in his magician dad's large, varied 78 collection, and having done so, he then delved into Jimmie Rodgers. Don is also a serious admirer of early acoustic blues and speaks readily of Blind Lemon Jefferson and Johnny Shines; he was struck by that blues side of Jimmie Rodgers' music and instinctively knew how to translate it into lonesome cowboy tunes.

"There were lots of people who would try to imitate the country blues artists," Don recalls, "but when Jimmie did blues, it was more the way I would sing it. I liked that, just felt that kinship . . . And in my cowboy music, I always included it. One thing in the traditional cowboy music that I had not thought about enough was pointed out to me by Jan Murray, a black woman from Mississippi who was then the dean of Davenport College at Yale. She walked up to me after a performance and said, 'That is *so* much like the blues; I just love those cowboy songs.' And a light came on. I realized that that was *why* I was singing cowboy songs and Jimmie Rodgers songs; that's what I was always drawn to—that lonesome, solitary sort of figure, a man and his guitar. To this day, I primarily play by myself, as Jimmie primarily did, too—and I don't do a show that I don't do two or three Jimmie Rodgers songs. It's just a natural thing."

When Edwards went on to meet a musically inclined old-time working cowboy and rodeo competitor like Glenn Ohrlin or a Hollywood stuntman with real connections to cowhand work like Walt LaRue (later a famed west-ern illustrator), they told him similar stories—that among the tiny handful of songs always useful for hushing a saloon full of rowdy cowboys, there were Rodgers ballads like "Waiting for a Train." That solo, cooling, quiet-ing aspect of Jimmie's music clearly spoke to Edwards; he was, for instance, stuck by Rodgers biographer Nolan Porterfield's description of an orchestra playing Jimmie onto a stage and then stopping, leaving Jimmie to continue on with the song quietly, his foot up on a chair.

Viewed in this light, that laziness and peaceful ease in the tradition of commercial, romantic cowboy songs is partly an extension of Jimmie Rod-gers' feel for the blues, an extension of the blues singers' ability to make themselves feel okay about their troubles by singing them out of their sys-tems. Even cowboys get the blues sometimes; just beneath the sagebrush surface, the blues' (and Jimmie Rodgers') heroic nonchalance lurks as a basic cowboy song element.

It would be "The Land of My Boyhood Dreams," "Moonlight and Skies," and the ballads, not more western yodels, that Don Edwards would bring to the cowboy music revival set off in the mid-'80s, as new cowboy poets were joined by singers of increasingly varied western musical styles at the National Cowboy Poetry Gathering at Elko, Nevada. Record labels became interested in the field again, as did younger audiences and knowing acts from varied backgrounds who were, nonetheless, well aware of the trends and history of popular culture. The sleepy little buckaroos were reawakening.

It seemed to be memories of those old '50s Saturday morning Gene and Roy TV broadcasts, as much as anything, that gave the singing cowboy harmony groups a nostalgic afterlife, exemplified by acts such as the pol-ished Riders in the Sky, founded in 1977 and led by the cowboy-crooning historian Dr. Douglas B. Green, in their notable, strikingly retro suits, hats, and sounds. The Riders have been the group most likely to be heard singing cowboy songs on the Grand Ole Opry, where they are cast members, for more than a quarter century.

Green, who was once a member of Bill Monroe's Bluegrass Boys, had interviewed a good number of the classic performers quoted in this book while he was working with the Country Music Hall of Fame and Museum's important oral history project, and he proved a knowledgeable author of notes for Jimmie Rodgers reissue LPs. The Riders' harmonies, however, would be more influenced by the Sons of the Pioneers and Gene Autry than by Jimmie Rodgers directly, though the Riders regularly perform "Mother, the Queen of My Heart" on the Opry around Mother's Day.

There is a more direct Jimmie Rodgers influence in the music of the somewhat similarly conceived band Wiley and the Wild West Show out of

Seattle, headed by horse-raiser Wylie Gustafson. The band would be a part of the rock-informed alternative country/Americana revival of the '90s and, like the Riders, was also accepted, to a degree, in adventurous mainstream country music circles. Montana-raised Wylie was the red-haired son of a rancher father who had sung cowboy songs for easterners at a Wyoming dude ranch and yodeled in the elaborate Elton Britt style. Astonishingly, Gustafson Senior had been taught the athletic sort of yodeling by a ski team from Austria staying at Montana University—which does not clarify the history of cowboy-Alpine interplay at all but is a true part of Wylie's own background. Wylie and the Wild West Show's 1997 CD *Total Yodel!* included cowboy versions of "T for Texas," "Waiting for a Train," and "When the Cactus Is in Bloom," all featuring pyrotechnic yodeling. Today, Wylie teaches yodeling and its context to young students.

"I describe the different styles of yodeling, and I always explain Jimmie Rodgers' style, which wasn't that complicated—but it was very, very effective," Gustafson notes. "He really imparted a trademark style of his own by using that yodel, a style I felt came from the black music. Growing up in the '70s, I was listening to rock and roll; I was listening to Delta blues—all of this different music. American music is such a melting pot.

"I first heard Rodgers music through other people; there seemed to be a lot of artists doing Jimmie Rodgers songs like 'T for Texas,' just as people did Hank Williams songs—and at the time I may not even have known who the songwriter was. And there was the Merle Haggard tribute album, too. I was living in Los Angeles, and kind of a yodeling hound; I wanted to find all varieties and buy as much of it as I could. And a guy at one of the stores with old records asked if I'd heard of Jimmie Rodgers and said that I should check all of his albums out."

The students in Wylie's classes are hearing his perceptive commentary: "Jimmie's guitar-playing is overlooked," Gustafson says. "He had a very strong guitar style, *un*-formal—which is part of what makes him so cool. He used his guitar playing, which was a part of *him*, to add to the music, just like he did the yodel. He was very talented, but that doesn't explain everything; there's a magic that happens with Jimmie Rodgers, when he does a song. He makes it his own, performs it, and makes it so it relates to people in a very strong way. That's the key to being a great pop artist—still."

Wylie describes his audience today as "next-generation and searching for something different." His band's most downloaded Internet-marketed song so far has been the rockabilly-tinged "Yodel Boogie."

Back when the singing cowboy movies ruled, Hollywood hardly made a distinction between the sounds of the cowboy pop balladeers and harmonizing groups and another sound entirely, born in Texas, in which

Jimmie Rodgers had a formative role. You could see and hear the result when Dallas-based guitarist and songwriter Bill Boyd—who had played guitar with Jimmie on such 1932 recordings as "Hobo's Meditation" and "Roll Along, Kentucky Moon"—wound up in a series of B-movie westerns later in the '30s; thereby making it forever necessary to clarify that he was not the William Boyd who played "Hopalong Cassidy." Bill Boyd's repertoire included Bob Nolan's Jimmie-inspired "Way Out There," performed in a rhythmic updated ragtime style more energetic than the Sons of the Pioneers' original, and also that novelty "Wah Hoo," as recorded by Ray Whitley. So there were some connections. But Bill and his band, the Cowboy Ramblers, would be best known as one of the hottest acts in that jazz-meets-country hybrid played by Texas stringbands augmented by steel guitars and, sometimes, horns—the ribald, danceable, hot, sometimes sophisticated, yet still downhome genre eventually dubbed "western swing."

Boyd, who had first met Jimmie while playing a lot of the more pop-oriented Rodgers songs on Dallas radio, along with his brother Jim, would record a Texas swing version of "Desert Blues," one of Jimmie's goofiest songs, underscoring the fun-seeking that would be central to this genre. Boyd would keep blues in his mix, too. His band would be second only to Bob Wills and His Texas Playboys in popularity; the two bandleaders shared a strong impulse to keep old square dance breakdown sounds alive within the jazzy modern mixture, even when others eschewed it.

A more jazz-focused Texas swing practitioner, fiddler Shelley Lee Alley, had been at Jimmie's remarkable 1931 San Antonio session, which included "Jimmie the Kid," "T.B. Blues," and a celebrated song written by Alley himself, "Travellin' Blues," on which Shelley and his brother Alvin played twin fiddles. Rodgers would also record Shelley's "St. James Infirmary" adaptation, "Gambling Barroom Blues." It takes no great stretch of the aural imagination to hear the origins of western swing stringband sounds in the original "Travellin' Blues" recording—or echoes of the earlier sound of Lonnie Chatman's blues fiddling with the Jimmie-friendly Mississippi Sheiks, either.

Alley's stepson, Clyde Brewer, himself an accomplished (and at the time of this writing, still-active) swing fiddler and mandolin player, recalls that "Shelly told me that Jimmie picked up him and his brother [Alvin] in the little town of Ramsey, Texas, in a car that he called 'The Blue Yodeler'; it had that right on the side. That was big time—like Garth Brooks driving up into my driveway and taking me someplace. And I do remember Shelly saying that there was a knock on his door after he got there, to that big Texas Hotel in San Antonio. He opened it—and it was Will Rogers looking for Jimmie Rodgers. Shelly talked about Jimmie treating him real well."

Meeting Jimmie Rodgers

Although Alley's music was jazz-oriented enough that he did not play the numbers himself, Brewer and his brother Shelly Lee Alley Jr. still receive royalties on "Travellin' Blues" (of which there have been more than forty recordings) and "Gambling Barroom." At annual Shelly Lee Alley memorial festivals in Columbus, Texas, in the '90s, they would play "Travellin'," and Rodgers' grandson Jimmie Dale Court would answer with "Barroom."

But then, Jimmie Rodgers' musical influence was evident in the very blueprint of western swing. If before the advent of that style you heard combinations of rural themes and sounds with elements of jazz or blues and sudden turns toward pop or Hawaiian, cowboy or comic novelty numbers, or if you heard horns meeting yodels, you had very probably been listening to Jimmie Rodgers—or one of his better imitators. Finding Jimmie interjecting "Pick it, boy!" into "My Good Gal's Gone Blues" or the spoken aside "It won't be long *now!*" into "California Blues" surely sends a pleasurable little shock of recognition right up the neck hairs of anyone acquainted with the collected works of Bob Wills.

By coincidence, it happens that in Dallas in February 1932 as the original Light Crust Doughboys, including Bob Wills and Milton Brown, went in to record for the first time (as the Fort Worth Doughboys), both Jimmie Rodgers and Jimmie Davis stopped by. It was within days of Jimmie's session with Bill Boyd, and it was the only time the future Texas swing giants would meet Jimmie Rodgers. (Davis would later sing with Brown's band.)

The seminal and remarkably long-lived Light Crust Doughboys would soon break into multiple bands and spread this style of music far and wide. The Doughboys themselves, as their long-time member Marvin Montgomery would recall, found themselves playing packed tent shows in which Jimmie Rodgers had appeared just a year or two before: "In Texas," Montgomery noted, "they just had the biggest crowds they ever had—on account of Jimmie."

The nonmusician politician W. Lee O'Daniel, the original Dough-boys manager and putative leader, having recording "Prairie Lullaby" and the Jimmie Rodgers memorial number, moved on along with vocalist Leon Huff to his next band, the Hillbilly Boys, and recorded "Peach Pickin' Time in Georgia," "Yodeling Ranger," and "Tuck Away My Lonesome Blues." The Hillbilly Boys would show a certain finesse playing the latter two Rodgers numbers as slow waltzes, but the vaudeville speed trap of "Peach Pickin'" utterly defeated them. The fiddler that day, either W. Lee's son Mike O'Daniel or Darrell Kirkpatrick, just saws away, underscoring the band's name, and the often effective Huff loses every nuance of the lyric in a sing-to-the-dance-rhythm rush. The problem of making Rodgers songs blend jazz and country breakdown, making them work for dancing while keeping the lyric meaningful, would not be solved by that band.

Nor would it be by the great Texas swing singer Milton Brown and his innovative Musical Brownies—for the simple reason that Milton chose not to record Rodgers material. As you might guess from the name, he had sung Rodgers songs with a predecessor of the Doughboys, "The Three Yodeliers"—while Jimmie was still alive, popular, and Texan—and continued to do so even in early Light Crust Doughboys broadcasts. A 1938 account suggested, however, that Milton had truly liked only a few Rodgers songs, more pop ones such as "My Carolina Sunshine Girl" and "Roll Along, Kentucky Moon,"and dropped even those from his repertoire as his band became jazz-oriented and his singing moved toward a sophisticated, playful, more Crosby-like, sometimes quite black-sounding jazz style. Milton Brown's yodeling was soon forgotten—and with that aspect so prominent in Bob Wills' band, he saw all the more reason to keep it that way. When the gifted singer died in a car crash, however, the Rodgers lovers lurking in the Brownies raised their heads again. Brother Durwood Brown's latter-day Brownies would record "The One Rose," as well as Rodgers-redolent numbers like "High-Geared Daddy," with Jimmie Davis on vocals.

The youngest of Milton's brothers, singer and bandleader Roy Lee Brown, would remain a Rodgers' fan and interpreter. "Back when I was growing up, Jimmie Rodgers songs were about the only thing I sang!" he reminisces. "I learned the songs from radio and records . . . In about the third grade, the teachers would have me sing sometimes; evidently they knew I was Milton's brother, and they'd say 'Now come up here and sing us a song.' And I'd get up there and sing prison songs, and the teacher would stop me, so I'd go into 'Waiting for a Train,' and *that* was okay!

"With my band, if I have a request for 'Waiting for a Train' I'll say 'OK, but I can't yodel' and turn around to the fiddle player and say 'You're going to have to do the yodeling!' And when it comes time, they do it on the fiddle. Jimmie's music itself wasn't old folk tunes, it was more of a blues, but not with improvisation—and without that, you don't really have western swing."

In that last comment is buried evidence of some caustic old band rivalry, since Roy Lee also describes Bob Wills, today the best-known western swing star of them all, as a man who could not improvise and was forced to hire musicians who could—part of a revisionist effort to have Milton, rather than Bob, deemed the "father of western swing." Wills biographer Charles Townsend provides a response: "But Milton didn't have the kind of a band that could take a Jimmie Rodgers song, like Bob could, and turn it into a great *dance* tune. Bob could have done that with 'The Old Rugged Cross'!"

Bob Wills would—almost uniquely—crack the problem of how to make Jimmie's music dance music while making use and sense of the lyrics at the same time. The charismatic Wills created a sound that encompassed a great deal of variety. He led the musical experimentation in the '30s that sought to blend the country string band with Jimmie Rodgers, Gene Austin, and Bessie Smith, taking that all the way toward horn-backed swing band pop of the '40s—whether performed by his own band or by a Bing Crosby. Bob was the epitome of smooth and cool in his region and always remained tied to it, despite the recordings, the crossover pop, the Hollywood success, and a move from Texas to Tulsa and then on to California. It was Bob whom all eyes followed whenever he was on stage or camera, and with those Jimmie-like spoken interjections, he was always the defining presence on the Playboys' records as well.

In short, Bob Wills, who didn't sing much and, it is sometimes argued, was not even the best fiddler in his own band, was nonetheless, along with Gene Autry, among the very first to achieve success as a roots music pop hero on the Jimmie Rodgers model. That was so even though it was his relatively unassuming lead singer Tommy Duncan, a lifelong lover and interpreter of Rodgers' music, who would truly absorb Rodgers' songs and musical style, make his mark on them, and insist that more of them came into the Playboys' repertoire.

Duncan, the next great western swing vocalist after Milton Brown, had been just one more of sixty-seven applicants who auditioned to replace him as vocalist in the Light Crust Doughboys, but he was recognized by the band's fiddler, Sleepy Johnson, as the forlorn guy whom he had seen playing one Jimmie Rodgers song after another, for tips, outside a Fort Worth root beer stand. And there were those back in the little Texas panhandle town of Hedley who recalled Thomas Elmer Duncan hanging around town in a stripped-down Model T, singing nothing but Rodgers songs with a cheap little foot-long guitar. He had heard Rodgers records early and accumulated a lot of them.

Duncan's brother, Glynn, who would eventually join him as bass player in the Wills band and then in Tommy's own, reports, "I've still got all but maybe a half a dozen of the things Jimmie did, which Tommy had, on transcriptions . . . Some record collector offered me a pretty good price for them, so before I sold them I had them all put on cassette tapes. Jimmie's wife sent the records to Tommy sometime after Jimmie died. I guess he had met her, and she'd got pretty well acquainted with him. They were still in the box she sent them in when I sold them. Jimmie Rodgers was Tommy's idol, as far as a singer was concerned."

Tommy had first reached out to Carrie Rodgers in a self-typed, idiosyncratically spelled (and previously unreported) letter of August 1933 on Burrus Mill stationery complete with Light Crust Doughboy cartoons. The young singer, still known only locally, sends condolences to Carrie regarding the (as it turned out, soon-solved) disappearance of her late husband's guitar; he says he will alert listeners about it on the air and requests a photo of Jimmie, who had died just a few months before.

"I guess you already know that my singing features his numbers altogether," he informed her. "I have studied his type of songs every since he has been singing on record. By this time you might be wondering who I am well I'm none other than Tommy Duncan with the LIGHT CRUST DOUGHBOYS. Inclosed you will find a copy of the song that we wrote about Jimmie. The original idea for the song was mine but I did not get the credit for writing it." ("Memories of Jimmie Rodgers" has always been credited to O'Daniel.) That Tommy could sing both Rodgers and Emmett Miller songs so well had clinched his being hired in the first place, and when Bob Wills left to form his own band, Tommy and his expert yodel came along. Repeatedly, and with growing finesse, Duncan and Wills would take Rodgers songs and jazz them, eventually driving them toward dance-driven swing. There was a slower, smoother, even-tempoed "T for Texas"; a truly boozy, cryin' "Drunkard's Blues"; and a "No Hard Times" that both etched the deep-Depression, no-money blues and overcame them, all on the same record. (As we will see, that last tune would be deemed by some folk and old-timey artists impossible to work as a band number. Apparently—not so!) Duncan's bluesy take on "Never No More Blues" was classic and much taken up by other western swing singers, yet he was equally comfortable with the novelty of "Everybody Does It in Hawaii."

While the musical attack became more driving over time (two different Playboys' turns on Jimmie's raggy "Mississippi Delta Blues" some years apart make this very evident), Duncan's increasing finesse in dragging and toying with notes when it mattered would still keep the lyrics' meaning clear, especially as he became more practiced. His approach would have considerable impact on later country singers.

Bob Wills, however, did not want to go on playing just the same sort of stuff. Rodgers numbers by the Playboys became scarce and then stopped being recorded, and it was a source of friction. "Bob was still developing western swing at about that time," recalls Herb Remington, a long-time steel guitarist with the Playboys whom Wills would order to room with the straight-laced Duncan when they were on the road to keep him out of trouble. "But once that *happened*, there was more of a wall there in the tunes they selected. I think Tommy probably hungered for [singing still more Rodgers tunes] while he was singing western swing with Bob."

Bob's wife, Betty, would talk about this, too, with Wills biographer Charles Townsend. "Bob could get so disgusted with Tommy," she told him, "like when he went through that Bing Crosby phase . . . and back when he was in his Jimmie Rodgers phase and all he wanted to do was be like Jimmie Rodgers."

Bob Wills, like Jimmie himself, sought continually to remake and expand his music through variety and through songs and sounds that were his own. Indeed, it is the outright western swing numbers of the '40s, not Rodgers or Bessie Smith adaptations from the '30s, for which Wills is best remembered. Duncan was more dedicated to existing repertoires—Jimmie's included—than Jimmie Rodgers would have been to anybody's but his own, and Tommy would not be a pop hero to many, partly for these very fixations.

"Tommy Duncan sang what *Bob* wanted him to do," Remington recalls. "Bob was the bandleader and Tommy was a singer, and Bob's music was dance music. Not that Jimmie Rodgers tunes couldn't be adapted to that; they were, with Tommy—true. But the thing Bob was always talking about was playing good dance tempos—and that's where the emphasis was, what he looked at first. When Tommy had his druthers it was different—and he tried to get me to join him when he left."

Remington would not go with Duncan when the singer left Wills in the late '40s, but Glynn Duncan did follow his brother into his new Western All-Stars, where Tommy immediately began to record Jimmie Rodgers songs again, including his biggest hit, a "jazz walk" tempo take on "Gamblin' Polka Dot Blues" for the new Capitol Records outfit in Hollywood. For a while after that chart success, Tommy would stick to wearing polka dot shirts on stage.

Another fairly adventurous late '30s/early '40s Texas swing adaptation of a Rodgers song was a "Blue Eyed Jane" adaptation ("The Sweetest Girl in the World") by the fiddle-driving Tune Wranglers out of San Antonio. The Wranglers mixed cowboy and swing songs, and their best-known tune, "Texas Sand," suggests a familiarity with Rodgers' blues. Also in those years, the Rice Brothers Gang out of Dallas came up with a version of another piece of Rodgers vaudeville, "My Carolina Sunshine Girl."

In the further reaches of western swing variations on Jimmie's music made in Hollywood were the still-surprising 1937 sides by the Rhythm Wreckers, who included some of the hottest jazz musicians of the '20s, such as Mugsy Spanier on cornet and Ben Pollack on drums, now slumming, in their own minds, by thumping out pop blues and a lot of exciting, twisty, nearly campy, but purely fun renderings of Jimmie Rodgers songs. The celebrated Hawaiian guitarist Danny Kalauawa Stewart was on steel, taking the lead on the Rhythm Wreckers' version of "Blue Yodel No. 2"; he would also appear on several Hawaiian-themed Bing Crosby records. The singer up front, sometimes understandably mistaken for a woman, is the thirteen-year-old boy wonder Whitey McPherson. With his spirited, strange, gravelly soprano singing and high-pitched yodeling, Whitey is simply one of a kind. "The singer was a hillbilly from Texas. Pretty bad!" an exasperated Spanier would note. Only the Rhythm Wreckers versions of "Desert Blues" and "Never No Mo' Blues" have been reissued, though several more have been available on western swing blog sites. Somebody ought to gather up the band's Rodgers sides and their other blues for postmodern posterity.

The McPherson boy has remained something of an enigma, in part because his story crosses lines genre historians rarely cross. He apparently appeared with Gene Austin in one of the musical featurettes the crooner was making at RKO at about the time of the Wreckers recordings. Los Angeles roots music was still a small world; this same teenager, less than two years later, was a member of an on-air country music band led by Woody Guthrie, which also included Woody's cousin Jack Guthrie and singer Lefty Lou. They performed regularly on Los Angeles radio and then, briefly, on the border radio station XELO out of Tijuana. Woody would say at the time that "Whitey McPherson [now fifteen] "made most of the good music."

Woody and Cousin Jack would split soon afterward, in part over the question of how much Hollywood cowboy music and hot, goofy western swing they would go on playing. Woody's career would veer into the urban folk arena, of course, another story.

Jack Guthrie, a lifelong Jimmie Rodgers fan and interpreter, would record at least fourteen Rodgers songs himself, many—the ones where he sounded best—with a smooth western swing band in the late '40s. He later worked with Ernest Tubb, that key Jimmie Rodgers advocate having emerged as a wartime innovator and leader of the new music that would do to big band western swing what Sinatra had done to expensive big bands in general—make them less necessary. The individual singer's vocal style was up front, a small, electrified group behind. And Jimmie Rodgers' influence would very much be there. They would call the stuff "honky tonk."

While there would be western swing revival acts in later years to match the harmonizing cowboy revivalist acts (most notably Asleep at the Wheel, a band more Bob Wills–fixated than Wills himself probably would have been), the Texan Hank Thompson, a member of the Light Crust Doughboys when he was young, is generally considered the last major performer to emerge who blended western swing with that incoming honky tonk style.

"Jimmie Rodgers was my *primary* influence," Hank recalled, very shortly before his death in November 2007, "and I can remember singing *his* songs as far back as I can remember singing songs . . . I had a neighbor that bought all of his records, and I'd line them up by that Victrola and listen to every one of them, and try to sing them all like Jimmie Rodgers did. That was by about 1933 or '34. 'Mother, the Queen of My Heart' [which he would record in the '50s] was always one of my favorites. Jimmie's songs were so popular; they were already standard songs back then, those things like 'Carolina Sunshine Girl.' These were things that people could identify with; the subjects were things everybody just accepted."

To twenty-first-century ears, John Lennon's comment that for a Liverpudlian of his generation "before Elvis, there was nothing" must come to mind when Thompson, speaking for the Texas kids of his generation, added, "If you didn't listen to Jimmie Rodgers, who were you going to listen to?"

In fact, Hank knew his Carter Family music well, too, as would be evident when his hit "Wild Side of Life" used the hoary tune of their "I'm Thinking Tonight of My Blue Eyes." By inclination and ability, he would become the king of the barroom singers, always keeping songs like "My Rough and Rowdy Ways" in his repertoire. He would prove a strong competitor in the oncoming age of Hanks, when Messrs. Williams, Snow, and Locklin would, like him, be making music that began to end the strong southwestern-southeastern division in the country music story—a split Jimmie had, if only half-wittingly, helped to create. If there were a "father of southwestern country," Jimmie Rodgers would be it.

Getting the hillbilly East to carry his music forward would take some doing, some time—and would not happen without some resistance.

Select Soundtrack

Jimmie Rodgers Recordings, Heading West

"T for Texas," "My Little Lady," "Waiting for a Train," "Desert Blues," "Jimmie's Texas Blues," "Yodeling Cowboy," "Blue Yodel No. 7," "Moonlight and Skies," "Mother, the Queen of My Heart," "The Cow Hand's Last Ride," "When the Cactus Is in Bloom," "The Land of My Boyhood Dreams," "The Carter Family and Jimmie Rodgers in Texas," "Prairie Lullaby," "Yodeling My Way Back Home," "The Yodeling Ranger."

Blue Yodelers Moseying into Jimmie's West

- **Cliff Carlisle:** "My Little Sadie," "When the Cactus Is in Bloom," "Desert Blues," "The Cowboy Song," "Cowboy Johnnie's Last Ride," "When It's Roundup Time in Texas,"

"On the Banks of the Rio Grande," and "On the Lone Prairie" are all on the JSP sets *Cliff Carlisle: A Country Legacy* and *Cliff Carlisle, Volume 2, When I Feel Froggie*, noted earlier. "Cowboy's Dying Dream" is on *Sounds Like Jimmie Rodgers* (also JSP).

- **Jimmie Davis:** "Cowboy's Home Sweet Home," "When It's Round-Up Time in Heaven," "Moonlight and Skies (No. 2)," "Prairie of Love," "Sweetheart of West Texas," and "In the West Where Life is Free" are all on *Nobody's Darlin' But Mine* (Bear Family).

- **Gene Autry:** "My Oklahoma Home," "Cowboy Yodel" (four versions), "Texas Blues," "Cowboy's Heaven," "The Yellow Rose of Texas," "Way Out West in Texas," and "The Dying Cowgirl" are all on *That Silver-Haired Daddy of Mine* (Bear Family). The film *Back in the Saddle*, featuring two Rodgers songs sung by Gene, is available on DVD (Image Entertainment, 2003), a part of the ongoing "Gene Autry Collection" series of restored Autry films. *Prairie Moon* was previously in circulation on VHS tape, and a new DVD format release is reportedly planned for the same series.

- **Goebel Reeves, the Texas Drifter:** "Little Joe the Wrangler" and "Cowboy's Lullaby" are on *Sounds Like Jimmie Rodgers* (JSP).

- **Jesse Rodgers:** "When the Texas Moon Is Shining," "My Brown-Eyed Texas Rose," "Old Pinto, My Pony Pal," "Rounded Up in Glory," "I'm a Roaming Cowboy" (all out of print).

The Cowboys' Jimmie Rodgers

- **Sons of the Pioneers:** "Hadie Brown (My Little Lady)," "The Yodeling Cowboy," "Rock Our Babies to Sleep," and "T for Texas," all with lead vocals by Len Slye (the future Roy Rogers) from 1934–35, are on *Under Western Skies* (Varese Sarabande). "Prairie Lullaby" was also among the Standard Radio Transcriptions from which those tracks were culled. Bob Nolan's "Way Out There" and its sequel, "One More Ride," are on various Sons compilations.

- **Hank Snow, Yodeling Ranger:** Hank's Canadian RCA Victor cowboy yodeler sides, such as "Lonesome Blue Yodel," "Polka

Dot Blues," "My San Antonio Mama," "The Texas Cowboy," "Goodnight Little Buckaroo," "There's a Pony That's Lonely Tonight," "The Hobo's Last Ride," and "Blue Ranger," are on the box set *The Yodeling Ranger* (Bear Family).

- **Wilf Carter (a.k.a. Montana Slim):** His Rodgers salute LP was discussed earlier; a generous sampling of Carter's cowboy yodel songs is on *Wilf Carter: Cowboy Songs* (Bear Family).

- **Ray Whitley:** "Blue Yodel Blues," "Big Bad Blues," "Wa Hoo," and "Just a Little Cough Drop" ("Rootin' Groundhog"), all Rodgers derived, are on *Ray Whitley: Back in the Saddle Again* (British Archive of Country Music).

- **Jimmy Wakely:** "For the Sake of Days Gone By" is on *Jimmy Wakely: Collector's Edition* (Simitar); "The One Rose" is on *Jimmy Wakely, Vol. 3*; *Country Masters* (Digital Musicworks); and "Roll Along, Kentucky Moon" is on *Vintage Collections* (Capitol).

- **Johnny Bond:** He is seen performing "Train Whistle Blues" on the DVD *Johnny Bond at Town Hall Party* (Bear Family).

- **Wiley and the Wild West Show:** "When the Cactus Is in Bloom," "T for Texas," and "Waiting for a Train" are all on *Total Yodel!* (Rounder).

- **Don Edwards:** "Land of My Boyhood Dreams" and "Moonlight and Skies" are both on *Moonlight and Skies* (Dualtone), and "Prairie Lullaby" is on *The Best of Don Edwards* (Warner Bros.).

Jimmie Rodgers Songs: Western Swing Style

- **W. Lee O'Daniel and His Hillbilly Boys (Leon Huff, vocals):** "Peach Pickin' Time in Georgia," "Yodeling Ranger," and "Tuck Away My Lonesome Blues" are on *Sounds Like Jimmie Rodgers.* "Prairie Lullaby," with the Light Crust Doughboys, is on *Let Me Be Your Sidetrack* (Bear Family).

- **Bill Boyd and His Cowboy Ramblers:** "The Wind Swept Desert (Desert Blues)," "I'm Gonna Hop Off That Train," "Wah Hoo," "Way Out There," and "Going Back to My Texas Home" are all on *Bill Boyd's Cowboy Ramblers: Saturday*

Night Rag 1934–1946 (Acrobat). Additional Boyd blues are on the follow-up CD, *Lone Star Rag*, on the same label.

- **Bob Wills and His Texas Playboys (Tommy Duncan, vocals):** "Never No More Blues," "Mean Mama Blues," "Blue Yodel No. 1," "Never No More Hard Times Blues," "Everybody Does It in Hawaii," "Gambling Polka Dot Blues," "Mississippi Delta Blues" (twice), and "Drunkard's Blues" are all available on the box set *San Antonio Rose* (Bear Family); there are also Tiffany transcriptions recorded for radio use, in collectors' hands, which include two versions of "Dear Old Sunny South by the Sea" and "I'm Free from the Chain Gang Now."

- **Tommy Duncan and His Western All-Stars:** "Gamblin' Polka Dot Blues," "In the Jailhouse Now," "Never No Mo' Blues," "Mississippi River Blues," and "Sweet Mama Hurry Home" are on *Tommy Duncan: Texas Moon* (Bear Family).

- **The Tune Wranglers'** "Sweetest Girl in the World" and the **Rice Brothers Gang's** "My Carolina Sunshine Girl" are both on the box set *Let Me Be Your Sidetrack* (Bear Family).

- **The Rhythm Wreckers (Whitey McPherson, vocals):** "Never No Mo' Blues," and "Blue Yodel No. 2" are both on *Sounds Like Jimmie Rodgers* (JSP); other recordings, originally on Vocalion, include "Desert Blues" "Brakeman's Blues," "Blue Yodel No. 1," and "Blue Yodel No. 3"; and as **Whitey Mc-Pherson Rhythmakers**: "Little Lady," "Brakeman's Blues," and "Blue Yodel No. 5." Some of the sides not released on disc have sometimes been made available on Web blogs.

- **Jack Guthrie:** "My Rough and Rowdy Ways," "Peach Pickin' Time in Georgia," "Muleskinner Blues," "Any Old Time," "Blue Yodel No. 3," "You and My Old Guitar," "Waitin' for a Train," "T.B. Blues," "Never No Mo' Blues," and "Travelin' Blues" are all on *Jack Guthrie: Milk Cow Blues* (Bear Family); "When the Cactus Is in Bloom" and "Answer to 'Moonlight and Skies'" are on *Oklahoma Hills* (Bear Family).

- **Hank Thompson:** "Mother, the Queen of My Heart" is on *Hank Thompson and His Brazos Valley Boys* (Bear Family); "My Rough and Rowdy Ways" is on *Smoky the Bar* (Dot LP); "In the Jailhouse Now" is on *Seven Decades* (Hightone).

nine

Back East
The Hillbilly Echo, 1933–1947

There are people who will swear to you, waxing nostalgic about it, that they grew up listening to Jimmie Rodgers on the Grand Ole Opry. They did not; he never appeared on the celebrated radio broadcast, although it had already been on the air two years when he first became a recording artist. Others, aware of that missed opportunity, have long wondered whether Jimmie Rodgers ever really performed in Nashville, Tennessee, the eventual "home of country music," at all. He did.

During his last year, Jimmie carried with him a little black ledger to track his appearances, expenses, and contacts. He also recorded the population of the towns he played and the weather he found as he arrived — useful, no doubt, for boasting about better-than-expected gates or explaining away any bad ones. The ledger notes two previously unchronicled Tennessee appearances in mid-1932, just a few weeks before the Atlanta recording session that produced "Peach Pickin' Time Down in Georgia" and "Whippin' That Old T.B."

Having played the Princess Theater in Springfield, Tennessee, on July 7 (the weather was fair), on the night of Sunday, July 10, at the stroke of midnight, he appeared on the 120-foot *Hollywood* showboat, which was docked at Nashville on the Cumberland River for an extended summer stay. An ad in the Nashville *Banner* that day listed him as an "Extra Added Attraction" for the special Sunday midnight show, following that week's live "modern family" melodrama *Hard-Boiled Husbands*.

Bill Monroe and the original Bluegrass Boys who took "Mule Skinner Blues" to the Opry, October 28, 1939: (from left) Art Wooten, Monroe, Cleo Davis, and Amos Green.

The *Hollywood*, which seated more than seven hundred and had done service since 1911 as the *American* and then the *Columbia*, carried an immense calliope, which generally was confined to playing nostalgia-inducing Stephen Foster tunes. It was one of the last major tugboat-lugged showboats still working the Mississippi and its tributaries, and by that point was enough of a curiosity that Fox Movietone news had shot a human interest report there just a few weeks earlier. It is too bad for posterity that they did not document the night of Jimmie's appearance. All summer long, Captain J. W. "Bill" Menke and manager D. F. Monroe had been featuring the same sort of fare seen in the tent rep shows of Jimmie's time. One week it would be *Camille*, with its elegant, romantic death by tuberculosis, the next *Broadway Butterfly*, a "Toby" character rural comedy. There were some burlesques of old-style melodrama and, often, vaudeville acts as bonuses. With some poignant synchronicity, the ad for Jimmie's showboat appearance was published on the same page of the *Banner* as a news report on WSM's first tests of their new fifty-thousand-watt transmitter, which was about to power the Opry to national prominence. It is a momentary real-life juxtaposition that reminds us again of that fictional mixture of flappers and steamboat hands in Buster Keaton's *Steamboat Bill, Junior* a few years before.

If Jimmie had listened to the Opry the night before his show, or even stopped by at its original home, the WSM studio, he would have encountered a lineup with a decided emphasis on rural hoedown instrumentals by the Fruit Jar Drinkers, DeFord Bailey, and the Crook Brothers. He also would have found the Opry's only vaudeville-seasoned singing star, Uncle Dave Macon, the first stirrings of modern country music sounds in the Dixieliners, a brand-new band that combined Fiddlin' Arthur Smith with Sam and Kirk McGee on guitar and banjo, and also the nearly pop vocal group the Vagabonds.

Macon and Rodgers worked the same sorts of venues often enough, from big Loews Theaters to dives in Florida, that they may well have crossed paths at some time. The admired fiddler Arthur Smith, probably the strongest competition Jimmie's pal Clayton McMichen then had, kept a day job repairing track on the Dixie Line railroad, hence the band's name. It would be nice to think that Jimmie sat down and hoisted one in Nashville with these characters so celebrated in country music history in those waning days of Prohibition, but we will likely never know whether he did.

What we do know is that until the late '30s Jimmie Rodgers' music was anything but a Grand Ole Opry mainstay. One of the first to sing Rodgers songs on the program was one of the instrumental-oriented Crook Brothers, Lewis Crook, who would occasionally switch from guitar to banjo and step out to sing. "T for Texas" and "Any Old Time" were apparently among the numbers he performed, but no Opry broadcasts of that early era have survived, so how he sounded singing them is unclear.

Cast member Sam McGee would work guitar finger-picking wonders with verses referencing trains in the Jimmie Rodgers way (though without yodels) in his most famous number, "Railroad Blues," recorded in 1934. Sam apparently learned whatever blues he knew from Rodgers, Cliff Carlisle, and Jimmie Davis records, though his brother Kirk was familiar with black blues singers such as Papa Charlie Jackson and Kokomo Arnold.

Nonetheless, with some irony, in the years following his death, Jimmie Rodgers' influence in the Southeast he had come from was a barely detectable echo rather than the crucial presence it was in his adopted Southwest. Southeastern country music was rapidly evolving toward a combination of traditional, fast-picked, stringband hoedown sounds and that next big thing, close harmony singing. There was generally little room in such arrangements for Rodgers' lazy guitar runs and varying rhythms, or his emphasis on individualized, by-the-lyric vocal stylings. He had not, as duo singers from over the years would note, written or selected songs with either fast picking or harmony singing in mind. The songs and the arrangements were designed for the solo singer.

An Eastern "mountain blues" act contemporary with Jimmie, the especially engaging and bluesy Darby and Tarlton, produced songs like "Traveling Yodel Blues" and "The New York Hobo" that had easily recognizable, laid-back Rodgers touches, but their sort of duet was becoming passé by the time Jimmie died. Jimmie Tarlton's sometimes driving, sometimes weepy slide guitar sounds progressive and involving today, and we can enjoy his country blues as easily as we can Cliff Carlisle's steel-driven records of the time. The record buyers' decreasing interest in the Darby and Tarlton sound and the ongoing shift away from arrangements in that style toward faster picking at least suggests that for eastern rural audiences in the mid-'30s, steel sustain was becoming something tired and tried; it just seemed to "drag things down," old-style. Moreover, Darby and Tarlton's vocal harmonies had always had more than a whiff of white-glove-clapping nineteenth-century plantation music—the sounds of minstrel shows and Old South choirs, tones now too musty to survive.

By the time Tarlton's disciple Howard Dixon (of the Dixon Brothers) and Frank Gerald recorded the Rodgers-like "Hobo Jack the Rambler" in 1938, the sounds of steel guitars and yodeling were apparently fresh enough to work for audiences again. By then, the harmonies in the duo's verse-ending train whistle yodels would show evidence of their having heard the Sons of the Pioneers pop Western records. No doubt their audience had now caught up with those sounds, too.

Meeting Jimmie Rodgers

Meanwhile, Rodgers' ghostly musical DNA found hosts where it could. This was the Depression, and the Bible Belt South, and times were hard, life too often heartbreaking. Wagons may have been heading for adventure farther West, but here they were circled—and that is not a situation favorable to Rodgers' music. This was the time in which restrictive codes were imposed on Hollywood movies in an organized attack on the more freewheeling and pleasure-friendly content of the '20s and early '30s. Even the cartoon character Betty Boop was being toned down.

Much of the material sung by the popular southeastern brother acts of the '30s and the way they sang it were both self-evidently bred in the environs of the fire-and-brimstone church, with the comforts its hard certainty on matters spiritual provides adherents and its distaste for the worldly and physical. In hillbilly music, as the genre now tended to be called, there would not be a rash of brother duet numbers climaxing with "This story has no moral." For example, the Bolick brothers, billed as The Blue Sky Boys, would be famous for singing the likes of "Turn Your Radio On" (to "get in touch with God"), not "Let Us Be Your Side Track." But there were acts that while not precisely immune to such influences, responded to them only moderately and were therefore comfortable keeping Jimmie in the mix. They just had to figure out how to make that work musically. The Delmore Brothers were arguably the most generally appealing act of the era, their success increasing through the boogying '40s. They would absorb what they wanted from Jimmie and put it to work, for the most part, in their content rather than their sound. Their recordings made in Chicago in 1933 and New Orleans in 1935 include obvious Rodgers-derived themes—jailhouses, fugitives, ramblers, old guitars, odes to southern climes and towns, smatterings of western fantasy, songs with "blues" in the title for a reason, not just for commercial convenience, and trains, lots of trains, including Jimmie's fabled old L&N.

Alton and Rabon Delmore, out of Northern Alabama, were as inclined as Jimmie had been to conglomerate their music from varied sources, increasing its variety in the process. Among the artists Alton would report learning recorded guitar licks from were Carson Robison and Riley Puckett at the backwoods end, jazzy Eddie Lang and Nick Lucas on the uptown side, and Jimmie Rodgers as a key influence down the middle. You can hear Jimmie in Delmore Brothers numbers such as "Down South" and "Lonesome Yodel Blues," the latter showing sophisticated assimilation of the jazzy "Jimmie's Mean Mama Blues."

In Alton's unique memoir, *Truth Is Stranger Than Publicity*, he devotes a chapter to a 1935 trip to Meridian in which the Delmores and Dave Macon meet some of the Rodgers family, such as Jimmie's brother Tal. They sing him a song that they had sent Ralph Peer, intended specifically for Jimmie to sing, which apparently had been accepted, but too late to happen. The number in question was "Blue Railroad Train," not only one of their best-known and most lasting songs, but also one of the most musically original responses to Jimmie's ideas.

Alton Delmore said of Jimmie, "There has never been one man in the whole history of entertainment that packed the wallop he did by himself . . . one man with a single instrument that could play and sing like he did . . . I don't believe there will ever be another just like Jimmie Rodgers. And I'm not meaning just style, either."

What the Delmores did not much do was look for ways to harmonize on Rodgers lyrics and yodels. The current consensus is that the fairly obscure team of Reece Fleming and Respers Townsend from just north of Memphis were the first to blue yodel in harmony on records—just on the yodeling parts. Fleming and Townsend certainly had the genre down; they sold thousands of records in the day, on Victor, and their obviously Rodgers-derived "I'm Blue and Lonesome," harmonized yodel and all, was even covered by Gene Autry and Frankie Marvin as early as 1931. Fleming would keep at it long enough to play piano for mid-'50s Sun Records artist Malcolm Yelvington and write more than a few of his bluesy songs, an interesting link between blue yodelmania and rockabilly.

The brother act most successful in singing Jimmie's lyrics in harmony—doing it well enough, in fact, to cast doubt on the frequent claims that doing so was a tough trick to pull off—was the Callahan Brothers, Homer and Walter, from around Ashville, North Carolina. When you hear them tear into "My Blue-Eyed Jane" or even "Mother, the Queen of My Heart" in close harmony, you know that you have caught up with a new, original mutation of Rodgers' music.

"I knew him personally," Homer Callahan recalled in a 1979 interview. "In fact, we was in New York recording when he died . . . I just worshipped the man; he just had something that I liked. Of course, I always liked the yodel; then me and my brother put that duet yodel thing together in harmony."

The Callahans were clearly familiar with Rodgers' music by the time they began recording in 1933, and it is sometimes suggested that they had run into him or heard him on the air in his prestardom Asheville period. Though they were just in their early teens at the time, they were already out playing. In oral history testimony for the Country Music Hall of Fame and Museum, Homer specifically denied ever having met Emmett Miller in Asheville, though the brothers did record "St. Louis Blues" and "Lonesome Freight Train Blues," Emmett style, as well. They would record such

Meeting Jimmie Rodgers

obviously Rodgers-derived numbers as "I've Rode the Southern and the L&N," "Gonna Quit My Rowdy Ways," "Mean Mama," and "Rounder's Luck," and they performed a wide range of Rodgers songs on various radio stations all through their long on-air career.

It is telling that, with their strong interest in the rowdy side of hillbilly music and Jimmie Rodgers' blues, and very limited interest in its churchy side, Homer and Walter's radio jobs relocated them increasingly westward. They eventually were among the earliest members of the important "Big D Jamboree" show in Dallas — changing their names along the way to the less hillbilly, more western-sounding "Bill," in Homer's case, and "Joe," in Walter's. Eventually, appropriately, they would appear with Jimmy Wakely in the singing cowboy picture *Springtime in Texas* and go on to tour with Ray Whitley and Lefty Frizzell — western Rodgers acolytes all.

It would be wrong to give the impression that all of the contributions to Jimmie Rodgers' music back East were by such anomalously adventurous vocal groups. There were also several important new individual exponents of the music, performers who were not simply '20s blue yodelers continuing on with their careers.

The percentage of railway workers' children who heard Jimmie Rodgers' music in their homes must have been staggering. One of these was Bill Cox, the son of a Charleston, West Virginia, railroad section worker. He was singing Rodgers songs and quirky, bluesy ballads on local radio by the time he was a teen, and he made dozens of records for a variety of companies from the early '30s through the early '40s under various names, solo at first, later with guitarist Cliff Hobbs. Cox's innovation was to apply Rodgers' musical stylings to material that was more topical. He could handle the Rodgers guitar runs, but he generally performed using a very simple guitar strum and a rack-mounted harmonica. He took up topics such as Roosevelt's National Recovery Act or what women would be like if they "held all the power." He had decidedly mixed feelings about the latter but offers a lot of arresting details. Among his most lasting tunes would be "Franklin Roosevelt's Back Again" and the original version of "Filipino Baby," which became a standard when covered by Ernest Tubb and Cowboy Copas a decade later. Cox even came up with a version of "Midnight Special" that mixes blue yodel trainman verses with the chorus of Lead Belly's version. This model of a topical song singer with his harmonica holder seems much less unusual now than it did then, so it will not be a surprise that while Cox remains an obscurity in country music history, he was eventually taken up in the folk world as a sort of Woody Guthrie prototype.

The singer-songwriter who was the key sonic link between the blue yodeler craze and the coming of honky tonk in the '40s was Rex Griffin.

Ernest Tubb, who would record songs Griffin wrote for him long after Rex's own recording career had ended, would note on his salute LP of Griffin songs, "In my opinion, his singing was second only to that of Jimmie Rodgers." For Tubb, this was saying something, but if you listen to Rex handling Jimmie's "Sweet Mama Hurry Home" or "The Lovesick Blues," where you can detect both traces of Emmett Miller and the blueprint for Hank Williams' future arrangement, you can see why. There is a simple poignancy in the singing, a sense of experience and emotional straight talk much like Tubb's own, though Rex's voice can veer either rougher or smoother than Tubb's does. In Griffin's own underrated song "An Old Rose and a Curl," time is crooned right out of joint. You cannot tell whether you are hearing a throwback parlor tune from 1895 or a prescient 1952-style country chart ballad—and it was recorded in 1939.

Rex Griffin would emerge as a major songwriter, author of the epochal pop suicide note "The Last Letter" and many more besides. First, however, he would write and record song after song patterned after Rodgers' material, often simple variations on Jimmie's more sentimental love songs with the patented guitar runs, very adeptly played, and the yodels. Such early Griffin sides as "Let Me Call You Sweetheart Again" and "Just for Old Times' Sake" are good examples. That the recordings sometimes included backing by a banjo, played with marked tremolo in an old mandolin style, only made them more retrospective and poignant.

Rex handled jumpier blue yodel style rhythm numbers, too, including "Mean Woman Blues" and his original version of "Everybody's Trying to Be My Baby." Yes; that rock standard began as a yodel blues before Roy Newman took it into western swing, and long before Carl Perkins, then Beatle George Harrison evolved it into a rockabilly and pop standard. Rex did a "Nobody Wants to Be My Baby," too.

He was born Alsie Griffin and was raised in a large, musically attuned farming family near Gadsden, Alabama. His dad bought him a $2.50 guitar—and when he heard Jimmie Rodgers records, which started coming out just as he reached the crucial age of fifteen, that was it, as far as Rex was concerned, for farming or working in the local foundry. He was very soon on radio, then, as the Depression deepened, on records, his first name changed to the more western-sounding Rex. He would never quite take off as a recording artist, and he had drinking and health problems—tuberculosis, in fact—but nevertheless, his striking songs like "Little Red Wagon," "The Last Letter," and "Just Call Me Lonesome" would last.

Also surfacing in this era was an artist as lastingly influential in country singing as Jimmie Rodgers had been, the Tennessean Roy Acuff. Here was a star who had paid his dues working medicine shows in tiny towns, a vaudevillian who could be relied on to take a break from breaking your heart by balancing a fiddle bow on his nose, and who loved train songs enough to add a few classics to the country repertoire, including "Wabash Cannon Ball" and "Night Train to Memphis." He had even learned to do his own famous train whistle imitation while working, briefly, for the L&N. So you would imagine that Acuff could not help being enamored with Jimmie Rodgers and his music—but in fact, he would always be ambivalent, at best, about his predecessor and sometimes would appear downright hostile to his memory.

When it came to singing, which was clearly Roy Acuff's primary ability as a performer, he was of the declamatory old school, from back before crooning—not just because of the way he was raised, singing church songs as the son of a Baptist minister who was also a judge, but also because he developed his style in live performance rather than in the recording studio. "My first training was on a medicine show," he explained to Doug Green in 1972, "and there was no microphones back in those days . . . I'd sing so that you could hear me at least a block away . . . Bing Crosby was very popular, and he was a crooner—and everybody wanted to be Bing Crosby [but] I had trained my voice to sing out, not to hold back . . . so when I came to the Opry, no one had ever heard a voice like mine that would come out, and with a lot of feeling, and seemed like a determination to do something." That determination was essential, not just an effect. Roy Acuff would remain just as determined to be a bulwark for the wagon-circling, Bible Belt sound and sentiments as to see country music become an immense industry. Jimmie Rodgers was never going to get caught preaching at you, but Roy Acuff was certainly willing to step up to the task.

The always insecure man who would co-own the vast publishing firm Acuff-Rose and have access to thousands of songs kept his own repertoire tight and rarely wrote any songs at all besides some new ones in the idiom that brought him fame, the "Great Speckled Bird" and "Wreck on the Highway" sort of moralizing parable, though he had written neither of those. There had been physicality in his music in its earliest, less sober period, when he called his band the "Crazy Tennesseans"; he had even recorded some down-and-dirty party songs with the band, incognito, as the Bang Boys. But increasingly he eliminated the earthy from his vocal repertoire, cleaving instead to songs rooted in church music. This was not the "school of Rodgers."

Still, transparently for public relations purposes supposedly good for the country music industry, Roy would sometimes have something nice to say about Jimmie Rodgers and what he had represented, as in his purported 1983 memoir, *Roy Acuff's Nashville*. The book almost never seems to be written in his own voice, and much of it reads less like an autobiography than a lengthy invitation to come and drop some bucks in Music City U.S.A. But there is a passage that describes how, when he was young, Roy had listened to Jimmie Rodgers records "every chance" he got, because he had "heard a lot of talk" about him. "There were many times I just sat and looked at those old, thick Victor records and tried to imagine how it felt to play and sing like that," Roy and his co-author, the auto-racing chronicler Bill Neely, tell us. "The Blue Yodeler was one of the few bright spots in a depression-torn land. Perhaps it was this overall atmosphere of sadness that contributed to the saga of the skinny little man from Mississippi."

More revealing of his feelings on the matter is the fact that Acuff virtually never sang Rodgers songs or anything much like them. Then, in a notorious live episode on cable TV in May 1987, he let loose with a public diatribe against Jimmie Rodgers and his ilk—in the middle of a salute to Jimmie on Ralph Emery's *Nashville Now* talk show.

"Well, I think that what really happened there is that Roy wanted to have people thinking more about the 'King of Country Music' [the title often attached to him] and had gotten tired of hearing about the *Father* of Country Music," Emery says today. He describes how Acuff became increasingly, visibly irritated as Jimmie's accomplishments and the breadth of his influence were detailed. When the time came for Roy to be asked what Jimmie had meant for him, he curtly replied "*I* wasn't that impressed . . . He was a pretty mean type person; he carried a pistol all the time, didn't he?"

Ralph and Minnie Pearl were helpless to do anything but beg, unsuccessfully, for a more positive comment as Acuff went on to suggest that if Jimmie had been anything special on the medicine show circuit he would have met him. In Ralph's recollection, Acuff then added how nobody in Meridian even remembered who Jimmie Rodgers was. As some who were in the audience remember it, he tossed in, while on this roll, that Jimmie was a drunk and the only people in Meridian who did remember him were a bunch of drunks themselves. Acuff was aware that a number of Rodgers' living relatives and others from Meridian were right there in the audience, visiting for the salute. Several of them would call that depiction of Jimmie Rodgers the most hurtful they had ever heard, and decades later people who were there still refer to the incident with considerable emotion, if perhaps with slight exaggeration.

Roy Acuff had, as a matter of historical fact, recorded one Rodgers song relatively early in his recording career in 1940—his own version of "Mule Skinner Blues (Blue Yodel No. 8)." Surprisingly, this now very familiar Rodgers song had not been particularly well-known or much sung before that time. In Acuff's version, a fast-picked guitar propels the song forward. He sings the "Good mornin', captain" opening with typical determination, but the vocal is unusually high-pitched, as are his somewhat anemic yodels.

Lyrically, there is a request for a "walkin' cane" to go along with the brand-new Stetson hat; Jimmie's "bottles of booze" have been expunged, as have the initials carved on a mule's behind. There can be little doubt that Acuff recorded the number only because a fresh new competitor on the Grand Ole Opry had been getting a tremendous response to his own updated, but as yet still unrecorded version. The newcomer was Bill Monroe.

Monroe was as southeastern as Acuff, and certainly an equally serious devotee of the church and churchy music — but when he got off of that, he got *off* of that. In hits with his brother, Charlie, recorded between 1936 and 1938, Bill had enthusiastically ventured into the likes of "Roll in My Sweet Baby's Arms" as a change of pace from the more typical "What Would You Give In Exchange [for Your Soul]?" — not a surprising combination for the man who would write and sing magnificently some of the great soulful songs and performances of earthly *and* spiritual depths in country music. His "Body and Soul" is an outstanding example.

The Monroe Brothers, one of the most accomplished of the '30s brother acts, offered soaring, riveting harmonies and, sometimes, manic mandolin playing from Bill that presaged the groundbreaking directions he would take next. Charlie had been buying Rodgers records in his teens, just as they came out, and had shared them with his younger brother. They recorded both a strongly Rodgers-influenced, yodeling take on the Carter Family's "(On Some) Foggy Mountain Top" and a faster version of Jimmie's "Dear Old Sunny South," retitled "In My Dear Old Southern Home," as two sides of a 1936 single. It is not difficult to fathom what in Jimmie's "Sunny South" had grabbed the Monroes' attention. His original version featured, in addition to a Hawaiian steel guitar intro, a break featuring a rhythmic, hard-chopped ukulele and mandolin combination. The arrangement sped along, providing an excuse for one of Jimmie's most extended, energetic yodels — all very provocative, forward-looking stuff, and that was Jimmie himself on the uke. The Monroes would record the song still faster and put Bill's mandolin pyrotechnics on display.

One Monroe Brothers Bluebird record, "Where is My Sailor Boy?" was actually a split single, with the "The Carter Family and Jimmie Rodgers in Texas," in its first release, on the reverse. The record company saw this combination as a straightforward audience fit, and indeed, neither the yodeling cowboy song nor the blue yodel passages contained in that Rodgers–Carters side would be foreign to Bill Monroe's emerging sensibility, any more than the Carter Family's material would be.

When Bill Monroe and the earliest lineup of "His Blue Grass Boys," the stringband he built after breaking with his brother, commandeered the Opry stage at Nashville's War Memorial Auditorium as guest artists on October 28,

1939, they just wrecked the place. With Cleo Davis on mandolin, Art Wooten on fiddle, Amos Garren on bass, and Bill, uncharacteristically, playing guitar, they triggered the first demand for an encore of a song ever heard on the broadcast show. Monroe won a permanent place in the Grand Ole Opry cast that day. The key audition number, the crowd-stunner on the broadcast, and, before long, the new band's first hit record, would all be the same song—his take on "Mule Skinner Blues," the most celebrated of all modified versions of Jimmie's song.

Monroe had been working on the number during a brief radio stint in Greenville, South Carolina, the arrangement evolving along the way from a loping, bluesy ballad into this new, aggressive version. The number many consider to be the first in the bluegrass genre begins with a revving-up guitar run, then rises to and sticks with a trainlike chug that keeps the rhythm furiously steady—all set in a high and relatively challenging key that highlights Bill's dramatic tenor, the cutting vocal, and the up-front yodel.

"I could hit the notes, I could yodel, and I just thought that would be good in bluegrass style," Monroe would explain. Famously laconic, on this subject he was relatively expansive. "Jimmie Rodgers, he was the first to come out with yodel numbers that I ever got to hear," he told Canadian radio interviewer Doug Benson. "He could sing 'em so good; had a wonderful voice, and he played a good guitar. I always liked his singing and playing, and I guess that's how come I wanted to do 'Mule Skinner.' I wanted to put the new touch to it . . . You know, I have a yodel . . . with a little laugh on the end of it."

The laugh was not all that little; it was almost manic, a natural extension of the braggadocio in the old blues lyrics and the "get the bucks to get back to my woman" structure Jimmie had given them. "I seen that that little yodel would help sell the number," Bill said. "Why, I knew then that we had something going that would be to my advantage on down through the years—with the *timing* of that number and everything."

As he once succinctly and strikingly put it, encapsulating his belief that the rhythm in bluegrass was what defined it, " 'Mule Skinner Blues' set the timing for bluegrass." He told author and musician Jim Rooney, "Charlie and I had a country beat, I suppose, but the beat in my music—bluegrass music—started when I ran across 'Mule Skinner Blues' and started playing that. We don't do it the way Jimmie sung it. It's speeded up, and we moved it up to fit the fiddle, and we have that straight time with it—driving time."

That laughing yodel and driving rhythm have fueled new versions of "Mule Skinner" ever after—some with electric twang and drums to match the Monroe yodel. The sturdy Rodgers song really enters the popular imagination broadly here, circa 1940. It is significant, in terms of the southeasterner Monroe's attraction to the Jimmie Rodgers line of attack, that he expressed admiration for the southwestern Bob Wills and the Texas Play-boys, who already had their own, more dance-friendly way of "straightening out" the Rodgers rhythms. Monroe would record Wills' "I Wonder If You Feel the Way I Do" the same day as "Mule Skinner," with Texas swing–influenced fiddle by Tommy Magness, and that is surely no accident.

It is at least as significant that Bill Monroe had been tutored as a boy by an African-American blues musician, Arnold Schultz, and had absorbed that music along with the old-time stringband idiom of his fiddler uncle, Pen Vandiver. Bill had come to prominence with a deep understanding of black blues and was prepared to reinject blues into southeastern country music, updated bluegrass style, in a serious, deliberate way. Jimmie Rodgers' blue yodels provided the perfect way.

Bill's own testimony was that he had been listening to jazz "all of my life" and very likely knew how, at this time, some of the hottest and most original of the popular swing bands were stopping dancing audiences in their tracks, leaving them standing there stunned, just concentrating on the instrumental solos. Inflammatory instrumental solos were going to matter in bluegrass, too—matter very much.

Without the central concern of pleasing dancers, Jimmie Rodgers' music could be taken fast and furious, yet the lead vocalist would still have room to stretch sounds and syllables as Jimmie had, in lyrics and yodels alike. In 1941, Monroe would record "Blue Yodel No.7" with a mandolin chop opening that presages Chuck Berry's rock 'n' roll and that may have been influenced by rhythm and blues swing king Louis Jordan. Shouts of "Play it, boy!" in the style of Rodgers' and Wills' interjections are tossed in, too.

In 1946, the classic postwar lineup of the Blue Grass Boys, including Lester Flatt and Earl Scruggs, would record something Monroe called "Blue Yodel No. 4," with syllables compacted or stretched—indeed, toyed with, especially in that allegedly "lonesome" upper register of Monroe's. The number was not in fact built on Rodgers' "California Blues," the actual "No. 4," but a combination of verses from "Blue Yodel No. 3" and "Jimmie's Texas Blues." By that time, Bill's blues-inflected mandolin solos on this sort of number and Scruggs' mind-boggling banjo rolls were generating yells and screams from the generally sedate Opry audience. This was physical music, body music—brash, unafraid, empowered music.

Rodgers numbers were dependable showpieces for music like that, given Monroe and his bands' skills, and they would always have a place in his repertoire. Airchecks and logs show that the band performed "My Blue-Eyed Jane" and "Sailor's Plea" on Opry broadcasts, and possibly "California Blues" as well. Later, Monroe would add his well-known version of "Brakeman's Blues."

The first chugging Blue Grass Boys train song was the famed instrumental showpiece "Orange Blossom Special," recorded by Monroe and company in 1941 and played live even earlier, not long after its originators, the Rouse Brothers, put it together. Unusually for the time, Bill sang some of the words rather than sticking to the instrumental pyrotechnics. He chose the verse the Rouses had taken from Jimmie's "Train Whistle Blues," the one that has you "looking over yonder" at the train "comin' down the track." There can be little doubt that the verse was a nod to Rodgers; Ervin Rouse's original published lyric, revealingly enough, even had the singer going to Florida not to lose "these New York blues" as Johnny Cash would later have it, but "these T.B. blues."

Bill Monroe would not be the only "hillbilly" with a modern, fresh feel for blues and swing who reached out to audiences in the big-time, fifty-thousand-watt radio arena. A masterful, jazzy, yet still very country guitar picker whom Monroe admired, Merle Travis, would popularize a flexible, simple, but sophisticated thumb-picking style people would come to call "Travis picking." He would write brand-new songs people were convinced were as old as the hills, work easily with markedly Western honky tonk backing when he wanted to, and sing blues and up-to-date novelties with panache. Appropriately, in light of these career similarities to Jimmie Rodgers, among Merle's first recordings were smooth, smartly phrased, jazzy versions of "Any Old Time" with clarinet and "T or Texas" with what might be called a swing yodel.

In the Southeast, this era initially associated with a sort of hillbilly music that had little room for the lyrical and musical themes of Jimmie Rodgers drew to a close with three key stars at the Grand Ole Opry, highly individual singers who fronted crack, modernizing string bands—Roy Acuff, Bill Monroe, and Ernest Tubb—and the latter two were major exponents of Jimmie Rodgers' music. Meanwhile, the equally innovative Merle Travis would find it so comfortable out West that he would soon virtually be a Californian, playing along amiably right beside Texan Hank Thompson in a Las Vegas casino, singing the blues in Hollywood movies, acting as a not particularly well-behaved mentor to Johnny Cash—all presaging a time not much later when Jimmie Rodgers' special place in country music's history would be reimagined. Meanwhile, curiously enough, a whole new set of people, many of them urban, were beginning to look at certain aspects of southeastern country and even some cowboy music from a different angle. Bill Monroe and Merle Travis would be two of the country acts they would adopt as their own, and a few advocates in their ranks could be found talking about Jimmie Rodgers' legacy, and the Bill Monroe and Merle Travis offshoots, as "folk music."

           Meeting Jimmie Rodgers

Select Soundtrack

- **Darby and Tarlton:** "Traveling Yodel Blues" (1928) and "The New York Hobo," "Touring Yodel Blues," and "Going Back to My Texas Home" (1929) are on *Tom Darby and Jimmie Tarlton* (JSP, 2005) and *Darby and Tarlton: Complete Recordings* (Bear Family, 1995).

- **The Rambling Duet (Frank Gerald and Howard Dixon):** "Hobo Jack the Rambler" (1938) is on *Dixon Brothers, Complete Works, Vol. 3* (Document, 2001).

- **Sam McGee:** "Railroad Blues" (1934) is on *Old-Time Mountain Blues* (County, 2003) and *Sam McGee, 1926–1934* (Document, 1999).

- **Delmore Brothers:** "I Ain't Got Nowhere to Travel," "Gonna Lay Down My Old Guitar," "Bury Me Out on the Prairie," "Lonesome Yodel Blues," and "Blue Railroad Train" (1933) and "Down South" (1935) are on *The Delmore Brothers: Classic Cuts 1933–41* (JSP, 2004).

- **Fleming and Townsend:** "I'm Blue and Lonesome" (1930), "I'm Leavin' This Town," and "Lookin' for a Mama" (1931) are on *Fleming and Townsend, Little Home Upon the Hill* (BACD); "Gonna Quit Drinking When I Die" (1930) is also there, and on *Sounds Like Jimmie Rodgers* (JSP). The Autry-Marvin version of "I'm Blue and Lonesome" (1931) is on *Gene Autry, That Silver Haired Daddy of Mine* (Bear Family).

- **Callahan Brothers:** "T.B. Blues" (1935) is on *The Callahan Brothers* (Old Homestead); "My Blue-Eyed Jane" (1939) is on *More Memories of the Callahan Brothers* (Cattle/Binge, 2003), as are "Gonna Quit My Rowdy Ways," "Mean Mama" (1934), and "I've Just Been a Brakeman" (1935). *In Memory of the Callahan Brothers* (Cattle, 2002) has "Lonesome Weary Blues" (1936) and "My Good Gal Has Thrown Me Down" 1934), also in Rodgers style. Collections of the radio transcriptions the Callahans made for Sellers in the early '40s include more than a dozen Rodgers songs (blue yodels and others), including their harmonized "Mother, the Queen of My Heart."

- **Bill Cox:** Rodgers-like sides such as "High Silk Hat and Gold Top Walking Cane" and Bill's take on "My Rough and Rowdy

Ways" (1930) are on *Sounds Like Jimmie Rodgers* (JSP). More
representative are the two dozen numbers on *Bill Cox, Rough
and Rowdy Hillbilly of the 1930's, Vol. 2, featuring Cliff Hobbs*
(Collector), which includes the Rodgers-meets-Lead-Belly
"Midnight Special," a version of "New Mama" (1933), and
topical songs such as "Franklin Roosevelt's Back Again" (1936).
Cox also recorded "Daddy and Home," "My Old Pal," "Travelin' Blues," "Train Whistle Blues," and "California Blues"—all
out of print.

- **Rex Griffin**: "Sweet Mama Hurry Home" (1936) and such
  Rodgers-derived numbers as "Why Should I Care If You're
  Blue?" "I'm Just Passing Through," "Mean Woman Blues"
  (1944), and the original version of "Everybody's Tryin' to Be My
  Baby" (1936) are on *Rex Griffin: The Last Letter* (Bear Family,
  1996), as are "The Last Letter" and "Lovesick Blues."

- **Roy Acuff**: "Mule Skinner Blues" (1940) and other early,
  raucous Acuff numbers can be found on the box set *Roy Acuff:
  King of Country Music* (Proper, 2004).

- **Monroe Brothers**: "In My Dear Old Southern Home" and the
  yodeling "(On Some) Foggy Mountain Top" (1936) are on
  *The Monroe Brothers, Volume 1: What Would You Give in
  Exchange for Your Soul?* (Rounder, 2000).

- **Bill Monroe and His Blue Grass Boys**: An Opry broadcast
  sound check of "Mule Skinner Blues" from just a few weeks
  after Monroe joined the cast appears on the box set *The Music
  of Bill Monroe* (MCA, 1994). The Bluebird releases of "Mule
  Skinner Blues" (1940) and "Blue Yodel No. 7" (1941), as well as
  "Orange Blossom Special" (1941), appear on *Country Legends:
  Bill Monroe* (RCA/BMG, 2002), and Monroe's so-called "Blue
  Yodel No. 4" (1946) is on *The Essential Bill Monroe and His
  Blue Grass Boys 1945–1949* (Columbia, 1992); all three are also
  on the box set *Bill Monroe: All the Classic Releases 1937–1949*
  (JSP, 2003).

- **Merle Travis**: "T for Texas" and "Any Old Time" (1946) are on
  Sweet Temptation, The Best of Merle Travis 1946–1953 (Razor
  and Tie, 2000).

Meeting Jimmie Rodgers

ten

Some Sort of Folksinger?

Jimmie Rodgers, it can be said with little equivocation, did not want to be a folksinger. It would be difficult to make a case that he ever demonstrated any particular interest in preserving and promoting traditional music for its own sake, or any old tunes and themes either, except to the extent that they still appealed to his growing audience. Even on the couple of occasions when he sings a snippet of pseudohistoric folk lyric about some hapless "maiden," the stilted phrase has got "*That* might get some of them!" written all over it, just as it would when Cliff Carlisle, for instance, borrowed the tactic from him. And one of Jimmie's rare "maiden" voyages was in an A. P. Carter adaptation, on a Carter Family duet side.

Overwhelmingly, when there was a chance to perform the music folk revivalists would come to love, whether old country reels or hoary Anglo ballads, Jimmie could be depended on to bolt—all the way into Ralph Peer's pop- and novelty-friendly arms. His first rise to a professional career and, then, fairly quickly, to roots pop stardom is marked by a pattern of choices and inclinations that steered him clear of the folk minstrel job description and, with a few notable exceptions, have kept his music outside of the urban folk song bag ever since.

Yet it is not surprising, in view of the eventual emergence of folk revival heroes who owed him something, that Jimmie himself is sometimes claimed as a hero of American folk music. Such portrayals almost always present him as a romantic railway worker and drifting hobo, and a reluctant, amateur

Performers in the folk music field had not often been at home with Jimmie Rodgers' music. Two who made that change: Bob Dylan and Jack Elliott.

performer—precisely the sort of "whistling plumber" character he wanted not to be mistaken for when he dropped the Singing Brakeman nickname. And since professional folk music tends to highlight nobility in those identified (usually from above) as "folk" and there was in Jimmie's day that growing identification of T.B. with poverty and unhealthy working conditions, his struggles with the fatal disease are sure to be emphasized.

The first intimation that an edited folk-friendly version of Jimmie Rodgers could emerge probably came in (of all places) the early-1945 Broadway book show *Sing Out, Sweet Land*, written by Walter and Jean Kerr, starring Burl Ives and Alfred Drake. Designed to track the impulse toward personal and even physical freedom in folk song, as regularly threatened by killjoys across American history, the show included in its score "Frankie and Johnny" (making a return trip to the Great White Way), "Casey Jones," and "Big Rock Candy Mountain," all circling around Rodgers musical territory and his anti-joy-killing nature. Solidifying the connections, a duded-down Burl Ives plays "the Jolly Tramp" for an episode set in the town of "Railroad Station, Texas," the character clearly modeled on Rodgers' acquaintance Goebel Reeves (the "Texas Drifter") and Jimmie himself. This revived construct of the romantic drifter hobo would prove especially useful when country singers wanted to speak to folk audiences, which, during the '50s to '60s commercial "folk scare," they would sometimes want to do, and which Johnny Cash could keep in play on his network show at the turn of 1970.

Given Jimmie's largely downhome audience and downhome imitators, it was predictable that academic folklorists taking to the "field," as it came to be called not long after his time, would regularly chance upon his music, often without recognizing it for what it was; such commercial material was among the last things they were looking for. It is also true that people down South were as likely to learn a folk ballad like "Frankie and Johnny" from Jimmie as from anyone else you might name, unless it was that noted cultural preservationist Mae West. In fact, however much Rodgers had wanted, justifiably, to avoid being identified as an amateur with a happenstance career, however much folklorists and folk revivalists strived to avoid the taint of musical contamination by supposedly ersatz mass-market product, his music would have a measurable impact in the evolving world of folk music. That this impact was restricted, and promulgated by a particular small group of interpreters, says much about what Jimmie Rodgers' music is—and where it reaches one of its limits.

It was in 1915, as Jimmie, halfway through his lifespan at age eighteen, was first working on the railroad and with medicine show performing already under his belt, that the folklorist John Lomax undertook to spell out the sources of the "types of American Folk-Songs." His article in an early issue of the *Journal of American Folklore* listed the miner, the lumberman, the sailor and soldier, the railroader, the negro (used, with no doubt unintentional accuracy, as if that were another description of a full-time job), the cowboy, and the "down-and-out," the last term explicitly referring to dope "fiends," jailbirds, convicts, tramps, and "outcast girls." This was a fairly daring list, in that it suggested to the era's fixated collectors of "pure," post-Elizabethan ballad lyrics that the songs of these semiliterate, certainly unliterary Americans could actually be of interest. John Lomax himself, like virtually all folklorists, was not yet much interested in nonstorytelling forms of African-American song—which would shortly come to include several thousand blues. Yet Jimmie Rodgers would have songs in his repertoire drawn from most of Lomax's listed sources—as well as plenty of those nonnarrative blues.

It was not until 1957, however, as the just-formed college boy group the Kingston Trio was heading toward the recording studio and the urban folk revival's commercial apogee, that John Greenway, an English-born anthropologist, sometime performer, and author of a maverick book on the modern protest song, informed *Journal of American Folklore* readers that Jimmie Rodgers had had decades of undetected impact as a "folksong catalyst." Greenway detailed how lyrics and lyric fragments introduced and popularized by this man Jimmie Rodgers (a name "unknown to many folklorists," he would rightly note) had been repeatedly mislabeled as "traditional" or "clearly from a negro blues song" in academic texts written by prominent professionals. Just one published folklorist had explicitly recognized Jimmie as a source, but in what would become a sort of tradition in the folk field of not quite bothering to get it right, he had misspelled the name.

Among the Rodgers songs Greenway identified as misattributed in folk lyric collections were "Waiting for a Train," Jimmie's version of Kelly Harrell's "Away Out on the Mountain," "The Soldier's Sweetheart," and blue yodels Nos. 1, 4, 5, and 8. That by 1957 anyone's blues had begun to be considered folk music and so worthy of attention (even if the extent and variety of black-white musical interaction remained virtually unexplored) is one indication of how far the academic folklorists had ranged, roamed, and traveled over forty-some years, becoming more accurate, less notably racist, and more sophisticated as to context along the way. In the process, they had been forced, if grudgingly, to admit that most of the "isolated" American folk communities required by their theories had not been isolated from mass media and mass culture at all, and that this had been the case for some time.

In practice, blues had been excluded from earlier academic definitions of folk music as much for being overwhelmingly impressionistic and non-narrative as for being non-Anglo. Variants of published—and, especially, commercially recorded songs—from the studied "folk" had automatically been

Meeting Jimmie Rodgers

excluded from documentation, whether written or recorded, along with much that was individually composed, improvised, and personal. (The noted blues authority and part-time musician David Evans would trace this evolution of what folklorists allowed themselves to see and hear from those they decided were "folk" and what they would brand "folk" in his seminal 1982 book on how blues communities balanced creativity and tradition, *Big Road Blues*.)

Folklore investigators who had been ignoring and even actively avoiding blues, almost all songs composed by individuals, songs designed for the popular music markets, songs sung in styles demanded by specific lyric content rather than by tradition, and songs made personal and novel by means of contemporary arrangements would, inevitably, be unfamiliar with the music of Jimmie Rodgers. He had, in every one of those respects, determinedly avoided being what they looked for as folky.

In the tantalizing sketch Carrie Rodgers offers us of her husband's honing of his skills and repertoire by studying piles of unidentified pre-1927 records, she quotes Jimmie being explicitly critical of the performing style of first-generation old-time country recording artists. And what were their performance sins? Failing to balance the vocal and the banjo or mandolin instrumental backup ("What's the use of having a good voice if it's all the time drowned out?"), crude understanding of vocal dynamics and clarity ("That guy's . . . singing is a pain in the neck. Too loud and wangy. 'Sides that, what's he singin' about, anyway? Can't make out a word he's sayin'."), and, most tellingly, lack of dramatic, emotional force ("*That* fella's got a good voice . . . You can make out what he's singin', too. Only thing is, no . . . tellin' if he's feelin' bad about it—or good.").

For an example of what Jimmie would have been referring to, we may not have to look further than a record he is very likely to have known, that first recording of the long-lived (often, simply *long*) old ballad he reworked into "Waiting for a Train"—"Wild and Reckless Hoboes" as recorded by George Reneau, "the Blind Musician of the Smoky Mountains," in 1925. Reneau's less than remarkable singing had been considered ineffectual enough by his record company, Vocalion, that for dozens of earlier sides, they had actually used a "ghost" vocalist as Reneau played harmonica and guitar—none other than Jimmie's friend and southern-raised pop competitor of a few years later, crooner Gene Austin. Austin had provided vocals at once more supple than most of that era and, with the intended audience in mind, twangier than either Reneau's or his usual own. Now George is on his own on this "Hoboes" single, and he sings not according to the sense of the song, but to the singsong rhythm of the meter—applied, as we have seen, to an uninvolving version of the story with a constantly wandering plotline and muddy point of view. Jimmie had effectively tightened and focused the material into a lasting popular song—one with all the more impact for being personalized in content and vocal style. It was emphatically *not* a simple variant of Reneau's record generated on the academics' model of song transmission, the so-called folk process.

In the months Jimmie spent in Asheville, North Carolina, immediately prior to his first recording session at Bristol, while looking for connections that would produce steady musical employment, he very briefly performed with a pair of old-time string musicians, the Helton Brothers. Osey and Ernest Helton had already made records of a few fast, rhythmically complicated old fiddle and banjo tunes, and they would become staples of the annual Asheville Mountain Dance and Folk Festival—where they would be recorded again in 1941 on one of Alan Lomax's first remote recording trips. Rodgers appeared on a few broadcasts with them, but their instrumental style was not designed for backing up singers; Ernest would just strum a guitar gently behind Jimmie, no doubt much as he does on his own rather whiny 1925 recording of the much-covered "Prisoner's Song."

Notoriously, the management of WWNC, the new Asheville radio station on which they had been performing, fired Jimmie, despite an outpouring of listener mail, preferring the restrained, "uptown" style (as Jimmie's biographer Nolan Porterfield put it) of Bascom Lamar Lunsford, the squirely lawyer and government official who collected and performed hundreds of old ballads and founded the local folk festival as an adjunct of the town's chamber-of-commerce-backed, touristy, tony, even intentionally precious Rhododendron Festival. (Lunsford claimed, incidentally, that he had sent his acquaintance Ralph Peer a note recommending that he hear Jimmie Rodgers, before Bristol. It is not impossible that this was true.)

As a performer, Lunsford had a way with a song, but it happened to be close to the direct opposite of Jimmie's—and for decades it was crucial in defining key aspects of that near oxymoron, professional folk singing. He was interested, above all, in "saving" the old songs as they had been made by the "folk" in supposedly gentler mountain times, and doing so for the sort of people who could "really" appreciate them now—namely, his educated, middle-class and upper-middle-class audience.

Lunsford was not suggesting, as some folklorists had before his time, that the purpose of collecting was to find new tunes to be raised into some great American symphony or opera for the upper crust. And, to his credit, he displayed little of the racism that marked another early promoter of old-time music, the industrialist Henry Ford, who believed—and he was not alone in this—that a supposedly "pure" Anglo-Celt musical culture needed to be defended against allegedly pernicious black and Tin Pan Alley Jewish influences.

Meeting Jimmie Rodgers

What Lunsford was very interested in was "getting it right," in saving "the real thing," as he understood it, whether that was some version of the ballad "Black Jack Davy" or the comic "Good Old Mountain Dew"—in the belief that without his intervention such authentic material would inevitably disappear and, very likely, soon. (In the folk revival world, song preservation is always a matter of dire emergency calling for immediate special ministrations.) Although Lunsford was a singer with more facility for this sort of approach than many who would follow with similar motivation, his documentary attitude colored almost every syllable he recorded. Jimmie Rodgers personalized and modified songs to make them more connected to himself and his downhome audience; he bent words and lines for dramatic impact and emotional credibility, made them something that came from him, whatever their original source. Lunsford's singing, by contrast, was dutifully careful; there was an obligation to stay out of the way, to document this artifact, this musical object, so that it could be heard "correctly."

Lunsford's mountain balladeer approach was soon followed by the troubadour Bradley Kincaid, who would perform on a succession of widely heard radio stations, including, eventually, WSM Nashville, on his own show and on the Grand Ole Opry. He could be charming; it could sound fine—and yet you would never, for a minute, suspect that the experience related by the music had much to do with the singer's life. You were not supposed to think it did. Not for nothing was one early folk favorite called "A Picture from Life's Other Side"; the title made a significant assumption about which side you, the listener, were on—establishing you as a spectator, not a participant.

There would be a strong strain of nostalgia in urban folk music, as there was in much of country music, for the preindustrial, preurbanized era, but with few exceptions, it would be nostalgia for somebody else's life—whether real or imagined. There would be a continuing emphasis on the otherworldliness of the old music, an attitude that has lasted to the present day, when a new generation has been persuaded to see Harry Smith's 1952 *Anthology of American Folk Music* set as the passageway to "the old, *weird* America."

Lunsford's "I Wish I Was a Mole in the Ground" would be one of the most referenced tracks on that set when it was rereleased on CD in 1997; Jimmie Rodgers, however, had never been included in the collection at all, except for a reference to his having recorded "Frankie and Johnny," noted, as usual, with his name misspelled. Harry Smith, as he explained to the folk revival performer and filmmaker John Cohen in a 1968 interview for *Sing Out!* magazine, had deliberately selected sides for the *Anthology* that would strike its audience as "odd" and "exotic." Jimmie Rodgers did not make that cut, failing to qualify as "mind-blowingly quaint and otherworldly"—a backhanded testament to the continuing power of his music to remain contemporary and accessible in 1952.

That date, as we can see more easily now, more than half a century later, was a pivotal moment in the history of popular culture, coming as it did so soon after the Depression, World War II, the advent of the Bomb, so much new technology, huge demographic shifts, and more; the relatively recent past could be presented successfully, if smugly, as very remote, strange, and innocent. Smith's *Anthology* was, in that sense, not so different from Hollywood's simultaneous reductive presentation of film styles and stars of Jimmie Rodgers' era, showing silent stars of just twenty-five years earlier as impossibly dated gargoyles in *Sunset Boulevard* and as cute, bad-voiced, superceded goofballs from days very much gone by in *Singin' in the Rain*.

It took Smith—who was, after all, essentially just selecting and reissuing some out-of-print commercial records of no more than the same quarter-century back—some fancy footwork to manage to avoid Jimmie Rodgers. For the introduction of the cowboy song, he would turn to Hollywood movie star Ken Maynard—an atypically mainstream choice. Vaudevillian Uncle Dave Macon, surely the least deadpan and timid of old-time singers, made the cut, as did the Carter Family, who though contemporary with Jimmie evidently seemed ancient enough. And, in keeping with Smith's admirably casual and unstated crossing of the folk color line—which, like the breaking down of artificial musical genre barriers, is one of his most important achievements—some of the very blues singers who knew and admired Jimmie's music, such as Mississippi John Hurt and Furry Lewis, were included as well. These performers were not from some other age, some repressed underground nation or lost "folk town" unavailable to Jimmie Rodgers. Yet there remained a serious enough reason why Rodgers did not fit in with the Harry Smith mission.

As both Greil Marcus in *Invisible Republic* and Robert Cantwell in his important examination of the folk revival, *When We Were Good*, explained in the late '90s, the *Anthology* was designed to show a progression from music that was flat, desexualized, and seemingly running on deadpan autopilot, to music on the brink of emotional modernity—yet all interrelated, and all standing in contrast to prevailing '50s culture. That was the *Anthology*'s job. It would have subverted this project to include Rodgers, whose work combined so many lively, unweird, pre–rock 'n' roll characteristics throughout the period the *Anthology* examined.

Harry, the merry prankster, was interested in making connections—but also in obfuscating the simple, which makes the *Anthology* particularly attractive to cultural interpreters; it screams for explication. Knowledgeable and tricky, Smith was quite willing to con Greenwich Village hipster provincials into believing scurrilous tales about Jimmie, no doubt for the sheer pleasure of it. One Smith protégé and experimental filmmaker, Henry Jones, related in print in 1996, without challenge or comment, how Harry had "taught" him that Jimmie Rodgers had been discovered by "Mr. Victor, of Victor Records" and utterly exploited—told he was performing to raise money for orphan kids' summer camps, so he would allow himself to keep on being carted around the country on "a special railway car with an oxygen tent . . . They'd wheel him onto the stage, . . . have him sing a couple of songs . . . put him back in the tent." Mr. Victor, Jones continues, finally brought this imaginary traveling contraption to a New York church where Jimmie recorded his last two sides—with the Carter Family on hand, incidentally—and then he died. Now that was a Rodgers story good enough for the weird new America—and for clueless sophisticates.

In a latter-day moment of poetic justice, when Smithsonian Folkways staged a live tribute to Harry Smith in 1999 following the much-heralded release of the *Anthology* on CD, in a show then itself issued on CD as *The Harry Smith Connection*, the African-American songster John Jackson was enlisted to perform "Frankie and Johnny"—and he proceeded to do it as he always had, not so weirdly, but in straightforward Jimmie Rodgers style, guitar runs and all.

Far from the enclaves of those who were playing such key roles in defining folk music but had no use for Jimmie Rodgers' music, however, there were others who did. In the places where the makers and consumers of unmediated downhome music lived and struggled to get by, Jimmie Rodgers music was out there, being played and adapted. And, inevitably, folklorists in the field, following in the footsteps of the Lomaxes, kept finding it.

For example, in 1940, while recording songs sung by Dust Bowl migrants in California, the researchers Charles Todd and Robert Sonkin encountered one Jack Bryant. Jack's song "Arizona," a self-penned tale of arriving West with money that "didn't last long," was an unreconstructed Rodgers-styled ballad with Jimmie-like guitar and echoes of "Desert Blues" and "Waiting for a Train" in the tune and lyrics. "I think the migrants were very much affected by Rodgers," notes Mike Seeger, who has performed Bryant's song for years, "because that was something they could do on their own—be a lone singer with a guitar."

Another lone singer working the same territory was Woody Guthrie, who was first introduced to Alan Lomax and Pete Seeger (like Mike, a son of the academic folklorist Charles Seeger, but older) at about the same time. Lomax and Seeger had tired of folklore's seclusion and fustiness and, for reasons roughly equally political and musical, had been looking for ways to encourage working, dispossessed, and middle-class left listeners alike to take

up and use folk music themselves, not just as an audience, but as partici-
pants. That they would run into Woody, an activist and maker of new songs,
an admirer of Jimmie Rodgers' friends Will Rogers and Goebel Reeves who
had already adopted some of the persona of each, seems predestined. Woody
was more in touch with music on hillbilly records and the country airwaves
than either of these new traveling buddies. Not long before, he had been on
those hillbilly radio shows in California and border radio out of Mexico himself. And he was, if by then with some significant and growing reservations,
a fan of Jimmie Rodgers' music — specifically of the blues and yodels.

Though it is not an incident recorded in standard Guthrie or Rodgers
biographies, Woody told his later musical partner and protégé Jack Elliott
that he had encountered Jimmie in person. "Oh yeah. I remember asking
Woody if he ever met Jimmie Rodgers, and he said yes he had — once,"
Elliott recalls. "It was, I believe, down in Corpus Christi, Texas. Woody was
down there working on a fishing boat. Woody was just hanging out, and a
train pulled into the station, and they set up a flat car, which made a natural
stage. It was somewhere at one end of the railroad station, on a little siding
perhaps, so trains could still come by. Jimmie Rodgers was performing right
there on the flat car — and Woody got to talk to him a little bit, but I do not
remember anything about what they talked *about*."

The timing and location make the reported meeting entirely possible;
the young Guthrie habitually took breaks from his working home in Pampa,
in the state's far north, to travel down into south Texas at around the same
time Jimmie was doing show after show there, many of them undocumented.
It was not just that Guthrie was a teenager eager to meet a southwest star;
this would have been at the very time, around 1931, when Woody — raised on
hymns, Maybelle Carter's guitar picking, old cowboy songs, and a handful
of Jimmie Rodgers records, and with some experience of performing in local
dance bands — was considering what he might do next, and how. Jimmie was
a model for working alone. Depending on the exact timing of the incident,
which is hard to pin down, Woody could also have been aware of the Will
Rogers–Jimmie Rodgers Red Cross tour of Texas, Oklahoma, and Arkansas
in early 1931 on behalf of drought-ridden Depression victims, though his
own involvement with and special concerns for such victims still lay ahead.

By 1940, however, when his recording career began, those interests were
crucial to him, and his hard-left political mindset would color his handling
of the Rodgers material he was about to introduce into the left-liberal folk
scene of the Popular Front era. Among his famous collection of *Dust Bowl
Ballads*, recorded in April–May 1940, would be "Dust Pneumonia Blues," a
song about environmentally caused lung disease that follows the basic pattern
of unadorned blue yodels like "T for Texas" and references "T.B. Blues."

Woody's verse, "There ought to be some yodeling in this song—but I can't yodel, for the rattlin' in my lungs" can still be taken as a teasing Jimmie salute, though it is interesting to contemplate how many folk followers of Woody, unaware of Jimmie, have wondered why there should have been yodeling.

His rendering of "California Blues" for Alan and Bess Lomax at the Library of Congress a few weeks later makes it clear that his doubts about Rodgers' role and the effect of his music were serious, that he had come to view Jimmie as not politically committed or aware enough—but that he would continue to use Rodgers songs for his own purposes, as Harry Smith would later ignore them for his.

Rendering is the precise word for this performance; in an introductory spoken rant, Guthrie describes how "several hundred thousand families" of Dust Bowl refugees had been misled by "pretty songs" like this "old Jimmie Rodgers piece" that sold them on how California was the golden place where "you can sleep out every night." As "evidence," he proceeds to sing a version of "California Blues" with Rodgers-like verses of his own devising, in part drawn from the first "Blue Yodel," twisted so that Jimmie appears to suggest that life in California is superior to various places—Oklahoma, Georgia, Texas. The agitprop gall reaches a crescendo as Woody tosses in, as an aside, "Notice how this song hits all of those southern states and welcomes them *all* to come to California . . . That was an old song that Jimmie Rodgers sang, and he put it on some kind of a phonograph record" (A black, flat one, perhaps?) "and I seen hundreds and hundreds of people gang up around an electric phonograph and listen to Jimmie Rodgers sing that song . . . and they'd punch each other in the elbow and say 'Boy; there's the place to go.'"

It was no accident that Woody Guthrie's music was much more often derived, if not gleefully stolen, from the southeastern, church-inflected tunes of the Carter Family, or even of the Monroe Brothers or Roy Acuff, than from Jimmie Rodgers' blues. These churchy tones apparently seemed more appropriate for delivering a message, and he was very much at home with them. There is something of the Carters' un-Jimmie-like ad copy "The Program is Morally Good" lurking behind the motto Woody famously inscribed on his guitar, "This Machine Kills Fascists." The music of Jimmie Rodgers (who had simply inscribed on his guitar "Thanks!") did not, finally, seem to supply Woody the right atmosphere for making moral points—any more than it seemed to serve Roy Acuff's different, but not so very different, needs. Ending a ballad like "Frankie" with "this story has no moral, this story has no end" is no more characteristic of Woody than writing a Will Rogers–like column of topical observations, as Woody did for the *Daily Worker*, would be of Jimmie.

The difference was not just in lyric content. As noted earlier, and as Woody's biographer Ed Cray points out, Woody's split from the California country act he had going with his more polished musical cousin Jack Guthrie was not so much over whether to be political or not, or about their real personal differences, but about different ideas as to the very sounds they should be pursuing. Jack, a hardcore Jimmie Rodgers fan, was leaning more and more toward the modern, orchestrated sounds of western swing, Gene Autry–style Hollywood cowboy, and early honky tonk; Woody, absolutely not. He now found such music slick and commercial, not "real country." Woody apparently made little or no distinction between the sounds of western swing and the professional harmonies of the Sons of the Pioneers, and he would certainly have been predisposed to skepticism about the latter, who were being advertised as the "aristocrats" of cowboy song, no less. Now that *was* "Hollywood."

In recording Jimmie Rodgers' songs solo and acoustic, Jack Guthrie was not particularly effective, but as has been noted, when he got a swinging, electrified band behind him, as he began to do in the mid-'40s, he was a star in the making and a very able Jimmie Rodgers interpreter to boot. There are tragic ironies in this conflict between Woody and Jack about Jimmie. Part of Rodgers' attraction to points West, especially California, had been the result of misleading advertising—about the health benefits of the place for tuberculosis victims. When Woody later began to succumb to the degenerative Huntington's disease, he too would head for the Golden West as a potential place of recovery—and similarly, to no avail. To complete the sad cycle, Jack Guthrie would die even younger, at age 33, in 1948—of tuberculosis.

Woody Guthrie and his friends' use of a short list of serviceable Rodgers blues did not end with the "California Blues" agitprop. One of the early, at first little-heard, even suppressed recordings of the Almanac Singers, a loosely-knit group that included Pete Seeger, Woody, and at various times Burl Ives, Josh White, Lead Belly, and future Weavers Lee Hays and Millard Lampell, was the antidraft "C for Conscription" sung by Seeger—an obvious rewrite or parody of "T or Texas" pressed into the service of the gang's unsustainable Stalinist opposition to "Roosevelt warmongering" during the period of the Hitler-Stalin pact. Such "songs for John Doe" marked a lamentable political low point for a group that would at other times bring much that was constructive onto the political scene.

Pete Seeger would maintain "T for Texas" and "T.B. Blues" as regular components of his shows for years to come and record them a number of times—most charmingly in live versions recorded at New York's Village Gate, joined by bluesmen Memphis Slim and Willie Dixon. (No one from the Almanac Singer/Alan Lomax scene, however, seemed to spot the Jimmie Rodgers allusions in Lead Belly's songs; they are never mentioned. John Lomax, as we have seen, had been aware of them—and did not like them.)

On the day of the 1949 event known as the Peekskill Riot, Seeger, Paul Robeson, and other assembled leftists gathered in support of Robeson and civil rights causes and were attacked by Ku Klux Klan and hard-line, thuggish anticommunist elements. It is a forgotten nugget of trivia—but also perhaps as unusual a place to find a Rodgers song as the Arctic Circle or Central Africa—that one of the songs Pete would manage to get out, as he would recall much later, would be "a country blues I learned from Woody, called 'T for Texas.'" That Seeger refers to the song as "a country blues" rather than "a Jimmie Rodgers song" is not an unusual way for it to be described in these folk circles. Since Jimmie Rodgers, given his very limited political involvement and sensibility, simply would not work as a promotable song-wielding political hero, as Woody or the Wobbly broadside writer Joe Hill could, it was just as well to assign songs Jimmie wrote or constructed to unnamable folk sources.

Despite his deep misgivings about Rodgers' mindset, however, Woody would go on to record a shambling but straightforward version of "Muleskinner Blues" with Cisco Houston during World War II, one without apparent reference to the new Bill Monroe version and including the uncensored "mule's behind" lyric from Jimmie's original recording. He had never given up the collection of Rodgers 78s he owned, either; his son Arlo would begin to learn those songs from records still around the house years later. Woody's "Muleskinner," meanwhile, would take on a life of its own as, it seems, the only version most people in the urban folk revival knew. Odetta, whose song choices may have influenced more folk-bag repertoires than the Smith *Anthology* initially did, recorded a languorous, dramatic "Muleskinner Blues" which, she recalled, just months before her death in December 2008, she had adapted from a version performed live, though never recorded, by nightclub pop and blues star Josh White. White had been a close associate of the Lomax/Seeger crew in the '40s and even appeared on *Songs for John Doe*. Odetta's version appears to be only the second recorded by a woman, after Rose Maddox—a performer who did know her Bill Monroe, and also knew Woody directly. Odetta's take was sensual and yodel-free and shared the pedigree of Woody's, but she realized once she learned the song that she had indeed heard the Bill Monroe version as well, since her stepfather was an avid Opry fan.

It was no doubt a consequence of Odetta's recording that there would be a dramatic, Broadway-influenced version by pop folk singer Harry Belafonte, with whip cracking yet, and there was one by a young, still "folk" José Feliciano in the '60s that followed that same line. Guthrie's cohort Cisco Houston would record his own flowing '50's version, and so did Jack Elliott.

But the apogee of the urban folk disconnection of "Blue Yodel No. 8" from its origins was at an Alan Lomax–staged show at Carnegie Hall in 1959, a prescient and impressive affair in many ways, which put Muddy Waters, country balladeer Jimmy Driftwood, and the first bluegrass band ever to play the august hall, Earl Taylor and His Stoney Mountain Boys, all on the same bill—a precursor of barrier-breaking Newport Folk Festivals to come. As introduced by Lomax onstage and restated in the notes to the extravagantly titled United Artists LP *Alan Lomax Presents Modern Folk Song Festival at Carnegie Hall*, "Muleskinner Blues" was credited to Woody Guthrie.

That 1959 show had marked Alan Lomax's return to the United States after nearly a decade in England, where he had gone to escape the political blacklisting era and to pursue his growing interest in British and European music. His BBC radio show would introduce and make legendary to U.K. audiences both Woody songs and Lead Belly records like "Rock Island Line," as well as other American folk and blues, providing song fodder for the sudden outbreak of the skiffle movement there. Alan himself had one of these loose skiffle bands, which all played energetic, if often instrumentally undemanding and limited blends of jug band music, folk jazz, and American folk and pop songs. This extension of Pete Seeger's "make your own music" philosophy inspired dozens of musicians and groups that would eventually transmogrify into the British pop bands, the Beatles included, that invaded the United States in the '60s. A staple in the skiffle repertoire was Woody's version of Jimmie's "Mule Skinner Blues."

The song would enter that musical realm through a 1956 recording by the jazz and skiffle bandleader Ken Colyer, and was further popularized by a live recording by the skiffle superstar Lonnie Donegan, which was eventually released on a widely heard LP. Donegan was a more gifted entertainer by far than many who jumped on the skiffle bandwagon—but skiffle, in anyone's hands, is all about the relentless rhythm and enthusiasm; the sense of the song virtually disappears, and it is approached as sheer novelty.

Both Donegan's and Colyer's skiffle music, including the vocals, emerged out of the British "trad" jazz scene, not folk. There were numerous bands around playing versions of '20s jazz, analogous to the Dixieland revival in the United States. The lines between jazz, blues, and folk music, all fairly clear back home even if they were now sometimes showing up in the same coffeehouses, were, at this point, still difficult for many British enthusiasts to distinguish. This was the world in which the visiting Big Bill Broonzy, formerly the leader of a fairly sophisticated blues outfit in Chicago, put on farmer overalls and played the role of a blues singer from the cotton fields. Then he was filmed singing "John Henry" with bopping British jazz fans sitting around snapping their fingers to it. Go figure.

This was not a bad situation for an adventurous American performer who showed up in 1954, having followed his new actress bride to England, who made little distinction between folk and country music, both of which he knew and cared about. As a protégé of Woody Guthrie and acquaintance of Lead Belly, Jack Elliott instantly found acceptance in the U.K.—and as a better guitar player than most anyone on that fledgling scene, he could teach everybody a thing or two. He had not been in the country a week when Ernest Borneman—an odd duck: a swing music historian and disc jockey, Reichian sexologist, and expatriate German communist—introduced him to the jazz bandleader Chris Barber, who invited Jack to join in playing a jazz show at the Royal Festival Hall. The show was already set to feature Lonnie Donegan's skiffle set. Jack would soon be touring with Donegan, whom he found to be much more engaging and knowing than most skiffle performers.

Jimmie Rodgers songs were among the resources Jack brought with him to England. He was born Elliott Adnopoz, the son of a Brooklyn surgeon, in 1931 and fell in love with the cowboy life after seeing Gene Autry's rodeo at Madison Square Garden. Unlike most other cowboy-struck Jewish kids from Flatbush, he followed up by running off to join rodeos at fourteen, to learn how to become a cowboy himself. Although he had learned, early on, some Jimmie Rodgers songs from Jimmie's records and some from a New Jersey–based, flat-picking radio cowboy, he had learned more, he recalls, from Rodgers-loving rodeo hands such as the bronco-riding champion Bill Linderman and bull rider Todd Fletcher.

In 1959, Jack made a record that effectively questioned and, in the long run, began to break down the folk-country divide for many listeners in the folk audience while serving as a more than creditable introduction to Jimmie's music. The LP bore a title that would previously have been impossible, *Rambling Jack Elliott Sings Songs by Woody Guthrie and Jimmie Rodgers*, and its selection of songs moved beyond the folk world's Rodgers short list to "Jimmie the Kid," "Mother, the Queen of My Heart," "Waitin' for a Train," and "In the Jailhouse Now." In an album of cowboy songs recorded the previous year, he had even included "Sadie Brown," his version of "My Little Lady," which had not been heard much since the '30s unless you knew the right cowboys. Musical expansiveness was basic to Jack's temperament.

"Yeah," he agrees, "I don't like to get locked into doing three dog songs and one train song. I try to get a little *variety* in my show." He rises to the challenge of that variety by bringing the singing of the songs back home to how it started, in the vital sense that the phrasing reflects his reading of the lyric content, as Jimmie's had. Jack declares, toys, shouts, and insinuates, as necessary, and even the yodels vary. The singing reflects knowledge and appreciation not just of Woody's music, but also of Jimmie's, and, at some points, of Bill Monroe's as well.

Equally notable is the musically adventurous arrangement approach of the Guthrie/Rodgers tribute album. Like only one other Rodgers-related record of that era by Hank Snow, the numbers are backed by a horn-centered jazz combo—even on numbers on which Rodgers had not used horns himself. In keeping with this approach, the jazzy violin on one tune becomes the sentimental violin on the next. "The jazz guys [on the session] from Scotland—Al Fairweather, Sandy Brown, and so on—had listened to the records of Jimmie Rodgers," Elliott remembers. "He'd had Satchmo on his records, and others, and we tried to copy *that* Jimmie Rodgers sound with our brass . . . When I met Merle Haggard later, when he was opening for Bob Dylan at a big theater in Oakland [in 2005], somebody had told him that I had done that tribute to Jimmie and Woody, and he wanted to know all about that, like what songs were on it."

Haggard's use of horns on Rodgers' songs later in the '60s would have serious impact on how Jimmie's music was understood among country and rock fans alike—just as Elliott's pairing of Jimmie and Woody and his knowing, exuberant take on both would set an example for folk rock and roots rock schools to come, and for at least some folk fans.

Bob Dylan would show up in New York in 1961, at age nineteen, sounding, many said, more like Jack filtering Woody than Jack did, and already singing not just the "official" short list of Rodgers songs, but "Southern Cannon-Ball," for instance, too. Dylan may well have picked that one up from Hank Snow's popular version; many of the songs he brought to Greenwich Village would reflect knowledge of country records, and Snow was a favorite. Dylan first learned Rodgers' songs, he notes in his memoir, from the record collection of a girlfriend's dad back in Minnesota. Arriving in New York, he initially showed a focused seriousness about accurately presenting old-time songs that was typical of a new wave of folk performers, reacting, in no small part, to the bland, often condescending, jokey frat-house versions of the music by hit-making pop-folk groups. Leaders of this contingent of the urban folk revival were the New Lost City Ramblers, including Mike Seeger and John Cohen, who would work to blend performing and scholarship. Also part of this new wing was musician, folklorist, and impresario Ralph Rinzler. Between them, they would reintroduce old-time stringband music into popular (and unpopular) culture, make bluegrass accessible to the folk scene at a time when rock's negative impact on country meant that bluegrass needed a new outlet, and, through organizational efforts like New York's Friends of Old Time Music, revive the working careers of a good many forgotten roots musicians, from Dock Boggs to Mississippi John Hurt.

Yet the only performer to be seen bringing Jimmie Rodgers songs into this revival of pre-1940 country and blues was Bill Monroe. His "Brakeman's Blues," for instance, is the only Rodgers song preserved on the Smithsonian's *Friends of Old Time Music* box set. There was an element of folk purism in this new wave of revivalism, which, in the case of the New Lost City Ramblers, for instance, was focused on resurrecting the old styles of Appalachian string-band playing, with the original instrumentation: Carter Family songs, old fiddle tunes, raucous sounds like Charlie Poole's, lone blues from Appalachian porches—material the band helped define as old-time music, creating a genre that has been active ever since. And that did not include Jimmie Rodgers.

"Jimmie's music was just a little too pop for a lot of people," Mike Seeger recalls. "We didn't do songs from what we perceived were not in the older traditions we were concentrating on. I thought it was more important to do something with the autoharp—which Jimmie Rodgers never did. John thought it was important to play the five-string banjo, and that was all getting further away from popular music, even of the singer-songwriter variety. Because singing a song like that takes a certain kind of presentation. Jimmie's songs were not singable by more than one person, usually; there's a hell of a dynamic range of expression—and there's got to be, to get the subtleties of his singing. So it's a solo kind of thing, I think . . . I considered that something for Jack Elliott to do.

"It also didn't fit, entirely, *philosophically* . . . The Carter Family were revivalist, in a way, with a slightly different approach to vocals. Their style was something they created out of older styles . . . with the tear between A. P.'s way-back sounds, and Maybelle's guitar pulling them forward. But with Jimmie, he was reaching towards being a creator, trying to get something that would grab people's attention—and *that's* pop. Jimmie was reaching for the big ring, by recording with a jazz band, by having all those corny, funny lyrics. But he did it; he happened to be the one who did it, in a brilliant way that *got* people."

Seeger, who has always followed developments in country music and bluegrass for his own pleasure, might play "T for Texas" or "No Hard Times" at home, alone, on the porch—but never in public, partly because he is not the sort of singer he sees as right for the songs. There is something slightly ironic about that since Carrie Rodgers reported that once Jimmie had turned to the guitar and the flexible style of flat-picking he applied to it, he never played mandolin or banjo in public any more. But he would for pleasure, in the old vaudeville styles he knew—at home, on their porch. All performers have their comfort zones—onstage and off.

It was also an issue that Jimmie Rodgers music displays plenty of sentimental attachment to old pals, the old home, Mississippi, and the sunny

South in general—but very little nostalgia for the preindustrial, premodern, rural life that was a key romantic or romanticized attraction for folk revivalists.

"His general approach to the music was one headed towards the city," Mike Seeger agrees. "Jimmie is a country boy trying to get citified." Seeger suggests that Cousin Emmy, a vaudevillian entertainer the Ramblers did foster in the revival, was, by contrast "a country girl trying to stay country and relate to country people." It might just as easily be argued, however, perhaps better argued, that Jimmie Rodgers was not walking away from country people in the least, but exploring the new ways in which music was engaging them in a changing world and seeing just how far that exploration could go.

The attitude common in the folk revival that country music, pop, and vaudeville, past a certain point of urbanization and polish, was outside of the folk revival's self-definition was likely to limit Rodgers' influence even where it was encountered. So in much of the urban folk revival, especially when it did not involve totally committed, talented, knowledgeable artists prepared to take a tough, imaginative leap (artists like a Mike Seeger), the performers simply sounded like city people trying to get *countrified*—and there is not going to be much Jimmie in that. As older folk artists were located and brought back to performing (one of the revival's very real and inestimable contributions), there would be no great interest in having them perform Rodgers-type music.

Dock Boggs, a major find of the revival by any measure, had been on that little Lonesome Ace label, the one that had gleefully promised "Without a Yodel." But Scott Boatwright, a smooth-singing guitarist from one of his bands who was still around in the '60s, had wanted, as Boggs' friend and promoter Mike Seeger would recall, to do Rodgers' songs back then, and again during the revival. He would be discouraged from doing so, simply to avoid falling into the Rodgers camp—sparse as that was in folk music.

North Carolina's Frank Proffitt, celebrated as the man who introduced to the revivalists the "Tom Dula" song that would be adopted by the Kingston Trio, also sang Rodgers songs. And when the hoots and hollers of competitive hollering competitions in North Carolina began to be noticed and collected, plenty of the contestants were found to be using Jimmie-like yodels in their routines. But as late as the mid-'70s, when sets of hollers were recorded for the Rounder Records LP *Hollerin'*, the producers still made known in the liner notes their deliberate avoidance of examples of the Rodgers influence, though one got in anyhow: Dewey Jackson's Rodgers-inflected, yodeling holler, "Cows in the Corn."

　　　　　　　　　　　　　　　　　　　　　　　　Meeting Jimmie Rodgers

Obray Ramsey, a North Carolinian who record buyers were told had been singing "all of his life" (no doubt true) but who had only started playing banjo and singing in public at Bascom Lamar Lunsford's Asheville folk festivals six years before his "discovery" at one of them, produced a 1964 album of Rodgers's songs he had long known, *Obray Ramsey Sings Jimmie Rodgers Favorites*. The album's notes, by the Jimmie-friendly John Greenway, notes that for many the banjo "will seem a rather odd instrument for songs of Jimmie Rodgers," but he praises Ramsey's constantly plucked, old-time five-string banjo style — which today seems rather plodding and rudimentary and seems to drag down every song on that now-rare Prestige International LP. Ramsey's diction is immaculate, his phrasing occasionally reminiscent of Hank Snow's, but when he tries something light and jaunty like "My Little Old Home Down in New Orleans," he is absolutely defeated. Ramsey is recalled today, if at all, for the cover of his "Cold Rain and Snow" by the Grateful Dead and for his bizarre appearance in the "psychedelic western" movie *Zachariah*.

Country artists who appeared at the centrally important Newport Folk Festivals and knew Rodgers songs, such as Johnny Cash, would not bring them up at that venue, even informally. One of the few cases anyone seems to recall of impromptu Jimmie-based jamming at Newport involved two "rediscovered" blues singers, Skip James and Mississippi John Hurt, in a backstage duet on "Waiting for a Train" recalled by David Evans as excruciating. ("One tried to play in waltz time and the other in 4/4.") The time clash is itself instructive — since the old "folk" setting of the George Reneau sort of "Wild and Reckless Hoboes" was in a cumbersome waltz time, whereas Jimmie's timeless, jazz-inflected "Waiting" moved toward a syncopated 4/4.

Two of the great Jimmie Rodgers interpreters of all time sang together onstage at Newport on several occasions, but Jimmie's music would not be on the program. Both were managed by revivalist Ralph Rinzler at the time: one was Bill Monroe and the other Doc Watson, who would bring utterly fresh, varied interpretations to Rodgers songs, opening up whole new possibilities for them within the folk realm — though most of that would have to wait until the '70s.

"That was kind of *hard*," Watson recalls. "The late Ralph Rinzler, the wonderful guy who helped me get started, said, 'Doc, play the old-time things till you get your foot in the door, and then you can expand.' He was a musicologist, and he knew what he was talking about! Most of the people didn't know *anything* about Jimmie Rodgers' music."

Doc would, rather typically, first be presented to the folk revival as the backwoods sidekick of the singer Clarence Ashley, two of whose recordings had been selected for the Smith *Anthology*, and as having learned all of the ancient Appalachian tunes from his own family. We now know better: Doc had been playing electric rockabilly music (including, he recalls, some electrified Rodgers songs) in local North Carolina bars when the folk opportunity presented itself, had been musically trained, and was even familiar with classical music. He had been handed the Harry Smith *Anthology* by Rinzler to make sure he knew the right songs for the market he was entering.

Doc has also described for many interviewers over the years how he had first switched to his characteristic, smooth as holy water and hot as holy smoke flat-picking style from Maybelle Carter–like thumb leads after realizing that Jimmie Rodgers had to have been using a flat pick on his records.

"My interest in Jimmie Rodgers started, believe it or not, when Dad used to bring the recordings home, even before I ever went to school. That goes way back there," he recalls fondly. "Dad and the boys worked at the saw mill, and got a little 'graphaphone,' we called it, a little wind-up job that sat on a table, and when Dad started it, I thought we had the king's treasure in the house. I think I was about six when they got that thing [around 1929], and I tell you, I was absolutely spellbound. I would be a-settin' close so I could hear it all. Then, when the Jimmie Rodgers recordings started to come into the home, I found something that I was *welded* to."

Tellingly, for Doc Watson, it is not the instrumental side alone that grabbed him, or the vocal, but the dynamic between the two and the result: "Jimmie Rodgers has always been a favorite; I liked the kind of songs he did. To me, they were adventure, and hobo trips, and all that kind of thing—besides the good sound, and those lyrics, the way they were put together. It was a different sound, totally different from all the other music . . . Listening to the records, I learned; by the time I was eleven or twelve, I could yodel in D! I'd go out and yodel so big you could hear it echo . . . I tried to stay pretty close to what Jimmie did with it. My yodel crossover from regular to falsetto wasn't quite as clean as Jimmie's; that's a gift given a person."

In another example of poetic justice, at the end of the '60s, when Doc had much more than a foot in the folk door, he got another offer of LPs to check out. Having heard of his interest in and special way with a few Rodgers songs, Peer International (most likely their energetic promoter Roy Horton specifically), sent Doc a full set of the Jimmie Rodgers reissue LPs, to make sure he had access to every song. He has recorded some eighteen of them to date—everything from a driving, memorable "Blue Yodel No. 3" with his son Merle adding some terrific slide guitar, to an "Any Old Time" that includes clarinets.

Doc never has a problem finding musical space for a smooth hand-off from his varied, celebrated guitar runs to his unmistakable, storytelling vocals. This is Jimmie Rodgers' music brought to a new "playing on the porch" intimacy never realized as successfully before. Watson had found the *ease* in the music—which set the stage for other musicians who would work in this new vein, such as Jefferson Airplane's Jorma Kaukonen or the Memphis soul and acoustic blues singer Sid Selvidge.

But then the variety in Doc's acoustic approach is as notable as the dexterity and ease. "I had a hard time convincing them that I wasn't bound in one corner," he says with a laugh. "They found out there's more to music than one little niche—and more to so-called folk music than one little niche!"

Doc had to wait until the '70s and '80s to unleash most of his Rodgers music—until a time when Bob Dylan had utterly transformed the place and the use of traditional music in pop and virtually demolished the urban folk scene in its original form. As onlookers from Mike Seeger to Merle Haggard have observed, Dylan's move, more than anyone's on the scene at the time, was in a Jimmie Rodgers direction. He proceeded to jump from genre to genre with each succeeding LP, producing a variety of public images to match—tramp blues kid, voice of a generation, high-speed rock star, country boy back home, singer-songwriter, old vaudevillian, even moving into gospel, where Jimmie himself barely ventured.

In the urban folk world, a performer was expected to have a single act and image and to stick with it, if they wanted to go on being accepted as folk. That's what Pete Seeger or Woody Guthrie had each had, whether it was acknowledged as such or not. No wonder, then, that Guthrie's trunkfuls of unpublished songs of rather different, pop-oriented sorts would have to wait until the '90s for public exposure by the English singer-songwriter Billy Bragg and the rock band Wilco. It was not Bob Dylan's much-dramatized and overanalyzed turning up the volume at Newport in 1965 that opened the door for more Jimmie Rodgers–friendly and–influenced singer-songwriters, roots rock, and pop music since. It was that Dylan had gone eclectic.

In that new environment, other performers were able to solve the folk-versus-country conundrum when they came to Rodgers' music. In the '90s, John Lilly, a veteran of fiddle-driven stringbands very much influenced by old-time music, regularly sang Jimmie Rodgers songs for old-time and folk audiences. In the era of Americana, the fuzzily defined but often lively musical idiom straddling country and folk, that is not a problem. Lilly had earlier teamed with the innovative East Tennessee longbow fiddler Ralph Blizzard, who had played in the '30s, stopped, then formed a latter-day New Southern Ramblers that could play Rodgers songs like "No Hard Times" in a perfectly engaging and workable fiddle band setting. Maybe nobody told them it was supposed to be difficult.

And then there was the unassuming, winning Bud Reed, from the Maryland-Pennsylvania border area, a country-friendly region rarely acknowledged as such. Husband of Ola Belle Reed, who long performed and wrote songs in a style variously described and marketed as folk, country, or bluegrass, he had watched her perform with her brother Alex Campbell all through the '50s at the celebrated music parks they had founded or run, New River Ranch and Sunset Park, but was too shy and nervous onstage to perform himself.

A lover of Jimmie Rodgers music since childhood, Bud watched, literally, without comment or question as many of the era's great country acts—Bill Monroe, Lefty Frizzell, Hank Snow, Ernest Tubb, Johnny Cash, Grandpa Jones, the Louvin Brothers—appeared on stages in front of him and performed Jimmie Rodgers songs in contemporary ways for that Mason-Dixon border crowd, an audience that included both folk music fans and hardcore country music followers. (In commercial country music, as Doc Watson noted, though most people in the folk world were unaware of it, a major Jimmie Rodgers revival had been building since the late '40s.)

After decades of this reluctance, pushed by Ola Belle, Bud Reed started to join her onstage at folk venues to perform short, modest, utterly charming Jimmie Rodgers interpretations—uninfluenced, it seems, even by Doc Watson, but rather in folk versions adapted from Jimmie's records for his own use. These would finally make it out to the wider world—or the small part of it that noticed—on his 1982 Folkways LP *Way Out on the Mountain: Jimmie Rogers' Songs by Bud Reed*. It was a great folk-style album of Jimmie Rodgers music. And yes, the name is misspelled on the cover.

Select Soundtrack

Jimmie Rodgers' Own Folk-Ballad-Style Repertoire

"Frankie and Johnny," "Those Gambler's Blues" (variant of "St. James Infirmary"), "Waiting for a Train" (variant of "10,000 Miles Away from Home"), "Away Out on a Mountain" (composed by Kelly Harrell), "The Mystery of Number Five" (composed by Rodgers), "Hobo Bill's Last Ride" (lyric by Waldo O'Neal), "Moonlight and Skies" ("Little Mo-Hee"/"On Top of Old Smoky" adaptation by Rodgers and Raymond Hall), "Ben Dewberry's Final Run" and "A Drunkard's Child" (both composed by Andrew Jenkins), "Hobo's Meditation" (lyric by

Meeting Jimmie Rodgers

Floyd Henderson), "I'm Free from the Chain Gang Now" (composed by Lou Herscher and Saul Klein).

- **George Reneau:** "Wild and Reckless Hoboes" (Vocalion, 1924).
- **Helton Brothers:** "Downfall of Paris" and "Leather Breeches" are available on the www.juneberry78s.com 78s Web site; Ernest Helton's "The Prisoner's Song" (1925) on the Web site of the American Folklife Center (Gordon Collection) at the Library of Congress, www.loc.gov/folklife; and, Osey Helton's "Green River" (believed to be from 1924) on *The Stuff That Dreams Are Made Of* (Yazoo).
- **Jack Bryant:** "Arizona" can be heard online at the Library of Congress, as part of "Voices from the Dust Bowl: The Charles L. Todd and Robert Sonkin Migrant Worker Collection, 1940–1941," http://memory.loc.gov/ammem/afctshtml/tshome.html.
- **Woody Guthrie:** "Muleskinner Blues" (with Cisco Houston) is on *Asch Recordings, Vol. 2: Muleskinner Blues* (1997); "Dust Pneumonia Blues" is on *Dust Bowl Ballads* (Buddha, 2000) and, in an alternative version, on the *Library of Congress Recording* (Rounder, 1992); the latter also includes "California Blues" and the related commentary by Woody.
- **Jack Guthrie:** *Jack Guthrie: Milk Cow Blues* (Bear Family, 2001) contains ten Jimmie Rodgers songs by Jack; *Jack Guthrie: Oklahoma Hills* (Bear Family, 1994), has his hits and a couple more Rodgers numbers.
- **Pete Seeger, with the Almanac Singers:** "C for Conscription" is readily available on various Almanac Singers or Woody Guthrie-Pete Seeger compilations and on the elaborate 1996 Bear Family box set *Songs for Political Action*, which also includes a very early Seeger take on "T for Texas." His version of "T.B. Blues" with Memphis Slim and Willie Dixon is on Folkways' *Pete Seeger at the Village Gate, Volume 2* (1962), and "T for Texas" is on *Memphis Slim and Willie Dixon at the Village Gate with Pete Seeger* (2007), both Folkways; the tracks are available online from Smithsonian Global Sound and elsewhere.
- **Jack Elliott:** *Rambling Jack Elliott Sing Songs by Woody Guthrie and Jimmie Rodgers* and his cowboy songs from the LP *Ramblin'*

Jack Elliott in London are combined on *Ramblin' Jack Elliott Sings Woody Guthrie and Jimmie Rodgers and Cowboy Songs* (Monitor, 1995), with seven Rodgers tracks; Elliott's version of "Mule Skinner Blues" is on *Country Style* (Fantasy, 1999).

Folk Revival Artifacts

- **Odetta:** "Muleskinner Blues" (1956) is available on *Odetta Sings Ballads and Blues* (Tradition, 1996). She can be seen singing the song on a 1960 Tennessee Ernie Ford Show, available on the DVD *The Ford Show, Volume Four,* via the ErnieFord.com Web site.

- **Cisco Houston:** "Hobo Bill" is on *The Folkways Years* (Smithsonian Folkways, 1994) and "Mule Skinner Blues" is on *Sings Songs of the Open Road* (Folkways, 1960).

- **Stoney Mountain Boys:** "Mule Skinner Blues" is on *Alan Lomax Presents Modern Folk Song Festival at Carnegie Hall* (United Artists LP, 1959).

- **Harry Belafonte:** "Muleskinner," credited as "traditional," is on *Midnight Special* (RCA Victor LP, 1962).

- **José Feliciano:** "Mule Skinner Blues" is available on a variety of his hits packages.

- **Bill Monroe:** "Brakeman's Blues" live, New York, 1963, is on the Smithsonian's *Friends of Old Time Music* box set (Smithsonian Folkways, 2006).

- **Frank Proffitt:** "Mule Skinner Blues" is on *Nothing Seems Better to Me* (Appleseed, 2000).

- **Dewey Jackson:** "Cows in the Corn" is on *Hollerin'* (Rounder, 1995).

- **Obray Ramsey:** *Obray Ramsey Sings Jimmie Rodgers Favorites* (Prestige International LP, 1964).

- **Skiffle:** The Ken Colyer Skiffle Group's "Muleskinner Blues" is available on *Ken Colyer 1956* (Lake, 2007) and the compilation *Great British Skiffle* (Smith and Co., 2007); Lonnie Donegan's influential live version is on *Donegan on Stage: Expanded Edition* (Castle, 2006).

- **Doc Watson's Jimmie Rodgers:** There is no compilation of Doc Watson's eighteen recordings of Jimmie Rodgers songs. Recommended are "Any Old Time," "Hobo Bill," and "California Blues," with Merle Watson on slide, on *Watson Country* (Flying Fish, 1996); "Anniversary Blue Yodel (Blue Yodel No. 7)" and "Never No More Blues" on *Trouble in Mind: The Doc Watson Country Blues Collection* (Sugar Hill, 2003); and "Daybreak Blues (Blue Yodel No. 3)" and "T for Texas" ("Blue Yodel") on *Songs From Home* (Capitol, 2002). Others of note, easily found, include "In the Jailhouse Now," "Miss the Mississippi and You," "My Blue-Eyed Jane," and "My Rough and Rowdy Ways." Doc can be seen performing "Miss the Mississippi and You" with Merle on slide on the DVD *Doc and Merle Watson in Concert* and "Blue Yodel No. 12" on *Doc Watson, Rare Performances 1982–1993* (both on Vestapol); the latter also includes Doc's performances of "Sleep Baby Sleep," "Dear Old Sunny South by the Sea," and "In the Jailhouse Now"; "Peach Pickin' Time Down in Georgia" is on the same label's *Rare Performances, Volume 1*.

- **Bob Dylan:** His versions of Rodgers songs from early '60s folk performances are among those that have circulated for years in various bootleg audio formats. "Muleskinner Blues," which he was singing as early as 1960, is on a tape made at Montreal's Finjan Club, 1962; "Southern Cannonball" shows up on an informal 1961 tape recorded in East Orange, New Jersey, where the ailing Woody Guthrie was spending weekends at the time. The widely heard and bootlegged 1969 Nashville sessions with Johnny Cash and Carl Perkins include Dylan and Cash playing with Rodgers blue yodel verses, at length. A 1992 Dylan performance of "Miss the Mississippi and You" was released on 2008's *Tell-Tale Signs* anthology CD (Columbia). Also see chapter 13.

- **Bud Reed:** His 1982 Folkways LP *Way Out on the Mountain: Jimmie Rogers* [sic] *Songs by Bud Reed* is currently available from the Smithsonian Folkways Web site.

- **John Lilly and Ralph Blizzard:** Ralph's "No Hard Times" is on Ralph Blizzard and the New Southern Ramblers' *Blizard*

Train (Appalshop); "Peach Pickin' Time Down in Georgia" is on their duo album *Blue Highway*; "No Hard Times" is revisited on Lilly's *Last Chance to Dance* CD and a "Whippin' That Old T.B.," much in the style of Hank Williams' "Ramblin' Man," on *Haunted Honky Tonk* (johnlillymusic.com).

eleven

The Father of Country Music

In April 1953, the pulp magazine *Country Song Roundup*, within the regular mix of song lyrics and star profiles it had been providing for six years, featured a salute to the man the editors called the "Father of Hillbilly Music." The slight but telling clash between the names used for the music in the magazine's title and the story's headline reflected an ongoing debate over just what to call this stuff that its many readers were listening to and learning to sing. But there was apparently no need to justify the choice of the man the story so casually dubbed the music's "father." That was Vernon Dalhart.

Hadn't Dalhart's two-sided 1924 hit "Wreck of the Old 97" backed with "The Prisoner's Song" (most often recalled as "If I Had the Wings of an Angel") sold more than a million copies and brought rural southern music new attention, including the competitive, money-making sort that had sent Victor Records and Ralph Peer out looking for new acts in that vein in the first place? Hadn't Dalhart recorded train songs, outlaw songs, jailbird songs, and even, let it be recalled, "There's a New Star in Heaven Tonight," a title that sets you trying to recall which beloved country singer had died early enough to be the object of this instant memorializing? (The star was actually Rudolph Valentino.)

The claim of Dalhart's fatherhood would not stick. His sales figures may have been attractive, much of his material predictive, but even if he had kept the provocative part of his true and startling American-badass birth name, (Marion) Try Slaughter, he was not a figure country singers or fans were

1957: The country music he fathered: national package tour stops in Portland, Oregon, packed with important and varied Rodgers interpreters, including (from left) Hank Thompson, Grandpa Jones (behind), the Everly Brothers, Hank Snow, and Merle Travis.

going to want to emulate, to have linked so tightly to what they loved, and, more importantly, to who they were.

He was a Texan, but not exactly downhome. He was the son of a substantial rancher, had enrolled in a conservatory, performed in Puccini operas and Gilbert and Sullivan operettas, and sounded, for the most part, as if he was visiting hillbilly territory from another country—some special citadel for syllables where enunciation was veddy, veddy clean. However many train whistles or human whistles were put on Dalhart's records, or fictional mountain homes, he sang with an upper-crusty old school squire's drawl left over from the days of cylinder recordings and minstrel tunes. Everything about the way the man spoke, dressed, and carried himself left the impression that he was more at home at Carnegie Hall than in a beer hall; the records reeked of the overly respectable gone slumming.

It should be stipulated, at this point, that "fatherhood" of any sort of music is, at best, a dubious notion; single progenitors of sounds that endure are rare—probably unicorn rare. The newgrass mandolin and fiddle player Sam Bush probably struck the right tone for the subject at a recent performance, referring in passing to Charlie Monroe as "the uncle of bluegrass." And there was that title Rodgers fans came up with for Carrie Rodgers, "the First Lady of Country Music," which suggests that her late husband should have been the President of Country. (Roy Acuff could still have claimed to be King.) Perhaps the closest anyone can get to fathering a commercial genre is to define an existing audience with identifiable tastes, then figure out how to keep marketing new music to it that is acceptable—which would make Ralph Peer as reasonable a choice as anybody for "Father of Country Music" (and of other genres, too).

Reason, however, has very little to do with what makes a "father" appellation feel right, or last. As sons, daughters, orphans, and knowing commentators from William Shakespeare to Ernest Tubb have pointed out, recognizing fatherhood requires two-way acceptance of credible *emotional* ties. In popular music, an audience will only share that sense of intimacy and connection with a very public, recognizable figure—and only a certain sort of public figure at that.

Vernon Dalhart had not done the truly crucial thing for seeming worthy of the Father of Country title. He had not committed himself in a defining way to serving the basic, core audience for that music—first, and above all other audiences. He was not convincingly more than a tourist in downhome music, and there was little about his lifestyle, his image, or where he chose to spend his time that suggested that he identified with the music's steadfast fans himself. He certainly had brought the general record-buying public plenty of rural songs, although even by 1953 few country fans could connect any of them to him, besides the two sides of his celebrated 1924 single. He had introduced "The Dying Girl's Message" and "The Mississippi Flood" to the middle-class public just as he had earlier brought them songs out of the Ziegfeld Follies, and "When Alexander Takes His Ragtime Band to France," and "(Who Put the Overalls in) Mrs. Murphy's Chowder." This was the issue Ralph Peer was raising when, in 1955, he wrote in the trade paper *Variety* that "Vernon Dalhart was . . . never a hillbilly artist. Dalhart had the peculiar ability to adapt hillbilly music to suit the tastes of the *non*-hillbilly population . . . a professional substitute for a real hillbilly."

As events would play out, from just a few weeks after that certitude-filled *Country Song Roundup* article about Vernon Dalhart appeared, almost no one would be raising his name as country's father again. The emotional connection and identification Jimmie Rodgers had had and kept with his audience, the dedicated advocates he had left behind who had felt that he changed their music and their lives, his key role as the model for what a roots music pop hero was and could be all came into play. In truth, however, the alternative, improved paternity case so taken for granted now was slow to take shape.

It seems clearer in retrospect that commercial country music's makers needed to feel secure about the staying power of their rural-come-to-town sounds before they could pause, even momentarily, to indulge in reflection, self-recognition, and knowing self-promotion. They needed time for a deeper understanding of their audience and its ongoing aspirations. It took a wiser child to know its own father.

As Diane Pecknold has demonstrated persuasively in *The Selling Sound*, it was not until the period from the 1950s into the early '60s that organized commercial country music came to emphasize and exploit the links between its history and the identity of its ongoing audience, the point being to underscore the respectability and ongoing commercial power of both. Jimmie Rodgers fit in with that emerging drive perfectly; it is not coincidental that it is since 1953 precisely that Jimmie Rodgers has most often been identified as "the father of country music." The fact was, however, that from the onset of World War II until as late as 1947, the year *Country Song Roundup* began publication, Jimmie Rodgers' records had not even been in print in the United States; that "hillbilly echo" had gotten very dim indeed.

With popular music usually ready, by design, to hurry right on to the next potential trend, there is a cycle of forgetting virtually built into it, a process that reverses the buildup that led to fame in the first place. Once that slide sets in, it virtually always takes time and tenacious advocacy for an artist or sound to grab attention again—if they ever do. For Jimmie Rodgers, the period of "late, great" memorial records and nostalgia for his day had inevitably ended, and

Meeting Jimmie Rodgers

a new generation had grown up who either barely knew or entirely missed his stardom; they were likely to find the sounds associated with him old hat. The postwar electrified honky tonk of Ernest Tubb; the charging bluegrass of Bill Monroe (though it was not yet called that); the somewhat fading love for the western swing of Bob Wills and Tommy Duncan (as for all big band music); the craze for hot country boogie exemplified in the records of the Delmore Brothers, Merle Travis, and many others; even a latter-day train song in the manner of Roy Acuff—none of these late echoes led most listeners back to Jimmie Rodgers himself any more. New hits kept on coming on a larger and larger scale, and through the war years and the years just after, those were only rarely updated versions of Jimmie Rodgers material.

Monroe or Wills, or some of their followers, might still pull out an occasional Rodgers number in the late '40s. In 1949, for instance, Tommy Duncan and his combo had that hit with their new version of "Gamblin' Polka Dot Blues." But there was no commercial advantage in advertising the fact that someone was reviving a Rodgers song.

Texas honky tonker Al Dexter's wartime multimillion-selling novelty "Pistol Packin' Mama," with its dancing-friendly, if rather square, accordion and muted trumpet solos, sounded nothing like a 1930 Rodgers record. Yet that song of a beer hall altercation, taken to a still broader audience by Bing Crosby, certainly derived some of its inspiration and alliteration from Jimmie's old "Pistol Packin' Papa." As it happens, the steel player on the Dexter disc was Frankie Marvin, an early maker of Jimmie Rodgers cover records, but that was a backward-looking Depression connection no one was interested in pointing out now.

After the war (to cram several thesis-loads of sociological understatement into a short declarative sentence), things were different—and in ways potentially hospitable to Jimmie Rodgers' music. Labor and royalty issues stemming from the use of jukeboxes instead of live acts in bars and deejays rather than live performances on the radio had led to prolonged disputes between the musicians' union and the radio and record industries, during which old public domain folk ballads (or new songs that passed for them) found a renewed place on the pop charts.

The upheavals of the war and the Depression done with, there was now rising affection for the very safely past Charleston era of the '20s, as in Jimmie Rodgers' day there had been a craze for the Gay Nineties, and later there would be for the rocking '50s—that last, unthreatening, nostalgia-inducing hot time in the old town tonight. The '20s were looking good. There would be success in the '50s and early '60s for films like *The Jolson Story*, TV series like *The Untouchables* and *The Roaring Twenties*, a Hemingway and Fitzgerald fad among the literati. Pop songs of the older era—"My Blue Heaven,"

"Love Letters in the Sand," "Blueberry Hill"—were hits all over again, and a less sophisticated, less edgy version of '20s jazz was being marketed successfully as Dixieland.

The mixing of northern and southern boys in army units and the exposure of many from around the United States to country music played near southern army and marine bases prepared the way for a substantial, ten-year flowering of country music, as well as the rock 'n' roll ascendancy that would compete with it and, for a time, damage it. Hit crossover versions of Hank Williams' songs by Jo Stafford and Tony Bennett were an early sign of the changing situation.

Indeed, one specific circumstance that surely contributed to the timing of Jimmie Rodgers' newfound recognition in 1953 was the death, just as that year began, of Hank Williams—another young man from the deep southeast who wore cowboy clothes Jimmie-style, another charismatic balding man with a dashing hat, another who sang the blues with gusto, reintroduced a meaningful yodel, took the music to a broader audience in a short time, lived fast and hard, died young (he was only twenty-nine), and became a legend.

Hank's relationship to Jimmie Rodgers seems obvious on the face of it. In fact, what linked them was not so much any direct, acknowledged musical influence, but an inheritance of style, sensibility, and approach, of how you would carry yourself as a roots music star along the path to fame that Jimmie had first defined and illuminated. And that was no small thing.

Williams' close connection to his core audience; his jauntiness, chastened by a degree of public suffering (some physical, some self-inflicted); his working relationship with Fred Rose, which in some ways paralleled Jimmie's with Ralph Peer's—these were all real similarities. Williams would soon have his own imitating disciples and, in time, apostles as outspoken and hardworking as Jimmie's. It seems in retrospect that being understood as a performer who wrote his own songs was so much a part of Hank's image and legend that Jimmie Rodgers' own role as a songwriter was almost certainly emphasized more, and even exaggerated, by sheer image association.

In truth, as Colin Escott explains in his definitive Williams biography, Hank had not even had much access to Rodgers records or a radio when growing up, and despite repeated assumptions in less careful writings about Williams that suggest he was a Rodgers disciple, any influence on his music clearly came at second hand, through his appreciation of the music of intermediaries such as Ernest Tubb and Rex Griffin. Hank is not known ever to have performed a Rodgers song publicly, and Don Helms, the steel player in Hank's Drifting Cowboys, confirmed that Hank was not particularly a Jimmie Rodgers fan and simply did not play those songs.

Helms' later employer, Hank's close friend and disciple Ray Price, on the other hand, would tell a reporter in 2006, somewhat surprisingly, "No one influenced me until I was about eight years old; the first one I ever heard was Jimmie Rodgers. Of course, for most of the guys of my era, he was *it*." In fact, if you were a member of that generation and had been regularly exposed to Rodgers' music, there was a good chance you were, like Price, from Texas, where western swing played on, where Carrie Rodgers still lived in San Antonio and was occasionally recognized, and where border radio cowboys might still be caught singing the occasional Rodgers song.

If Jimmie's influence—beyond the understanding that jazz and hill-billy music were not really from separate planets—is seldom detectable in Ray Price's honky tonk or later crooner-style music, it certainly was in the repertoire of his fellow Texan and Hank Williams friend Billy Walker. That long-time Opry member's last album, just before his death in a car crash in 2006, was a *Tribute to Jimmie Rodgers*—full of polished, mellifluous tenor crooning.

Hank Williams was no Texan, nor a Rodgers acolyte, but his death was the first loss since Jimmie's of a downhome music star of that caliber, a loss so substantial that it shook the music and its fans alike and accentuated a connection that *was* there in a new round of memorial records in which one loss recalled the other. Willie Phelps and his brother Norman, of the Virginia Rounders from the Chesapeake Bay area, both released versions of "Hank Williams Meets Jimmie Rodgers." (They would also record "So Long, Pal Jimmie" and "Jimmie Rodgers Will Never Die" together for good measure.) Just a few years earlier, they had been sidemen and backup singers for that cowboy-crooning Rodgers fan Ray Whitley. Riley Crabtree, a second-tier Texas honky tonker and Rodgers admirer, rushed out the more fait accompli "When Hank Williams Met Jimmie Rodgers." (The time element kept shifting in these songs.) In Australia, bush balladeer Buddy Williams seemed to be reaching for generation-skipping simultaneity with "The Death of Hank and Jimmie," and the harmonious Hawking Brothers offered the slightly less committed "Will Hank Williams Meet Jimmie Rodgers (in Heaven)?" with a lyric that wondered aloud if "old timer" Rodgers somehow knows who Hank Williams has been, and if the angels will introduce them so they can sing together a "round-up of their songs" of "life we see every day."

Back in the United States, the short-lived, unrelated "Cochran Brothers" act—future rockabilly Eddie Cochran and country songwriter Hank Cochran—recorded "Two Blue Singing Stars," once again focused on that meeting in heaven above. "One is a true blue yodeler, the other is from Alabam'; we need not call his name," it went. And in 1955, that was probably true. If '90s-style punk rocking alternative country bands had been around, there no doubt would have been a "Hank Williams Meets Jimmie Rodgers in Hell," intended as a compliment to both.

By the time he became a star, Hank, as was almost inevitable, did know something about Jimmie Rodgers blues, even if he kept the fact mainly to himself, and he was certainly aware to some degree of what then remained of the Jimmie Rodgers legend. As his friend and frequent opening act, the Texan Big Bill Lister recalls, "Hank and I always had a family fuss going on about Jimmie Rodgers. He wouldn't admit that Jimmie was *any* influence to him, and I'd tell him, 'Ah Hank, come off that.' And he'd say 'Nah, I didn't pay no attention to him.' And I said, 'Where did [the intro to 'Lovesick Blues'] come from?' That's pure Jimmie Rodgers, just Don Helms putting it up on steel.' And we'd laugh and kid each other."

As clearly evidenced by a photo that still hangs toward the back of the Ernest Tubb Record Shop in Nashville, Hank had even met the widow Rodgers; he is seen sitting at the head of a table of revelers sporting that enormous "Boy, I've made it now" grin of his, circa 1949 or so, and Ernest Tubb and Carrie are among the other identifiable partygoers at the table. Whether the evening captured was during a short tour by Hank and Ernest in Texas or back in Nashville is unclear. Whether the volatile Audrey, Mrs. Hank Williams, had met Carrie at that point is not on the record, though they certainly met at numerous memorial events for country greats by 1955. By then they were both, sadly, in the "widow of the legend" business and, according to Audrey's daughter Lycrecia, friends.

In a January 1975 on-air interview with Nashville deejay T. Tommy Cutrer, Hank's chief competitor, Lefty Frizzell, an out-and-out lover of Rodgers music and another Texan, recalled: "In 1951, I was booked for two weeks with my band, myself, and Hank Williams and his boys. And for the first job, I flew into Little Rock, Arkansas, and Hank already had his room, next to my room . . . I was settin' there, just pickin' guitar, and Hank and Big Bill [Lister] come by and come in, and I was doing a blues and yodeling and everything—and Hank did a Jimmie Rodgers number . . . Since I was doing a yodeling thing, he said, 'Let *me* try that.' And then he did *another* [Rodgers] number; see? Now things like this is a beautiful thing, because you're sharing beautiful songs together . . . It reminds me of a whole family around a piano, sharing music, the way that our ancestors did."

Here you have two of the greatest names in the history of hard country music, competitors (and not, it is said, particularly friendly ones), at the very time they were both the rage, comfortably ensconced in a downtown hotel suite—and, given who they were, very likely well-oiled, too—sitting around trading Jimmie's blue yodels, and what Lefty is reminded of by this scene is the old folks learning songs from each other at home in the parlor. Swapping oldies with the family around the piano was not, however, even the way he had picked up Jimmie Rodgers songs himself.

He was born in 1928, and so was five years younger than Hank. His father Naamon was a subsistence farmer in the depths of the Depression, and the family barely got by. Things reached their nadir while they were living in the ironically named town of El Dorado, Texas; Lefty was about six, and it was only a year after Rodgers' death. Naamon traded the family's aging cow, since it was costing more than it was worth to feed it. What he decided to trade it for sounds apocryphal, the apogee of those "I'll have a loaf of bread and the new Jimmie Rodgers record" stories, but it is apparently true. Lefty's dad traded that cow for an aging Victrola and "some old, thick records of Jimmie Rodgers."

For this future master of honky tonk singing, hearing Jimmie Rodgers' music would not be the experience it was for many of his contemporaries, secondhand and filtered through some other singer in-between. Rodgers' sound would be, he said, both an inspiration and a comfort. "I'd trade all my yeah-yeahs and slurs for his yodeling, anytime . . . absolutely," Frizzell admitted to reporter Geoff Lane in the last interview he gave, not long before his death in July 1975. "Jimmie Rodgers—just his voice, the guitar and the yodel—shaped my part in life. I knew when I was twelve years old what I was gonna do; I was gonna sing. I'd come in frustrated from school and it'd help me. It has always helped me . . . I'd yodel and harmonize with him and it gave me peace. I can truly say he was the biggest influence in my life. Frustrations you can't talk about, you can sing about," said the man whose early smash hit "I Love You, a Thousand Ways" was written in a jail cell.

"Jimmie was known for the blues because he had some hard times. He was sad. I become sad too; we all do," Lefty continued. "I'd give anything if I could yodel and sing like Jimmie Rodgers, but I'm like Ernest Tubb. My voice changed till I couldn't yodel good no more. Course—I can *still* yodel better than Merle Haggard!"

By 1938 or so, as Frizzell's biographer Daniel Cooper notes, there is little doubt that the boy known as "Sonny" would have been found pressing on the headphones of the family's crystal radio set, not so much to hear Roy Acuff on the Opry, as his father did, but to catch Bob Wills and the hot, horn-augmented Texas Playboys, with those distinctive vocals from Tommy Duncan cutting through the static from Tulsa. By that point, remember, Tommy Duncan's exciting versions of Jimmie Rodgers' songs were a regular part of the band's repertoire. His dragging and fondling of notes at key moments, as heard in the Playboys recording of Rodgers' "Gambling Polka Dot Blues" and other Playboy numbers, including that alternate American national anthem, "Trouble in Mind," were crucial touchstones for Lefty.

Also, Al Stricklin's jazzy, Earl Hines–influenced pumping piano stands out in the Playboys' arrangements of that time—and a similar plinking keyboard sound would be heard on Lefty's honky tonk records years later. Tapes exist of Lefty, in his very last years, sitting around with Sanger "Whitey" Shafer, cowriter of his last great songs in the '70s such as "I Never Go Round Mirrors" and "That's the Way Love Goes," trading random blue yodel verses like: "I'd rather drink muddy water . . . than to be in Nashville, treated like a dirty dog," as well as "T.B. Blues."

Whether glued to that headset in childhood or, as his family recalled, learning the nuances of that pile of Jimmie Rodgers records with his head stuck deep inside the Victrola cabinet (to filter out the noise of his rambunctious siblings), Lefty acquired Rodgers' music not by some person-to-person hand-me-down process, but by an up-close-and-personal relationship with the hardware of the new mass media. If a boy in Texas had wanted to have the same sort of encounter with Jimmie Rodgers' music ten years later in 1948, he would have found it difficult. It was the period in which Jimmie Rodgers records became virtually unobtainable—a software crisis.

The effort to make that experience less challenging, to return the music to circulation—which would also be, as it proved, the first serious step toward enshrining Jimmie Rodgers as the "father of country music"—came, appropriately enough, from the grassroots. It was sparked by a devoted amateur, Jim Evans, who had begun to assemble his own set of Jimmie's 78s in 1938 and would eventually do enough to bring Rodgers back to a larger audience that a 2002–2003 exhibit at the Country Music Hall of Fame in Nashville ("Treasures Untold: Unique Collections from Devoted Fans") focused in large part on his achievement.

As a child in Abernathy, Texas, Evans was grabbing up Rodgers records, especially taken with Jimmie's unique yodeling. "I bought every record of Jimmie's as they were released," he would recall. "They came out by twos to Pinson's Drugstore. There was a big crank-up Victrola . . . and if I got to play a record a couple of times right after I bought one, I'd sing it all the way home [from town] on the wagon seat. If I got to play it one more time before I had to milk the cows and slop the hogs, I could fill in what I couldn't remember on the way home, and then I knew it forever."

The Evans family moved to Lubbock the year Rodgers died, and as his records and memorabilia got harder to come by, Jim advertised in the city's daily *Avalanche-Journal* his interest in owning a copy of each of Jimmie Rodgers' records. People who still had them, he found, did not part with copies easily. "I soon found out that most people bought Jimmie Rodgers records to *play*, not to fill a record cabinet!" One Lubbock lady whose affection had moved on from Rodgers to Roy Acuff was willing to trade, and "a little horse swapping" resulted in the first substantial addition to Evans' original Rodgers collection. He went further, placing ads in national magazines such as *Popular Mechanics*. A Japanese-American army reservist, one of whose two precious sets of Rodgers releases on Bluebird and Montgomery Ward was destroyed while he was overseas, sold Evans the second set of forty-eight just to make sure they would be preserved. The numbers show that Jim was now getting close to having a clean set close to the total 111 released sides. A few more that would be added to his total were supplied by fans who responded from abroad, far down the international trail Rodgers' music had traveled. Records were still in print in England, Australia, Argentina, Japan, New Zealand, even Panama, and American soldiers based in India during World War II could still find good quality pressings for sale there on local labels. It took Jim Evans ten years and a thousand dollars ('40s dollars) to complete a mint set.

"One thing I learned quick," Evans noted in 1980, "was that all the people that were interested in Jimmie Rodgers records didn't have any to sell—they were looking *for* them . . . They just wouldn't hardly part with 'em, and fans everywhere was writing saying they wanted 'em. So we hit on the idea of trying to *reproduce* them for fans, at cost." Evans started churning out Rodgers records on blank discs that cost him eighty-five cents. The hundreds of letters that came in as a result started him thinking that there should be a Jimmie Rodgers Fan Club to share information and thoughts. When he wrote to Ernest Tubb and Hank Snow asking if they could start such a thing, both responded that he was really the man to do it. Carrie Rodgers, still living in San Antonio, agreed to be honorary "first lady" of this proposed club, which Evans started in September 1947. The club journal followed, *The Blue Yodeler*, professionally produced, with photos, cleanly printed by Evans himself, and full of important new information, such as that report on the unknown details of Jimmie's early-'20s work (and blue yodeling) with Billy Terrell's traveling tent show, contributed by Terrell.

The newsletter would report that early issues had reached print runs of close to five thousand, and it appears that many of Evans' privately manufactured records were now reaching that growing readership. The entire set-up inevitably brings to mind the world of fifty or sixty years later, of Internet e-mail lists and fan boards, downloaded mp3s of out-of-circulation recordings from specialist blogs, of fanzines and fan-based marketing "street teams," of dedicated Web sites. So it will probably not be a surprise that Jim Evans soon heard from an RCA Victor lawyer.

"Somebody reported, I guess, that we were dubbing Jimmie's material, and I got a letter from the legal department of Victor telling me that that was illegal. Course, we knew it was supposed to be—but we also knew that they was supposed to be putting them out, or [else], it felt like, then *we* should. I wrote 'em a nice long letter explaining how . . . if they would just release them, they wouldn't lose any money on 'em; they were a sure sale. And they decided that we knew what we were talking about."

A 1947 missive from RCA to Evans, preserved in the Country Hall of Fame Museum's Frist Archives, informs Jim that he must stop bootlegging records but also gives some good news: plans had begun for new albums of Jimmie Rodgers' music for legitimate release. It would take almost two years for the promised albums to begin to appear, even with heavyweight support for the idea from Ernest Tubb, Hank Snow, Carrie Rodgers, and Ralph Peer. Tubb wrote to Evans in the summer of '48, saying, "I'm still after Victor to get the album out. I can hardly wait myself." Finally, in the spring of 1949, live, on the San Antonio radio show *Hillbilly House Party*, Carrie was presented with the first copy of an album of three 78s titled *Yodelingly Yours — Jimmie Rodgers: A Memorial Album to a Great Entertainer, Volume One*. Harry Truman was playing piano in the White House, and with the sole exception of a wartime Bluebird reissue of "The Soldier's Sweetheart/The Sailor's Plea," obviously intended to appeal to older men in uniform, no Jimmie Rodgers record had then been released in the United States for fourteen years — since Franklin D. Roosevelt's first term. It would take another fifteen years to get all of his original work back in American record stores.

Examining Victor Records' sales figures for Rodgers' original 78s, it becomes clear that the postwar reissues were selected on the basis of previous success; among the six sides on the first *Memorial Album*s were huge hits such as "T for Texas," "Daddy and Home," and "The Brakeman's Blues." But for anxious fans waiting for more, the next three volumes were released excruciatingly slowly; the return on the first had not been great, and the project was evidently considered risky. Indeed, in a November 1954 letter to Jimmie Rodgers Fan Club member Thomas Woodrich of Austin, Texas, RCA Victor's now legendary A and R man Steve Sholes suggested, essentially, that he would be wise not to hold his breath for more releases from Jimmie. "Thank you for your suggestions," Sholes wrote. "As you probably know, we have made available, during the last few years, twenty-four of the Jimmie Rodgers recordings. The sales on these records and albums have been so disappointingly small that we do not feel it is feasible to consider a Limited Edition on this artist at this time."

And so, as late as 1956 when the reissues slowly started up again, songs that now seem to be obvious Jimmie Rodgers standards, including even "Mule Skinner Blues" and "Miss the Mississippi and You," were only just coming back into circulation; the original singles had not sold in enormous numbers, so the reissues had to wait in line. "Any Old Time" would only

return in 1958, and some songs that seem to us today to be most emblemati-
cally Jimmie's would not be back in print until the '60s—"My Rough and
Rowdy Ways" in 1960, "T.B. Blues" in 1962, "Gambling Polka Dot Blues" in
1964—all on vinyl LP albums.

For the very many listeners who first came to Jimmie Rodgers' music
in the years when those albums of old singles were slowly being released,
1949–64, what songs were available affected the understanding of who Jimmie Rodgers was, what his music had been, and how it might still matter.
But then, because of the capabilities of that extended, multisong album format, there were, increasingly, people ready to try to explain those things to
you—through track selection and sequencing, cover art imagery designed
to leave specific impressions, and liner-note commentary. The commercial
introduction of the microgroove long-playing record in 1948, initially in the
form of ten-inch, eight-cut albums, then the more familiar twelve-inch LP of
ten to twelve cuts, did not just make possible records with a point of view, it
virtually demanded it. It was in this technological context that Harry Smith's
Anthology of American Folk Music appeared in 1952.

An early signal of the sort of contextualizing to come was not the liner
notes on the *Memorial Albums*, which were scanty, but scripts provided to
radio stations by Peer International out of New York, so that the new collections could be featured in special half-hour radio presentations with a
familiar local announcer mouthing the furnished commentary.

In case you somehow did not know that you could buy one of these
albums for yourself now, the often overheated script prose let you know that
"More than sixteen years ago, the scourge of tuberculosis leveled this great
spirit to the ground, and the man who was beloved by millions . . . found
eternal peace. But because of the magic of recordings, Jimmie Rodgers
will never die. For so long as one phonograph machine still plays, and one
recording of his music is still to be played, Jimmie Rodgers will be alive.
By means of this magic, and because he was so great a part of American
music, we bring you today a new album of the favorite all-time recordings of
America's Blue Yodeler. (PAUSE)."

Among the interesting half-truths and outright misinformation that listeners to these broadcasts were offered was that Jimmie was a unique "truly
American *ballad* singer," how the young Jimmie had learned "salty soil-
sprung songs of the grownup world" such as "Frankie and Johnny" from
his dad's railroad buddies (not from that Frank Crumit record), how he and
his family conquered loneliness and heartache as he wrote songs like "Away
Out on the Mountain" (actually written by Kelly Harrell), and, better still,
how the comic and quirky "Desert Blues" reflected the Rodgers family's
quest for dry air in Arizona. Well, a segue is a segue, however tenuous—and,

after all, these albums' tracks had not been chosen for thematic links or track-by-track airplay.

Appropriately, though, the radio scripts for all of the albums went for the big finish with that staple vaudeville era closer, the flag drop: "The story of Jimmie Rodgers . . . is that of a man who rose to great heights, in spite of his background, in spite of his health, . . . a story of these United States . . . that lives to reaffirm our faith in democracy and in man's dignity and freedom, the story of a man who believed in himself and a gift that God had given him a gift that he shared with lonely and troubled people." Step-right-up hoopla aside, much of that analysis happens to be true.

The first appearance of Rodgers music on long-playing records was delayed, briefly, by the fact that Jimmie was on RCA Victor. Columbia was the original LP promulgator; RCA initially promoted 45-rpm singles as the preferable new format. When, reluctantly, they began releasing short 33-and-1/3-speed ten-inch LPs in 1951, among their first albums—which targeted upscale early technology adopters and were dominated by light classical, opera, and jazz sides that audience generally favored—would be one that stood apart, *A Treasury of Immortal Performances: Folk Singers*. It offered two hits each by "folksingers" Jimmie Rodgers, Vernon Dalhart, and Gene Austin. On the liner notes, the jazz critic Leonard Feather explained to record buyers who these performers were and how, as this lineup of polished professionals suddenly dubbed "folk" made obvious, the "folk singing art form" had become "a broad term."

In the early '50s, fans of the music that was coming to be called country were likelier to be reintroduced to Jimmie Rodgers' music not through the slowly emerging reissues, but through a series of competing thematic collections by four of his greatest interpreters—Ernest Tubb, Lefty Frizzell, Hank Snow, and, in fascinating sessions that never quite became the projected album, Bill Monroe. What may not be apparent now is that, except for some old hits taken up by Lefty, virtually none of the songs covered in these salutes were in circulation in Jimmie's original version at the time and had not been for years.

One previous obscurity, "Why Did You Give Me Your Love?" would show up on both *Jimmie Rodgers Songs Sung by Ernest Tubb* (1951) and *Hank Snow Salutes Jimmie Rodgers* (1953). E.T. would later call this not particularly distinguished ballad "an extra special favorite of mine," perhaps because it suited his singing so well, but the likely reason it received this new attention is that its theme had become more relevant, and probably more suggestive. The musings of a man left in the lurch, perplexed and hurting, after having been "given" love for "just one day," may, when the song was first recorded, have seemed to listeners to refer only to a brief declaration

Meeting Jimmie Rodgers

of love, but in the era of cryin'-in-your-beer cheatin' songs, it was undoubtedly taken to be about the aftermath of a one-night stand. Elsie McWilliams, uncredited, had supplied the lyric; it may be one of the songs she was glad not to be associated with, given that its content was now perceived as daring.

The original record, produced in Atlanta in November 1929, featured Jimmie singing over some rather sophisticated—and overdone—guitar chording by Billy Burkes, the very model of how not to make a good Jimmie Rodgers record. Jimmie is not well that day, and you can hear it; his voice is full of phlegm and even cracks at times, and the effort defeats him. The arrangement is damagingly sluggish; there's no real interplay between the vocal and the intrusive guitar part, nothing to clarify the emotions in the song, make it Jimmie's, bring it home. The outtake that has survived is no better. The single was released in 1935, one of the last of the posthumous recordings, and apparently sold fewer than eight thousand copies. You probably had to be Ernest Tubb or Hank Snow to remember this one at all, or to see how to sing it now.

Snow's version, which begins with a seemingly incongruous, satisfied hum, profits from the patented clarity of his elocution and storytelling, which mesh with the sounds of violins and steel guitar to produce an effect of thoughtful wistfulness. This singer, you can tell, had had, well, kind of a special day and night back there one time with the woman in question, but he has survived the bad outcome with just a lingering touch of the blues about it. Hank, in the phrase of his monster hit of the time, has mainly moved on, a little bent, but not broken.

Ernest Tubb cannot count on the vocal precision that was Hank Snow's gift, but he does demonstrate his often underestimated skill at getting to the heart of a lyric through simple but idiosyncratic, knowing phrasing. The song in Tubb's hands is that of a sturdy man who has truly been set back by that one-day affair, and he is pleading now, more fervently than even Jimmie would have done on a good day: "This is my last . . . ap-PEAL dear!" He can hardly get the phrase out; that word *appeal*, when he is forced by emotion to let it loose, explodes from some air pocket deep in his lungs—as he owns up to his need. Sympathetic steel guitar by Dickie Harris ends the phrases and verses, underscoring Tubb's emotional points.

With these performances of a generation later, a minor Jimmie Rodgers song became less minor. Both singers understood Jimmie's material well enough to know they could bring new meaning to a song that had not worked in its original presentation, and each applied his particular performing style and temperament to it. Over time, the divergence between the two styles would lead to quite different notions of where the strength of Rodgers' music lay—indeed, what it *was*. Much the same could be said of Lefty Friz-zell's and Bill Monroe's approaches to Rodgers songs. All of these sessions happened within a brief time span, and all added to the resuscitation of the music. They also added up to a new list of ways to enter Jimmie Rodgers country.

Ernest Tubb was the first into the studio. He had promised Carrie Rodgers, the fan club's Jim Evans, and Victor Records (although he was on Decca) that he would promote Jimmie's music however he could, if they would just bring Jimmie's records back into circulation. He was in a position to do that, at the height of his impact and commercial success, with a string of genre-shaping hits such as "Walkin' the Floor Over You" and "You Nearly Lose Your Mind." Over the years since Carrie Rodgers had managed and intro-duced him, he had established his own unmistakable style, yet kept close to some of his musical origins. He recorded songs by such Jimmie-inspired writ-ers as Elsie McWilliams, Rex Griffin, Jimmie Davis, Gene Autry, Tommy Duncan, and Jimmie Skinner, and even credited "Mrs. Jimmie Rodgers" with a few songs—1947's "A W-O-M-A-N Has Wrecked Many a Good Man" was one—just to keep some cash flowing in her direction. That year he took a first tentative stab at something he had surprisingly never done—recording Rodgers songs himself—specifically, "Waiting for a Train" and "The Won-derful City." For more than a decade, he had been unable to see himself as capable of bringing something to his idol's music, being worthy of it, or, apparently, even attempting to perform it without the yodels, which he could not tackle since having had a tonsillectomy. But he was a star now, and he had promises to keep.

First, as Ronnie Pugh delineated in his penetrating biography, Ernest instituted the practice of seeing that at least one Jimmie Rodgers song would be sung or played from records on every episode of his weekly WSM show following the Grand Ole Opry, the *Midnight Jamboree*. More than fifty years later, Rodgers songs are still regularly performed there. In the 1947 feature film *Hollywood Barn Dance*, E.T. clearly brandishes Jimmie Rodgers' Mar-tin guitar, the one with "Thanks!" on the back, in the closing moments of the picture. (There is also a guest appearance, his only one on film, by Jack Guthrie.)

In 1950, Ernest republished Carrie's book, *My Husband Jimmie Rodgers*, and sold it through his record shop and mail-order business out of downtown Nashville, essentially at cost. From midway through that year, on into Janu-ary 1951, came the LP sessions of Rodgers songs at Nashville's Castle Studios. Carrie would provide liner notes expressing gratitude for Tubb's tribute, "reveling" she said, that, still, after seventeen years, "so many well-known entertainers credit Jimmie with being their inspiration . . . remind[ing] me that his style and his songs have influenced either indirectly (or directly) all artists in the field today."

The eight recordings on the *Jimmie Rodgers Songs* LP are riveting, prime-time Tubb. A chastened, mellow "I'm Free from the Chain Gang Now" is particularly good, the inimitable Billy Byrd playing a modern, jazz-influenced, single-note break on electric guitar as he does at pointed moments throughout the LP, while, in a sign of the new times, Dickie Harris contributes smooth but chiming steel that is in almost constant conversation with Tubb's vocal. Crucially for this sound, the steel guitar finishes off vocal lines, provides intro runs before the vocals, comments in keeping with the tone of the numbers—does, in short, exactly the things that Jimmie's yodels used to do, and that the fiddle did for western swing, without nostalgia or any deliberately retro approach restraining it. This was simple, direct honky tonk.

There is a very sweet, jaunty change of pace turn on "Any Old Time." As does almost every interesting singer who has ever performed that song, E.T. toys with the vaudeville phrasing; "once were" in "all you once were to me" becomes almost one word; in "prove what you can be" he pops the p-word, and the final "Come back home" ends "ho-ho-home," an amused Bert Williams–style alternative to a yodel. Owen Bradley, a future promulgator of the much more uptown, urbane Nashville Sound, appears on the track, adding some old-time piano.

The Rodgers songs Ernest Tubb has chosen to sing, now that he has finally done some, are almost uniformly downbeat, either broken-hearted admissions ("I'm Lonely and Blue," "Why Should I Be Lonely"), or sad stories related of others ("Hobo's Meditation," "A Drunkard's Child").

Not until years later, in the late '60s and '70s, would Ernest come to record the two Rodgers songs probably most associated with him, which seemed to have been written for him and which he would perform most often until his own end in 1984—"In the Jailhouse Now" and, especially, "Women Make a Fool Out of Me," which he always titled "Jimmie Rodgers' Last Blue Yodel." The emphasis and flavor encapsulated in his singing of "the whi-MINNNN . . . make a fu-*hool* . . . out of *muh-ee*" virtually define the charming, winking, just-between-us vocal approach that made his name; they may even have been its point of origin. Both Rodgers songs are built on amiable if slightly embarrassed acceptance of a series of personal disasters. "Winding up in the hoosegow or being left hanging, like a fool . . . well, I guess that's just what happens to a hapless guy like me," they seem to say, especially in Ernest Tubb's hands. There is self-mocking—and also living with the situation.

At heart then, Tubb's Rodgers take is a straightforward blues expression of the central, sturdy sort that is about overcoming or living through the blues. That is what he finds he responds to most in Jimmie's work and, maybe more importantly, can use best. It is also, at root, why honky tonk — for many, to this day, country music's most distinctive and potent style — is sometimes referred to as "white man's blues" or "workingman's blues." Anyone introduced to Jimmie Rodgers' music by this route, by Tubb or anyone carrying the Tubb emphasis further, will find that tone in Jimmie's music and persona, too. In a real sense, the postwar renewal of interest in Rodgers' music as "country" depended on it.

The very different sounding and feeling Rodgers salute LP by Lefty Frizzell was recorded in Dallas by producer Don Law for Columbia Records over one night on June 1, 1951, just a few months after Tubb's. The album extends this honky tonk image and sound, and modifies them. Lefty's massive popularity at that time is a reminder that this was not 1931 or 1941, and that virtually all pop vocal approaches and styles of phrasing that seem emotionally credible and sincere to audiences when fresh will sooner or later, with repetition and adoption by uninspired followers, come to seem just an overfamiliar, tired set of tics and tricks. That descent was as inevitable for the innovative vocal styles of Jimmie Rodgers, Roy Acuff, and Ernest Tubb as for, say, early '40s swing band "girl vocalist" singing, early '60s British Invasion rock group harmonies, or late '60s R & B soul. (Though sometimes, given enough rest, the same approaches strike later generations as fresh and freshly credible all over again, becoming less tried and more true.)

In 1951, Lefty employs his then shockingly new, deliberate, even contrived, and often breathtaking vocal attack. Those melismatic "yeah-yeahs and slurs" he could joke about would stretch once familiar words to more syllables than anybody suspected they could have, every stretch leaving the responsive listener no choice but to let the words startle again.

Now, that is one large thing to do for an old song — force you to encounter its very meaning anew. Lefty's new vocal approach made it possible for new listeners to be struck by the emotional specifics in Jimmie's songs all over again and introduced new ways to listen to Jimmie Rodgers tunes ever after.

Only a week before those eight sides were set down in one long session, Lefty had recorded the remarkable double-hit single "Always Late (With Your Kisses)" backed with "Mom and Dad's Waltz," adding two more to the string of classics he had been coming up with since "If You've Got the Money, Honey" just the year before. Don Law, a veteran British producer of American roots music, knew that this young man, who as a kid had privately vowed to learn every Jimmie Rodgers song (back fourteen years before, when Law himself was busy recording blues legend Robert Johnson in Dallas), was now itching to do an album of them and would jump at his offer to do just that — in Dallas — now.

"At twenty-three," the LP's liner notes would say of Lefty, "he is one of the country's foremost folk-singers"—so *that's* what he was, like Austin, Dalhart, and Rodgers, according to RCA—"and his tribute to Jimmie Rodgers in this collection takes on a distinctly personal atmosphere, for it is to him that Lefty owes much of his own immense success."

The offer to make the album was not just a reward for having hits, though it was surely that in part. Historian Charles Wolfe noted the timing: Columbia was, at that moment, making a hard marketing push for their new ten-inch LPs. There is an irony here: Jimmie Rodgers' recording career had happened in part because rural audiences were relatively slow to switch from buying a lot of records to listening to music on the radio; the demographic, and the lag, had both been identifiable. Now *Songs of Jimmie Rodgers Sung by Lefty Frizzell* would appear as a Columbia pop record, advertised along with offerings from Jo Stafford and Duke Ellington; the label had not yet introduced a regular series of purely country LPs because the country audience was not among the early adopters of LP record players.

Wolfe quoted Lefty as saying, "The first thought I had was, first chance I get, I'm gonna do an album of Jimmie Rodgers' songs, and I started recording at eleven o'clock and didn't finish until seven the next morning . . . Some of those songs—you can *tell* when it was getting to be seven in the morning."

Maybe so; there are slower sentimental songs ("My Old Pal," "Treasure Untold") that are perhaps a little sleepy, but the overall result has understandably been reissued time and again—always with an additional, potent set of four more Rodgers songs Frizzell recorded in 1953, including "Never No More Blues" and "California Blues." The slower ballads still show that this is a singer who knew the original Rodgers records intimately; they are not exactly imitations, but they are less played with, less divergent and fresh. Where Frizzell scores, and in grand style, is on the harder-charging blues numbers; "Travelin' Blues" was a 1951 hit for good reasons. The small combo behind him, referred to as a stringband, though there is effective, prominent Dixieland piano by Evelyn Rowley, has about the same lineup as was used for recording new songs at the same Jim Beck Studio the week before but reverts to the old Dobro sound rather than steel guitar. Steel player Curley Chalker has denied he is the Dobro player, but no other musician has ever stepped forward to claim credit for the flowing acoustic lines that so help keep Lefty in a time zone that is not exactly '30s nor exactly '50s, either, throughout the original session. On the added 1953 cuts, Lefty is comfortable and at home enough to toss in hip, rhythmic spoken asides, midlyric ("*I* ain't goin' to stay at home *no* how!"); the talented guitar player is Roy Nichols, a future long-time associate of Merle Haggard, drums and steel are onboard, and Wayne Rainey adds harmonica. The sound of these straightforwardly modern cuts anticipates some of what Haggard will do with Rodgers material, including some of the same songs, fifteen years later, even as some of Lefty's vocal touches recall the jazz-inflected singing of Tommy Duncan and the interjections of Bob Wills.

There is a chain to be followed there—but Bill Monroe, taking on Jimmie Rodgers material anew at about the same time, was thinking about *breaking* one. Monroe's credentials as an interpreter, promoter, and invigorator of Jimmie Rodgers' music were unquestionable by 1951; he had continued to add new, hard-driving touches and favors to his chosen (and often virtually remade) Rodgers tunes for a dozen years, and as we have seen, he would go on to steer the music—his way—into the commercial folk revival in the '60s. Since he had moved from RCA Victor to Decca the year before, a key Monroe recording, in lasting impact and quality if not in initial sales as a country single, had been the freshly updated "New Mule Skinner Blues," featuring the extended, bluer-than-blue fiddling of young Vassar Clements, the latest hot addition to the ever-evolving Bluegrass Boys.

Since Bill and his first-generation Blue Grass Boys let loose "Mule Skinner Blues" on the Opry in the late '30s, other country bands working in that supercharged stringband mode (nobody was yet calling it bluegrass) had occasionally visited a circumscribed list of Rodgers songs. Most often, they would choose precisely the yodeling blues "Big Mon" had picked first for close copies or further reworking, such as the still more manic, show-stopping late '40s version of "Mule Skinner" by the Maddox Brothers and Rose—based on Monroe's, certainly, but also pointing toward rockabilly. Alternatively, early bluegrass musicians might choose Rodgers songs that were like the ones Bill chose, as was the case with Jim Eanes' Monroe-style version of "T for Texas."

For Monroe himself, and therefore his followers, the Rodgers set list had begun short and remained so, as he would specify in typically laconic fashion for Charles Wolfe in a 1974 radio interview: "People like Jimmie Rodgers touched me . . . with *some* of the songs they sang." He certainly seems to be referring to the blues. But in 1951, Monroe would tackle some different Rodgers songs, employing sounds that would venture beyond acoustic bluegrass instrumentation. That was partly because of commercial pressure. Decca chief Paul Cohen was looking for ways to present Monroe that would get him hits again on the mainstream country music charts, which he had not revisited for a while. There were the immediate examples of Ernest Tubb's Rodgers salute, just released on the same label, and the oncoming Frizzell LP for Columbia, which Decca seems to have heard about, suggesting that Rodgers' music could be the focus of a successful album.

And so Bill Monroe returned to Jimmie Rodgers material in a highly unusual series of sessions through the first half of '51—five in all, some with the Bluegrass Boys of the time, including Rudy Lyle on banjo and Jimmie Martin on guitar, and others nobody would label bluegrass. Still written off today as beyond the instrumentation pale by some hardcore bluegrass-only aficionados, they featured an early lineup of Nashville's studio A-team, including Grady Martin on electric guitar, Owen Bradley (also the producer) on piano, and Farris Coursey on drums. The latter two had played, only weeks before, on Ernest Tubb's Rodgers salute sessions.

Monroe's '51 Rodgers experiments have been characterized by his biographer Richard Smith as "a near disaster"; Smith quotes Bradley as saying, "We had no idea what the hell we were doing, to be honest. I think Bill was as bewildered as we were." The actual results, however, are often highly entertaining, certainly surprising, and singularly enlightening as to how and where Bill Monroe left his mark on Jimmie Rodgers' music—and where he did not.

Four sides were released on two singles at the time, and four more—doubtless conceived as finishing off an eight-cut, ten-inch LP—were never heard until Bear Family's completist set of Monroe's '50s recordings was released nearly forty years later. They are a mixed bag, but not in the way often suggested, with the bluegrass sides passable and everything else awful.

Monroe is not thrown by the unaccustomed instrumentation. On "Peach Pickin' Time in Georgia," for instance, which is pure '20s vaudeville updated slightly with a walking bass rhythm and a string-of-single-notes guitar break from Grady Martin, he sounds not only comfortable, but amused and amusing—a reminder that Monroe was something of a vaudevillian himself, first hired as a dancer rather than as a mandolin player or singer, and enjoyed being emcee of a whole, varied show.

"My Carolina Sunshine Girl," unreleased at the time, was another vaudeville-styled number, not so much bad in any way as undistinguished; the musicians cannot get a handle on it, and Bradley's Gold Rush–era piano never gels with what Monroe is singing. No telling if they could have made it work better if they had kept at it, but they didn't. What is missing on such cuts is the vocal-instrumental interaction, which is one of the key strengths in Monroe's bluegrass concept.

"When the Cactus Is in Bloom," another released side, is far from bluegrass with its primordial cowboy content, though it has now been accepted into the bluegrass repertoire because Monroe sang it. Why *did* he? Well, the recording is a winning, jaunty, fiddle-driven romp, with Bill giddily zigging and zagging lines like "I drink m'coffee fromma can" with a fast, clipped vocal equivalent of his mandolin chop. His comments on another seemingly incongruous cowboy number he recorded, "Goodbye Old Pal," purchased from Cliff Carlisle, seem instructive here: "Well, it had a good tune . . . and it was a good wording . . . I just thought it would be a good story to tell to the people, you know, along about roundup time, the Texas Wild West and just stuff like that." Monroe might well have been familiar with the earlier western swing version of "Cactus" by Jack Guthrie, rhythmically similar to his, but in the end, he liked the song and in particular, he liked that other people who buy records would like it—simple as that.

Few have ever questioned the effectiveness of the Rodgers blue yodeling numbers Monroe took on at this time. These include "Brakeman's Blues" and "Travelin' Blues" (both released on singles that competed with Frizzell's more widely heard versions of the same songs) and the unreleased "St. James Infirmary" variant "Those Gambler's Blues," with its large helping of "ho-ho, hey-heys," in which electric instruments can be heard playing near-bluegrass and outright blues lines.

The songs that do *not* work for Monroe at all are the narrative ballads, "Ben Dewberry's Last Run" and "The Sailor's Plea"; the latter a released side. They remind us that Bill Monroe was not a singer-songwriter who liked to get caught up in a whole lot of exposition. Whereas Jimmie Rodgers might take an old, more or less "folk" ballad and simplify its narrative line for easier following so that the listener might care all the more, that was not something Monroe cared to do; it was not what his music was about. Take an old ballad like the racehorse story song Monroe transformed into the seminal "Molly and Tenbrooks." He offers us not a cleaner narrative line, but a series of images, impressions, snatches of (horse) conversation—and, through the astounding music that comes racing out, Earl Scruggs' banjo and all, an overall sensation of speed and heat and trauma. There are people who have known this song for decades and never quite followed the narrative. And it does not matter to them in the least.

This cumulative, "adding up the effects" approach, common in African-American ballads and normal in seminarrative blues, whether by Jimmie Rodgers or anyone else, is concerned primarily with creating a general impression by the sound of the song, including the sound of the words— elements the early folklorists ignored. As with the jazz music with which bluegrass has much in common, in the sound sometimes lies the whole point. Bill Monroe is audibly uncomfortable with Jimmie Rodgers' narrative ballads because the words needed to detail the narrative are for him, almost literally, stumbling blocks in the way of a flowing, rhythmic line.

The early '50s Rodgers' resuscitation program did, however, include a singer gifted at handling precisely the aspects of Jimmie's music, and

Meeting Jimmie Rodgers

precisely the songs, that were not in Bill Monroe's natural repertoire, who was most effective in relating and updating Rodgers' narrative ballads and the sentimental story songs most dependent on storytelling. With neat symmetry, of the four singers then working on Rodgers tributes this singer was least obviously equipped vocally for delivering emotionally riveting blues; in fact, on a blue yodel like "Anniversary Blues," he left the song sounding less like a cry and more narrative than it had been in the first place. This singer was Hank Snow.

The young Nova Scotian balladeer who had started out as the Yodeling Ranger with a repertoire heavy on blue yodels and with a tinge of the cowboy, whose own career outside of Canada had been stymied for so long, had finally attained stardom in the United States in 1950, recording for American (rather than Canadian) RCA Victor and joining the Grand Ole Opry cast, in part because of the backing of Ernest Tubb, who had learned of their common intense interest in Jimmie Rodgers.

Yet for all of the clearly Rodgers-influenced and -derived songs Hank had recorded since the '30s, first in Canada, then in the United States, he, like Ernest, had not yet gotten around to doing many Rodgers songs as such. It was as if those had to wait until he had really found himself. Characteristically, his first flurry of activity in that direction was making singles and four-song EPs that featured some of Jimmie's train sagas— "Hobo Bill's Last Ride," "The Mystery of Number Five," "Ben Dewberry's Final Run"—the last being the very song that was proving so problematic for Bill Monroe at about the same time.

With his huge new hits like "I'm Movin' On" and "The Golden Rocket," Snow became so associated with railroading songs, including Jimmie Rodgers' train songs, that it is easy to forget that he had not worked on the tracks himself but on the waves, that he had actually been a boatman.

"That he was," agrees his son Jimmy, born Jimmie Rodgers Snow. "And when he did his paintings, he always painted ships, not trains. That was Jimmie's influence on Dad, there, but [also] he had that big hit ["I'm Movin' On"], and therefore that became his signature. So he pretty much hung in there with trains after that!"

His son's given name speaks volumes about Hank's devotion to the first Jimmie; that the younger Snow, now past seventy, simply calls himself Jimmy Snow today speaks to having gotten tired of telling people the right spelling. In the Snow household, Jimmie Rodgers songs had never gone out of fashion. "He rehearsed every day, and he catalogued *all* those Rodgers songs," Jimmy recalls of his father's early Nashville years. "I'd *hear* him. He'd done a lot of the blue yodel things; that was a lot of his repertoire, in fact, throughout his entire career—and that's why he named me after him. . . . 'Cause my dad started out emulating Jimmie Rodgers, playing those old guitar licks, and he got the yodeling going too."

That Hank Snow probably knew every record Jimmie Rodgers made, and intimately, is evidenced by his record collection, which his son still keeps intact. He would eventually record more than sixty of the songs. How, then, should we understand the order in which Snow chose to record them—the selection of songs, for instance, for his entry in the Rodgers tribute album competition, the 1953 RCA Victor ten-inch LP *Hank Snow Salutes Jimmie Rodgers*?

"Those first songs," Jimmy Snow says, "would have been like his favorites. Dad's choices *were* made, given all that he could have done . . . There were certain ones that stood out; he practiced all of those songs—and picked the ones that had the strongest influence on his mind and his career."

And so, in keeping with Snow's preferences, story songs and sentimental love ballads would dominate the album. Hank would also use it as an opportunity to introduce the singing of seventeen-year-old Jimmy—in quite sweet father-son harmony on the old memorial ballad recorded by both Dwight Butcher (its coauthor) and Gene Autry, "When Jimmie Rodgers Said Goodbye," and on one solo, Rodgers' "Treasures Untold."

Recorded in Nashville over the two days before Valentine's Day 1953 and released just a few weeks later, the LP seems now to mark the turning point between two sonic eras, the country music that had been and the more urbane sound Nashville studios were just starting to create. Forward-looking, ubiquitous steel guitar by Joe Talbot swells under Hank's vocal verses, seeming to duet with them, even as more traditional fiddle breaks by Tommy Vaden punctuate them. Fast-picked and strummed acoustic guitar is tightly coupled to clickety-clack, hand-dampened steel guitar licks to produce an original driving break (one that seems to predict the eventual use of "tick-tack" bass guitar in the fully-developed Nashville sound) on the album's best-known track, "The Southern Cannonball."

Now, nobody who has heard Hank Snow bend the word *southern* in that song into three syllables (usually rendering it "southerin") could imagine his singing being mistaken for anyone else's. Indeed, Snow's phrasing has been the subject of countless instantly recognized comedy impersonations. But, as Hank had to have been acutely aware, he did not possess any kind of a Dixie drawl to mark his singing as hillbilly, and he was wise enough not to try to invent one, as, for example, Tex Morton had in Australia. That clean, clear far-northern tone actually made Snow stand out from the established Opry stars Tubb, Monroe, and Acuff, even as his generally unfrilly singing and elegant diction, which years later would make possible the verbal gymnastics on "I've Been Everywhere," differentiated him also from more baroque stylists like Frizzell or Floyd Tillman. Hank had found his sweet spot.

The aural evidence is that Snow's vocal simplicity and emotional restraint suggested both to him and to his expert producers (Steve Sholes on this first Rodgers LP, Chet Atkins later) the importance of variation and innovation in the settings and backgrounds of his music. If he would not offer the personally revealing close-ups that Monroe, Frizzell, and Tubb did, in their differing ways, he could offer a large, colorful set of Cinemascope wide shots instead. This predisposal toward graphic, pointedly varied settings would be one way Hank Snow would change our understanding of how Rodgers' music could be taken forward. (It also meant that Snow made a great many sonically perfect and adventurous, innovative records.)

Of these four routes back to Jimmie Rodgers' music at this midpoint in the twentieth century, three were essentially blues-based: in Ernest Tubb's case, in attitude and that breezy creation of empathy for the dire situation he sang about; in the cases of both Lefty Frizzell and Bill Monroe, in highly expressive (and eventually much-imitated) singing styles that employed blues, gospel, jazz, and soul singing devices—following a direction Jimmie Rodgers had taken in the first place. But Hank Snow's ease in relating stories that needed to get the listener from here to there, and in adapting to varied musical arrangements, settings, and sounds, had been within Jimmie Rodgers' range as well. These four divergent interpretations, and the rerelease, however slowly, of Jimmie's own records, were heady reminders of the wide ground he had covered, the talents he had encompassed, and some of the lines of possible development he had set in motion—just within country music.

Finally, with the help of these same advocates, people began to notice.

Snow followed Ernest Tubb in becoming a friend, admirer, and protégé of Carrie Rodgers. (Jimmy Snow recalls frequent stop-by visits to her place in San Antonio as he and his dad headed for broadcasts with Paul Kallinger at the powerful border station XERF in Villa Acuna, Mexico.) Carrie would refer to Tubb and Snow as her "guardian angels" in an apparently self-penned October 1952 piece in Country Song Roundup, in which she detailed the extent of their continuing generosity; Hank had given her a "lovely RCA television combination set" (a TV with a radio and record player built in), and Ernest had recently provided a 1952 Cadillac sedan. She expressed amazement at how, over the nineteen years since Jimmie's passing, public and performer interest and "reflected glory" still "keeps me part of the whole thing."

Months before, Ernest Tubb had suggested quietly to Hank that they should split the cost of an elaborate memorial marker stone with bas relief of Jimmie to be erected at Meridian, Mississippi, and then, as Snow put it in his memoir, "have a big celebration with a huge country music show and invite a lot of celebrities, so we could draw a big crowd and get lots of media attention." Hank would recall for Tubb's biographer Ronnie Pugh that Ernest had used some fateful words in proposing the idea, very possibly the first time the thought had been expressed out loud: "We need to do this for Mrs. Rodgers, as well as to the memory of the late Jimmie Rodgers; he was the daddy of country music."

The Meridian daily paper, the *Star*, already had plans to retire a steam locomotive as a memorial to railroad men who had died on the job, and the two projects would now be conflated. There was considerable input from the Meridian city council and one member in particular, Carrie Rodgers' brother, attorney Nate Williamson, as to where this statue would go (not on the courthouse lawn, for one thing) and other logistical details. Thus began plans for what would amount to a second "big bang" in the life story of Jimmie Rodgers' music and reputation—the Bristol Sessions being the first for him and, as many contend, for country music as a genre. May 26, 1953, the twentieth anniversary of Jimmie Rodgers' death, would prove a crucial turning point in the recognition of his contributions and, not accidentally, a milestone in country music's self-recognition and self-promotion.

It seems somehow appropriate that the event, generally referred to simply as the first "Jimmie Rodgers Day," had a variety of names, reflecting competing, even conflicting interests. The printed program called it "Jimmie Rodgers and Railroadmen Memorial Day." It was also, thanks to a bill submitted by Mississippi Congressman Arthur Winstead who had evidently never been sufficiently informed that Ernest Tubb, among others, could not stand the term, officially deemed "National Hill Billy Music Day." (In its publicity, RCA Victor would refer to that designation as "one of the highest tributes to American *Folk* Music in its history.") A year later the issue would be put to rest when the general title of the continuing celebration became "National Country Music Day."

How short a time has passed between the era of legendary heroes of country song lore and the ratcheting up of promotion of an industry was underlined by the participation in the railroading part of the event of both Casey Jones' widow and Jones' working fireman, Sim Webb, who had survived the train wreck commemorated in the old ballad. On the other hand, how long the passing decades could seem since country music began was exemplified by the historic—and quite overlooked—reunion performance that night of the original Carter Family, A. P., Sara and Maybelle, a full ten years after most accounts, including the 2005 Zwonitzer-Hirshberg biography, say they had performed together in public for the last time. A photo in *Hoedown* magazine's coverage shows them there, and an aircheck tape, surviving in the hands of collectors, shows how even history makers could be left stranded if they were lacking advocates.

"I guess you people have kind of *forgotten* the old Carter Family name," says a rueful-sounding A. P. to the crowd that overfilled the Meridian Junior College stadium that night. "A good many years ago, about twenty-five years ago, the Carter Family and Jimmie Rodgers was two of the very first acts that started in Bristol, Virginia. I know I didn't meet Jimmie at the time we recorded, but I seen a letter written just a few days after . . . and the Victor people said they figured they had found two good talents in the South; one was Jimmie Rodgers, and the other was the old Carter Family. So this is the old Carter Family; we've been out of the eye for a little while, but in order to pay tribute to this good friend of ours, we came down here to sing . . . for ya. The first number will be a hymn, 'Anchored in Love.'"

They proceed to sing it, sounding noticeably older than when last heard together, and then A. P. adds, "Time is running short, but we're gonna sing for you a number that is one of Jimmie's favorites"—a somewhat dubious but convenient assertion—"and it's another hymn, 'God Gave Noah the Rainbow Sign.'"

It would be several years more before such Carter Family admirers as Earl and Louise Scruggs, Lester Flatt, and then Johnny Cash would help to restore the Carters to the level of recognition that Jimmie was getting this day. Meanwhile, the second-generation June Carter and her beau, Carl Smith, were among the touted headliners of the Jimmie Rodgers Day show.

The list of performers who rode convertibles in the daytime downtown parade that the organizers staged, attended the unveiling of the Rodgers monument, and performed at that big stadium-jamming show that night is a testament to the growing reach of Jimmie Rodgers' music, a summoning of the troops who had carried the music forward and cared about it most since the '20s. "Every hillbilly and his brother is here!" WSM radio announcer Grant Turner tossed out on the regional broadcast of the night's speeches and musical performances. Bill Monroe and his brother Charlie were there, in one of their infrequent reunions, and from the folk/bluegrass borderland came Jimmie Skinner. From the western end of country and western came Tommy Duncan, Leon McAuliffe, Moon Mullican, and Hank Thompson. In the honky tonk contingent were Lefty Frizzell, Little Jimmie Dickens, Webb Pierce, and Hank Williams' mother, standing in for her late son. Such new-style pop-influenced crooners as the young Marty Robbins, Jim Reeves, and George Morgan were there, too—and old Jimmie Davis, and even, with a relatively low profile, Roy Acuff.

To welcome Rodgers fans and followers globally, the teenaged Jimmie Rodgers Snow and Justin Tubb were sent to New York to meet a young British Rodgers fan, Ian Lee, and accompany him to Mississippi. (In later years, the Australian Rodgers imitator Tex Banes would travel halfway around the world to appear as a regular feature of the shows, sponsored by the International Singing Brakeman Society fan club.)

Carrie publicly expressed her thanks for the tribute; Elsie McWilliams was naturally on hand, but then so was baseball's southern hero and pitching legend Dizzy Dean. Sadly, Ernest Tubb, after all of his contributions to making this festival of Rodgers recognition happen, was not. Overwhelmed by the succession of Hank Williams' death, his own USO tour in Korea, and the planning of the event, he had gone on a bender (described at the time as flu) and was not in shape to make it, a major embarrassment. (He would be at the Rodgers' Days immediately following; but if you see a photo of him there, it is not 1953.) His son Justin would join Hank Snow in unveiling the Jimmie Rodgers monument, with its statue depicting the thumbs-up Singing Brakeman with his guitar.

Nashville *Banner* reporter H. B. Teeter, who in that day's paper pointedly described Jimmie as "a country singer who fathered the type of music that put Nashville, Tennessee on the map," also wrote the often-quoted, flowery inscription on the monument that now marked Jimmie Rodgers as, more literally than most to whom the term is applied, a national icon: "His is the music of America . . . of the people he loved, thundering boxcars, lonesome prairies, great mountains . . . bayous and cotton fields . . . wheated plains, little towns, cities . . . winding rivers. We listened. We understood."

Amidst all of this new "father" talk, the *Birmingham (AL) News* reporter Thomas Hill came up with another descriptive phrase that would endure, referring to Rodgers in his report on the event as "the man who started it all."

The song lyric chiseled on to the back of the monument was, of all things, "Home Call," accurately attributed in stone to Elsie McWilliams as well as Jimmie, and clearly put there as a nod to Mrs. Rodgers, since she always referred to that ballad, with its reference to "Carrie, Anita, and me," as her favorite song of Jimmie's. Carrie was visibly in tears, the reports have it, as Hank Snow dedicated the monument on behalf of "the industry." "It's an honor to be here to pay tribute to the daddy of us all," he intoned, "the daddy and originator of hillbilly and folk music, the one and only Jimmie Rodgers. He led the way for all of us, including Hank Williams—who's been called home. Jimmie Rodgers handed it over to Hank, who bridged the gap between hillbilly and popular music, who did *that* part."

And that is some interesting framing. From Hank Snow's perspective, hillbilly music, southeastern-style, had gotten farther away from pop since

Jimmie's day—and Hank Williams' songs, in crossing over to general audiences, brought it back closer. That is a coherent argument, one not always grasped by those who would later romanticize Williams as a "pure country" martyr, if somewhat ironic coming from Snow, who favored the more folklike, less pop side of Rodgers' music himself. The liner notes to Snow's *Salutes* LP, just released at the time, make the point even more explicitly: "The days when there existed a gap between Country and Popular music seem beyond recall, now that Folk tunes are making every hit parade."

Despite the recurring references to the music as "folk," common at the time, no one from the soon-to-emerge commercial folk revival was at this event, nor were there any allusions to the cross-racial character of American music that urban folk enthusiasts were discovering in the Harry Smith *Anthology*. Nor were African-American blues musicians or other performers onstage in segregated Meridian in 1953, making speeches or singing as they had been on Jimmie Rodgers' (and also Jimmie Davis') records back in the day.

In fact, the term *folk* would not be applied to commercial country music by many people for much longer, except by those who deliberately kept a foot in the separate folk world—in part because most country performers, whatever their politics, wanted no confusion with acts like the politically left-leaning Weavers, who had just called it quits at the end of 1952, their career as pop hit makers ended by political blacklisting.

Politicians, on the other hand, were not shy about appearing at Jimmie Rodgers Day, before crowds estimated by various news organizations as numbering somewhere between ten thousand and one hundred thousand. The thirty thousand reported by *Newsweek* was likely about right. The Democratic presidential candidate Adlai Stevenson would find Jimmie Rodgers Day a useful annual stop; during the second edition, the *Meridian Star* published a photo of him strumming Rodgers' guitar while Ernest Tubb held it.

The officeholders and -seekers were so omnipresent that when Universal-International shot a theatrical newsreel segment about the first Jimmie Rodgers Day, clips of speeches by the Mississippi and Tennessee governors dominated it. No country performers even appeared, and the music chosen was an orchestral "I've Been Working on the Railroad." With the memorialized hero's name misspelled "Jimmy Rogers" in the title (as it was in some press coverage), this was a perfect encapsulation of how the mainstream media were still treating country music at the time.

Not everyone on hand was thrilled by the large political presence. "That didn't set too well with folks there that were with me," Hank Thompson recalled. "We came there for a country music festival, not to hear some politicians!"

Organizers had, in fact, enticed the officials to the show to add that respectable "official" touch. Charlie Walker was a popular, working deejay in San Antonio at the time, though starting to come up with the records that would make him a honky tonk hero and Opry star. He and his wife had become close fiends of Carrie Rodgers and named their own daughter Carrie Lucinda for her and songwriter Cindy Walker. There is a photo of Charlie on the day carrying around Anita Rodgers' infant son, Jimmie's only grandson, the future performer Jimmie Dale Court. "I got hold of the governor of Texas and got him to make a presentation at the festival," Walker recalled.

Tubb and Snow had commissioned Charlie Lamb, then working as the Nashville correspondent for *Cash Box* magazine, to promote the event, and he had made flights down to Meridian with them during the organizing stages to see what might be done. Later dubbed "the Mayor of Music Row," the affable Lamb was at the time establishing Nashville as a working music reporting beat, something it had not been considered before, and was also creating the close link between the Nashville press and the local music industry that would be a part of Music City journalism for years to come. It was Lamb who arranged for a bevy of Tennessee officials to fly to Meridian along with the Opry stars.

Tennessee governor Frank Clement's old-school southern stem-winder of a speech started off, "The music of the people, *that's* what I prefer to call the music of Jimmie Rodgers, the father of the music we love so well, a man who is a legend in America today!" He then went on to say, in so many words (actually, many, many words) that if Ernest Tubb says Jimmie Rodgers is good for this business that is rising in my state, then good for Jimmie Rodgers. The cosponsoring Meridian Chamber of Commerce must have been slightly stunned, however, when Clement went on to advocate that National Hillbilly Day be relocated in the future. "We invite you to visit the *real* birthplace of country music—Tennessee." He tossed this relocation notion in, according to an approving Nashville *Tennessean* report, "after a late morning conference with Roy Acuff." What a surprise.

"It more or less looked," Charlie Lamb admits today, laughing about this apparently unforeseen effect, "as if Nashville, in the artists and support that was there, were claiming Jimmie Rodgers for *themselves.*"

Although he had never recorded in Nashville and his showboat appearance there was long forgotten, Jimmie was now officially claimed, in effect, as the father not just of country music, but also specifically of the emerging Nashville-based and -defined industry. Music City's huge Fan Fair shows would eventually emerge from that "keep it up here" thinking, but the Jimmie Rodgers/Country Music Days were, for a time, country music's main annual get-together.

A forgotten sidelight: in 1956, in what must have been seen by the locals as a satisfying speck of Mississippi payback for Nashville's attempted hogging of their spotlight, Ernest Tubb and Hank Snow were photographed breaking ground near the Rodgers monument for what was going to be, it was announced, both a Jimmie Rodgers museum and a more general (and this phrase *was* used) "Country Music Hall of Fame." The Rodgers museum would not open for another twenty years, in Meridian's Highland Park, across the city from the original monument site, and the monument would be moved there (as well as the train—on one huge flatbed truck) to join it. By then, an actual Country Music Hall of Fame was very well established—in Nashville.

For most of the people who were there, though, the first Jimmie Rodgers Day and the festivals that followed were simply celebrations. Lycrecia Williams, who would ride in parade cars with her mother Audrey and brother Hank Williams Jr. in the mid-'50s, recalls, "They were fun trips, because there were a lot of people there, a lot of the entertainers who'd been over at the house—so it was like old friends all getting together. I was just becoming a teenager, so I was flattered that people were saying how pretty I was, what a nice young lady I was turning out to be. I really did enjoy it."

"It *was* fun," her contemporary Jimmy Snow agrees. "You got to meet with *all* of your peers. Everybody who was in the business was there; you rubbed shoulders in the hotel with everybody. And there was a lot of great music, big crowds, parades."

Jimmy had a key role in the 1953 proceedings himself, a career starter for him. Bill Bruner, who had substituted for Jimmie Rodgers back in the day at several live shows that he missed because of poor health, performed for the last time, singing "My Old Pal," then passed the guitar Rodgers had given him in thanks on to young Jimmy. A simple, cheap Oscar Schmidt model autographed and dated "September, 1929" by Rodgers, it is one of the half-dozen or so instruments referred to as "Jimmie Rodgers' guitar." It went up on Hank Snow's wall, the younger Snow not being particularly interested in such things yet, and stayed there for decades, sometimes misidentified in print as a "Little Martin." Sold to Tim White of Bristol in 2007, this particular "Jimmie Rodgers guitar" now has a new home in the Mountain Music Museum there, as part of the Virginia-Tennessee border town's ongoing salute to the now celebrated Bristol Sessions. The presentation of that guitar in '53 lent an extra measure of sentiment to the closing line of the Snows' live duet performance: "He left his guitar behind him, when Jimmie Rodgers said goodbye."

The Rodgers memorial, publicized as much as any country music event of its time, was designed not just to enshrine the man, but also to stimulate a future for his music. "The celebration at Meridian," Jimmy Snow says, look-ing back, "gave Jimmie so much notoriety, and the fact that everybody who was in the business came there, that by the time that took off, with crowds that were humongous—these were the things that turned that around."

Charlie Lamb had been able to line up record executives and perform-ers from multiple labels to ride the convertibles in the parade, and they could not fail to notice the response. Jimmie's own label left a plaque (or was it a bronzed ad?) for the Singing Brakeman "whose great talents are preserved forever on RCA Victor Records," depicting a "big-hole" 45-rpm format single Jimmie would not have recognized. Ralph Peer was an active participant in the Meridian events and had every reason to be; the most immediate effect of this second Big Bang would be an upsurge in new recordings of Jimmie Rodgers songs, which were all published by Peer International.

Peer, along with Tubb, Snow, and Carrie Rodgers, was among those who contributed pieces to an unprecedented multipage Jimmie Rodgers trib-ute spread in *Billboard* magazine just before the Meridian event; indeed, he used his bylined article "Discovery of the Hillbilly Great" to suggest that his prescience and influence regarding Jimmie's musical possibilities were greater even than they no doubt had been.

It was from this point that the legendary promoter Roy Horton, man-ager of Peer's country and blues division, began the active pursuit of new placements for Jimmie Rodgers' songs. Raised in Pennsylvania coal min-ing territory and a working musician, Horton had become a song plugger for Peer in the '40s, having previously played bass for the Rodgers imitator Red River Dave in the '30s and formed the hillbilly band the Pinetoppers with his brother George Vaughn Horton. As George Vaughan, that talented brother would write or cowrite such country and pop hits as "Hillbilly Fever," "Mockingbird Hill," and "Sugarfoot Rag," and confuse a lot of people for years to come by being listed as the cowriter of "Mule Skinner Blues" "with" Jimmie Rodgers. In fact, he had composed the toned-down, cleaned-up, alternative lyric used on Bill Monroe's "New Mule Skinner Blues," with its "haw-haw-hey-hey" and deletion of all references to a mule's behind. Mon-roe rarely used the new lyric when performing, but that mysterious George Vaughan name or Vaughan Horton has tended to appear in the credits for all versions of "Blue Yodel, No. 8" since the '50s. The Peer organization's song placement efforts, which included Ralph Peer himself directly encouraging artists to record Rodgers' songs, worked.

In late 1954, the ultimately twangy honky tonk singer Webb Pierce, who had already made clip-clopping, declarative versions of "California Blues" and "In the Jailhouse Now"—though for a small label, so they were little heard—recorded what turned out to be the biggest hit of his career, a sales phenomenon for Decca Records that topped all the official country charts and stuck around for months, including a stay atop the jukebox chart for twenty-one weeks. This was Webb's new version of "In the Jailhouse Now," with call and response backup from the Wilburn Brothers and verses gathered by Webb from Jimmie's version of the old vaudeville standard and his follow-up, "In the Jail-House Now—No. 2."

Jimmie Rodgers' "Jailhouse" sides were not yet back in circulation on LP, nor was "Any Old Time," which Webb handled deftly in 1956. It was no accident that he had attended the first Meridian bash, recorded the songs, and felt comfortable enough to play around with the lyrics; he had been a fan of Jimmie's music since boyhood. "My mother," he would later tell Ralph Emery in an interview, "had just about every Jimmie Rodgers record in existence, so I played them a lot!"

Webb's near-rockabilly fiddle-and-steel-dominated "Any Old Time," which brought back a tune that so smacks of old-time vaudeville that it had dropped off the musical map since the '30s, would attempt to simplify and make contemporary the complicated point of view of Jimmie's lyric for '50s country music audiences. The roaming woman could now appear to be a domestic goddess *driven* away, and the reactive male bravura of the original was removed, as it so often was in the hurtin' side of honky tonk. All that stuff in the original about what appears to be the woman's unexplained, "unfair" roaming, in which Jimmie has no expressed complicity and about which he certainly expresses no guilt, instead announcing cavalierly that he was willing to forgive all that and let her once more "prove" what she can be, if she would come back home—that is all "updated," '50s-style. Webb modifies the story so that he admits he misses the woman and is guilty about driving her away; he is still hurting and begging for a letter like the one that sets off Rodgers' lyric. He even admits that he is no good (unlike Jimmie) at putting up a cheerful front: "When you left me sweetheart, I never thought I'd really care . . . Now that you're gone, I don't know what to do. Won't you please come back, 'cause I'm still in love with you."

That Jimmie was, very probably, consciously or not, singing from a long-suffering woman's point of view, contemplating a rounder much like himself who (conveniently) is easily forgiven is momentarily beside the point; Webb felt the need to deal with the way '50s audiences were likely to hear the song—and he turned the singer into the explicitly guilty, crying party. (Despite this effort to appeal to contemporary audiences, it sold less than "In the Jailhouse Now.")

Meanwhile, the vocal harmonies Webb added to "Jailhouse" suddenly made the old song a natural for a brother act—the great, harmonious Louvin Brothers, who kept it in their live shows, as captured in a lively 1956 recording at Bud Reed's New River Ranch. "Yeah; it's the version Webb Pierce did," Charlie Louvin would recall more than fifty years later in a 2007 interview after he had cut a verse-alternating version of "Waiting for a Train" with George Jones (Charlie's first ever studio recording of a Rodgers song). "It's true; that's the first. We never recorded a Hank Williams song either." And for the same reason: "Hank never did have a good harmony part, which lent itself to a good tenor singer." In that, Charlie Louvin was basically in agreement with Mike Seeger rather than the Callahan Brothers: Rodgers songs were made for soloists.

Another tonal approach entirely, virtually the opposite from Webb Pierce's, was soon taken by Jim Reeves as he moved from his early novelty-number period to become one of the central smooth-voiced crooners of the Nashville Sound era. Reeves' "Waiting for a Train" explored every sweet and even bouncy angle in that old tune, and the single reached the top of the country chart at the beginning of 1957.

Curiously, Gentleman Jim's friendly competitor Eddy Arnold, raised on Jimmie Rodgers from childhood in Tennessee, as Reeves had been in Texas, never cut a single of a Rodgers song in this period, for all his enthusiasm for Rodgers' music—which seems all the stranger when you remember that he had sold a million copies or so of his version of the old Emmett Miller hit "Anytime" in the late '40s. Eddy would eventually record "Roll Along, Kentucky Moon."

In any case, other new-era country crooners were turning to Rodgers songs. Marty Robbins, a rising young singer with his own pliable voice, would record "Mother Was a Lady" in this period, and he would later perform a number of Rodgers songs, including "Mississippi River Blues," on his syndicated television series, demonstrating the finesse with the material that would make him one of Merle Haggard's favorite Rodgers interpreters. Ernest Tubb's sometime duet partner, Opry costar and Decca stablemate Red Foley, had recorded, probably at Ernest's urging and just in time for the Meridian event, a single with oozing, almost Hawaiian-style steel, fiddle, and tinkling piano that coupled "Treasure Untold" and, unusually, "I'm Sorry We Met." Red's vocals are not dissimilar to the crooning Jimmy Wakely had been applying to Rodgers songs, though they are notably more southern and molasses-laced.

It was during 1955 that Hank Snow hit on a way to offer fans, including the thousands who were showing up at the ongoing Rodgers Day extravaganzas each year, "new" Jimmie Rodgers records. There would be no artificial, overdubbed vocal duet, but an updated musical setting, a new background—exactly the approach you would expect Hank to suggest. Eight Jimmie Rodgers sides, beginning no doubt with Webb Pierce's huge hit with "In the

Jailhouse Now" as inspiration, were overdubbed by key members of Snow's own band—Joe Talbot on steel, Ernie Newton on bass, Tommy Vaden on fiddle, and Chet Atkins, leader of the sessions, on guitar. Six of the sides would be released on singles attributed to "Jimmie Rodgers and the Rainbow Ranch Boys," and they amount to a working demonstration of where Jimmie's music could be meshed into current country sounds of a quarter of a century later, and where it was a sonic squeeze.

Jimmie sounds surprisingly natural singing "with" the steel-fiddle combination—a reminder that he had introduced an early, working version of the vocal-with-steel sound himself. The extensive yodeling on the original fits right in with Talbot's fluid, circular, modern steel playing, sounding at home with the sorts of filigree decorations that, in Ernest Tubb's tribute LP, for instance, had replaced the yodeling entirely. Similarly, with "Mule Skinner Blues," the frantic fiddle and steel just about approximate the Bill Monroe arrangement by which the song was best known. "Memphis Yodel," unheard until Bear Family released it on a box set in 1992, receives a similar jolt of fresh excitement. Modern sounds seemed to fit with Jimmie's blue yodels easily.

On the other hand, very little is added to the already full sound of "Peach Pickin' Time Down in Georgia." The direct sentiment of "Daddy and Home" and "Mother, the Queen of My Heart" is lost in the overbusy accompaniment, the new "background" gravy too much in the foreground. Much the same can be said for an attempt, also unreleased at the time, to update that first of all blue yodels, "T for Texas"; the busy fiddling, right through the verses, gets in the way of the singing, amply illustrating why it was never there in the first place.

These recordings, which apparently sold quite well, can be considered either harmless commercial keepsake novelties or cheeky overreaching on the part of Hank Snow and Chet Atkins—but that pair's continuing adventures in finding settings for Rodgers' music would produce some very satisfying results a few years later. In the 1958 sessions for Hank's second LP of Rodgers material, released in 1960 as *Hank Snow Sings Jimmie Rodgers Songs* (with the legend "In Living Stereo" on the blue cover almost overwhelming the title), they brought in Bill McElhiney on trumpet and E. R. McMillan on clarinet, joining such Nashville stalwarts as Chubby Wise on fiddle, Bob Moore on bass, and Buddy Harman on drums on about half of the tracks. The return of horns to an outright country LP looks, in retrospect, more like a peek into the sonic future a decade or more later than a retro Dixieland exercise, though it is possible that the Dixieland fad of the '50s prompted this isolated experiment.

Hank Snow is at the height of his vocal prowess in those sessions, demanding attention for the tight pairing of his phrasing and tone with the varied instrumental sounds used. The horns, particularly McMillan's swinging clarinet, and Marvin Hughes' energetic piano playing with its hints of the incrementally faster-than-ragtime World War I–era stride style, edge Hank toward a sort of cool jazz blues approach on the blues numbers, which works better for him than attempts at something emotionally hotter. "You and My Old Guitar"; "Any Old Time," with its original lyric restored; "Gambling Polka Dot Blues"; and "Travelin' Blues" are all favored with strong readings that go well outside what was considered country music at the time. ("This album is not just for the country-and-western fan," says veteran country musician Ted Daffan, a fan of Rodgers and friend of Snow, in the LP's liner notes.)

An admirably loose Hank throws in a "you *know* it baby" and even "I must be *rootin'* right") as a sly aside on the piano-driven "Blue Yodel No. 10," but he cannot quite allow himself to boast about his "regular grindin'" as Jimmie had. But then, what he sings instead, "my regular lovin'," probably seemed nearly as shocking in the heyday of *Ozzie and Harriet*—a reaction that Webb Pierce had assumed and avoided in his changes to lyrics.

By the beginnings of the '60s, a number of country artists who had found a second, often much-needed home in the commercial folk revival (and outlined much of the territory later called "Americana" while they were at it) were finding Jimmie Rodgers songs and themes a useful resource. If Bill Monroe could bring "Brakeman's Blues" to the bluegrass-intrigued New York folk revival scene, others could follow that example.

Johnny Cash, who, like Monroe, would be welcomed at the Newport Folk Festivals that were soon to come, recorded many train songs in the mid-'50s during his years with Sun Records in Memphis, but an aborted version of "Brakeman's Blues" produced by Cowboy Jack Clement was his only early attempt at a Rodgers cover. By 1959, he was recording with Columbia Records—because of the variety of music and the special projects the move enabled him to do—and based in Los Angeles, looking for Hollywood opportunities. Appearing on the hip *Town Hall Party* TV show out of Compton that August, he wondered aloud if the audience would even accept the more detailed, narrative story songs he was just starting to try on record.

Dressed in what appears to be, even on black-and-white television, a light cream-colored suit, he offered his new "Frankie's Man Johnny," the updated Johnny a "guitar-picker with a wicked, wandering eye," Frankie's man *"almost* all the time." He first warned the crowd, "I rewrite a lot of songs; [this one's] actually an old folk song, you know, that was rewritten . . . Some of the best folk entertainers have passed on—like Jimmie Rodgers and Hank Williams—and I haven't been feeling too good myself."

He would soon be promoting the idea of a Hollywood feature film on the life of Jimmie Rodgers with himself in the lead, which took him (as described back in this book's introduction) to the stage of Carnegie Hall in Jimmie's brakeman's suit, provided by Carrie Rodgers. While neither of those efforts worked out very well, Cash had two hit singles in 1962 with a freshly comic, well-timed, absurdist "In the Jailhouse Now," which includes a call for the guitar to yodel, and a wistful "Waiting for a Train." (These recordings did show some debts to the Webb Pierce and Jim Reeves precedents.)

Jimmie Skinner, a lifelong Jimmie Rodgers devotee, is today best remembered as the author of bluegrass standards like "You Don't Know My Mind" and "Doin' My Time," and for his Cincinnati-based mail-order record store, which was important for sales of Jimmie Rodgers reissues and bluegrass records alike. He was also a singer of middling success and middling individuality, most of that distinctiveness derived from his bluesy midrange tone, and one model for Johnny Cash's practice of walking the country/folk borderline. (Skinner's tendency to go slightly flat when dropping to the lower notes in his reach and thin when stretching for the top, which comes off sounding pretty bluesy, would recur in Johnny Cash's singing as well.)

Skinner had had some success with the Rodgers-saluting single "Jimmie's Yodel Blues," basically a version of "Never No Mo' Blues" on the tiny Radio Artists label in 1950. In 1962, he came up with a full LP for Mercury Records, *Jimmie Skinner Sings Jimmie Rodgers*, the album dedicated to Carrie, first lady of country music, who is said to have encouraged the project but died soon afterward. When younger, Skinner had been quite a good yodeler; at this stage, he still has a voice break that yodels within a word, much as Jimmie Rodgers had. The song choice is eclectic, as befits someone who knows all the songs and figures this will be his one chance to record ones he likes. "Miss the Mississippi and You" makes an appearance on the LP, with some particularly oozy steel from Rusty York, and also "Dear Old Sunny South by the Sea."

It was also in 1962, in a similar context of appealing to the commercial folk market with old-timey tunes, that Grandpa Jones recorded his nearly all-Rodgers *Yodeling Hits* LP for Monument (as described in chapter 4)—and scored a hit single with a breakneck, holler-and-growl version of "T for Texas." Possibly it was not the best idea to include in the liner notes a crack about Grandpa's dislike for "phony folk song singers," but that was intended to place him as a real sort of folk singer—which seemed to mean a working vaudevillian showman rather than a mild college frat boy in a sweater.

These varied versions of Jimmie's songs, many of them hits, were but one important indication of the revival of interest in him within country music in the decade after Meridian's first memorial event. There were also incremental, official moves toward institutionalizing Jimmie Rodgers as "the father of country music." A clear indication of his growing stature in Nashville came early, in late November 1953, as the new self-recognition and self-congratulation continued. At a ceremony at the Ryman Auditorium during the annual country disc jockeys' convention, marking also the twenty-eighth anniversary of the Grand Ole Opry, *Billboard*'s Paul Ackerman handed out eight scrolls to performers dubbed the "All-Time Greats" of country singing. There to accept this honor, a clear precursor of induction to the Country Music Hall of Fame years later, were Ernest Tubb, Roy Acuff, Hank Snow, Eddy Arnold, Red Foley, Carl Smith (who would have to wait quite awhile to be so honored at the Hall of Fame), and representatives of two who could not attend—Fred Rose accepting for Hank Williams and Carrie Rodgers for Jimmie. In a photo spread on the event in *Hoedown* magazine, the unrewarded Carter Sisters and Mother Maybelle are shown among the attendees, with little comment besides "June Carter is married to Opry Star Carl Smith." As the second Jimmie Rodgers Day approached in May 1954, Jimmie was on the cover of *Cash Box* as the "Father of Country Music," and there was an accompanying article fostered by Charlie Lamb. By now, labels for both the music and the man were more or less settled.

The changing pop music scene of the mid- to late '50s would throw the country music Jimmie was now said to have fathered into a fight for its very survival as potential new fans were being grabbed by rockabilly and rhythm and blues instead. The number of radio stations playing country records plummeted, and in 1958, forward-looking executives and artists out of the fledgling Nashville industry founded the Country Music Association (CMA) to fight for the reinvigoration and acceptance of the music.

An early, primitive little offset-printed issue of the organization's *Close-up* newsletter (still active but now a four-color magazine), described the opportunity to piggyback publicity at the 1959 Jimmie Rodgers Day Festival, where Johnny Cash, Jimmie Skinner, Johnny Horton, Mac Wiseman, Skeeter Davis, and Porter Wagoner were among those performing. There was discussion in a 1960 issue of the origins of the British country publication *Country Western Express*, founded by two Jimmie Rodgers fans. And then, at a CMA meeting in Miami in the spring of 1961, where the organization was staging its own country music spectacular for fans, the decision was taken to establish a Country Music Hall of Fame, patterned after the successful Baseball Hall of Fame. This institutionalizing of country history was seen not only as a means to put current-day music in a context for fans, but also to further legitimize the industry and its core demographic base commercially.

A selection process was decided on for induction, and it was announced in June 1961 that for the first year—no doubt to avoid controversy at the outset—all of the inductees would be deceased. The first three whose image and career summary would be etched onto the famed Hall of Fame plaques would prove to be Hank Williams, publisher Fred Rose, and Jimmie Rodgers. There was not yet a Hall of Fame building, so the marker visited by thousands annually was initially displayed in Nashville's Tennessee State Museum, where it was unveiled in November 1961. The words on that plaque are well known now, almost a half a century later, and rarely if ever challenged. It had taken a considerable amount of effort—and reconsideration—to put them there: " 'The Singing Brakeman' Jimmie Rodgers' name stands foremost in the country music field as 'The Man Who Started It All.' His songs told the great stories of the singing rails, the powerful steam locomotives and the wonderful railroad people that he loved so well. Although small in stature, he was a giant among men, starting a trend in the musical taste of millions."

What the citation has no room to suggest is that Rodgers' contributions to the southwestern branch of country music had long been so much easier to trace than those to the southeastern school; this was a father of country music who gave very short shrift to gospel music or to sentimental evocations of farm life per se—preferring salutes to one southern region or another and, tellingly, depictions of life as experienced not so much in the country, but in the sorts of small towns where most of the audience increasingly resided. But after World War II, and especially after 1953, the East/West division in country music, while still present, was far less important. There were hot players, from Monroe to Chet Atkins, who were Eastern based, crooners like Reeves and Arnold who could fit in anywhere, and Texans on the Opry, while an artist as assertively southwestern as Buck Owens might include gospel numbers along with the rougher stuff in any of his shows.

It was this nationalized, robust genre of many flavors that had earned the name "country music," rather than "hillbilly" or even "country and western"—and Jimmie Rodgers made a very credible father for it. He had established a deep relation with the audience that would come to be understood as country music's, and as the Hall of Fame citation suggests, he had carved out a set of themes and musical approaches to them that would remain potent in the developing field over time. He was such a hero and model to many who performed country music that he spawned emotionally committed advocates who saw him as the father and who made the title stick.

But even then, as other people would be pointing out, country music was not all that the rough-hewn little man had set in motion.

Select Soundtrack

Tommy Duncan

"Gamblin' Polka Dot Blues," "In the Jailhouse Now," "Mississippi River Blues," and "Never No More Blues" (1949–51) are on *Texas Moon* (Bear Family, 1996).

Jimmie Rodgers Meets Hank Williams

- **Norman Phelps/Virginia Rounders:** "Hank Williams Meets Jimmie Rodgers." Out of print.
- **Willie Phelps:** "Hank Williams Meets Jimmie Rodgers," "Jimmie Rodgers Will Never Die," "So Long, Pal Jimmie." Out of print.
- **Buddy Williams:** "The Death of Hank and Jimmie." Out of print.
- **The Hawking Brothers:** "Will Hank Williams Meet Jimmie Rodgers?" is on the *You And My Old Guitar* tribute CD (Jasmine, 2008).
- **Eddie Cochran and Hank Cochran (Cochran Brothers):** "Two Blue Singing Stars" is widely available online.
- **Riley Crabtree:** See *When Hank Williams Met Jimmie Rodgers* (Cattle/Binge, 2006) for Riley's own Hank/Jimmie memorial song and his versions of Rodgers songs.

The Jimmie Rodgers Country Revival

- **Billy Walker:** *Tribute to Jimmie Rodgers, the Father of Country Music* (Gusto, 2006).
- **Ernest Tubb:** *Ernest Tubb Sings Jimmie Rodgers Songs* (Decca), released August 1951. All cuts also appear on the Ernest Tubb box set *Let's Say Goodbye Like We Said Hello* (Bear Family, 1994). "In the Jailhouse Now" and "Jimmie Rodgers' Last Blue Yodel" appear on numerous anthologies.
- **Lefty Frizzell:** *Songs of Jimmie Rodgers Sung by Lefty Frizzell* was released as an eight-song Columbia LP (1951), as

an expanded twelve-song LP on Columbia's Harmony label (1960), and on Koch/Sony CD in 1999.

- **Bill Monroe:** "Brakeman's Blues/Travelin' Blues" was released in 1951, "Sailor's Plea"/"When the Cactus Is in Bloom" in 1952, and the remaining four Rodgers sessions cuts on the box set *Bill Monroe: Bluegrass 1950–1958* (Bear Family, 1990), on which they all appear. "New Mule Skinner Blues" is on various Monroe anthologies that include Decca sides.

- **Hank Snow:** *Hank Snow Salutes Jimmie Rodgers* (RCA Victor LP, 1952); all cuts and songs from the earlier EP *Hank Snow Sings Famous Railroading Songs*, also appear on *Hank Snow: The Singing Ranger, 1949–1953* (Bear Family, 2003). *Hank Snow Sings Jimmie Rodgers Songs* (RCA Victor LP, 1960); all of its cuts also appear on *Hank Snow: The Singing Ranger, Volume 3* (Bear Family, 1992).

- **Webb Pierce:** "In the Jailhouse Now," "Any Old Time," and "California Blues" are on the box set *Webb Pierce: The Wondering Boy 1951–1958* (Bear Family, 1990). The earlier small-label versions of "Jailhouse" and "California Blues" appear on *Webb Pierce: The Complete 4-Star/Pacemaker Recordings* (Acrobat, 2006). Pierce can be seen performing his hit version of "Jailhouse" on the Shanachie DVD *Webb Pierce and Chet Atkins*, derived from Albert Gannaway filmed performances; Pierce sings the song with Red Sovine and Doyle Wilburn. A much later *Country Music Caravan* telecast tape survives in which he sings it with Del Reeves.

- **Jimmie Rodgers recordings overdubbed by Hank Snow's Rainbow Ranch Boys:** 1955; "In the Jailhouse Now — No. 2"/"Peach Pickin' Time Down in Georgia" (which also appears on the JSP CD set *Sounds Like Jimmie Rodgers*), "Muleskinner Blues"/"Mother, the Queen of My Heart," "Never No Mo"/"Daddy and Home" (RCA Victor singles), and two further overdubs unissued at the time are all on the box set *Jimmie Rodgers: The Singing Brakeman* (Bear Family).

- **Red Foley:** "Treasure Untold"/"I'm Sorry We Met" (Decca, 1953). The latter is on the *Let Me Be Your Sidetrack* (Bear Family) salute set.

- **Jim Reeves:** "Waiting for a Train" (RCA, 1957). Various compilations.

- **Marty Robbins:** "My Mother Was a Lady" is on the box set *Marty Robbins Country 1951–1958* (Bear Family, 1991). Robbins also performed "Roll Along, Kentucky Moon" and "Mississippi River Blues" on his 1968–69 TV series.

- **The Louvin Brothers:** The 1956 "In the Jailhouse Now" is on *Live at New River Ranch* (Copper Creek, 1996).

- **Johnny Cash:** "In the Jailhouse Now" and "Waiting for a Train" (Columbia, 1962) are on *Johnny Cash: The Legend* (Sony/Legacy, 2005). "T for Texas," "The One Rose," and a late-in-life "Waiting for a Train" are on *Unearthed* (Sony). "My Mother Was a Lady" is on *Johnny Cash/Personal File* (Sony BMG, 2006). His ballad singing comments are on *Johnny Cash at Town Hall Party* (Bear Family DVD).

- **Grandpa Jones:** "T for Texas" is from *Grandpa Jones Yodeling Hits*, his Rodgers salute (Monument LP, 1962) and is on the *I Am Sad and Weary* Rodgers tribute set (Bear Family, 2003).

- **Jimmy Skinner:** *Jimmie Skinner Sings Jimmie Rodgers* (Mercury, 1962) and all of its songs are on the *Doin' My Time* box set (Bear Family, 2003).

twelve

Rough and Rowdy Ways
To the Rock and Roll Hall of Fame

It was not a coincidence. Just two weeks before that first Jimmie Rodgers Festival got under way in May 1953, and reinvigorated Jimmie's music within the country music industry, Bill Haley's rave-up, "Crazy Man Crazy," first entered the pop music charts. The Chester, Pennsylvania hillbilly-by-choice was no longer being referred to as Yodeling Bill Haley, and the band behind him was not dubbed the Downhomers or even the Saddlemen any more. Haley's Comets were streaking overhead, flying too high to be saddled or kept down on the farm. The record was thought of as rhythm and blues, and from its Louis Jordan–inspired drum blast opening, basically, it was.

Just a few years later, the liner notes on the RCA Victor album *Elvis* would make explicit the genuine connection between Jimmie Rodgers' music and image and what was coming to be called rock 'n' roll, if with a vagueness about genre titles that was typical of the time. "Of commercial folk music," the cover suggested to potential album buyers, "Presley is perhaps the most original singer since Jimmie Rodgers. His rhythmic style derives from exactly the same source of Deep South blues and jazz as that which inspired the late Blue Yodeler."

Jason Ringenberg, lead singer and whirling dervish of the incendiary early-'80s Nashville-based "cowpunk" rockers Jason and the Scorchers, recalls the first time he and his band checked out a Jimmie Rodgers hits LP for potentially useful hard rock fodder: "When the band first started, we were messing around, hopping up country songs. On that Jimmie Rodgers compilation, some things just popped out. 'She rubbed my back with alcohol just to cure my cough—I almost broke my back trying to lick it off'! I swear that's the best rock 'n' roll line *ever written*. That's better than the Stones' 'Honky Tonk Women,' better than anything Springsteen or anybody ever wrote." That liquor-soaked line from Jimmie's "Long Tall Mamma Blues" would be permanently stapled onto the Scorchers' trailblazing punk version of "Jimmie Rodgers' Last Blue Yodel."

The renewed rerelease of Jimmie Rodgers recordings through the '50s and into the '60s, and the upsurge in new versions of his songs in the country music world, happened precisely as broad American pop tastes, and those of white, Southern pop audiences in particular, were threatening to become seriously rowdy and physical once again. As had been demonstrated by the advent of blue yodeling blues, western swing, bluegrass, country boogie, and honky tonk, when white southern music makers feel that sporadic urge to get rougher and rowdier, to bring the body and humor and ego more into play again, they tend to look across the tracks, to the sounds of the other side of town, the African-American part. That now meant looking to rhythm and blues, as it once did to the "Deep South blues and jazz" mentioned by that anonymous *Elvis* annotator.

Things had been moving in this direction ever since World War II. The recently deceased Hank Williams' first propulsive, blues-based record, "Move It on Over," had charted as country in 1947, and in retrospect, the famed cut seems to anticipate key aspects of Chuck Berry's musical attack. In New Orleans, the emerging rhythm and blues star Fats Domino, soon to be an extraordinarily popular pop star, would comfortably and very successfully record Hank Williams songs. But long before Hank came into earshot, Domino, like so many blues performers before him, had been a Jimmie Rodgers fan.

Asked today about his early encounters with Jimmie Rodgers music, Fats instantly quotes lines from "Waiting for a Train" with relish, and the yodel, too. In 1955, he recorded "Helping Hand," a rolling, hobo-free version of the song with a New Orleans rhythm and blues arrangement, including honking saxes, worked out with his regular collaborator Dave Bartholomew. Fats had grown up with his family's old 78s, Rodgers records among them. As he recalls, when the spring broke on the household Victrola in the late '30s, he would spin the old records with his own fingers, so he could learn them in any case. "I didn't know whether he was white or black," Fats says, "but I know I liked him. I liked everything he done." He mentions "T for Texas" and "Any Old Time" in particular; he has recorded the latter himself, with a fresh, pounding beat. Asked what the specific attractions of those Rodgers records were for him, he says, "I liked *everything* about them."

When Chuck Berry was high on the short list of those competing with Fats Domino to see who could extend this powerful rock 'n' roll idiom the furthest, he was already steeped in Jimmie Rodgers music himself. Rockabilly great Carl Perkins recalled in his memoir that once when he broke into a blue yodel on a rock 'n' roll tour bus, Berry leaned over and corrected him about the verses, informing him, "That second verse belongs in 'Blue Yodel Number 4'!" Carl added, "Chuck knew *every* blue yodel."

The case would be made, gradually but eventually routinely, that Jimmie Rodgers was, as the Rock and Roll Hall of Fame labeled him at his induction in 1986, a key "early influence on rock and roll." Even putting the musical impact aside, the picture of Jimmie Rodgers as a rock precursor was never difficult to sketch. It is simply a matter of emphasis. The sexual boasting and touches of explicit violence in his blues give you a clue, as does his mixing of those blues with white country balladry and pop, while the Bob Wills/western swing interpretations show that you can dance to the Rodgers mix if it is handled right.

Honky tonk country, from Ernest Tubb and Ted Daffan forward to Hank Williams, had emphasized the "been done wrong" elements in Jimmie's blues, the situations that left you lonely and crying in your beer, with, as they sang it, a treacherous female often the suggested cause. Now rockabilly turned that around, emphasizing another side of the Jimmie Rodgers blues—that rather than just sitting and crying or walking the floor, you could shake the feeling off or even kick back with a "won't take it any more" attitude. Rodgers' music, words, or sound had never *just* cried.

The irrepressible, even irresponsible rounder image adds to the picture of Jimmie as rocker. The song "My Rough and Rowdy Ways" in particular, in addition to providing a phrase useful for many in the rougher and rowdier kinds of country music, offers a convincing, knowing portrait of the centrifugal "keep you on the rough side" force at work on the less genteel side of town—right down to the "friends" there who try to drag the settled or reformed ex-rounder back into that life at every turn.

There was, from early on, that rebel outsider, Huck Finn aspect to Rodgers' life. When he tackled these subjects, he knew what he was talking about, and sounded like it. As his biographer Nolan Porterfield has pointed out, plenty of photos have surfaced, published and unpublished, of Jimmie with some record executive's wife or some other unknown lovely on his arm while he is out on the road, sometimes hanging by a fancy car or even by a train, with bottles of booze in hands all around. There are specific, credible stories of Jimmie arriving in a town, meeting a few women, and leaving several new divorces in progress in his wake. Clayton McMichen reported helping to administer morphine shots to Jimmie toward the end

Rowdy ways in Texas: Jimmie and unidentified friends.

of his life, and there was clearly plenty of drinking in Jimmie's general vicinity.

As for evidence that he was carrying with him the image of the transgressor in his own day, there is the suggestive fact that Jimmie Rodgers was a personal favorite of his contemporary Bonnie Parker, of the beloved, notorious Texas outlaw pair Bonnie and Clyde. Her sister, Billie Jean Parker, would recall, "Bonnie was musically inclined. [She] could hear a song and she'd go home and play it [on the piano]. She liked Jimmie Rodgers; she had every record that he ever made." You would figure that Bonnie would have found a number like the gangbanger saga "Pistol Packin' Papa" attractive, if not downright familiar in content. In fact, some of the self-publicizing doggerel Bonnie Parker wrote, which was picked up by newspapers at the time, feature rhythms and rhetoric closely resembling Rodgers record lyrics such as "Mother, the Queen of My Heart." The Bonnie and Clyde connection to Jimmie Rodgers may well have been closer than shared musical or rhetorical interests. Frank Ballinger, an authority on the Barrow gang, has a copy of a photo of the fabled pair in hiding, inscribed as taken by none other than Jimmie Rodgers' friend and song collaborator Carey D. Harvey. Clyde's sister Marie confirmed that Harvey had taken it. Did the couple who, as the '60s movie ads put it, "were young, in love, and robbed banks"

Meeting Jimmie Rodgers

ever meet Jimmie? They reportedly did manage to catch some early Texas swing by Milton Brown's band at the Crystal Springs Dance Pavilion in Ft. Worth, when not distracted by the pressing need to dodge bullets. It was just the sort of spot Rodgers frequented as well.

Whether they ever met or not, Jimmie Rodgers would not have minded suggesting he was acquainted with their like; from early on, he understood, as so many rock 'n' roll stars would later, the image value of seeming to be a vaguely dangerous near outlaw, a man who hung around with people you might not be ready to spend time with yourself. It was an especially useful image addition for a man often in pain, sapped of energy, and waylaid by tuberculosis. Elsie McWilliams, who knew Jimmie as well as anyone, always suggested that apart from his high-stakes gambling, Jimmie's exploits tended to be amplified, even exaggerated by fans who loved to think of him as something of a wild one—with his agreement. "He wanted to *appear* very rough," she recalled. "He wanted everyone to think that he was a rough sort of fellah."

An industry would be built on such suggestions. One of the prime movers responsible for "breaking" rock 'n' roll had been a Florence, Alabama, ten year-old, already in love with blues, hillbilly, and gospel music when Jimmie Rodgers died—Sam Phillips. The first record he could remember listening to, Phillips told the author Peter Guralnick, was Jimmie's "Waiting for a Train," which, like so many others, he proceeded to sing as he recalled it. It says much about Phillips' sensibility that of the blues artists he recorded in Memphis, Tennessee, early in his career, circa 1951–52, the one he often said he was proudest of having helped bring forward, his favorite artist of all, was Howlin' Wolf—whose Rodgers influence was self-proclaimed. Another artist Sam recorded early on, B. B. King, was also, as we have seen, a Rodgers fan. A third Phillips find, the African-American protorockabilly Junior Parker, had a pretty good blues song about a railroad both real and metaphorical, "Mystery Train."

Whenever and however exactly Sam Phillips made some version of the often quoted, much debated, and easily misunderstood remark about knowing he could "make a million dollars" if he could find a white boy who could "sing like a Negro," he certainly was well aware that this commercial trick had been pulled off before, that Jimmie Rodgers had ridden that train successfully. What's more, he knew that what made it work was not blatantly derivative, exploitive imitation of African-American vocal styles, but identifying an artist comfortable with the material and with the world it came from, someone who could yield a different, individual interpretation.

Phillips' recordings of the obscure, folksy Harmonica Frank Floyd have sometimes been pointed to as early, failed attempts to find a synthesis of rhythm and blues and country for the '50s. Listened to today, they seem like dispatches from the era of Goebel Reeves, coming from a man whose talents did not translate into the record medium particularly well. Floyd's "Great Medical Managerist," recorded by Sam, is the focus of a full chapter of Greil Marcus' celebrated *Mystery Train*—built up as an artifact of Phillips' striving, it seems, mainly so it can be knocked down. It is portrayed there as the work of a country musician stuck in that genre's allegedly inevitable constriction, as compared to the liberating rock 'n' roll that is just around the corner. Frank was not really an artist who could carry all of that weight and significance well, but his background was interesting. He had been a Depression-era hobo who took up music only after hearing Rodgers and may have met Jimmie in person, out on the road. He could sing blues, but he certainly did not have Jimmie's rhythm and aggression—and he did not have much to do with rock 'n' roll, either. He would eventually record an outright Rodgers tribute and Blue Yodels Nos. 6 and 7. That Sam Phillips, given the artists he did discover, ever took him to be a possible answer to the "million dollar question" is highly doubtful. Nor, exactly, were two other Sun artists who recorded some Rodgers tunes. Johnny Cash, who recorded "Brakeman's Blues," was to Phillips' discerning ear a country artist, relatively pure and strikingly simple, not a man to cross the lines of genre, race, and national border and some potential pop monster. The less widely known rockabilly Sonny Burgess recorded an incendiary version of "My Little Lady" at Sun, too, as "Sadie's Back in Town," but stardom was not his destiny.

Sam's artist at Sun records who would fit the "million dollar find" bill was, of course, Elvis Presley. Elvis' connections to Jimmie Rodgers and his music, as touted by RCA in those *Elvis* album notes, are real but subtle. We know that Elvis was exposed to Jimmie Rodgers' records and songs from early on. There is ample testimony that his father Vernon and, particularly, his mother Gladys Presley, who especially loved "Mean Mamma Blues," were Rodgers fans. That would be expected, given that they were poor working folks from Tupelo, Mississippi, and of the right generation. Still only regionally famous, Elvis himself appeared at the Jimmie Rodgers Memorial Festival in Meridian in May 1955 while on tour with the Hank Snow Show and rode in the parade on the hood of a Cadillac with his friend, Hank's son. Jimmie Rodgers Snow confirms that Presley was in very comfortable and familiar territory when the subject of Rodgers music was raised—which was bound to happen around Hank Snow, let alone on the streets of Meridian. Elvis performed both sides of his latest Sun single, "Baby Let's Play House" and "I'm Left, You're Right, She's Gone" among other well-received numbers, none of them apparently Rodgers songs, at the festival's big junior college stadium show.

Jimmy Snow and Elvis Presley "Cadillac-in'" in the Jimmie Rodgers Day parade, Meridian, Mississippi, May 1955.

Unreported in detail has been the virtually private show Presley gave while in Meridian, backstage at the Hamasa Temple Ballroom later the same night, for a small audience close to the festival organizers. According to eyewitness Carl Fitzgerald, a veteran Meridian music reporter and talk show host, Elvis sang duets with local fifteen-year-old singer Patsy Norman on a selection of mainstream pop ballads from the "great American songbook"— material he was not yet generally known for. As with Hank Williams, there is a single photo, which also includes Jim Reeves among others, showing Elvis meeting Carrie Rodgers at a get-together in Meridian sponsored by New Orleans radio station WBOK.

Ken Berryhill, who as a local radio executive would help revive the festival in Meridian after its temporary suspension in the late '50s and would come to know Carrie Rodgers and Else McWilliams and even manage Jimmie's grandson Jimmie Dale Court, was working in television in Memphis during this period. Not many weeks after Elvis' 1955 Meridian appearance, he spent some time with the Presley family at the first house they bought with Elvis's early hit-making money, the one before Graceland. As Ken recalls, "The person in that family who was the big fan of Jimmie Rodgers was his mother, Gladys. I drove by there one night, stopped in there, heading home from the TV station, and Elvis was back in his room with two girls. He just poked his head in and said hi. Gladys had had a few, still had the beer bottle, in fact, and never got off the couch. They may have been playing a Jimmie Rodgers record; something like that made his name come up, and she said, 'Well, *you* were a good friend of Jimmie Rodgers.' And I said, 'No, I was only about five when he died.' Vernon was talking about something else, but then Gladys interrupted and asked, 'Well then, where did you *meet* Jimmie Rodgers?' It kept going round and round. Vernon just looked at her, and then Elvis, who'd heard this, came back in the room and said 'Mama, he's told you four times—he *never met* Jimmie Rodgers!'"

One colorful Rodgers-related Elvis story, which has been related in a half-dozen books, is inaccurate on all counts—but where there are legends, there are legends about them. In this one, Presley, within a week of graduating from high school, hitches to Meridian, for the first 1953 Jimmie Rodgers Festival, a complete unknown, takes part in the talent contest and wins second prize, a guitar. As mythically appealing as it would be to place Elvis at that historic event, the story is a combination of handed-down misinformation and fanciful embroidery. To set the record straight, there was no talent contest at the 1953 festival. They did not begin staging those until 1955, the year Elvis actually appeared there—not competing in an amateur show, of course, but as a highly publicized, rising young regional star. It seems that the young girl who won the contest in 1955 revisited Meridian years later and reminded people she had won the year Elvis was there. Some locals thought she was referring to having competed against him in the amateur contest and began repeating it that way, and one Meridian photographer, understanding that there was no sense to that, spread the amended tale of Elvis appearing as an amateur two years before. Some writers bought into that fantasy without checking.

Elvis never recorded a Jimmie Rodgers song; his much updated version of "Frankie and Johnny" for the movie of the same name was as close as he got. But that tells us nothing of the ways in which the Jimmie Rodgers model created a space for Elvis to happen—for Presley was as perfect a realization of the roots music pop hero as Jimmie and, arguably, in certain ways, more so.

Elvis, like Jimmie, maintained his local and regional identity while finding ways to speak to the world. In Elvis' wake, when we hear Jimmie Rodgers sing of going "Cadillac-in'," in "Jimmie the Kid," it is difficult not to wonder, at least momentarily, if they were already available in pink. Presley's role as unelected representative and hero of the working-class south has barely wavered to this day, even in the aftermath of massive wealth, Hollywood fame, an increasingly secluded lifestyle, death, and biographical

Meeting Jimmie Rodgers

revelation. His music transcended genres, and he took a variety of American musical styles to places they had never been, for ever-widening audiences. There was in him that same image-straddling Huck Finn–Tom Sawyer concatenation Jimmie had displayed—the lip-curling, leather-clad rebel who says "Yes, ma'am" and loves his mama. Indeed, with Presley's continuing love for and interest in gospel music, he brought a Christian element to the mix that Jimmie had not, thereby adding a certain worshipful quality to his lasting adulation.

Nowhere can we see more clearly how Elvis' career was made possible by the Rodgers model than in his becoming an international multimedia star—particularly through his movies. "Elvis is Back—and He's Got More Women Than a Passenger Train Can Haul!" was not a selling line for any of them, but it easily could have been; it has the tone, even if Presley worked with race cars and motorcycles instead of trains. It is tellingly easy to substitute Jimmie Rodgers song titles and themes for Elvis Presley movie titles. If "Frankie and Johnny" gets you precisely to *Frankie and Johnny* in this game, "In the Jailhouse Now" yields *Jailhouse Rock*. "Gambling Polka Dot Blues"—that's *Viva Las Vegas*. "My Little Old Home in New Orleans"— *King Creole*. "The Sailor's Plea"—the navy-based *Easy Come, Easy Go*, and "Soldier's Sweetheart"—*G.I. Blues*. "Women Make a Fool Out of Me"— *The Trouble with Girls*. And "Everybody Does It in Hawaii," or maybe "Elvis Does It in Hawaii," could just as well have been the title for *Blue Hawaii* or *Paradise, Hawaiian Style*.

However, the genuinely rough and generally rowdier performer at Sam Phillips' Sun Records, the one who would truly, knowingly absorb the music of Jimmie Rodgers and prove to be one of its great all-time interpreters, was not Elvis Presley. This was the man who is reported to have roared from the stage in 1994, "I wanted to be Jimmie Rodgers reincarnated, but they wouldn't *let* me!"—rock 'n' roll's master of mass destruction, creation, and preservation, Jerry Lee Lewis.

In Lewis's nimble hands, as in Jimmie Rodgers', songs from as far back as the mid-nineteenth century or as fresh as the current pop charts all become live, immediate entertainment—and his own. And in the matter of perpetuating yourself and your image in your material, if "Jimmie the Kid" had heard the way Lewis has gotten the talismanic phrase "Jerry Lee" into practically every song he has ever performed, toyed with, and recorded, he would have been downright envious. Pressed to declare which performers have mattered to him most, for over fifty years now Jerry Lee has responded with some variation on the comment "There have been many great performers, but only four great *stylists*—Al Jolson, Jimmie Rodgers, Hank Williams, and Jerry Lee Lewis."

Lewis' friend and producer at Sun, Cowboy Jack Clement, notes of Jimmie Rodgers' appearance in that oft-repeated, exclusive list, "Well, Jerry Lee *would* say that, wouldn't he? Because he doesn't play like other boogie-woogie piano players. One thing that's different is that, a lot of times, that left hand is playing Jimmie Rodgers guitar runs."

While this is not a musical analysis that it seems wise to raise with the "Ferriday Fireball" directly, Jerry Lee does agree today that "Jimmie Rodgers was great accompanying himself, *great*. And when he recorded with that jazz band, man, I love that Dixieland sound, like on that song 'Blue-Eyed Jane.' But his yodel, that's what still gets me every time. He had a great singing voice, too."

What Lewis has always meant by a "stylist" is a performer who puts his stamp indelibly on virtually any sort of material or song he takes on. Indeed, Jerry Lee's characterization of Rodgers speaks to the close link between a distinctive stylist and a potential star—or even a popular hero: "Yeah; Jimmie Rodgers had to be a strong personality, driven. He was special, and I'll bet he stood out in a crowd—in a *good* way. People connected with him; they could identify themselves with him. Hard-working people understood where he was coming from."

Jerry Lee Lewis heard Jimmie Rodgers' music from his childhood in Louisiana in the '30s. His father, Elmo, had a set of original Rodgers records and would sing along with them, strumming a guitar. Jimmie's original version of "The One Rose," released posthumously in 1937, was Elmo's favorite, and it's a song Jerry Lee has always performed with romantic depth and delicacy. With Rodgers songs, he has had a lot of practice. "When I was in my teens," he recalls, "I was [already] playing his songs in clubs where I was performing. I made them my *own* style though."

The choice of Rodgers songs Lewis has chosen to record over the years—standouts include "My Carolina Sunshine Girl" and "Waiting for a Train" at Sun, and a majestic version of "Miss the Mississippi and You" later on—shows a certain predilection for the ballads over blue yodels. But Lewis has a firm handle on where Rodgers fits into the rock 'n' roll story, particularly in its beginnings:

"Back in the '40s and '50s he had an influence. But what they call rock 'n' roll today has become something so different, [that] there are not that many artists out there that have ever even heard of Jimmie Rodgers. At least their music does not *sound* like they've ever listened to him. They need to get back to the original rock 'n' roll! He was one of the main ones who paved the way." And to hammer the point home, Jerry Lee adds, "Don't just remember that Jimmie Rodgers mattered; remember *he still does*."

However, the act that would first take a Rodgers song to the top of the pop charts in unabashedly propulsive rock 'n' roll style would not be a legend and creative force like Jerry Lee, and they would not have all that much to say about Jimmie Rodgers. They would not be from the South, either. The year was 1960, the band was a duo from out of Wisconsin, the Fendermen, and the song was "Mule Skinner Blues," in a rumbling, thumping, electrified version that pushed the manic yodeling and cackling introduced by Bill Monroe and Rose Maddox to unexplored, electrified limits. The famous "Ha-ha-hahs" on the single are still pretty unnerving, and fun, the total sound now seeming to predict the attack of some punk rock bands twenty years later.

"When I first met up with Jim Sundquist," recalls the Fendermen's jubilantly crazed singer Phil Humphrey, referring to his Fender guitar–playing partner, "we started playing bars for free beer. When they started paying us five bucks a night, we started playing every weekend! That was the first time we were doing 'Mule Skinner Blues' publicly. After we'd done it about a month, people were going nuts, and we had to play it four or five times a night. Everyone in the bar kept saying, 'Why don't you record that song; it would be a hit.' So, what the heck, we went into the garage and put a tape recorder down and recorded it."

The story from there is garage-band rock legend. After the number was rerecorded more professionally by a local record store owner, with added echo, the tiny Cuca Records put it out—if only five hundred copies of it. Then deejay Lindy Shannon, out of nearby LaCrosse, Wisconsin, played the record, the story goes, for twenty-four hours straight, until it reached number one locally. Their number was then recorded and released yet again, with improved sound quality and, especially, volume, by the middle-sized Soma Records, which was in a position to push the single hard and fast. The Fendermen's "Mule Skinner Blues" soared to the top of the national pop charts, selling, depending on whom you want to believe, many hundreds of thousands or several million copies. The two guys who had been playing in a Wisconsin bar a few months earlier appeared on Dick Clark's prime-time Saturday-night TV show and were put on tour with Johnny Cash and Johnny Horton. Not long after, they were already over as a hit-making band—one of the most often cited, anthologized, and affectionately recalled "one-hit wonder" acts.

It has often been assumed, reasonably, that the raucous Maddox Brothers and Rose version of "Blue Yodel No. 8," hyped up from Bill Monroe's, was the inspiration for the Fendermen's aggressive rock 'n' roll take, but that is not the fact. These were not the most historically minded or particularly curious guys who had come down the pike.

"No; I've never heard *that* one," Humphrey says today of the Maddoxes' record. "I've still never heard Jimmie Rodgers' record, or *any* Jimmie Rodgers record. I liked country music—but that meant Buddy Holly or the Everly Brothers . . . I had heard the song from just one place. Joe D. Gibson had a recording of it that was similar; that went 'OOm-plech, OOm-plech" . . . I just happened to see his record one day and picked it up. I know why now— *divine intervention!* When I heard it, I played it all the time. I thought, 'This is great!' It was already upbeat . . . So I mentioned it in the studio—though nobody knew what the hell I was talking about."

The allusion seems obscure now, too. Phil had found himself, or been presented by God with, a copy of the now generally forgotten single "Good Morning, Captain," recorded, as its label, Tetra Records, a little company based in New York City, had it, by "Joe D. Gibson." Tetra was owned by Monte Bruce, the son-in-law of the famed deejay and rock promoter Alan Freed. The 1957 Gibson single had been released and distributed only in the Middle Atlantic and New England states but had sold 475,000 copies. Though acoustic and featuring Gibson's hard-plunked (or, if you prefer, "OOm-pleched") banjo, the arrangement is indeed essentially the one the Fendermen used to rock with in 1960, from the opening shout to the almost verse-long "Hey-hee" laughter after the yodel. Who Joe D. Gibson was and how his "Mule Skinner" version came to be is a singular saga in itself and, in part, an unsolved mystery.

The singer and banjo player, born in 1929, had grown up a neighbor of Monte Bruce's in Brooklyn, New York. As a performer he was calling himself Jody Gibson, but Bruce could not believe that Jody could actually be anybody's name, a very regionally rooted Brooklyn misconception, so he put "Joe D." on the record label instead. Gibson was not the name the artist was born with, either; that was actually the name of the guitar brand he *did not* favor. He had wanted to call himself "Joe Martin" after the guitar he did play—but that was too reminiscent of a U.S. Speaker of the House he hadn't much cared for. That's how the man born Joseph Katzberg became Jody, or Joe D. Gibson.

By the very early '50s, Joe-turned-Jody was playing guitar, then banjo, in Greenwich Village, in the nascent Washington Square folk scene that included friends such as Tom Paley, later of the New Lost City Ramblers, and Roger Sprung, later one of a handful of banjo players who would introduce Earl Scruggs–style picking up North. At the time, Katzberg could still run into Woody Guthrie and Lead Belly, and apparently did. His recording career began during a break between enlistments with the U.S. Air Force, where he had begun to work as an air traffic controller for the Strategic Air Command. During the 1956–57 break when he waxed "Good Morning, Captain," Jody also toured Canada backing Elton Britt, the country yodeler and Jimmie Rodgers disciple, and even did some radio with Britt out of WWVA in Wheeling, West Virginia. That is an interesting Rodgers coincidence, but it was not the source for his fresh attack on "Mule Skinner Blues." Nor was the Bill Monroe version, at least directly, though people who knew him best agree that Jody had been familiar with it. The problem is that decades later, Gibson (who died in 2005) would point out in notes to a self-made collection of his recordings, "Truthfully, I didn't dream up this 'wild' arrangement. I learned it from a guy I heard at the Eastern States Exposition in 1955. To my everlasting shame, I cannot remember his name. If he ever contacts me, I'll make sure that he gets the credit he deserves."

In that era, quite large-scale country music shows were attached to that fair and rodeo in Springfield, Massachusetts, New England's answer to state fairs elsewhere. None of the regional acts listed in the program for the 1955 event—Smilin' Wade Holmes, Buddy Hawk, the Woodward Brothers—were the sort who might have been doing near-comic versions of "Mule Skinner Blues." Not everyone who appeared would necessarily have made it into the printed program, of course. The producer of that 1955 show, it turns out, was Aubrey Mayhew, decades later the producer of Johnny Paycheck, Jeannie C. Riley, and others at Little Darlin' Records in Nashville, and still very much around today. Mayhew suggests that the yodeler behind the man behind the Fendermen's hit might well have been none other than Cowboy Jack Clement. Jack had only recently been doing a comedy-bluegrass duo act with Scotty Stoneman, son of Rodgers contemporary and fellow Bristol sessions artist Ernest V. Stoneman, on a Boston radio country show Mayhew produced. Cowboy Jack confirms that he had come back from Memphis and his work at Sun records to appear at the New England fair but points out that he did not yodel, still can't—and what he introduced to the region in the summer of '55 was not a crazed acoustic "Mule Skinner," but the first Elvis Presley numbers likely to have been heard so far North. So the mystery of who did invent the rock-ready arrangement remains. The closest thing to a folkloric missing link in the whole Rodgers music story turns out to involve the entrance of this song into rock 'n' roll.

A coda of relevance: in 1957, Jody Gibson was transferred by the U.S. Air Force to England, where he eventually put together a racially integrated, Rodgers-referencing rock band, Jody Gibson and the Muleskinners. They performed electrified versions of songs of mainly country pedigree—"San Antonio Rose," "Company's Comin'," "Hillbilly Fever." A British producer by the name of George Martin liked what he heard in them, which seemed to move more than a step past British skiffle, so beginning in 1959, with Martin producing, the band had several singles on Parlophone. (Some were cut not very long before Martin produced another band with a certain country-influenced, postskiffle tinge to them that he liked. They were called the

Beatles.) Some of the music of Joseph Katzberg of Brooklyn, New York, immediate progenitor of "Mule Skinner Blues" in rock 'n' roll, can now be found on compilations of pre-Beatles *British* rock.

The first-generation rock performers most taken with Jimmie Rodgers had been, like Rodgers disciples in all genres over the years, strongly individual, dominating singers—sometimes soloists but more often with propulsive, electrified backup bands. In the '60s, as harmonizing Beatles-influenced pop bands started coming into their own all over the world, even though elements of American country and blues were increasingly prominent in the pop/rock mix, Rodgers songs were rarely in the foreground. The same thing had happened in other genres when group sounds were predominant. Yet the songs could prove quite useful in making roots-pop connections and, since this was the '60s, even statements.

It is telling that Rick Nelson and the Everly Brothers, two of the biggest pop acts of the late '50s, used Jimmie Rodgers songs as stepping stones while they evolved from their '50s careers to late '60s comebacks as innovative country rockers. Nelson, who sang both rockabilly ballads and rhythm numbers in a light but effective style, had been one of the highest-selling of all first-generation rock acts, mainly because of his teenage-idol looks and his talented band, with James Burton on lead guitar. Another reason was his regular national exposure on the family situation comedy *The Adventures of Ozzie and Harriet*, in which he grew up before the public. Ricky, as he had been known, found his career sputtering somewhat in the mid-'60s, and he had tried classic country as an alternative. He found a number with which he could convincingly get in touch with the madcap side of the mid-'60s, the Beatles-movie-meets-the-Monkees comedy style, in Jimmie Rodgers' goofy old pop number "Desert Blues" ("Big Chief Buffalo Nickel"). Nelson delivers the song in a wacky arrangement, with country Dobro and a background chorus chanting "Keemo-Sabe, Keemo-Sabe," a reference to the TV series *The Lone Ranger*, in "sock-it-to-me" style. Not long after, his image evolution and his transition to modern country rocker complete, Nelson staged a significant comeback.

His contemporaries, the Everly Brothers, had their ups and downs through the Beatles era and staged their own comeback at the tail end of it, just as Nelson did, in Los Angeles–based country rock. Raised in the Rodgers-friendly, downhome but modernizing Kentucky milieu of their dad, Ike Everly, and his musical cohorts, they had always known Rodgers songs. As Phil Everly recalls today, "With where we came from, and my Dad, Merle Travis, and Mose Rager there, these were the songs we sang all our lives—and on the radio, as kids, with our parents."

The Everlies' strong recasting of "T for Texas," a Rodgers song they had performed for years, on the seminal 1969 LP *Roots*, marked their entry into an experimental new era. Their deliberately ragged, rhythmic deconstruction of their own earlier harmonizing style (which had influenced the Beatles) smacks at once of Dylan intonations and of the helter-skelter guitar sounds Jimmie Rodgers had produced in the instrumental break of the original "Mule Skinner Blues." The contextualizing of the songs on the *Roots* album, with flashbacks to childhood recordings, made the whole enterprise a now much-valued touchstone of creative, historically minded album realization. *Roots* was wholly in keeping with contemporary trends in music framing of the time, a theme that will be further explored in the next chapter.

"It's a shame, in a way," Phil Everly says, "that people think of Jimmie Rodgers as the root of just *one* thing, when he was a root for so many things. People will talk about how rock 'n' roll is just a black thing—but here's your story of how it's more than that. There's so much of that country in it. I can tell you, Chuck Berry always wanted to be a country singer."

In May 1965, the Sir Douglas Quintet, a band named and first marketed to give the impression that they were part of the British Invasion, revealed themselves to be a typically impure product of Texas, and San Antonio–based Tex-Mex, border-music-influenced Texas at that, by announcing the fact live on NBC's prime-time TV rock show *Hullabaloo*. Their recording of Jimmie Rodgers' music was almost as blatant a declaration. The Rodgers spirit had never entirely faded in the San Antonio area, and Doug Sahm, Augie Meyers, and the rest of the band delivered a hopping, organ-pumping, maraca-shaking version of "In the Jailhouse Now" that presaged some '80s cowpunk recordings. The Quintet proved to be an outstanding American roots and rock band, unusual for its time, with a dominant leader in Doug Sahm. "Sir Doug" would also record a fairly straightforward, Wills/Duncan-influenced version of "Never No Mo' Blues" during the 1973 Atlantic Records sessions in which he worked with Bob Dylan and Dr. John.

The eclecticism and muscle Dylan had inspired with his '65 Newport appearance would reveal themselves most clearly in the works of individual singer-songwriter school vocalists, many of whom, as we will see, would take new, often electrified approaches to Jimmie Rodgers material, but the roots rockers—folk, blues, and country rock bands whose impulses Bob had done much to foster—showed similar interests. Most such bands included members with backgrounds as solo folk or blues singers, or in bluegrass, jug, or country bands, who knew, valued, and had assimilated Jimmie Rodgers' music. In their music, this would play out subtly, as textural or lyric coloring—the Grateful Dead's train and cowpoke references; the Allman Brothers Band's seamless interweaving of southern music from blues and country sources; Creedence Clearwater Revival's whole ethos, their sense of

American life and experience across the decades made new and empowering by imagination, that big metaphorical train or big-wheeled steamboat coming up around your bend.

In roots rock, Jimmie Rodgers lurked just below the surface. Passing references to him in band interviews furthered the prevalent notion that he was always out there, mixed into the American or American-derived musical landscape. There was a rock press now, asking musicians about such matters as their cultural touchstones. But there was more telling evidence about how close Rodgers lurked in the surface of the musical mix. Time and time again, when these bands broke up, as bands do, or key individuals embarked on side projects of their own—they would turn to Rodgers material.

If the Beatles were the band that did most to foster group sounds, George Harrison was arguably the Beatle most connected to American roots music as opposed to pure pop. On his own, he would join the country-and soul-blending Delaney and Bonnie, perform and maintain a longtime friendship with his guitar mentor Carl Perkins, and join the Traveling Wilburys, along with Bob Dylan, Roy Orbison, and Tom Petty. He would report that his own first favorite recording artists, even before he picked up his first guitar at twelve, were Jimmie Rodgers and Hank Williams. Many Liverpool lads' dads brought home American records, but Harrison's brought home those. Among the songs he toyed with at the sessions for his first, post-Beatles solo album, 1970's *All Things Must Pass*, was "Down to the River," a sort of joking parody of Hank William's throat-catcher, "Long Gone Lonesome Blues." Among the very last recordings he made before his untimely death in 2001 was "Rocking Chair in Hawaii," a remade, evolved version of that very song, chosen to salute a place he dearly loved—and to appeal to and tease a woman or deity in the vicinity of that chair. The farewell song's form was not Hawaiian music or the Williams tune, but an unmistakable Rodgers blue yodel with Jimmie-style guitar runs, though Harrison reminds us of his Eastern, mystical side as "Hare, hare" takes the place of any yodels. The whole startling, touching song serves as a sort of summoning up of the man's delights in life—sung in Jimmie Rodgers style, the first style he had taken to and the final one he turned to.

The Grateful Dead were not known for performing Jimmie Rodgers songs any more than the Beatles were, but Rodgers was all over their map. Jerry Garcia sang and played banjo on a Bill Monroe–style "Mule Skinner Blues," in the early '60s bluegrass band the Wildwood Boys, an outfit that also featured the future Dead lyricist Robert Hunter. In the San Francisco rock band's early incarnation as Mother McCree's Uptown Jug Champions, a West Coast answer to the Jim Kweskin Jug Band back East, they performed the Memphis Jug Band version of "In the Jailhouse Now." Garcia, like

Harrison, would get around to recording a Rodgers song toward the end of his life; a version of "Blue Yodel No. 9" recorded with David Grisman would be his last studio recording.

No one would have expected the generally far-from-rootsy San Francisco psychedelic-era band Jefferson Airplane to break into Jimmie's "I'm Free from the Chain Gang Now," even though, like Elvis Presley, they were a rare rock act on Jimmie's RCA Victor label. Their lead guitarist, Jorma Kaukonen, and bass man Jack Cassidy, however, had the band Hot Tuna to show off the acoustic guitar mastery they had developed on the Washington, D.C., folk scene, featuring Jorma's dexterous finger-style blues and rag picking. Hot Tuna recorded such tunes as "Hit Single No. 1" and "Funky No. 7," which suggested familiarity with Victor song titling practices for Jimmie's records. Jorma finally stepped up to Rodgers music as such in 2002, playing a half-dozen of Jimmie's songs, "Free from the Chain Gang Now" among them, along with such adventurous Nashville-based newgrass instrumentalists as Béla Fleck, Sam Bush, and Jerry Douglas. Long known for blues picking influenced by Reverend Gary Davis, Kaukonen proves equally at home with the laid-back, porch-style approach to Jimmie Rodgers tunes created by Doc Watson, adding his own lazy, smart singing. The vocal on "Gamblers' Blues" and the Dobro-guitar collaboration with Douglas on "Waiting for a Train" are particularly effective.

Creedence Clearwater Revival, the most commercially successful American roots rock band in history, frequently nominated as the best rock band produced in America, period, kept a country flavor in their "swampy" rock, soul, and twang, California-born, Deep South–inspired musical gumbo, if discretely. But as soon as leader and songwriter John Fogerty went out on his own in 1973, he made an album's worth of Nashville and California country, under the guise of the Blue Ridge Rangers, a "band" in which he happened to play all the parts. In that set was his Dobro-and-drums-driven take on "California Blues," with a trumpet solo he also played himself. The sound suggests that Merle Haggard's salute to Jimmie Rodgers had been played a few times in the Fogerty household, as it had by that point in so many.

Rodgers' submerged, yet clearly integral influence was more intriguingly employed in the music of the Allman Brothers Band—a group that gave its audiences even fewer direct clues about its very real country music influences than Creedence, instead foregrounding masterful electric blues and soul. Though they were an archetypal album rock outfit, with their live albums their most celebrated releases, their biggest hit single, "Ramblin' Man," suggests in its essence that somebody in there knew something about Jimmie Rodgers' rounders and drifters—and country blues. The now very familiar song is, after all, narrated by a southern man who's "tryin' to make a livin'" and "doin' the best [he] can," a goal much more commonly noted in country music than rock, particularly than in hippie-friendly jam band rock. He is also always leavin'—a Rodgersesque characteristic of both country and rock 'n' roll. And the singer is headed to New Orleans where, in a direct quotation from "Jimmie's Texas Blues," lest you have not gotten the connection so far, the "women think the world of me."

That "somebody in there" writing and singing the song was the guitarist Richard Betts—a lifelong Jimmie Rodgers devotee and the member of the Allmans who kept the closest ties to Nashville singer-songwriters and country music. Singer-songwriter Steve Forbert, running into Betts while on tour, once spent an entire evening with him swapping Rodgers songs. Steve Earle recalls, "I first met Dickey Betts, literally, at a Waylon Jennings gig at [Nashville rock venue] the Exit/In, at a benefit Waylon was doing there. We and Bonnie Bramlett [of Delaney and Bonnie] wound up in a caravan of cars going to get eggs in the middle of the night . . . Dickey would hear songs in Nashville, learned a lot of country music—and yes, he knew his Jimmie Rodgers songs; no doubt about it. He was then [in the '70s] a main connection between us singer-songwriters who landed in Nashville and rock 'n' roll." Twenty years later, Betts' quite traditional—and accomplished—version of "Waiting for a Train," which appeared on the same Bob Dylan–produced Rodgers salute CD as that final Jerry Garcia track, was greeted with a good deal of surprise by reviewers. It shouldn't have been. Off with his own band Great Southern, Betts has also recorded a version of "No Hard Times," that most rural of all Rodgers songs—in a screaming rock guitar-driven version that nevertheless employed both yodels and horns.

There was genuine interplay and mutual influence between the "outlaw" country acts of the mid-'70s and the exponents of what came to be called southern rock, and the lines between the two were often deliberately blurred. Audiences who might have been the grandchildren of Jimmie Rodgers' original listeners were often fans of both of these parallel country and rock contingents, and Jimmie Rodgers songs would be a notable medium of exchange between the two camps.

What a record coming out of Nashville could sound like heading into the 1970s, in truth, had already evolved considerably, the lines between the Nashville Sound, pop, and rock 'n' roll having become less sharply delineated at least as far back as 1966 when Bob Dylan chose to record *Blonde on Blonde* on Music Row. A top sideman like electric guitarist Jerry Reed could play a country session one day, back Elvis Presley the next, and also have gritty, rhythm and blues–flavored hits of his own such as "Amos Moses." Reed's 1971 version of "Mule Skinner Blues," with Chet Atkins joining him on second guitar, is a perfect example of how blurry the country/rock/soul lines could become during the heyday of such artists as Reed himself, Tony Joe White, Joe South, and Bobby Gentry in the late '60s to early '70s. Since blues, story-telling, and rural themes had all been elements in Jimmie Rodgers' reper-toire, his songs fit into this updated, soulful, country pop style quite naturally. Jimmie's own grandson, Jimmie Dale Court, began, at that time, to perform a great many of them precisely in the soul-tinged, funky storyteller style. It is still not uncommon to hear musicians cite Jerry Reed's "Mule Skinner," with its bluesy vocal and hard, precision-picked guitar lines, as a musical model.

If Music Row sounds were more fluid and unpredictable than they had been, the system behind the sound would be shaken up further by the efforts of such country music "outlaws" as Waylon Jennings, Willie Nelson, Jessi Colter, Tompall Glaser, and Hank Williams Jr., who by this point looked like Wild West desperadoes ready to be booked for rock tours. Jimmie Rod-gers would have understood the look very well. They fought for and, to a degree, won the right to record their own way and with their own bands, con-trary to the standard Nashville practice of assigning top studio musicians to most recording sessions. The outlaw crew were not, in fact, so far outside the country music industry mainstream as some took them to be, but they bran-dished images and songs that had more than a little of the badass character of rockabilly and rock; and they often did appear in rock venues. The outlaws, peaking commercially, were certainly well-appreciated by members of the southern rock bands whose way was cleared by the Allmans' roots rock—Lynyrd Skynyrd, Molly Hatchet, Charlie Daniels, the Marshall Tucker Band, and so on. These bands offered sounds that were more varied than their regular bundling on arena bills might lead you to believe, with tinges of blues rock, country, and even jazz that would not have been alien to Jim-mie Rodgers. For all these bands' musical differences, however, they shared themes and audiences, and they all emphasized their home roots—as did the country outlaws.

Waylon Jennings, as he reminds us in his memoir, was the son of a Texas Jimmie Rodgers fan who played guitar in Rodgers style. When Way-lon was himself signed by RCA Victor, he was pleased in part because it was the brand of the many Rodgers 78s he had grown up with. Jennings' leathery, pounding take on "T for Texas" opens his classic live LP recorded in Austin in 1974, an album so good that it has been repeatedly rereleased in new, further expanded editions. Waylon would regularly nod in Jimmie's direction in salute songs, too, such as "Waymore's Blues," a chugging train blues that has Jimmie's ghost yodeling up the track, or his song "Rough and Rowdy Days."

On that celebrated live "T for Texas," Jennings asks rhetorically, "Do you wanna hear me yodel?" then answers himself with a guitar lead, not a throat trick. He also, leaves out the particularly rough verse about shooting poor Thelma, perhaps because of its content but just as likely to leave more room for the blistering instrumental. For all of the rockabilly in him, Jennings rarely showed anything like belligerence toward women in his songs or in his personal stance, which was that of a strong man looking for a strong woman to match, so dropping the signifying "jump and crawl" lyrics may well have been deliberate. "If you don't want me, woman," Waylon sings instead, "just say so—*that's all*." No problem, no fuss, since, of course, he can get more women than a passenger train can haul.

The change in the lyric would stick; this was one of the most heard versions ever of "Blue Yodel." Jennings' buddy Tompall Glaser, formerly of the Glaser Brothers who had regularly sung behind Marty Robbins, recorded a boogie beat version of "T for Texas" for the million-selling compilation *Wanted! The Outlaws*, the LP that defined outlaw country territory for those who had not spotted it already, many of them rock fans. Tompall does not mention shooting anybody either, but he does toss in that "women make a fool out of me" and trails off with a message for one "Lucille from Atlanta, Georgia"—very possibly a close relative of the lovin' gal Lucille in Rodgers "Blue Yodel No. II"—that (no reasons provided) she can go to hell. Glaser also recorded a version of "Mother Was a Lady" that updates the song to put two cowboys in "the Holiday Inn West End"—situated near modern Nashville's Music Row. That this was a Rodgers-associated number also recorded by Marty Robbins may have been a coincidence; the Glasers did not sing on his earlier version.

Another of Waylon's buddies, Hank Williams Jr., then in the process of remaking himself into the rougher and rowdier figure he has generally embodied publicly ever since, recorded a smooth, energetic, partially electrified, yet string-laden version of "Muleskinner Blues," which reflected a love of Bill Monroe—and some banjo lessons he had been getting from Earl Scruggs at around this time. "I sure *did* sing his tunes," Hank notes. The song that springs to mind and comes to his lips, however, is not the usual "Waiting for a Train," but the more pop than country "My Carolina Sunshine Girl." "Moon, moon, I can see you sinkin' low," Williams sings, and adds, "Oh *yeah*. I *love* Jimmie Rodgers!"

Hank Williams Jr. can recall, as does his sister Lycrecia, when they rode in Jimmie Rodgers Day parades in Meridian in the late '50s with their mother Audrey. By the '80s, Hank would headline there for a number of years running, singing his own songs and Rodgers' numbers, too, as did Waylon Jennings. Hank Jr. had recorded a not entirely different, whip-cracking pop/folk duet version of "Mule Skinner" with Connie Francis, no less, as far back as 1964, when he was just fifteen.

Williams, who does not mind displaying some regional, good ol' boy defiance in his tougher numbers, has appeared frequently, since the turn of this century, with surviving members of the band that for many epitomized southern rock, Lynyrd Skynyrd. Their live 1975 version of "T for Texas," often performed in locales where Confederate flags and other expressions of southern separateness and recalcitrance were not difficult to spot, turned out to be another nod toward Waylon in that it left out the shooting of poor Thelma. Skynyrd's version, then, is actually less threatening than Jimmie Rodgers' original. The late Ronnie Van Zandt used to begin singing the song in the style of a football cheer: "*Give me* a T for Texas; give me a T for Tennessee," which seemed to please the band's stadium-filling crowds.

How the song entered the band's repertoire is recalled by one of the two men who put it there, Skynyrd's bass player of the early years, Ed King. King was not a southerner, but a refugee from that primal Californian surfer band, Dick Dale and the Del-Tones, and from the psychedelic pop band Strawberry Alarm Clock. "The arrangement of 'T for Texas' was mine," he recalls. "We worked it up at a rehearsal in Arizona. I was working on a blues arrangement, and then Ronnie suggested that we use 'T for Texas,' specifically, which I didn't mind at all! By the time it was all together, it sounded like 'One Way Out' by the Allman Brothers, anyway. I only performed it with them two or three times at most, because two weeks later I left the band." But King and Van Zandt had already coauthored "Railroad Song," a number built on rail and hobo imagery out of the Rodgers bag—boxcars; a hungry, guitar-carrying hobo; a policeman who does not want him around. Rodgers-influenced themes ran in Van Zandt's stream of consciousness.

"In early 1975," Ed recalls, "I was in a hotel room in Atlanta, writing this music track, and I asked Ronnie to come down to my room, because it sounded to me like it should be about a train; the rhythm just propelled it that way. Ronnie Van Zandt *was* a country singer—in a rock 'n' roll band. His roots were based in country; he loved Merle Haggard and most any country singer. He was into vocalists—and somebody like Ry Cooder, too, who liked all that musical history. Ronnie wrote the 'Railroad Song' lyric all the way through in one pass, in fifteen minutes, without writing anything down; he *never* wrote anything down . . . I mean, most of the guys in Skynyrd were not really so much into country music, and their basic rock 'n' roll influences were actually very British—Jimmie Page, Eric Clapton. But we would feed Ronnie these rock 'n' roll guitar riffs, and he would bounce off of them perfectly, with his country vocals." The much-played live version of that Skynyrd number would make "T for Texas" a sort of southern identification song; for instance, the nearly as familiar version by Molly Hatchet, derivative of Skynyrd and Clapton, was introduced on a live recording with the comment, "I've got a feeling you've heard this one somewhere before." Now this southern rock band was headed in the direction of thudding, harder-than-hard-rock heavy metal, and somehow, appropriately, the gun with the shiny barrel returns to their version of the lyric.

The same live Molly Hatchet CD on which that gun-bearing "T for Texas" appears also features their song "Big Apple," in which New York City's "punks and high heeled steppers"—the latter suggestive of '70s disco fans who were not necessarily women, or white—are given notice that this southern boy band is headed that way with "pistols loaded," feeling "rough." It is not difficult to trace a line from Jimmie Rodgers' presentation of himself as potentially violent in the original "T for Texas," and his joking "Pistol Packin' Papa," to the bar fight in Al Dexter's "Pistol Packin' Mama" and on to this pistol packin' threat song. There is, however, a key difference: There is not a trace in Rodgers' music of tribal belligerence, of that zero-sum regional confrontation game that goes "if we're OK down here, other places must not be" that is common in southern rock and even outlaw country lyrics.

Thumbs-up Jimmie Rodgers, for all of his pre–rock 'n' roll macho, was never a performer (or a man) to draw a line in the sand; he ignored and even worked to erase such lines and to expand the boundaries of his own and his people's acceptance, in as many places as possible. He would not be alone in that. In this same mid-'70s period, the Tennessean country singer James Talley, contemplating outlawry from a different angle in a period of oil crisis and economic dislocation, would invoke a stream of specific Jimmie Rodgers references in his "Are They Gonna Make Us Outlaws Again?" to reach out to working-class people in trouble anywhere, even those in places where they have not "picked no peaches" or "worked out on the road gang."

Steve Earle, a rocking Texan Rodgers fan who relocated to Nashville in the '70s, adds: "Jimmie Rodgers finds the common ground between poor people in the South—and make no mistake, his music is *southern*, which means it could have been ugly and divisive, from the place where words like *white trash* and *nigger* come from. But there's this other side of the place, where people realized, 'We may as well be the same color, because we *all* ain't got nothin'.' I'd say just calling Jimmie Rodgers 'the father of country music' is almost doing him an injustice. He could record a little bit of everything; he was in a prototypical category with a handful of people who happened to be from the South and incorporated that into the music, who were really the beginnings of rock 'n' roll. If you believe—and I do—that rock 'n' roll brings about a nexus of black music and white music, then Jimmie Rodgers is one of the people who made *that* happen—from 'Jump.'

"As for me, growing up," Earle adds, "I was listening to the Beatles and the Stones, just like everybody else—but I lived in San Antonio, Texas—so,

God, I don't think I remember ever *not* knowing about him." Earle's own career would regularly blur and cross the lines between singer-songwriter, hard rocker, rockabilly, mainstream country star, bluegrasser, and folksinger. As a child, he found Jimmie Rodgers records in the collection of his dad's brother, a western swing piano player. He owned Merle Haggard's Rodgers salute LP but also heard singers performing Rodgers tunes solo at the Kerrville Folk Festival in the early '70s. "Jimmie Rodgers has been huge for anybody from Texas who ever played guitar and sang at the same time," he recalls. "And back *then* I could yodel—so within a few years of learning to play guitar I was playing 'Waiting for a Train' and 'Blue Yodel Number 9' and five or six other Jimmie Rodgers songs."

What's not generally known is that Earle had more direct Rodgers connections: "My grandmother was director of a halfway house for alcoholic women in San Antonio, in Alamo Heights, and her neighbor from across the street was Anita Rodgers Court, Jimmie's daughter, who would spend a lot of time visiting, befriending my grandmother and a lot of women who lived there. So I knew Anita fairly well when I was thirteen to fifteen, in about '68, '69, and '70. I was playing guitar, and I can remember seeing and actually handling at one point Jimmie Rodgers' triple-aught 45—one of the two; Anita still had it." (It was almost certainly the Martin that now resides as a "precious jewel" at the Country Music Hall of Fame in Nashville, the one Jimmie had played at Bristol.)

"Anita Court would play me Jimmie Rodgers recordings at her house; she was just taken with the fact that I knew who he *was*. She scared the hell out of me once at my grandmother's house. In the middle of a sentence, she just reached around back, unfastened her bra, pulled it off through the sleeve of her blouse—and put it in her purse. And I was eleven or twelve; I was *impressed!*"

Earle recorded "In the Jailhouse Now" as a straightforward rocker with the roots rock band the V-Roys, having been asked to take on the song by Bob Dylan's "people" for Bob's Rodgers salute CD. After Steve served time on drug charges and become an advocate for prisoner's rights, the song had seemed an inevitable choice—perhaps, he says with a laugh, a little too inevitable. He had long been performing "Blue Yodel No. 9" with his own hard-charging band the Dukes, sometimes in its entirety, sometimes as a smooth lead-in to his own "The Other Kind," an outsider song that references Jack Kerouac. The Rodgers blue yodel, marking Earle's transition from working-class country singer to hard rocker, was captured on a live album in 1991.

The reference in that Molly Hatchet number to those New York "punks" they would take on, if only in their imagination, was a sign of the changing face of rock music in those years. Punk rock, New Wave, and modern rock in general have often been less than friendly toward the blues, which tends to be viewed through an '80s lens as a tired, baby-boom generation obsession. You might think, therefore, that Jimmie Rodgers would have seen decreasing rock interest from that point. The opposite was the case. When Steve Earle and Dwight Yoakam were being introduced to country audiences as the new, historically informed representatives of that genre (Earle refers to this brief New Traditionalist country period as "the Great Credibility Scare"), both were playing in venues where the next act on the bill might be in that emerging cowpunk genre. For Earle, in Nashville that might mean a markedly fresh kind of band like Jason and the Scorchers letting loose their pounding version of "Jimmie Rodgers' Last Blue Yodel," with an all-shook-up "the women make a fool out of me" tagline that owed nothing to Ernest Tubb. Members of that band had quietly enjoyed Skynyrd but were more obviously taken with the direction of New York punks the Ramones.

"I can't say I remember my first exposure to Jimmie Rodgers' music for sure," Jason and the Scorchers leader and front man Jason Ringenberg says, "but it was probably Waylon doing 'T for Texas' that I heard first. Also, Jimmie Rodgers would come up as a reference in Dylan biographies and things like that . . . I still am immensely proud of our version of that 'Last Blue Yodel.' We interpreted the song totally in a rock 'n' roll context; we weren't thinking about it as anything else. We *saw* it as one of the first rock 'n' roll songs; I'll swear it's the first rock 'n' roll song ever written." More recently, Ringenberg rerecorded the song with the British heavy metal band the Wildhearts—who had learned it from the Scorchers in the first place, and with no particular idea of who Jimmie Rodgers was.

"Jimmie Rodgers," Jason posits, "was a huge cornerstone of rock 'n' roll—and in that respect, he's completely underrated. Lyrically mostly I think, but yes, with ego; yes, with *drive*. The way he twists those words, rhythmically, really predated the rockabilly and the whole male attitude of the rock 'n' roll singers and even the '60s bands. And there *is* that cocky side that shows up big time in the punk rock world."

Out in California, where Kentuckian Dwight Yoakam first found an audience, the frantic band of relevance was the edgy, neo-rockabilly and rhythm and blues band the Blasters, headed up by the working-class, Southern-California-raised Alvin brothers—Dave Alvin on extraordinary electric guitar and Phil, on searing, bluesy vocals. The Blasters would seize Rodgers' "Never No Mo' Blues" as a cornerstone number to rock out with. They would go on to explore almost every corner of American music with that punk-rock-related aesthetic.

"Our version of the song was kind of a combo of the Jimmie Rodgers version and the Bob Wills version," Dave Alvin recalls. "We had both 78s. Phil always had a band, as a teenager, that basically did Chicago blues and Kansas City stuff, but he started doing solo gigs as a ragtime and blues guitar player—and he'd yodel 'Lovesick Blues' and 'Never No Mo' Blues' and yes, also Jimmie's 'Frankie and Johnny.' Phil and I were record collectors at a very early age; I was eleven or twelve, and he would have been thirteen or fourteen [i.e., 1966–67]. We knew a lot for our age, but we didn't know everything, and one way that we learned was if an old 78 said 'blues' on it, whether it was 'Columbus Stockade Blues' or 'Wang Wang Blues,' whatever it was, we'd check it out. And we first found a scratchy copy of one of the blue yodels that way."

Bringing Jimmie Rodgers songs into the sort of venues that would book the Blasters was not without hazards. "Nobody was doing anything like that," Alvin recalls. "And *nobody* yodeled! . . . In 1980, we were playing at a bar in Hollywood. We'd just made a record in a garage on a rockabilly label called Rollin' Rock, and 'Never No Mo' Blues' was on that record. So we were in this bar, and the guys from Queen were there—yeah, *them*—and they saw us, and they decided they wanted us to be their opening act. So we had this tour of the West opening for [arena rockers] Queen. In Phoenix, we played an outdoor amphitheater kind of thing, where people could bring blankets and chairs, an ice chest—*ammunition*. They *didn't like us*. Somewhere between the blues and rockabilly stuff it didn't equate to them as music, and when we did 'Never No Mo' Blues,' the place really, really went berserk. Negative berserk. We'd gone off the scale with the yodel.

"When you get booed by twenty thousand people and you're assaulted with beer cans and everything, you try to figure out where you went wrong, and what we came up with is that the yodel was too close to home. For people who wanted to consider themselves 'progressive rock fans,' to suddenly have these guys up there yodeling, what could be more *uncool*? 'My grandfather liked that!' It was really ugly—but for us it was like a bonding thing. It made us start to think that we were pretty *good*!"

Whether this is how that yodel showed up in Queen's monster radio staple "Bohemian Rhapsody" remains unrecorded. But the fact is, Jimmie Rodgers' music has been taken, in rock's latter-day, so-called modern period, to the furthest reaches of the genre—as when the studiously decadent "psychobilly" leather band the Cramps decided that no version of "Mule Skinner Blues" had gone quite far enough. They battered the Fendermen's version into a raspy, almost retching vocal rant, matched by twangy guitar that might have come off a spaghetti western soundtrack. That they performed the number on television with their lead singer, Lux Interior, dressed primarily in a leather brassiere certainly demonstrates how far Jimmie Rodgers' Huck Finn outsider aspect might be extrapolated. But apparently there were limits. When leader Iggy, of the seminal punk band Iggy and the Stooges, decided to transform himself into Iggy Pop, to be either seriously or only ironically more commercial sounding and pop oriented, "Mule Skinner" was also one of the numbers he toyed with, if only by referencing the lyric, in one of his less-crazed demos, "Old Mule Skinner." Rock, having gone out so far, was now beginning to bounce back toward Jimmie Rodgers.

A similar impulse lay behind the alternative country idiom that established itself in the mid-'90s, with a historical knowingness and postgrunge sensibility, which still reverberates, if less strongly, at this writing. There was a pull to reconnect, not necessarily with an "old home place"—that generation rarely having experienced such a thing—but certainly with American roots music and culture. Jimmie Rodgers remained useful for attempting that sort of connection. Jeff Tweedy, of Uncle Tupelo, one of the founders and leading lights of the alt.country movement, and, as his popular band Wilco would prove, one of its more pop-oriented exemplars, would take on the task assigned to him by the Guthrie family of bringing into modern pop some unrecorded, urban lyrics Woody had written while living in Brooklyn. Tweedy would also record a version of Ernest Tubb's early Jimmie Rodgers pastiche "The T.B. Is Whippin' Me" as a gently rocking duet with the indie rock chanteuse Syd Straw. The ever-busy and knowledgeable Jon Langford, of the Mekons, the head-banging British punk band that always demonstrated that it had actual heads to bang, and of its American country punk offshoot the Waco Brothers, could comfortably join the Austin, Texas, alt.country artist Alejandro Escovedo for a new version of Jimmie's "California Blues." Nobody could claim that such acts were typical of modern indie or college rock in general, but some of what made them different—that attraction to claiming their place in a historical/cultural line—drew them, too, toward the music of Jimmie Rodgers.

Cary Hudson, the Mississippi-raised lead singer and songwriter of the long-lasting and recently-revived alt.country band Blue Mountain, explains, "I grew up being into classic rock and, later, alternative rock of the late '80s—the Replacements, Hüsker Dü. Then I moved to Los Angeles, and there I started to get interested in indigenous Mississippi music. I didn't realize that I *had* a culture, that I came from one—until I moved to Los Angeles. I said then, 'I get it; I'm not like these other white people out here, and I need to see the difference.' I went out and started buying Jimmie Rodgers records with Laurie, the girl I started Blue Mountain with." Hudson not only learned the Rodgers songs; he studied the man through Nolan Porterfield's biography, a carefully chosen gift from his grandfather, a harmonica-playing farmer from just outside Hattiesburg. Whereas most alternative country bands derived from that alterative rock line would eschew blues, Blue Mountain reveled in the form, as much as in country and grunge rock. Although they have not, so far, recorded a Rodgers song as such—the closest they have gotten has been their proficiently feisty electrified version of Cliff Carlisle's blue-yodel-style "That Nasty Swing"—they were invited to perform at the Jimmie Rodgers Festival in Meridian in 1995, precisely for their contemporary mix of sounds that seemed entirely relevant to the proceedings. For their performance there, they delivered a hard rock version of a song that has been waiting for the treatment, Jimmie's "Pistol Packin' Papa."

The story of Rodgers and rock has not ended. Perhaps the youngest working musician to add to it, as of today, is Taylor Hollingsworth, who heads a twenty-first-century metal band around Birmingham, Alabama. For a break in a set of screamers, a few of them referencing rockabilly, Taylor regularly performs a perfectly contemplative version of Jimmie's "Gambling Barroom Blues." "I'm not sure if my audience even knows who Jimmie Rodgers *is*," he notes, a little ruefully. "But I get lots of compliments on that song—sometimes that 'It's my favorite song you wrote.' I have to tell them 'Yeah, well thanks—I didn't write that one, but you should totally check this Jimmie Rodgers out.'

"He's one of my heroes, actually. I first bought a cassette tape at a thrift store for like twenty-five cents or something and had just heard of him, but for so cheap a figure I figured, what the hell. I'll listen to this and throw it away if it sucks . . . Shortly later I was driving to the beach and had a tape player and like five hours to kill, so I threw it in, and I really didn't take it out the whole drive; I just played it over and over and over. The first song on the tape was 'Soldier's Sweetheart,' and I really thought it was the saddest song I'd ever heard . . . It also had 'Ben Dewberry,' which I also now cover. I was just fascinated and started to read about him and learned all about his life and then just became temporarily obsessed."

Another young contemporary performer, "Crazy Kid" from the Michigan hip hop group Trick Hatin' Click, has attracted considerable online attention with a rapped version of, what else, "T for Texas." "Talk about *old* school," he notes, starting off the thumping number. Thelma crawls one more time—and Ronnie Van Zandt's football cheer version of the song and the bootcamp-style shouts of Jimmie's gander dancer co-workers vibrate in the historic distance.

The Rock and Roll Hall of Fame in Cleveland inducted Jimmie Rodgers as an elder statesman and vital early influence in 1986. Jerry Wexler of Atlantic Records, the very man who had gotten the terms "hillbilly" and "race" music changed to "country and western" and "rhythm and blues" when he had worked as a columnist at *Billboard*, delivered the induction speech. "Jimmie had a tremendous appreciation of the blues," Wexler noted. "His most popular songs—which you won't hear in heavy rotation now—are marvelous. He traveled the United States as a brakeman in the Depression, a time when soul was very close to the bone. Somebody said that with soul, you had to feel bad before you feel good—and Jimmie Rodgers felt plenty bad before he could feel good . . . It's good for us, as we get further and further into highly developed rock music, to keep one eye on the root. Jimmie Rodgers *is* the root."

In 1997, the Rock and Roll Hall of Fame and Case Western Reserve's American Studies program held a joint conference on Jimmie Rodgers in rock, "Waiting for a Train: Jimmie Rodgers' America"; later, the conference was the taking-off point for a book of essays of the same title. Some attendees reviewing the proceedings in the popular press indulged in the classic "rockist" argument, which assumes that all musical roads lead up to fulfillment in album-era rock. It suggests that Jimmie Rodgers was a forerunner of rock 'n' roll because all country music is but a predecessor of the rock apotheosis, and Jimmie is country.

One glaring thing wrong with that point of view is that in saying what he wanted to say, in offering his fans a liberating, empowering musical vision and a new sense of themselves, Jimmie Rodgers was already accomplishing things in the '20s and early '30s that are often attributed to the power of rock 'n' roll alone. It requires no ill-informed reduction of country music to "prerock" to recognize that accomplishment. Jimmie's very venturing into such territory contradicts the notion that personal liberation was offered only by American pop music during "the rock revolution," and certainly not by anybody called "country." That Jerry Wexler should cite Jimmie Rodgers' soulful, knowing take on the blues was much to his and the Rock Hall's credit. At the Case Western conference, a combination of leading music historians, including Nolan Porterfield, Charles Wolfe, Bill Malone, and Rodgers' musical interpreters from Steve Earle to Lynyrd Skynyrd, Jimmie Dale Gilmore, and Alejandro Escovedo were on hand to keep the discussion straight.

Earle's caveat that calling Jimmie Rodgers the father of country music is "almost doing him an injustice," given his actual musical breadth, applies to rock and his influence in it as well. Jimmie Rodgers' music is broader in its emotional range and subject matter than much of contemporary rock; the rocker-rounder vision of Rodgers is myopic if it is not part of a wider view. Rodgers' songs also contain forthright statements of sentiment and appealing portraits of domesticity—neither of which are the stuff of twenty-first century rock. Asked how sentimental songs about mom and home and orphan kids

Meeting Jimmie Rodgers

could comfortably coexist in the works of a first-generation rock 'n' roll wild one—or of a 1930 vaudevillian—"the Killer" Jerry Lee Lewis replies, "I can't explain that any more than to say that I have more than one side to me. *Any performer who is real will understand that.*"

Presenting the multifaceted Jimmie Rodgers in his totality to audiences of a very different time became a task not just for rock bands, but also for commentators and interpreters of many stripes. Some of the most effective at the job were solo artists who, like Jimmie Rodgers, were not committed to any single genre. They, like historians and critics with a broad view, helped restore Jimmie Rodgers' music and the range of sentiments he could evoke. That process has been going on for some forty years.

Select Soundtrack

The Rock 'n' Roll Era

- **Fats Domino:** "Helping Hand" (his 1955 "Waiting for a Train" variant) is on *Imperial Singles, Volume 2* (Ace, 1997); "Any Old Time" is on *Fats Domino 1980* (FD Records, 1980).

- **Harmonica Frank Floyd:** "Blue Yodel No. 7" and "Blue Yodel No. 6" are on *The Great Medical Menagerist* (Adelphi/Genes, 1997); "Tribute to Jimmy Rogers" [*sic*] is on the LP *Blues That Made the Roosters Dance* (Barrelhouse, 1975).

- **Jerry Lee Lewis:** His Sun records recordings of "Waiting for a Train" (1962), "My Carolina Sunshine Girl" (1957), the Rodgers-influenced "High-Powered Woman," and "Frankie and Johnny" (1958) all appear on the box set *Classic Jerry Lee Lewis* (Bear Family, 1989). The 1971 "Mother, the Queen of My Heart" is most readily available on the compilation *I Am Sad and Weary* (Bear Family); "The One Rose" is on several live Lewis show recordings. "Miss the Mississippi" is on *Young Blood* (Elektra, 1995) and Time-Life's 2006 Lewis collection, *A Half Century of Hits*.

- **Sonny Burgess:** "Sadie's Back in Town" ("My Little Lady") is on his *Arkansas Wild Man* (Charly/Sun UK, 1996).

- **Joe D. Gibson:** "Good Mornin' Captain" ("Mule Skinner Blues") was a Tetra single, not anthologized thus far. Jody

Gibson and the Muleskinners' "If You Don't Know" Parlophone single is on *British Beat Before the Beatles, Vol. 5* (EMI, 1993).

- **The Fendermen:** "Mule Skinner Blues" is available as a single online, on various compilations, and on their *Mule Skinner Blues* (Sundazed, 2000).

The Rock/Album Rock Era

- **Rick Nelson:** "Big Chief Buffalo Nickel" is on his 1967 Decca LP *Country Fever* and *Bright Lights and Country Fever* (Ace, 1998).

- **Everly Brothers:** "T for Texas" is on *Roots* (2005) and the compilation *Walk Right Back* (1993), both Warner's.

- **Sir Douglas Quintet:** "In the Jailhouse Now" is on *The Crazy Cajun Recordings* (Edsel, 1998); Doug Sahm's "Never No Mo' Blues" is on *The Original Texas Groover: Complete Atlantic Sessions* (Atlantic/Rhino, 2003).

- **George Harrison:** "Rocking Chair in Hawaii" is on *Brainwashed* (Capitol, 2002); the 1970 "Down to the River" demo has been widely available in bootlegged versions.

- **Jerry Garcia and David Grisman:** "Blue Yodel No. 9" is on *The Songs of Jimmie Rodgers: A Tribute* (originally Columbia/Egyptian, 1997, now included on the *Let Me Be Your Sidetrack* box set, Bear Family) and also by Garcia and his band on *Almost Acoustic* (Arista, 1995).

- **Jorma Kaukonen:** "Waiting for a Train," "I'm Free from the Chain Gang Now," "You and My Old Guitar," "Gambler's Blues," and "Prohibition Has Done Me Wrong" are all on *Blue Country Heart* (Columbia, 2002).

- **John Fogerty:** "California Blues" is on *The Blue Ridge Rangers* (Fantasy, 1991).

- **Dickey Betts:** "No Hard Times" is on *Bougainvillea's Call: The Very Best of Dickey Betts* (Raven, 2006). "Waiting for a Train" is on the *Songs of Jimmie Rodgers* tribute disc, as above.

- **Jerry Reed:** "Mule Skinner Blues" is on the LP *Georgia Sunshine* (RCA Victor, 1971) and the compilation *Guitar Man* (UK BMG, 1996).

- **Tompall Glaser**: "T for Texas" is on *Wanted! The Outlaws* (RCA/BMG, 1996) and *Another Log on the Fire* (Bear Family, 2005); "My Mother Was a Lady" is on the *I Am Sad and Weary* compilation (Bear Family, 2003).

- **Waylon Jennings**: His "T for Texas" opens *Waylon, Live* (Buddha/BMG). It is also, with his original song "Rough and Rowdy Days" and "Waymore's Blues" are all on the multilabel box set *Nashville Rebel* (BMG/Sony Legacy, 2006). The "Me and Jimmie Rodgers" version that includes a verse by Waylon is on *The Old Dogs* (Warner's, 1998).

- **Hank Williams Jr.**: "Mule Skinner Blues" is on *Living Proof: The MGM Recordings* (Mercury, 1992). The 1964 version of the song is on *Hank Williams Jr. and Connie Francis Sing Great Country Favorites* (Bear Family, 1994).

- **Lynyrd Skynyrd**: "T for Texas" is on *One More for the Road* (2001) and *Lynyrd Skynyrd* Box Set (MCA, 1991); "Railroad Song" is on *Nuthin' Fancy* (MCA, 1999).

- **Molly Hatchet**: "T for Texas" is on *Live at the Agora Ballroom 1979* (Phoenix Gems, 2000).

- **Steve Earle and the Dukes**: "Blue Yodel No. 9" is on *Shut Up and Die Like an Aviato*r (MCA, 1991); "In the Jailhouse Now" (with the V-Roys) is on the *Songs of Jimmie Rodgers* salute.

- **James Talley**: "They're Gonna Make Us Outlaws Again" is on his LP *Tryin' Like the Devil* (Capitol, 1976), available as a custom CD on his Web site.

The Modern Rock Era

- **The Blasters**: "Never No More Blues" is on *American Music* (Hightone, 1997).

- **Jason and the Scorchers**: "Jimmie Rodgers' Last Blue Yodel" is on *Jason and the Nashville Scorchers: Reckless Country Soul* (Mammoth/Praxis, 1996). The later metal version, by Jason Ringenberg with the Wildhearts, is on Ringenberg's *Best Tracks and Side Tracks* (Yep Roc, 2007).

- **Iggy Pop**: "Old Mule Skinner" is on his *Nuggets* demo compilation (Jungle Records, 1999).

- **The Cramps:** "Mule Skinner Blues" is on *Stay Sick!* (Capitol/Enigma, 2001).

- **Jeff Tweedy and Syd Straw:** "T.B. Is Whippin' Me" is on *Red Hot + Country* (Polygram, 1994).

- **Alejandro Escovedo and Jon Langford:** "California Blues" is on Escovedo's CD *Boubonitis Blues* (Bloodshot, 1999).

- **Blue Mountain:** "That Nasty Swing" is on their CD *Roots* (Black Dog, 2001).

- **Taylor Hollingsworth:** "Gambling Barroom Blues" is on his CD *Tragic City* (Brash Music, 2005).

thirteen

Sentiments in Context
The Return of Vaudeville Jimmie

In American roots music by the turn of the '70s, as in the broader culture in which the music lives and sometimes thrives, something had happened. There was a strong cross-genre impulse at the time to try to recapture the flavor not just of folklore, but also of pop culture past, to reframe and find new uses for it. A careful, informed accuracy as to background detail and texture was the tool favored by a variety of individual artists.

"I guess I was being a sort of professor in some ways while trying to spread the news about that music," says Merle Haggard, looking back at the time of the recording of his extraordinarily influential, sonically eclectic Rodgers salute album *Same Train, A Different Time*, a project very much of that moment. "I had an unconscious urge to make sure that people heard it and knew it, because Jimmie Rodgers was just the biggest thing that was totally American that had ever happened." Merle, as few would dispute, has been the single most ardent advocate of Jimmie Rodgers' music over the decades since that double LP's release on May 1, 1969. With its sounds and framing narratives belonging to that "different" time, the album has been a common place of first encounter with Rodgers' music for performers and listeners ever since.

"Ours was a *return*; it was not an invention," says Arlo Guthrie, whose early assimilation of styles and songs of his father Woody's and cousin Jack's generation led him to explore American musical styles farther back and farther afield. "We've always tried to do songs that were true to the times that

271

Saluting Merle Haggard's Rodgers salute, Meridian, early '70s: Peer Music's Roy Horton, Anita Rodgers Court, Merle, and songwriter Vaughan Horton.

they were written," he adds, referencing not just the defined set of instrumental backings and songs that had been integral to the folk revival he was born into, but also a more expansive, varied, often playful set that could be rock 'n' roll physical.

"Well, I always thought I was doing the songs the way *Jimmie Rodgers* would have done them," says the sly, generationally dislocated crooner Leon Redbone. "It wasn't really accuracy I was after, it was the *sentiment*." And yet Redbone, as much as any frequent interpreter of Jimmie Rodgers songs, applied considerable care to putting that music back into the vaudeville context in which it had risen in the first place, while building a public persona for himself to match. In Leon's hands, Jimmie Rodgers songs were reintroduced alongside numbers from Bing Crosby, Gene Austin, Sophie Tucker, Johnny Mercer—and Ernest Tubb, too. On the cover of his very first, typically languorous album, which had the railroad-themed title *On the Track*, he explicitly sent a "very special thanks for their music" to an interesting pair, "the late Jelly Roll Morton and the late Jimmie Rodgers." The album was released in 1975, when Jimmie had been "late" for forty-two years.

Today, the late '60s and much of the '70s are often cited as the heyday of the LP, particularly as a vehicle for ambitious, even overambitious, self-contained pop statements, both musical and editorial. This period saw Nashville responding to rock; rock itself going retro-rootsy with blues, country, and rockabilly reconnections; former folk artists toying with pop; the success of everyone from B. B. King to Flatt and Scruggs in rock venues; vaudeville excursions of British rock stars; and the advent of a new sort of knowing, retro-pop songster exemplified by the Pointer Sisters and Bette Midler, performing—enacting—what Midler called *Songs for the New Depression*.

This era of crossovers and time-warping identification with past styles proved to be, perhaps inevitably, a friendly environment for new appreciation and interpretation of Jimmie Rodgers' music and life. This time around, his tunes and tones would transcend the strict pop genre divisions that had grown in his wake. As country, rock, jazz, blues, folk, bluegrass, and the emerging singer-songwriter school all experienced a softening of the boundaries that music marketers had erected, Jimmie seemed, in retrospect, to have crossed them, nonchalantly, before they even were designated.

If this longing to recapture aspects of an earlier musical era seems somewhat reminiscent of the '50s when Harry Smith and others pointed a direction for the folk revival, chroniclers and interpreters were now much less coy about dealing with old pop and vaudeville elements as such, and no longer tried to represent them as supposedly primordial, noncommercial "folk." Much more pre–World War II music was back in circulation, including virtually all of Jimmie Rodgers' records, and having had access to the music

and been seized by it, more performers were moved to play it as it had originally been played. The quest for musical accuracy—one sort of so-called
authenticity—presents its own challenges, in particular that of keeping the
old songs and sounds lively, not being so focused on accuracy as to embalm
the material—the challenge of making art, not artifacts. The social and
political context may have helped; a great many musicians and albums from
both sides of the Atlantic seemed to focus on capturing the past accurately in
order to calm down or at least loosen up a tumultuous, paranoiac present—
the aftermath of the assassinations of John and Robert Kennedy and Martin
Luther King Jr., the subsequent investigations, and the Vietnam war, where
facts were both disturbing and continuously disputed. Getting things right,
it was felt, could help to reconnect the disconnected.

The '50s task had been to rediscover less romanticized, less gussied-up
music that delivered straight talk about sex and death, but by this point rock
'n' roll and the tougher end of country had long been handling that well.
The new mission was to reconnect to a different part of the Rodgers legacy—freely and openly expressed sentiment. The looser sentiments and more
painstaking research alternately clashed or complimented each other, sometimes producing albums full of half-serious love/hate camp ('20s vaudeville
as revisited by the New Vaudeville band of "Winchester Cathedral" fame or,
arguably, the work of Tiny Tim, for example), sometimes entirely fresh
experiments, sometimes reeducation.

To use the often useful analogy of the movies once more, an engaging western, circa 1960, could still be an aggressive, leathery, no-excuses
Hollywood heroic movie like *The Magnificent Seven*. In 1970, it was Robert Altman's *McCabe and Mrs. Miller*, the bowler hat, mud-caked period
background of which had rarely been seen in the movies before, but there it
was—and married to '70s-style California sentiment, which, in that instance,
played out like despair. The attention to authenticity of detail had an additional benefit: It made the past a better metaphor for the present, which is
quite relevant here. By this time, Jimmie Rodgers was more a metaphor for
writers and performers than a memory.

No artifact is more illustrative of the moment and its methods than that
1968 pop masterpiece *The Kinks Are the Village Green Preservation Society*.
The theatrically inclined, role-playing Ray Davies and band mix a variety of
familiar retro motifs, pleas for comfy domestic culture, and gentle, carefully
worded demands to "protect the new ways" as well. This very British album
is not far removed in style from that of the simultaneous resurgence of interest in Jimmie Rodgers and his world; witness its cut "The Last of the Steam-
Powered Trains." With double-edged metaphors in place, the preservationist
song includes "the last of the good old renegades" among the things worth

preserving or renewing. The theatrical, British, vaudeville-inclined Sensational Alex Harvey Band would easily work Jimmie's "Gambling Barroom Blues" into their rock set list in this period. If this music was about nostalgia, it was nostalgia with a modern mission—and once again, what Jimmie Rodgers had made fit the time and helped foster the project.

In terms of musical attack, Hank Snow's experiments of a decade before, focusing on the backgrounds at least as much as the style of the singer in the foreground and connecting country sounds past and current, even bringing back horns on the record, now looked prophetic. It is telling that in the hands of Leon Redbone, Merle Haggard, and Arlo Guthrie alike, Jimmie was back with the horn section intact. That horns should be reappearing within the more Caucasian-dominated areas of popular American roots music was itself the sign of a beneficial sea change. Their use in commercial country music had been rare for some time, novelties such as the "mariachi" horns heard on Johnny Cash's "Ring of Fire," some Herb Alpert–produced Waylon Jennings sides, and those Hank Snow Rodgers cuts aside. The Nashville Sound had concentrated on adding strings and choruses in an effort to go uptown—not a brass section. (That Danny Davis, a former member of the Gene Krupa and Bob Crosby bands was encouraged by Chet Atkins to form the Nashville Brass in 1968 is not accidental timing, though the Brass would more often produce their own LPs of Nashville Sound songs than back country singers.) In commercial folk music, horns had been virtually anathema. In rock 'n' roll, unforgivably given the racial connotations, horns had been regarded as appropriate for soul but not for guitar-slinging bands—segregated, in a sense, in the music of African-Americans.

The appearance of Otis Redding and his racially integrated Stax-Volt Memphis band, including brass, at the 1967 Monterey Pop Festival may have been the significant boundary-breaker; within a year and a half of that performance, roots music–influenced bands such as the Electric Flag, the Paul Butterfield Blues Band, and the original Blood, Sweat, and Tears were bringing horns back into American blues-rock. Meanwhile, the eclectic trend Dylan had set off at Newport in 1965 had moved singer-songwriters to look at a variety of musical sources broader and more pop oriented than traditional folk had. Indeed, outside of the increasing focus on the personal, that broadening instrumentation palette is essentially what distinguishes '70s singer-songwriters from earlier commercial folksingers. Then Glen Campbell—pop friendly, soul-aware, and ready for prime-time television— introduced horns into the mix on his 1969 single "Galveston," a country smash that also climbed the pop charts.

Practically, the road was cleared for this new interplay of sounds, and the musical return of "vaudeville Jimmie" with it, by the coming to power of a new generation of producers and record-company executives. The New Jersey–raised Joe Boyd, one of the young record collecting blues enthusiasts of the '60s, started his career when he found the great bluesman Lonnie Johnson working in a Philadelphia restaurant kitchen and got him back onstage at Princeton. He would soon be booking an acquaintance of Jimmie Rodgers, bluesman Hammie Nixon, and key acolytes such as Doc Watson and Jack Elliott in the lively venues of the Cambridge, Massachusetts, folk scene such as Club 47, then go on to manage blues revival tours. His close friends, such as Geoff Muldaur, Tom Rush, Jim Rooney, and Jim Kweskin, would all sing the occasional Rodgers song at Club 47. These were performers of a mind-set that treasured old jazz, jug band tunes, and the more rooted kinds of frolicsome pop as much as anything "traditional." Boyd not only admired Ralph Peer; he also tended to see the folk contingent led by Alan Lomax and Pete Seeger as rigid, Old Left, stick-in-the-mud New York sticklers.

"Bostonians loved Rodgers," he recalls. "Feelings that Jimmie Rodgers' songs were 'impure' were limited to people like Lomax and his ilk . . . Jim Kweskin might have been the first one to show me an LP of just Jimmie Rodgers; the Jim Kweskin Jug Band became hugely popular, and the thing about them, and the Rolling Stones for that matter, is that they quoted from the past because they loved it . . . Boston and England were always more interested in the intrinsic value of the music."

Boyd was close to players in the folk revival sector that was most open to the comical, raucous, and physical, the jug and blues band outskirts, and he would be backstage, as the production manager of the Newport Folk Festival, when Dylan and band stepped out with those electric instruments in 1965. Joe liked it, a lot. A few years later, when the Kweskin band broke up, he was the producer of albums for Warner Brothers featuring his friends Geoff and Maria Muldaur, key singers from that outfit. Their 1970 duo LP *Pottery Pie* would feature Geoff's blue, midnight-dark, uncowpokelike version of Jimmie Rodgers' "Prairie Lullaby," with horns and strings as backup, possibly influenced by the version Leon Huff had sung with the Light Crust Doughboys. Maria recorded the song as well some years later. "Geoff and I were never very interested in 'folk music,'" Joe says now. "We liked jazz and blues and commercial recordings of the past of all kinds. So that's a pretty good example of Geoff's fundamental aesthetic." In 1973, Boyd produced Maria's hit first album under her own name for Warner-Reprise, featuring her memorable version of Jimmie's "Any Old Time," reviving the number as the opening track in a set of songs with explicit old-time show business references, including Wendy Waldman's "Vaudeville Man" and Kate McGarigle's "The Work Song." As the B-side of her "Midnight at the

Oasis" single, "Any Old Time" reached jukeboxes everywhere. Warner's, under the direction of the eclectic-minded producer Lenny Waronker, was particularly hospitable to these excursions, and the Rodgers-reviving Leon Redbone and Arlo Guthrie recordings were on the same label. But Warner's was not alone.

At Capitol Records, veteran producer Ken Nelson was overseeing the groundbreaking Los Angeles–based country music unit that brought the world Buck Owens, Glen Campbell, and Merle Haggard. Nelson was hardly adverse to jazz and pop elements; he had spent a good part of his youth playing jazz banjo at parties thrown by Jimmie Rodgers' friendly competitor Gene Austin and had worked for Austin's publishing company in Chicago. He had clear memories of Jimmie Rodgers as a popular star.

"Ken was the guy who gave me the green light to do all that," Merle recalls fondly regarding the horns, the spoken narration that told Jimmie's story, and the whole size and concept of his album *Same Train, A Different Time*. "He had the insight that allowed me to be myself . . . There were a lot of people who didn't know about Jimmie Rodgers who ought to. It didn't satisfy me—and it doesn't satisfy me *yet*. About the horns, well, with me that was just coming from my heart. I didn't really give a great deal of scientific thought to it—but you can't have the real deal without the *whole* package."

In fact, the "real deal" album subtly and effectively mixes and matches sounds from Jimmie's era and his original recordings, from interpretations by Haggard's touchstones for singing Rodgers' music, Lefty Frizzell and Tommy Duncan, and elements of entirely contemporary, driving, Bakersfield country. The most unifying sound throughout the album's several dozen Rodgers interpretations, marked by quite varying amounts of instrumentation, is the plaintive Dobro, sounding like an old-time steel guitar. (The Dobro name, it should be acknowledged, is technically a brand name for one sort of resophonic, or resonator guitar, owned today by the Gibson Guitar Corporation; it is a brand that has become as much a part of common speech as Kleenex has for tissue.) Often, on Merle's LP, it is an acoustic Dobro played by Norman Hamlet, with a nod toward the prominent use of the instrument in the 1951 Lefty Frizzell recordings of Rodgers tunes. When Merle interjects "It's like the 1930s!" during a particularly notable Dobro break on "Blue Yodel No. 6," however, that's no Depression-era instrument taking the lead, but a new-fangled electric Dobro played by Elvis Presley's soulful guitar ace James Burton. Burton's Telecaster guitar is all over the album as well, adding a near-rock aspect to pieces like "Frankie and Johnny."

A series of specific influences brought Merle Haggard to the project and to Rodgers' music in the first place, beginning with the tastes of his father, Jim Haggard, an Oklahoma fiddler who sang Rodgers songs at schoolhouse dances. Merle did not learn that his dad sang those songs until well after he passed away in 1946, when Merle was only nine. Jim and his wife, Flossie, Merle's celebrated mama who "tried," had migrated to California in the '30s, as so many Okies had. Some of Merle's earliest days were spent living with his parents, brother, and sister in a converted refrigerator car—or as the hoboes called them, a "reefer."

"My dad was my hero," Merle still stresses. "I had a dream one time that I died and I got to the other side and my dad met me. It was like a train station, and he helped me out of the train and said, 'Now come on; we've got to hurry up.' 'Why are we in a *hurry*?' And he said 'Well, you're on a show with Jimmie Rodgers and Lefty Frizzell—and you're opening!' "

Merle did not learn Rodgers songs from his father's records, as some have reported; the Haggards were too impoverished at the time to own a record player. But he heard on the radio some songs that he would later learn were Jimmie's—the driving, danceable versions performed by Tommy Duncan and Bob Wills. One of Haggard's first professional gigs was playing guitar for Tommy Duncan in the '50s, and the two would be friends and mutual admirers.

"When Tommy would sing a Jimmie Rodgers song to me," Merle says, "it seemed like he *leaned* the right way. Some of the old bands that Jimmie Rodgers had with him weren't *that* good, but with Bob Wills' help, Tommy would lean in the right direction. It was good to know that somebody you admired like that felt the same way about the music that you did." Collecting then hard-to-find Tommy Duncan/Bob Wills versions of Rodgers songs would eventually lead Merle to make a separate album saluting Bob Wills. The radio that was his first source for hearing Duncan was also where he came to hear the other chief influence on his own soulful, jazz-tinged, honky tonk vocals, Lefty Frizzell.

"I was really knocked over by Lefty when I was about fourteen years old," Merle recalls. "And then one day my mother and I were standing in the kitchen and on the radio he came, singing 'Blue Yodel No. 6.' And I said, 'That's Lefty with a new record; Mom—*Lefty's got a new song*!' And she had a funny look on her face and said, 'That's Jimmie Rodgers' song.' She had some sort of indifferent posture about it, so I said 'I don't understand. Who's Jimmie Rodgers?' And she said 'Why he's—the *best*!'

"So I love Hank Snow's way of singing like Jimmie; I love Tommy Duncan's way," Merle elaborates, "but I guess I loved Lefty's interpretation better than anybody's. I liked his voice already, and somehow or other our voices were alike. Our families' dialect and the way they expressed themselves were identical. He grew up in the oil fields, and so did I; we heard things the same way." Frizzell, on the verge of a last comeback, would be a friend and sometime imitator of his own younger disciple by the time Merle's Rodgers tribute came out. He told deejay T. Tommy Cutrer, "Merle does a marvelous job on these numbers . . . I was going over to the studio, and he had me drop by to give me a copy of his Jimmie Rodgers album. And it's real terrific."

To a very Lefty-like vocal on "Travelin' Blues," Merle added, as he would on "Nobody Knows But Me" and a number of other tracks, a break by a Dixieland jazz band—on this country LP. That was news—and all the more so since the Haggard album climbed both the country and pop charts. The band was evidently the same group that backed him on a *Johnny Cash Show* TV appearance, at the very time Cash was doing on-air Rodgers tributes.

There is a curious moment in that jazzy "Travelin' Blues" arrangement: at one point the brass plays precisely the same downward-spiraling blues line that had kicked off Bob Dylan's hit single "Rainy Day Women No. 12 and 35" three years earlier. That had been a novelty incursion of Dixieland vaudeville sounds into album rock on a key artifact of that genre, the *Blonde on Blonde* double LP, recorded, as we have noted, in Nashville. It is possible that the song's cryptic title was a joking reference not to recording-log take numbers, but to Rodgers' blue yodel numbering, much like the Flying Burrito Brothers' "Hot Burrito No. 1 and No. 2," recorded, like Merle's album, in 1969.

That a recording by the one-time singer of "Masters of War" should be referred to by the singer of "The Fightin' Side of Me" was not something anyone would particularly have expected or even noticed at the time, four decades before Haggard and Dylan happily toured together. Regarding Dylan, Merle told documentary filmmaker Benford Stanley during the first of those tours in 2005, "I think our connection is real clear; Jimmie Rodgers and Woody Guthrie influenced both of us—I just took it in one direction, he took it in another. Now we've come full circle." Stanley, while working on a long-brewing film documentary about Rodgers, was present when Bob and Merle actually met for the first time. He reports, "Bob walked up, offered Merle his hand, and said 'Haggard, I want you to teach me how to hop a freight train!'"

On his salute album, Haggard brought back into circulation Rodgers songs such as "Nobody Knows But Me," "Miss the Mississippi and You," and "Blue Yodel No. 6," and they have become considerably more familiar because he did. He has continued to record Rodgers songs occasionally ever since, typically with some new approaches: closer to Jimmie's originals but stripped down; on the 2005 *Peer Sessions* CD, for example, and acoustic oriented on his 2007 *The Bluegrass Session* CD. He still gets excited when suggesting reasons why we should "pay closer attention," as he puts it, to Jimmie Rodgers' music.

"The tempo and the attitude never sag!" Merle says. "In some of those very last records Jimmie made, even then, lying on a cot, he still knew where the beat was. A tremendous beat sense. And his articulation was amazing; there's nobody ever beat him. The songs share a total corner of the history of blues in America. They are a group of songs that you can sing in New York or you can sing in Nashville—or you can sing in London. And people will respond, in any of those places, 'Yes; you have touched a nerve with me.'"

Crooner Leon Redbone has great affection for Merle's interpretation of Rodgers' tunes and singles him out as "a sincere singer able to put a song across without too much noise." The main interpreter of the songs for Leon was, of course, Jimmie himself. "I think the reason why I was attracted to Jimmie Rodgers," he says, "was that my musical interests have always been the likes of Paganini and Chopin; you can't get any more sentimental than Chopin! So, sure, Jimmie Rodgers' music has certainly taken up a lot of my life. From my point of view, Jimmie Rodgers is the Chopin of his time. I see a clear parallel between them, as far as sentiment goes. And they both went the same way, by the way [tuberculosis] . . . I think knowing that your time is more or less up tends to make you a more reflective person, though, by nature, Jimmie Rodgers was probably a sentimental sort in any case."

From the time he first showed up at folk festivals in Toronto and then across the northeastern United States with a clarinet player in tow, to his prominent television appearances ever since the '70s, Redbone certainly has shown great interest in musical style as well as content. He has recorded more than a dozen Rodgers songs through the years, everything from "Big Chief Buffalo Nickel" to "The One Rose" and "T.B. Blues," accompanied by musicians as varied as western swing steel guitarist Leon McAuliffe; the blues pianist Little Brother Montgomery; Nashville studio musicians such as bass player Roy Huskey Jr. (who played on the Haggard album, too); jazzmen of the caliber of Milt Hinton, Jo Jones, and Joe Venuti; and the adventurous bluegrassers Jerry Douglas and Béla Fleck. That suggests he pays careful attention to getting styles and backgrounds just right, but Redbone will tell you, in his deadpan way, that all of that is secondary.

"What I have always been interested in, really, is more covering the sentiment than covering the song. Some people are loud, braggadocious, pain-in-the-neck kind of characters—and some people have a different character to them. Jimmie Rodgers obviously had his limitations, and knew them, and he had his strengths, but he's the *perfect* example of the sentimental gentleman." This may be the most laid-back, quiet Jimmie Rodgers we have heard described. The portrait certainly matches the emphasis in Leon Redbone's take on Rodgers' music, which seems to be fundamentally derived from his own character—the mysterious, avuncular, young-old guy that Leon, who has always been very guarded about his own background and life, plays in public.

Arlo Guthrie's Jimmie is more complicated, has more spin on him. Woody Guthrie's own Rodgers 78s were around the house during Arlo's childhood. He also wore out the western swing recordings of Rodgers songs by Jack Guthrie. Because of the visits to his hospitalized dad and the family by the Minnesota kid Woody called "the boy," Arlo was also permanently influenced by Bob Dylan's music, whether acoustic or electric. Another musical guide was Woody's last sidekick, Jack Elliott.

"I started doing songs like 'Waiting for a Train' in shows when I was thirteen or fourteen, in around 1961 or '62," Arlo recalls. "It's still one of my favorite songs. Something about it is just wonderfully sad; the imagery is just perfect." As a son and heir of a legend, he had admirers who wanted him to be an unreconstructed folk scene performer, embodying the ethos and sobriety of that world, but it was not going to be that way, for all of his own political seriousness. "There have always been the sort of folk police who sort of guard the bastions, but I certainly never had any hesitation about trying to push the limit of the genre-exclusive world, to bust through that," he says, "because to me that's just a load of crap."

He would record quite varied-sounding versions of Rodgers songs, the first a 1973 treatment of "Miss the Mississippi and You" that starts out sounding rather extravagantly tired of big-city glamour and expands to include far from tired clarinet by the L.A. jazzman Buddy Colette and an expansive background choir. "The example that I used as inspiration for 'Miss the Mississippi,'" Arlo says, "was Ramblin' Jack's. He had done a record one time called *The Songs of Woody Guthrie and Jimmie Rodgers*, and he didn't really have horns; he had one clarinet on that record, and I thought it was brilliant, because *that* sounded like the old records. And for somebody like Jack to do it made it so much easier for somebody like me to come upon it."

Arlo, with some notable emotional fence-straddling, also sang "Mother, the Queen of My Heart." In some live performances, he has been known to ponder out loud, "What did I *like* about that song, anyway?"—and then proceed to do it, after some more characteristically comic monologue contextualizing, with all the sentiment intact. The released live recording of the song, recorded from a stage shared with Pete Seeger, sets it up as a generation gap number.

" 'Mother, the Queen of My Heart'? I always thought that was kind of funny," he starts to say, simply enough, before putting a little spin on it. "Well, the old-world sentimentality is funny; it's not that the *song* is funny. That somebody would write that is interesting, with a certain sentimentality that we find odd today. It's the juxtaposition between knowing it's real and how odd that can sound; *that's* what makes the song work for me."

Is he suggesting that a singer of his generation could have it both ways—sing the song knowing there would be those who would take the sentiment straight and also those who could digest it only with a slight but protective smirk? "Yeah; that's what I'm sayin'."

Other musicians on his album on which "Miss the Mississippi and You" appeared, in addition to Colette, included rockers such as drummer Jim Keltner, bottleneck guitar master (and promulgator of musical variety) Ry Cooder, bluegrasser-turned-Byrd Clarence White, Nashville guitar ace Grady Martin, and Buck Owens' Buckaroos, including Buck's alter ego Don Rich on guitar and fiddle. When Arlo wants a band that sounds like the patched-together, genre-jumping, jazz-meets-hillbilly bands of the '30s, he takes care to get one.

"To get something to sound authentic," he says, "you have to go back in time and really understand what they were playing, what they knew. And they knew enough that this music wasn't dry; it's so freakin' *juicy*. Obviously, they wouldn't have had somebody like Ry Cooder playing slide, but there's something great about getting those instruments playing together that we don't hear any more . . . My father's cousin, Jack Guthrie, had recorded 'When the Cactus Is in Bloom,' and when I went out to Sacramento and played a few tunes with the Buckaroos—who were terrific—that was one of the ones we did with them . . . We may have said to them, 'Listen; we really want this to sound like the 1930s.' That's how I generally approach these things." (Arlo later recorded a second, more cowboylike version of "When the Cactus Is in Bloom.")

But why was he recording and performing Jimmie Rodgers songs, right then and in that way, at all?

"Ultimately, it's because I like the *guy*. Something about that man comes through in the songs, in the melodies, in the words, something about his heart. To me, that's what resonates—not the style of his songwriting, or what chords he played. That *he* comes through is a hell of an accomplishment . . . You listen to the guy who rings true, and he is certainly one of the three guys in whose style I'm most comfortable today—along with my dad and Stephen Foster."

The impulse to reintroduce Jimmie Rodgers' songs to new audiences in a way that emphasized their origins in a heterogeneous pop context was not confined to any one genre. For example, Jim Eanes, who had recorded "T for Texas" in the earliest days of bluegrass development, closely following the original Bill Monroe manner, now recorded Rodgers songs less obviously suited for bluegrass treatment such as "Gambling Polka Dot Blues" and even "Everybody Does It in Hawaii." What's more, he recorded those and other Rodgers tunes alongside songs from Bob Wills, Emmett Miller's

"I Ain't Got Nobody," "Yum Yum Blues" (a jazzy number associated with Clayton McMichen and Slim Bryant), as well as traditional bluegrass and heart songs. Between the late '40s and late '60s, Eanes had found that his rounded, croonerlike tone gave him pop capability and turned toward more mainstream country music. He revisited the bluegrass format with his 1968 album *Bluegrass Favorites*, backed by the first-generation bluegrass musician Red Smiley (of Reno and Smiley) and his band the Bluegrass Cut-Ups—but the album title was somewhat cheeky (or misleading) given the varied and, in the case of the Rodgers numbers, vaudeville-tinged material. The sound is spacious, with nearly as much reverb as on many '60s pop records, and Rodgers songs dominate, as does Eanes' yodel, which is more like Jimmie's than Monroe's.

Putting Jimmie back in his proper context was not just a musical initiative; the process of getting his biography right began in these same years. The now familiar narration Merle provides on *Same Train, A Different Time* was written by the country disc jockey and Rodgers enthusiast Hugh Cherry, who provided the liner notes, as well. Haggard had already recorded several Rodgers tunes when the idea came up of expanding the project to a full album, even a double album, with contextualizing narratives about Jimmie's life and music. Cherry claimed that this was his own idea, but as Merle recalls, "At my request, Capitol Records asked him to come in and give me some correct history to read off there."

Cherry's father had worked for the L&N railroad and idolized Jimmie, who had worked for the same line, so Hugh had grown up with Rodgers records in the house. He was a lifelong enthusiast. Even so, making the history more correct than what Carrie Rodgers had provided years before was not an easy task in 1968. Shortly before writing the narratives for Merle— more of them, in fact, than made it onto the album—Cherry had broadcast a two-part program on Jimmie's life and music for his Armed Forces Radio show *The Many Faces of Folk Music*; the broadcasts may well have led to the invitation to provide the album narratives. Cherry featured a knowledgeable selection of Jimmie's music on those shows, but his commentaries were riddled with errors concerning Jimmie's underexplored life, most of them then common. He had Earl "Fatha" Hines joining Louis Armstrong on "Blue Yodel No. 9" rather than Lil Hardin, he reported the year of the *Singing Brakeman* film as 1932 instead of 1929 or '30 as he broadcast the soundtrack of the supposed "sole surviving copy," and he referred to "Blue Yodel No. 3" as "California Blues," which is actually "No. 4." The narration on Merle's album, by contrast, is entirely accurate—but that may be in part because it sticks to generalities.

Serious research and writing on country music or anything thought to resemble it were in their infancy, and there had been some premature deliveries, such as accounts of Jimmie learning music from "spiritual" song chorales that somehow happened to be working the boxcar circuit. A substantial obstacle to getting the story right was that blues research in the '60s—what there was of it—was mostly conducted either by academic folklorists venturing gingerly outside the ballad terrain or by jazz historians who saw the blues as a subset—or crude antecedent—of what they were really interested in. Neither faction paid much attention to country music; they often loathed it. Folklorist John Greenway's 1957 article on Jimmie Rodgers' impact in blues and John Cohen's 1963 essay on black-white song interchange still stood as daring, isolated efforts.

The beginning of creditable reporting on Rodgers' life, beyond Carrie's memoir and those occasional folklore journal entries, was a chapter of a photo-heavy 1966 book by the music journalist Robert Shelton, *The Country Music Story*. Much of the content was derived from Carrie's book, but Shelton also called on and credited the earliest research of a young professor at Southeast Missouri State College, Nolan Porterfield, who had written him asking whether a piece on Jimmie and the blues would be suitable for *Hootenanny*, a folk revival magazine Shelton edited. The chapter's photos were supplied for the most part by that collector of Rodgers memorabilia, Johnny Cash.

Then, in 1968, a historian (and singer) from East Texas, Bill C. Malone, delivered the first serious, comprehensive history of the genre, *Country Music, U.S.A.*—still, in revised form, the standard reference book on the subject. Jimmie had his own detailed chapter, in which he is portrayed as the first country singing star. Also a key moment for "the story of the story" was the beginning, at the same moment, of systematic examination of the musical interchange between American whites and blacks. That this topic could have been so generally neglected seems wildly improbable now, yet it had rarely been visited.

The breakthrough book, vital for grasping where Jimmie Rodgers really came from musically, was Tony Russell's *Blacks, Whites and Blues*, which gave more attention to Jimmie, Cliff Carlisle, Dock Boggs, and other white blues singers than anyone had before—and put them in a context of blues interchange and a song stock and music heritage shared with key African-American performers. Russell—British, and perhaps less stymied by American musical category rigidity for it—was the man for the job. He was versed and immersed both in old-time American country music and in blues, and remains devoted to writing and researching both. The book's focus was on recordings, in part because the young Russell *was* approaching the subject from the U.K and had not been able to conduct on-the-spot research or observation in the United States.

Some of the photos and recordings for Russell's research were furnished by another British fan of old-time country music, Chris Comber, who, with Mike Paris, performed in an outfit called the Southern Eagle String Band. They had begun, simply out of the avid interest of fans, to research Jimmie Rodgers' life, though, again, from a transatlantic distance. The project was another product of the power of Jimmie Rodgers' music across time — and oceans. Part of their work first appeared in the 1975 biographical anthology *Stars of Country Music*, edited by Malone and Judith McCulloh. That was followed in 1977 by the book *Jimmie the Kid: The Life and Times of Jimmie Rodgers* by Paris and Comber, the first Rodgers biography. Time has not been kind to that effort, which filled in a large number of underinvestigated blanks with speculative "must haves" and "surely did" stories. But with that reservation, the book did offer an often entertaining introduction to much of the Rodgers story, and it took a cursory look at what became of the music after Jimmie's death. Decades later, coauthor Chris Comber is, if anything, overapologetic about the whole effort.

"Neither Mike Paris nor I," he says, "were professional writers or entertainers. Mike was a schoolteacher, and I was an adjuster of marine claims — a job I still do now . . . I recall introducing Mike and Tony Russell to the world of old-timey music long before reissues were available . . . as I had (and still have) a large collection of 78s. I began playing solo around 1958, having acquired the ability to yodel — a novelty in these parts. I met Mike at a mutual friend's house around 1965, and with another musician, the late John Runnells, we formed the band.

"[As] we researched and wrote the book, neither of us had been to the States. I had a copy of the Carrie Rodgers book in the late 1950s, and found it a useful start . . . Our claim to fame, such as it was, was that we were U.K. citizens producing a serious work on an icon from across the water. Our drawback was that we did not have the time or the money to visit the U.S.A. Mike did correspond with Nolan Porterfield; it was ironic that Nolan's book came out hot on the heels of our own; we beat him to the draw . . . [but with] his superior knowledge and research ability . . . his book was far better than ours. I viewed ours as no more than a labor of love. My own views of Jimmie's life and music have not and will never alter; he was an innovator and sang to ordinary folk, and for them."

Nolan Porterfield had grown up with a dad whose seven brothers all played string instruments and "a lot of Jimmie Rodgers songs." Since this was in West Texas, he heard Jimmie's songs on local radio as well, even before getting copies of the RCA *Memorial Albums* in the late '40s, when he was about nine years old. "What I heard in Jimmie Rodgers," Nolan recalls, "was authenticity—however you want to use that word in a positive way, not as a buzzword. I was nine, but I heard something real and it appealed to me. It felt like 'He's been there. He knows that. He's done that.'"

At fifteen, Nolan noticed that according to one of the "Jimmie Rodgers Society" ads in *Popular Mechanics*, the society founder, Jim Evans, lived only forty-five miles away in Lubbock. "I got in touch with him," Nolan recalls, "and he was much taken that a kid my age liked Jimmie Rodgers. He had this Saturday afternoon record show called 'Uncle Jim's Memory Lane' on KDAV, arguably the first full-time country music station on the air, and he invited me to come and be on his show. That really went to my head." While Porterfield was attending grad school in the late '60s, Archie Green, one of the most respected early historians of country music, encouraged him to pursue the Rodgers research that had been mentioned in *The Country Music Story*. In fact, his biography of Jimmie Rodgers was sparked by questions that kept coming his way on Rodgers topics—including those from Mike Paris and Chris Comber.

"They got in touch with me," he recalls, "while their book was still in manuscript and posed questions to me, some of which I couldn't answer. It set me thinking seriously . . . I thought, 'These guys are sitting over in England and doing a book, and I'm a day's drive from Meridian, Mississippi' . . . What I didn't know about Jimmie Rodgers in 1966 you could fill a room with—but by the time I wrote my book, I knew more about Jimmie Rodgers than any other human being. I'm not bragging about it; when you write a book, you should be able to say that."

He certainly could. After years pursuing and interviewing the many Rodgers friends, relatives, and coworkers who were still alive, searching newspapers, record-company files, court records, and more, he completed what remains the definitive Rodgers biography, published in 1979, *Jimmie Rodgers: The Life and Times of America's Blue Yodeler*. That the research would present a new picture of Jimmie had already become clear when Porterfield wrote an introduction for the 1975 republication of Carrie Rodgers' book by the Country Music Foundation and revealed for the first time information about Jimmie's first wife, Stella, and their child, about Carrie's ghostwriter Dorothy Hendricks, and Carrie's little-known second marriage. Since both Anita Rodgers and Stella (who, once located, consented to a single interview) were irate about the inclusion of unvarnished details of Rodgers' first family in the biography, it took considerable courage and integrity for Porterfield to tell the tale straight, as he did. More importantly, no one reading his biography could come away clinging to the notion that Jimmie Rodgers was by choice a railroad man, who had only turned to performing when there was nothing else that he could do. Nolan Porterfield delivers a portrait of a born, ambitious entertainer. There is a small irony of timing though: Porterfield, by his own admission, had always, since his childhood, preferred to hear Jimmie in his least produced manner, one man and his acoustic guitar, and that preference is often reflected in his book—which emerged in the very era when interest in the *variety* of Jimmie's recorded music seems, in retrospect, to have been rapidly regaining performers' attention and new affection.

It has become commonplace for performers who delve into Jimmie Rodgers' music to any significant extent to turn to Porterfield's book for background. That is not to say that they will necessarily have taken in all its facts or accepted its revealing picture. The book's publication did not put an end to manipulation of Jimmie's music and image for performers' or producers' own ends; there was just more good information to use if someone wanted to do so. Old reliable Hank Snow, for example, claimed to have read the book a half-dozen times; but that is not reflected in his three '70s albums of Rodgers songs, which can be seen, thematically, as a three-act playlet about Snow's increasing cultural conservatism in a complicated era, the attitude that made him a target for satire in Robert Altman's film *Nashville*.

The first, *Hank Snow Sings in Memory of Jimmie Rodgers*, showed Hank on its cover going over Rodgers songbooks and memorabilia. The liner notes by Hugh Cherry, who in 1970 was still the natural choice for the commentary, rightly salute Snow's mix of the familiar ("Mother, the Queen of My Heart") and less familiar ("She Was Happy Till She Met You") and, quoting Ralph Waldo Emerson, peg Jimmie as a true, empowering friend to Snow, though they had never met, "somebody who can make us do what we can." Hank's singing is at a peak of flexibility, smoothness, and subtlety on this record, and with Chet Atkins producing and top Nashville musicians such as Jerry Reed, Pete Wade, and Buddy Spicher on board, as well as the regulars from Hank's band, it is a thoroughly contemporary country album—drums included. The next LP in this sequence, *The Jimmie Rodgers Story*, reflecting an interest in documentary audio narrative that had been initiated by Haggard's salute album, intersperses the songs with audio testimonials of Jimmie's railroading friend Albert Fullam. It reflected Hank's growing predilection for associating Jimmie with railroad songs in particular, emphasizing that side of his story and speaking of those fading railroad days and Jimmie's role in them in increasingly nostalgic terms.

The third LP, released in 1975, *All About Trains: Hank Snow and Jimmie Rodgers*, paired five train songs—almost all ballads—from Jimmie on one side and five from Snow on the other. To frame the songs Hank's way, there is, once again, narration between them, this time by his son Jimmy. From the train whistle that opens the narration, the monologue portrays

Rodgers not only as a man of the grand old lost trains, with railroading his "way of life," but as a fellow who was religious to a degree that would have bemused the real Jimmie.

"I can't help but realize," Jimmy Snow tells us on the record, "the *faith* Jimmie Rodgers had found. Even in his saddest songs those beliefs seem to live." The younger Snow had long since become a committed preacher and evangelist. By the '70s, he was best known to audiences outside of the gospel music and traveling revival arenas for that often-used film clip, captured just after he had stopped singing rockabilly, where he is railing against "the *beat*, the beat, the beat" that was enticing teens into rock—preaching right on the beat, of course. So it might appear that these thoughts were Jimmy's own, but in fact, he recalls, his dad recruited him for the job and the script was provided. Personally, he does not see Jimmie Rodgers as having had any special Christian commitment. "I don't think that it was likely," Jimmy submits, "probably because he started out so young and his life was so short that he never had a chance."

The Jimmie Rodgers of memory, who had represented so many character traits attractive to his audiences, who was many things for many people, had almost inevitably become, and has more or less remained since, an object ripe for cultural analysis and exploitation from one fixed viewpoint or another. At times he seems like a Rorschach inkblot ripe for interpretation. His story had now been told in more detail, and step-by-step, his complete recordings, including the revealing outtakes, were falling into the hands of interested listeners. Bootleg LPs made available to collectors included significant alternate takes, such as the version of "Let Me Be Your Side Track" featuring Clifford Gibson, even before careful labels such as Bear Family and Rounder Records filled in all the gaps with complete sets. Yet his songs, sentiments, and image were still going to be pushed around, poked at, and reframed at will. Jimmie Rodgers was now as much a metaphor as a presence—and metaphors are put to use.

There was perhaps no better example of that than Sly and the Family Stone's number "Spaced Cowboy" on their seminal 1971 rhythm and blues LP *There's a Riot Going On*, wherein a very Jimmie Rodgers–like yodel appears at the end of each line, judging by the bitter lyrics, to stand for nothing less than the final burial of the line-repeating blues, now assumed to have been taken over by white folks. As with most things concocted by Sly Stone, however, the metaphor was more complicated than that. The enthusiastic delivery of the song shows you that he feels free to play with the Jimmie Rodgers blues at will and that the racial background is of little consequence. He himself had taken to donning a "spaced" cowboy hat— and he was a Texan.

Rockers who wanted to associate or reassociate themselves with coun-try could do so through the songs of the freshly "current" father of country music. Michael Nesmith, the Texas-raised member of the television-born pop phenomenon the Monkees, emerged at this time as leader of the country-rock-oriented First National Band, recording in Nashville in Dylan's wake, and found "The One Rose" a useful touchstone. His version, on an album revealingly titled *Magnetic South*, is more obviously country and steel-guitar drenched than Jimmie's had ever been, and has an overstated crooner melodrama about it that suggests some familiarity with the playful, comic side of Jack Clement or Tompall Glaser.

Leon Russell and Dr. John (Mac Rebennack), veteran, deeply south-ern, piano-pumping singers more associated in the early '70s with rhythm and blues and psychedelic rock than with country music, brought their barely suppressed twangy sides out of the closet with craggy, soulful versions of "In the Jailhouse Now" and "Waiting for a Train," respectively, in the context of country music salutes. Jerry Lee Lewis's interpretations lurk not far below the surface in both. Arguably, Leon and Dr. John were themselves particular influences on the country- and blues-friendly southern rock trend just beginning to emerge at the time. There was a similar countrified move by another Texas white boy associated with rhythm and blues, Boz Scaggs, when he recorded his own version of "Waiting for a Train" with Duane All-man on Dobro. As with Nesmith, there were elements of exaggerated vaude-ville in the singing. Muscle Shoals keyboard player Barry Beckett, who later became a fixture in Nashville, took the piano solo. The soulful piano on these recordings was almost as telling a signifier of crossover as the horns.

Jimmie Rodgers had also become a point of cross-generational con-versation and common ground—a significant thing to be in the wake of the '60s' intergenerational upheaval. For example, the West Texan Jimmie Dale Gilmore was just emerging as a significant countercultural singer-songwriter with a special, even peculiar ability to blend folk, cowboy music, and '60s rock 'n' roll with a tinge of Eastern mysticism. "Radio had obliter-ated a lot of boundaries," Jimmie says. "In Lubbock, where I grew up, we basically were the first generation off of the farm, but we were living in an actual city, with about 150,000 people, and a university—so we had the same influences that every other middle-class town in America had, pop and mass culture along with the influences of lonesome cowboys . . . I always was a rock and roller. I didn't like the Beatles any more than Hank Williams and Jimmie Rodgers—but I didn't like them any *less*. My dad and I differed in every way, politically, and in all of those respects, and I liked a lot of music that he could never get a hold of and understand, but there was this one strain of music that my dad and I both loved equally."

Jimmie Dale was another of those boys named for Jimmie Rodgers at birth, and Rodgers' music, from the original through the Ernest Tubb and Lefty Frizzell honky tonk versions, was a lifelong connection between father and son. When Gilmore, established both as a solo artist and as a member of the Flatlanders, got around to making an album of classic country as a salute to his father, "Blue Yodel No. 9" was on it. There had long been a variety of Rodgers songs in his act; on a 1992 Rodgers salute on the Nashville Network cable TV show *American Music Shop*, he performed a set that included "California Blues" as a Texas shuffle, an "In the Jailhouse No. 2" that referenced Webb Pierce, and a bemused "Peach Pickin' Time Down in Georgia," which he seemed born to sing.

There were then and would continue to be country veterans who found common ground with younger country stars or the rock world by using Jimmie Rodgers' music as an amicable meeting place. Webb Pierce himself recorded "In the Jailhouse" yet again, this time in a duet with the '70s crossover superstar Willie Nelson—and the piano player there was Richard Manuel of Dylan's former backup rock group, the Band. Ernest Tubb took a new stab at his emblematic version of "Women Make a Fool Out of Me" in a duet with Mississippian Conway Twitty, a former rockabilly turned soulful, chart-topping country balladeer. If a record was ever set up to represent the voices of experience concerning a song's subject, that was it. Rising, younger country stars with a sense of history—something you cannot always spot in twenty-first century country—continue to find Rodgers connections useful. Brad Paisley's hit 2007 CD *5th Gear* ends with a track, "Mr. Policeman," that begins as a frantically picked, high-speed chase taunting a policeman to "catch me if you can" and finishes by turning into "In the Jailhouse Now," at once a sweet musical joke and a claim on tradition.

When Marty Stuart and his Fabulous Superlatives wanted a tune that was seminally country and could easily switch from honky tonk to bluegrass (a switch the versatile band can make at will) they recorded "No Hard Times." As both a rocking country modernizer and a thoughtful student and preserver of the culture from which he has come—Philadelphia, Mississippi, just thirty-five miles from Meridian—Stuart feels a particular connection to the implications of that Rodgers song.

"'Corn . . . crib . . . hog . . . lard'!" Marty reels off, in an inventory of rural references in the lyric. "That was a refection of a way of life, and one of the things that I admire about Jimmie Rodgers very much is that he had the courage to bring his culture to the table—who and what he was and where he came from. And now it can seem like you have to check it at the city limits line, you know!" In the tradition of those who care about meaningful tradition, Marty sang Jimmie Rodgers songs at Hank Snow's funeral in 1999 and, during the ceremony, lit Jimmie's brakeman's lantern—which Carrie had given Hank and Hank had since passed on to him—and placed it by Snow's casket.

Before the '70s were over, there were some users of the nostalgic railroad man image who had gone further than Hank Snow ever had—to the point of attempting to embody it. Before the assault of the Elvis impersonators a few years later, there were performers who staked their careers on Rodgers' image. Singer Van Williams, raised in Louisiana and blinded during World War II, made a career out of his Jimmie Rodgers impersonation, peaking in the '70s and '80s as he appeared at festivals and on television specials and salutes (including the one Jimmie Dale Gilmore had starred in). He was billed as "America's Foremost Purveyor of Jimmie's Rodgers' Music," and, dressed in brakeman's clothes, regularly gave the crowd the thumbs-up. Most of the reviews Williams received praised him for, allegedly at least, duplicating the sound of Jimmie's records so exactly. Among his recordings and regularly performed numbers was "Prohibition Has Done Me Wrong," of which Rodgers' original recording had famously been lost, making this the one way to "hear" Jimmie do it—although a version by Clayton McMichen, who wrote it, turned up and was released in 1993.

A more celebrated performer working this territory was Boxcar Willie, who became an international celebrity by playing at representing the "old-time hobo," which he had never been. His repertoire emphasized traditional country styles and songs from Jimmie Rodgers to Hank Williams, also embracing pastiche songs about those performers, or about loving but losing them, or loving hobos who had loved them, or being one of those hoboes—and so on through Box's rather postmodern hall of mirrors. "Boxcar Willie" was originally the subject of a ballad written by this Air Force veteran born Lecil Martin, who performed without much effect as Marty Martin, before he decided to assume his fictional character's identity. People loved the act and his genuinely smooth, evocative singing—and it appeared that the less the audience knew about the realities of hoboing across America, whether in Jimmie's day or the present, the better they liked it. It was possible to romanticize the homeless drifter once again.

Boxcar Willie recorded quite contemporary-sounding, steel-driven versions of half a dozen Rodgers songs, and others by Rodgers' followers. He also established himself early on in the developing country nostalgia resort at Branson, Missouri, where he set up a little Jimmie Rodgers museum of his own, with memorabilia provided by Anita Rodgers Court. "Jimmie Rodgers," Boxcar Willie said, quite sincerely, "is the foundation of the rock and roll as we know it today, country music as we know it, and heart songs as we know them."

It could be argued that these Jimmie imitators were simply establishing performing identities, as Jimmie had himself, that Boxcar Willie played the hobo as Jimmie had the cowboy, or as Sarah Cannon played the Opry's Minnie Pearl, while letting people know that she was an educated, sophisticated, even upper-crusty woman in her civilian, nonperforming life.

It is a fair argument, but it is worth noting that Jimmie Rodgers' image was not built on a character patterned on one somebody else in particular, real or imagined. He was *somebody*, and the exploitation of his *own* personality was fundamental to his success, as it would be for other roots music heroes who have followed his model.

Now, in a subtle corollary to marketing imitative acts that were built around being "like Jimmie," some discounter record companies began to put out Rodgers salute LPs that were, for all practical purposes, by *nobody* in particular—utterly generic productions simply playing on Jimmie's appeal. Rather than aping the sound of Jimmie's records or his distinctive vocal attack, as imitators had back in the days of the blue yodel craze, the producers of such albums used generic, contemporary Nashville instrumentation, and the vocals were exercises in a lack of personality. Examples were the albums put out by studio vocalists under the evocative, but apparently trumped-up names of "Slim Boyd" and "Jessie Clifton," the latter a man, despite the spelling. The Slim Boyd record actually delivers an innovation—putting guitar-driven Rodgers ballads on one side and blues on the other; Jimmie Rodgers has finally been diluted to mood music, for two moods, with "true stereophonic" sound. The "Clifton" album mixes Rodgers songs of various kinds—setting them all to the same medium tempo, with the same Dobro-abetted sound, and with the same pallid, disconnected vocal approach—quite like "Slim's" as it happens, but pitched a shade higher. These depressing artifacts of disembodied reference, commodities that treat Jimmie and his work as commodities themselves, are a sort of pop music product—but one that misses the essence of Jimmie Rodgers' music in virtually every way. And they still sold some of them.

Lest it seem that we were stumbling, toward the end of the LP album's heyday, into an era of hopeless nostalgia and utter cynicism, it is worth naming a couple of fine, well-versed, and emotionally connected new interpreters of Rodgers songs who began lasting solo careers in this period. Steve Forbert and Sid Selvidge—both teenaged garage band rockers with twists in their musical biographies, both raised in Mississippi—brought fresh thinking to the handling of Jimmie's music.

Forbert was a Meridian native, and while it was natural that he grew up hearing Rodgers music around town and at the annual festivals, it was not inevitable that he would learn guitar from Jimmie's cousin Virginia, interview Elsie McWilliams at length, and gradually incorporate Jimmie Rodgers songs into his lively, varied shows. Born in the mid-'50s, his own models were Bob Dylan, the Rolling Stones, and the Texas blues rocker Johnny Winter—but he owned Merle Haggard's Rodgers salute LP, too. As Forbert emerged as a successful singer-songwriter and FM radio staple with records such as "Romeo's Tune" and "What Kinda Guy?" he was reading the Porterfield book and buying the reissued Rodgers LPs, and he came away familiar enough with the core of Jimmie Rodgers' music to be able to play with it. If it was fun to do "Rough and Rowdy Ways" in the pop style of Buddy Holly, he would do it. If he saw clear Rodgers connections in the Rolling Stones' "Honky Tonk Women," his take on the song might feature Rodgers yodels and guitar runs.

Forbert would not make his own Rodgers salute album, *Any Old Time*, until 2002, by which time he had ways to make the varied numbers included his own. There was no hesitation to feature the vaudeville side of Jimmie in numbers such as "Desert Blues," "My Blue-Eyed Jane," and that title track— the side of Rodgers he was particularly captured by. Onstage with his band, he might do Jimmie's two versions of "In the Jailhouse Now" back-to-back, making plenty of time for solos and jokes with the band members—a show. Forbert could say of Rodgers' career, "It was the Great Depression, and here you had this guy who brought all this *levity* to the listening public . . . He was dying of tuberculosis the whole time and knew it, yet he brought great joy to people. The equation there is insane . . . Jimmie Rodgers just *had* it; there aren't that many people who can tell a personal tale and enchant a million record buyers doing it. 'I'm a Tennessee hustler, and I don't have to work'? That's a Keith Richards attitude, all the way! And when he sang it with that voice, with his soul, millions of people believed it."

Sid Selvidge is best known in some circles as a major rock innovator, as lead singer of the legendary Memphis band Mudboy and the Neutrons and producer of Alex Chilton's recordings during Chilton's move toward early power pop in Big Star. But then, there are those who know Selvidge best as a professor of anthropology, or as a Memphis blues disc jockey. He also owned a collection of Gene Autry 78s almost as large as B. B. King's; they both donated their cowboy records to the University of Memphis, at King's suggestion.

Sid's story is somewhat comparable to Joe Boyd's; Joe started out working in the '60s acoustic blues scene and eventually produced the ultimate southern indie rock band R.E.M., while Selvidge's musical beginnings were in coffeehouse blues, opening for Furry Lewis and Mississippi John Hurt, songsters with broad repertoires who loved and played Jimmie Rodgers songs. He first took up the acoustic guitar when he was forbidden to play his electric in a military school dorm. Sid's singing style is a wistful, blissful meld of Memphis soul balladry, country, and acoustic blues, heard on a series of recordings that come out at the unhurried rate of about one per decade, all to tremendous critical acclaim. Among the short list of numbers to which he has applied that style are memorable, influential versions of "Miss the Mississippi and You," "Waiting for a Train," and "Hobo Bill's Last Ride."

"I think of Jimmie Rodgers as a song *stylist*," Sid says. "He did write some songs, but I've never really paid much attention to who wrote what with him. He could have sung any decent song in his own style and owned it; he had the ability to figure out what worked for him. I think of myself as a stylist too—because I don't write a lot of my own material, maybe ten percent of it. But I can find a song that I can identify right away as a Sid Selvidge song, and when I take that song on, it's because I have confidence that I can make people identify my version of it with me . . . I knew Furry Lewis very well, and he sang "Waiting for a Train," of course, and Jerry Lee Lewis has done it; that was some of what I was going for. I can remember hearing 'Miss the Mississippi' for the first time and just being overwhelmed by it; I *knew* I had to do it, right away. I believe I borrowed the Rodgers record at a party, played it, and put it back. It's still one of the most called-for songs; if I don't do it, I get beat up! With another song I do, 'The Outlaw,' most people don't even realize the influence of Jimmie Rodgers on it—but the opening lick is a tribute, a direct lick steal."

Selvidge has always been both a student and promulgator of black-white interchange in American music, a factor that has made him an institution in Memphis. "The story of American music is fundamentally about the *collusion* between black and white cultures," he says, "and Jimmie Rodgers is right in the middle of that."

In 1996, the fellow who had played such a pivotal role in the growing eclecticism of story-singing solo performers—and in making entire albums matter—finally got around to making a direct album statement about Jimmie Rodgers. Bob Dylan had, by that time, adopted and discarded as many musical and self-presentation styles as Jimmie had. Now his first album as a producer of other artists would be his Rodgers salute—and it would bring together artists as varied as Dickey Betts, Aaron Neville, Iris DeMent, and Dwight Yoakam. It included his own first Rodgers song recording that you did not have to explore the bootleg archive world to hear, "My Blue-Eyed Jane." Dylan's liner note comments about Jimmie Rodgers, in an almost stream-of-consciousness mode, focused on Jimmie's eclecticism and gifts for empowerment: "Though he is claimed as the Father of Country Music, the title is limiting and deceiving . . . He was a performer of force without precedent . . . he gave hope to the vanquished. He sings not only . . . his bawdy, upbeat blues and railroading songs, but also Tin Pan Alley trash and crooner lullabies . . . Jimmie was alive in a way that others were not and are not. His message is all between the lines and he delivers it like nectar that can drill through steel . . . We love the man."

Beck (Hansen), a standard-bearer and star of turn-of-the-twenty-first-century indie rock and singer-songwriter pop, sometimes came up with a Jimmie Rodgers number when called on to open for Dylan, to whom he has tended to be compared for his "roots music here/no roots there" zigs and zags and for the ways he was attracted to and handled variety. If the shape-shifting of Jimmie Rodgers' image was a model for Dylan's protean album-by-album changes of image and sound, it was the Dylan variation, fused with some Kinks-style British vaudeville theatricality, that opened the door for a '70s shape-shifting pop star like David Bowie. Bowie assumed a series of temporary stage and album identities, "Ziggy Stardust" and so on, and what held them all together for audiences was his central image as a knowing, controlling modern artist who had created all the other faces. In the '90s, Beck went a step further, taking audiences for a dizzying ride through a wide variety of musical styles and performance approaches while leaving the details of who the heck he was himself and where he had come from as vague and irrelevant as possible. He was of a generation willing to raise doubts that a core personality could be known or created, or was vital for stylizing a song. With his interest in American roots music, an artist with that attitude was bound to bump into the legacy of Jimmie Rodgers.

A hero of self-conscious, postmodernist pop, he emerged as a performer from the small antifolk movement in New York's East Village, a school of soloists who eschewed folk music's earnestness (yet again) and brought something of a feisty punk rock aesthetic to their acoustic presentation. When Beck reached pop stardom, one of his most celebrated CDs was *Odelay*—the title, he would admit in a radio interview, a direct reference to Jimmie Rodgers' ready-for-many-things, much-used yodel. In a move of true deconstruction, "Beck's" recording of "Waiting for a Train" was not sung by himself at all but taped and sampled from a passing panhandler he asked to sing the song—and who turned out to know it. (Maybe he had finally located Slim Boyd or Jessie Clifton.) A brief narrative that frames the song snippet suggests we may have a space alien singing here—a passing spaced cowboy far from home if there ever was one. Thus, by 1997, this exemplar of an obscure old song that Jimmie Rodgers had personalized so well that he had made it his own had become useful as a means of indicating and isolating the impersonal and estranged. Beck seems to suggest that it might as well be this anonymous drifter singing it, or someone grabbing a ride on a UFO, as Beck "himself," whoever *that* is. But to make sure that this arm's-length treatment of Rodgers' songs is not hardened into habit, fixed in place, Beck sometimes does sing "Waiting" himself. He also performed and recorded a quite straight-ahead duet version of "Peach Pickin' Time Down in Georgia" with Willie Nelson at a Farm Aid fundraiser quite far removed, geographically and sentimentally, from the bars and sensibilities of the East Village.

There was now elasticity in, or even debate about, how straight the music and sensibility of a Jimmie Rodgers could be taken. A more obviously tradition-respecting young singer-songwriter, Mark Brine, wrote a new Rodgers pastiche with a title that says it all for one approach: "New Blue Yodel." But a brash contemporary alternative country rock band, Slim Cessna's Auto Club, expressed the opposite attitude equally straightforwardly in the title of a song that they recorded: "Goddamn Blue Yodel No. 7."

Had the music of Jimmie Rodgers become so tried, however true, that it could no longer be performed without postmodern quotes or commentary attached to it? One fervent latter-day acoustic band identified with both traditional music and punk rock certainly has not seen it that way. Based in Austin, Seattle, and other towns, the modern old-time band the Bad Livers, when they are able to get together in one place, are fronted by two highly knowledgeable and skilled music makers—though they might not always want you to be aware of the fact—in Mark Rubin and Danny Barnes. Since it was formed as a sort of postbluegrass punk band in the '90s, this outfit has been determined to put all of that irony and quotation and contextualizing to bed. They have Jimmie Rodgers blue yodels in their permanent set list— and Rubin is as likely to bring his tuba to the band's updated old-time sound as his stand-up bass. No "strings versus horns" arguments for these boys—for sure—and no self-conscious games either.

"I'm forty-one now, and the music I was formed by," emphasizes Rubin, "was not some punk rock band trying to do this stuff, some 'postmodern' goof on something that was old, or even by Merle Haggard being nostalgic and trying to turn back the clock. My experience was with people who saw it as a living, breathing actuality, expressing sentiments that were timeless. 'I had a dream last night; I dreamed my baby was gone' is absolutely *present* for us, common for all people at all times."

Rubin was raised in Oklahoma and first heard Rodgers tunes as change-ups at amateur square dances. When he made the Austin music scene his home, he found an aging fellow not much known outside that town, Bill Neely, singing Jimmie Rodgers songs, blues and yodels especially, and telling stories about how he had met Rodgers as a teenager in Texas and was taught his first guitar chord by him. Neely is recalled now as "the original" Austin-style singer-songwriter; beginning in the '60s, he had frequently performed Rodgers songs, sometimes imitating him, with Kenneth Threadgill, both in Austin venues and at the Kerrville folk festivals. Threadgill would found the restaurant and music venue (Threadgill's) that was home for Austin roots music personalities from Janis Joplin to Jimmie Dale Gilmore.

"If you're going to operate honestly as an American music performer," Rubin says, "you're going to have to have at least a passing acquaintance with Jimmie Rodgers. I was actually taken aback that the more you found out about him, the more you realize that you can't put him in any one particular bag. You *could* say he was like a lot of southern Americans trying to co-opt African-American popular traditions—and you'd be right. You could say that he was a cosmopolitan person, trying to evoke southern and western rural traditions for the *city* folk—and you'd be right. Or you could say that he was a dyed-in-the-wool southern musician introducing northeastern pop traditions to his fellow southerners—and you'd also be right."

The young mandolin player and singer Chris Thile, who might seem at home on stage with either Beck or the Bad Livers, was raised in bluegrass, having been featured as a player from early childhood, and reached stardom as a leader in the boundary-breaking, turn-of-the-twenty-first-century acoustic band Nickel Creek. When he made a move in 2006 toward founding a very different band, later named the Punch Brothers, that sometimes got closer to traditional bluegrass but had a rock 'n' roll edge, he employed a Monroe-derived "Brakeman's Blues" as a pivotal transition number. The high, sensitive vocals he had been specializing in needed some reshaping for the tougher new sound; taking the high end of his voice into that Rodgers blue yodel and turning it toward a shout, midsong, brought him to rock 'n' roll's door—which was where he wanted to be. Jimmie Rodgers tunes remain useful and empowering today to performers coming into their own at the points where pop and tradition meet.

"The bottom line," says Arlo Guthrie, "is that Jimmie Rodgers is a *deep well*. You have a lot of people drinking from it still, taking away from it in different ways—and they may not even know it. They may be getting it from Jerry Lee Lewis, or from me, or from Ramblin' Jack, or somebody else. The wonderful thing about the modern world is that you can find something on the Internet that rings true to you and say, 'Well where did *he* get that?' And you go find it—and that becomes a new source for you . . . So Jimmie Rodgers hasn't run dry yet."

True enough. What's more, in the years since the LP's heyday, the range of artists invigorated by waters from that Rodgers well has not just continued to expand, but in one very significant way, potentially doubled. That is because, at long last, female performers have been able and have felt ready to make as much of Jimmie Rodgers' music as the eighty-year procession of men.

Select Soundtrack

- **Merle Haggard:** the complete original Rodgers salute album and additional Rodgers songs from the period are on *Same Train, A Different Time* (Bear Family, 1993), which also serves as the first disc on the label's box set *Hag: Concepts, Concerts and the Strangers, Capitol Recordings 1968–1976* (released 2008). Merle's live "T.B. Blues" is also included in that set. The 1995 Koch CD of the salute LP is sometimes in circulation, too. For twenty-first-century Haggard, *The Peer Sessions* (Audium, 2002) includes "Peach Pickin' Time Down in Georgia," "Anniversary Blue Yodel," "Miss the Mississippi and You," and "Whippin' That Old T.B." The 2007 "Jimmie Rodgers Blues" is on *The Bluegrass Sessions* (McCoury Music, 2007) and has been available as a single download.

- **Leon Redbone:** "Sweet Mama Hurry Home" and "Big Chief Buffalo Nickel (Desert Blues)" appear on his first Warner Brothers LP, *On the Track* (1975). "Mississippi Delta Blues" and "Mississippi River Blues" are on *Double Time* (1977), and "The One Rose" with Leon McAuliffe and "T.B. Blues" with Little Brother Montgomery are on *Champagne Charlie* (1978, both Warner Brothers). "My Good Gal's Gone" and "Somewhere Down Below the Dixon Line" are on *No Regrets* (1988), and "Roll Along, Kentucky Moon" is on *Sugar* (1990; both Rounder). "In the Jailhouse Now" and a live "Desert Blues" are on *Live and Kickin'* (Master Classics, 2004). "Prairie Lullaby" is on *Branch to Branch* (Atco, 1990).

- **Arlo Guthrie:** "Miss the Mississippi and You" is on the 1973 *Last of the Brooklyn Cowboys* LP. "When the Cactus Is in Bloom," first version, is on the 1974 LP *Arlo Guthrie*; the '90s cowboy version is on *Son of the Wind*, and "Mother, the Queen of My Heart" is on *Pete Seeger and Arlo Guthrie Together in Concert* (all albums rereleased on CD by Rising Son).

- **Jim Eanes:** "Everybody Does It in Hawaii," "Gambling Polka Dot Blues," "Tuck Away My Lonesome Blues," "My Carolina Sunshine Girl," and "My Mother was a Lady," as well as the Emmett Miller, Bob Wills, and jazz tunes, are most readily available on the cassette *Jim Eanes with Red Smiley and the Bluegrass Cut-Ups: 20 Bluegrass Favorites* (Rural Rhythm, 1968). Some LP copies of the album are still in circulation.

- **Hank Snow:** his first LP of Rodgers songs in this era, *Hank Snow Sings in Memory of Jimmie Rodgers (America's Blue Yodeler)*, was released in 1970; *The Jimmie Rodgers Story*, with narration by Rodgers' friend Albert Fullam, followed in 1972 (both RCA Victor). Tracks from both albums, without the commentary, are on the box set *The Singing Ranger, Volume 4* (Bear Family, 1995). The 1975 Hank Snow/half Jimmie Rodgers LP, *All About Trains*, with narration by Jimmie Rodgers Snow, is also on RCA Victor.

- **Geoff Muldaur:** "Prairie Lullaby" is on Geoff and Maria Muldaur, *Pottery Pie* (1967), available as an online download and a few leftover CDs.

- **Maria Muldaur:** "Any Old Time" (1973) is on *Maria Muldaur* (Warner Archives). "Prairie Lullaby" is on *On the Sunny Side* (Music Little People, 1992).

- **Jim Kweskin:** "Travelin' Blues" (1968) is on his *Whatever Happened to Those Good Old Days at Club 47?* (Universe Italy).

- **Boz Scaggs, with Duane Allman on Dobro:** "Waiting for a Train" (1969) is on *Boz Scaggs* (Atlantic, 1990).

- **Leon Russell:** "In the Jailhouse Now" (1973) is on *Hank Wilson's Back* (Capitol/Right Stuff, 1995).

- **Mike Nesmith:** "The One Rose" (1970) is on his "2fer" *Magnetic South/Loose Salute* CD (Camden International, 2000).

- **Sly and the Family Stone:** "Spaced Cowboy" (1971) is on *There's a Riot Goin' On* (Sony Legacy/Epic, 2007).

- **Sensational Alex Harvey Band:** "Gambling Barroom Blues" (1975) can be seen on the video *Supersonic* (1976) and has been available as a single video online.

- **Dr. John:** "Waiting for the Train" is on *Dr. John Plays Mac Rebennack: The Legendary Sessions, Volume 2* (Clean Cuts, 2002).

- **Ernest Tubb and Conway Twitty:** "Women Make a Fool Out of Me" is on *Ernest Tubb and Friends, Volume 2* (Pair, 1996).

- **Willie Nelson and Webb Pierce**, with Richard Manuel: "In the Jailhouse Now" is on the Nelson 2fer *In the Jailhouse Now/ Brand on My Heart* (DCC, 2000).

- **Charlie Louvin and George Jones:** "Waiting for a Train" is on *Charlie Louvin* (Tompkins Square, 2007).

- **Slim Cessna's Auto Club:** "Goddamn Blue Yodel No. 7" is on *Jesus Let Me Down* (Smooch, 2004).

- **Mark Brine:** "New Blue Yodel" is on *Fortunes: The Best of Mark Brine* (Shut Eye, 2004).

- **Chris Thile:** "Brakeman's Blues" is on *How to Grow a Woman from the Ground* (Sugar Hill, 2006).

- **Jimmie Dale Gilmore:** "Standin' on the Corner (Blue Yodel No. 9)" is on *Come On Back* (Rounder, 2005).

- **Marty Stuart and His Fabulous Superlatives:** "No Hard Times Blues" is on *Live at the Ryman* (Universal South/ Superlatone, 2006).

- **Brad Paisley:** "Mr. Policeman/In the Jailhouse Now" is on *5th Gear* (Arista Sony/BMG, 2007).

- **Van Williams:** *Van Williams Salutes Jimmie Rodgers at His 50th Anniversary of Death,* with fifteen Rodgers songs, was a Cattle Records LP (1983). (Clayton McMichen's original "Prohibition Blues," as he called it, is on *White Country Blues* [Columbia Legacy, 1993].)

- **Boxcar Willie:** *Boxcar Willie Sings Hank Williams and Jimmie Rodgers* (1979) (Column One or "Big R" U.K. LP).

- **Sid Selvidge:** "Miss the Mississippi and You" is on *The Cold of the Morning;* "All Along the Watertank" is on *Waiting for a Train;* "Hobo Bill" is on *Little Bit of Rain* and *Live at Other- land* (all Archer).

- **Steve Forbert:** *Any Old Time* (Koch), his Rodgers salute CD, has twelve Rodgers songs. "Years Ago," by Forbert and the Rough Squirrels, is on *Here's Your Pizza* (Paladin).

- *The Songs of Jimmie Rodgers: A Tribute:* This Bob Dylan– produced salute (Egyptian/Columbia, 1996) contains Rod- gers tunes performed by Bono, Alison Krauss, Dickey Betts,

Mary Chapin Carpenter, David Ball, Willie Nelson, Steve Earle, Jerry Garcia and David Grisman, Iris DeMent, John Mellencamp, Van Morrison, Aaron Neville, Dwight Yoakam, and Dylan himself. Now available on the *Let Me Be Your Sidetrack* set (Bear Family).

- **Beck:** the sampled "Waiting for a Train" (1994) appears on *Stereopathetic Soulmanure* (Flipside/Revolver, 2000). Beck sings the song himself on a Web-archived broadcast on KCRW Santa Monica of June 19, 1996. His "Peach Pickin' Time Down in Georgia" duet with Willie Nelson is on *Farm Aid: Volume One Live* (Turn Up the Music, 2003).

- **The Bad Livers:** "Travelin' Blues," "T for Texas," and "Women Make a Fool Out of Me" are all on live performance recordings by the band, archived online.

- **Bill Neely:** the 1973 recording of his Rodgers-recalling "Blackland Farm" is on *Texas Law and Justice* (Arhoolie, 2001); a live version is on *Bill Neely: Austin's Original Singer-Songwriter* (Lost Art, 2003), along with his version of "Hobo Bill."

- **Kenneth Threadgill:** "Waiting for a Train" is on *Kerrville Folk Festival: The Early Years* (1998), and "Mississippi Delta Blues" is on *Blues at Kerrville* (1999; both on Silverwolf).

Jimmie Rodgers Anonymous

- **"Slim Boyd":** *Nashville Express* (Coronet/Premier Albums LP, 1964).

- **"Jessie Clifton":** *The Jimmie Rodgers Story: Songs Written by the Famous Blues Yodeler* (Cumberland/Mercury LP, 1965).

fourteen

High-Powered Mamas
Women and the Music of Jimmie Rodgers

"I'm thinking about the *testosterone*," said the soulful folksinger Odetta, speaking of Jimmie Rodgers, "his singing, and that falsetto of his. It's kind of surprising, with all the macho-macho stuff that goes on in this country, that that wasn't *turned* on." She had a point.

There were indeed screeds published back in Jimmie's day by puzzled and repelled men with traditionalist attitudes, attacking the lazy, intimate, and often higher-pitched vocal emanations of pop crooners such as Gene Austin and Nick Lucas (and later of Bing Crosby and Frank Sinatra) as effeminate—a threatening break with long-held, self-protective notions of American masculinity. The new, close-to-the-mike crooning style was all the more scary because so many women were responding so strongly to it. No specific attacks of that nature seem to have targeted Jimmie Rodgers' related style of vocal intimacy with its emotional voice breaks, high yodels, and openly displayed sentiment. Yet he was arguably being even more daring in employing all of those devices without reservation in front of a rural and small-town southern audience that still shared plenty of traditionalist sentiments themselves.

"That *affected* people," Odetta added, "and very positively."

The abundance of "rough and rowdy rounder" songs and bluesmanlike sexual boasting in Jimmie's repertoire probably served to limit negative reaction to his casually and publicly displayed vulnerability—another notable instance of the man managing to have it both ways: now manly bordering on macho, now vulnerable. Yet that balancing act did not and probably could not work its usual magic when it came to extending the appeal of his songs to female performers, especially during the first forty years after his first records were released.

Why, then, the long-standing gender gap?

"There *was* a gender question there," says Rhonda Vincent—as forceful a female exponent of bluegrass music as there has ever been, when she chooses. Her band is not called the Rage for nothing, and a raging version of "Mule Skinner Blues" has been a staple of her shows for years. Yet she notes of women's general reluctance to perform Rodgers' music, "It wasn't ladylike! How many women do you think *are* out there, a thousand miles away from home, waiting for a train?"

Dolly Parton, whose pivotal 1970 version of "Mule Skinner" Vincent later built on, recalls how her own recording originated. "One day when I was with *The Porter Wagoner Show* we were all playing around. Porter and Buck Trent [Porter's celebrated electric banjo player] were singing 'Mule Skinner Blues,' and I remember Buck saying, either as a joke or as a serious comment, 'You should record this song. That would be funny for a girl.'"

Maybe not many women are known to have been mule drivers, but that alone was not what was supposed to be entertainingly incongruous. Any of the aggressive blue yodels, and, as Vincent suggests, plenty of other Rodgers numbers as well, might be taken to be just as "funny for a girl."

Still, it does not seem that assigned sex roles, in songs and outside them, can account on their own for the relative lack of interest in Rodgers' music that lingered among female performers. Was it maybe something Jimmie said?

Even a casual glance at Jimmie Rodgers' lyrics reveals portrayals of women, characterizations of them, attitudes toward them (individually and collectively) that were no more uniform than Jimmie's sounds, genre jumps, and themes. For every "triflin' woman" or "meanest gal in town," there is a "sweet angel" and "sunshine girl." Unusually, in any era, most of the women in Rodgers' songs are defined and described by neither of those commonplace extremes, but as "the best pal I ever had," "my good gal," "friends until the end," and if the relationship was especially sexual, "my sweet mama."

These characterizations of gals that are pals have a remarkably modern ring to them—and they provide handholds for women to get a grip on the material from the other side of the gender divide. There is not a lot to work with if you choose to typify Jimmie Rodgers' songs, as John Pankake did "Mean Mama Blues" in his notes to a 1998 Hazel Dickens and Alice

Gerrard CD, as "misogynistic." The duo had transformed the jazzy song into a rollicking "Mean *Papa* Blues," where for once the woman grabs a train and leaves the man behind. Hazel does not agree with Pankake's characterization.

"I don't think Jimmie was anti-*anything*," she says. "I think he was trying to find his place, and he wanted to do music, be popular—not to wave some sort of flag. We were just saying that women can point out these things, too—and when men talk about women, they'd better look at themselves! They can find it very hard to get along with women, and they're not conciliatory sometimes, and they think then they have to be aggressive. But I don't think Jimmie was trying to be aggressive that way. We wouldn't have sung that song if we didn't feel immensely what it does say."

It is highly tempting, but perilous, to identify the women touched on in Rodgers' songs with the ones he knew best. Maybe there is something of Carrie in the woman in "Blue Yodel No. 11" who likes shopping so much that she would "break a millionaire." And there may be more than a little of his Scarlett O'Hara–like first wife, Stella, the beauty who would wind up as an Oklahoma socialite, in all of those "high-powered" women who take him to be or make him feel like a fool. Stella was something of a real-life femme fatale; her second husband would be convicted of manslaughter for shooting a man who "said something insulting and provoking" about her. And doesn't "Any Old Time" make a whole lot more sense if seen as a sort of wish-fulfillment—as the letter saying "come back; all is forgiven" that Stella never wrote?

Except, except, except . . . Jimmie Rodgers' repertoire famously includes a good many sentimental numbers about boys disappointing their "poor old mothers," but he had lost his own in early childhood and had virtually no experience of a relationship with one. Sentiments about Mom have been material for popular songs in most eras of pop, particularly in socially disrupted times such as Jimmie's. There were queens of various children's hearts—sons' hearts mainly—in plenty of songs of Jimmie's day, in places quite far removed from Meridian, Mississippi, such as the Yiddish theater and Irish-American vaudeville.

Jimmie's often-recorded "Mother Was a Lady" was actually written back in 1896, principally by Ed Marks and Joe Stern, Jewish songwriters from New York City who had previously been in the dry goods business. They are said to have had had some help with the song from young William Fox, who went on to found Fox Pictures in Hollywood. And sentimental songs about mom are still very much with us, exemplified by hip-hop mother-love hits such as Tupac Shakur's "Dear Mama," L. L. Cool J's "Big Mama, Unconditional Love," and Kanye West's salute to his late mother in a version of "Hey, Mama." The several decades following World War II, in which such direct statements of feeling about Mom or Dad were considered too corny, were something of an anomaly.

In any event, songs about women, subcategory "mothers," clearly did not require Jimmie to have personal experience to sing them well and to move people doing so; imagination ultimately rules in these matters. But let us not overstate that, either; there is little doubt that Jimmie Rodgers' own varied experiences at least informed the emotional credibility that audiences detected and responded to in his telling of such stories—and his boasts and complaints, as well.

It is also worth recalling that close to forty of Jimmie's songs were written or cowritten by a woman, his sister-in-law Elsie McWilliams—some of them sentimentalizing the nuclear family and home but others in the rough and rowdy or even jailbird mode. No one has ever suggested that the rougher material was directly derived from Elsie's life—and it was not. It does seem significant, though, that Elsie was as lasting a close friend and working collaborator as Jimmie Rodgers ever had, that he could sustain a constructive relationship like that. Elsie's point of view is in her material, tailored though it is with him in mind, and that viewpoint played a strong role in the songs that are part of his legacy. Intrinsic to that legacy, as we have seen, is the expression of strong self-confidence and the way Jimmie could take so many real experiences and popular fantasies and make them all credible, personal, and closely attached to who he was. For his many fans, he could seem not just entertaining, but also, in the attention he paid to their lives and fantasies, empowering.

For female performers of his time and for many years after, however, it was as if there were a hidden and limiting factor in Jimmie Rodgers' personalization of his own songs. Their Jimmie-ness, the very elements that made them the personal repertoire of a roots music pop hero, worked against the material being accessible to most female performers given the thematic and stylistic roadblocks women were encountering. It was, however, by no means inevitable that this would remain so since the songs contained material women would eventually be able to take on.

What's more, the prevailing '20s idea of what constituted ladylike themes clearly did not apply, in record producers' or buyers' minds, to black women. Consider all those verses about grabbing trains and even hoboing that the early female blues singers recorded, gleefully, purposefully, and very much in keeping with the public's taste. And some homeless women really had been out there, waiting for a train. The main attraction of hot uptown white imitators and emulators of the vaudeville blues style—Sophie Tucker, Mae West, Lee Morse—was that they were transgressing established propriety at least as much as Jimmie Rodgers. That no raunchy, self-empowered, vaudevillian hot mama, black or white, ever performed a Rodgers song can not be proved, but it is clear enough that they were not recording any. In effect, they simply did not need to do it.

The few women who did perform Jimmie Rodgers' music and extended it their own way, especially in its first decades, would come almost entirely from the realms that would be defined as country music and folk, where there were particular, traditional constraints on women. They knew what the musical rules for girls were supposed to be and proceeded, to some degree, to break them, in the process becoming some of the feistiest, most ground-breaking women those fields would ever produce. The high-powered, down-home, corn-fed mamas Jimmie often sang about would be the very ones to take him up at his own game—pushing the limits of what was acceptable, working, as he had, to divine how far they could breach propriety with-out losing their audience. They had to deal with those issues—whether consciously, deliberately, and blatantly or more cautiously. The results are performances of Jimmie Rodgers' songs that remind the listener of their capacity for sheer gall and, at the same time, their reserves of surprising tenderness.

Moonshine Kate, born Rosa Lee Carson, the daughter and rambunc-tious performing partner of hillbilly music pioneer Fiddlin' John Carson, appears to have been the first woman to record a Jimmie Rodgers song, pulling together some of his blue yodel verses and employing the Rodgers guitar runs and yodels. As it begins with the opening lines of "T for Texas," the recording in question was released in 1930 as "Texas Blues." From verse one, Rosa Lee has to deal with the issue of gender translation head-on, and does so with impressive offhandedness, simply eliminating the references to "Thelma," then twisting Jimmie's great, incendiary line from "Brakeman's Blues" into "Where was you, Papa, when the train left the shed?" It is just the man who has now been left wishing he were dead. She also applied Jim-mie Rodgers' guitar runs and song structure in her appropriately themed, charming, and hilarious "My Man is a Jolly Railroad Man" in 1931.

At about the same time, Sara Carter became the only woman, in fact, the only singer at all, ever to record duets with Jimmie himself. The pair-ing of the Carter Family with Jimmie on record was, naturally, Ralph Peer's idea. It added another novel angle for these acts he managed, capitalizing on their fame and exposing each to the other's audience. The recorded skits are notoriously awkward, but when your mood is right there is a charm in them still and a sense of history being captured. In 2003, Bob Dylan and Mavis Staples could still have fun parodying the Carters' and Rodgers' forced attempts at casualness in their own joint recording of Dylan's "Gonna Change My Way of Thinking," and it was still cute.

Meeting Jimmie Rodgers

As the session results would show, Peer was particularly interested in getting Sara, whom he considered the sharpest of the Carters and whose singing he considered the linchpin of the act's success, on record with Jimmie. There would be no spotlighted Maybelle Carter-Jimmie Rodgers guitar showdowns or trade-offs; Maybelle's appearances on the two "visits" records would, however, make her the answer to the trivia question, "Who alone performed along with Jimmie Rodgers, Hank Williams, Johnny Cash, Elvis Presley, and Bob Dylan?"

Jimmie and Sara sound good together, a provocative but underexploited blueprint for a much later pairing of a Deep South Mississippi man and an Appalachian woman, Conway Twitty and Loretta Lynn. Two of the four songs Sara and Jimmie recorded come from the Carter side of the fence. One, A. P.'s version of an old lament, "Why There's a Tear in My Eye," is a sonorous but inconsequential "once there was a maiden" song. Much better is "The Wonderful City," a hymn written by Elsie McWilliams in the Tin Pan Alley waltz vein of "Sidewalks of New York." It is rather obviously introduced here, given Jimmie's avoidance of such religious material, as a sort of Rodgers song that the Carters could like and handle, and on which Sara would harmonize well—which she does, even on the yodels.

The other two numbers incorporated into the skits have a harder edge and are both from Jimmie's side, "T for Texas" and "A Hot Time in the Old Town Tonight." Sara and Jimmie do not so much harmonize as combine shouts, slamming home and amplifying the presence of both voices. Sara cannot quite bring herself to sing the words of "A Hot Time," so she "duh-duh-dums" the verse. On the blue yodel, she leaves poor aggravating Thelma in there, without special comment or turning her into the woman "we'd" shot, as she sings along with Jimmie, just telling a tale—in keeping with the folk tradition that allows a woman to sing a man's lyric and vice versa, precisely because the singing is not personalized, and so no gender issues are raised.

Years later, Sara recalled the Louisville, Kentucky, session with relish—the restaurant Jimmie took the Carters to for a chicken dinner, the little dog Mrs. Rodgers was babying so much that it kept her up in the hotel room most of the time, and, especially, singing with Jimmie Rodgers. "Jimmie was a wonderful *singer*. I think he's the world's best—and the world's best yodeler; I don't think there's *ever* [going to] be anybody that can yodel like Jimmie Rodgers, or sing like him either; I don't *think* so! He sure had a wonderful voice."

We can only wonder how potent the result might have been if a Sara Carter had approached a Rodgers song from her own point of view. In truth, Sara was very different from the domesticated person she portrayed for her audience. She was a modern, independent, pants-wearing, cigarette-smoking woman who would divorce A. P., leaving her kids and taking off to find her lover in California, where she remarried. A nominee for potential material might have been "Lullaby Yodel," one of the first songs Elsie wrote for Jimmie on demand. As he sings it, a workingman—a performer perhaps—is far away from home, worrying about and desperately missing his baby, wishing he could be singing the child a lullaby, but the mother has taken the infant from his arms and is apparently keeping him far away. If that sounds maudlin or dated, consider how powerful it would still be if a woman had sung it from that viewpoint—a Sara Carter, for instance, missing an infant at the end of a working day, a child she is being kept away from by its father. But there was no such record. Indeed, one of the only versions of that song done by women underscores the lost opportunity—or, more exactly, the possibility female performers did not yet have or take. Dorothy and Millie Good, the harmonizing Girls of the Golden West, well known from the National Barn Dance broadcasts out of WLS in Chicago, recorded it (as "Baby's Yodel") in 1933. Even if, as is sometimes suggested, their cowgirl image and more urban, ethnically mixed radio audience gave them a degree of freedom compared to their southeastern hillbilly counterparts, this song was still too hot to make their own. In their rendering, "she" still takes the baby away; it is a disengaged exercise—and also one free of blues influence—in narrating the man's complaint again. The only modernization is the Goods' use of more up-to-date, pop-crooning-influenced sounds than the Carters were attuned to.

At about this same time, seventeen-year-old Beverly Long, the daughter of Jimmy Long, sidekick of WLS's star Gene Autry, recorded Rodgers' "Soldier's Sweetheart" with no gender adjustment needed since it had been written from the female's viewpoint in the first place. The most celebrated cowgirl on those '30s WLS National Barn Dance broadcasts, Patsy Montana, would always credit the launch of her performing career to her ability to sing and yodel Jimmie Rodgers songs well enough to win contests. As Patsy recalled in her memoir, while still Ruby Blevins back in Hope, Arkansas, she cherished the stack of Rodgers records she owned and memorized them all. She was quite perceptive and specific as to why that was relatively easy to do: "Some songs we learned as kids had a zillion verses, while most of Jimmie's had [just] a certain number of verses. Jimmie Rodgers also had a certain structure to the way he wrote songs, [though he] never gave a name to his particular style of music. It may be because the music was a conglomeration of different styles."

Patsy would win her first talent contest singing Jimmie's version of "Mother Was a Lady." For all of her relative oomph, her way of dealing with

Hazel Dickens accompanies Patsy Montana, Vancouver Folk Festival, 1987. Between them, they've sung Rodgers songs from his day to ours.

the assertiveness in Rodgers' music was essentially avoidance. She would stick almost exclusively to his tamer songs, especially ones commemorating mom and dad. She earned her first chance to appear on the radio by singing "Whisper Your Mother's Name," and rendered smooth versions of "Daddy and Home" and "Treasures Untold" on the air after she reached national prominence. But Patsy Montana would sing "Yodeling Cowboy," too, a gutsy step for the young woman best recalled for wanting to be a "cowboy's sweetheart" rather than a cowpuncher herself. She had tentatively ventured across the gender barrier already with the story of "The She Buckaroo," so why *not* play at being the yodeling cowboy? Though she recorded early on with Jimmie Davis and appeared regularly on air and then on film with Gene Autry, Patsy would only get around to putting a Jimmie Rodgers song on record, the pop-slanted "Roll Along, Kentucky Moon," in 1988. At that time, she was still yodeling away and appearing at Rodgers Festivals in both Meridian and Kerrville, Texas.

Recordings of women singing Rodgers songs through most of the '30s are indeed few. Radio was the main home for much of downhome music at the height of the Depression, particularly for "girl singers," as they were called, but we know of some radio performances that were gutsy, self-assertive, and make a contribution to the story of Jimmie Rodgers' music. For example, as uncommon as hearing Jimmie Rodgers songs on the Grand Ole Opry was in the '30s, you might have caught Little Texas Daisy, reputedly one of the best yodelers around, singing and strumming Rodgers songs such as "Roll Along, Kentucky Moon" when she appeared with Pee Wee King's Golden West Cowboys, beginning in 1937.

Yet another act that could be heard on the WLS National Barn Dance in the '30s was the DeZurick Sisters, Mary Jane and Carolyn, from out of Minnesota. This pair bolted not so much across the gender divide as across the species barrier and out into the barnyard of the surreal. If yodeling had always been, in part, a way to leave audiences with something special they would remember you by, nobody succeeded in that quite like the DeZurick Sisters. Heard on the air more than on record, they found their widest audience beginning in 1937 when they were signed by Purina Checkerboard for broadcasting on stations across the nation, via prerecorded transcription discs. They appeared on these much-heard shows through the early '40s as the Cackle Sisters, and the pseudonym was more than apt. They had built their act, and most of their yodeling songs, on pulsing, triple-time, harmonized chicken cackles; they even answered announcers' questions in pure, indecipherable Poultryese. A lively, if bent, "Peach Pickin' Time Down in Georgia" was among the tunes they gave the cackle-then-sing treatment, as was the Rodgers-Carlisle "Shanghai Rooster" number. The latter was considered off-color, but they must have been unable to resist its theme, dedication to the chicken gimmick overcoming propriety. Nobody else extended the Rodgers yodel quite so exotically.

Among the female radio performers it would be most interesting to hear, though no transcriptions seem to have survived, is one Mattie O'Neal who was regularly singing "Peach Pickin' Time," "Mule Skinner Blues," and such at 5:30 a.m. on Atlanta's WSB around 1940, accompanying herself on hot banjo. A member of the Hoot Owl Holler Girls on the *Farm and Fun Hour*, "Mattie" was actually an incarnation of Opal Amburgey, one of the celebrated Amburgey Sisters, who were billed variously as part of the Coon Creek Girls, the Hoot Owl Holler Girls, and the Amber Sisters. The sisters changed their individual stage names several times; Irene Amburgey would eventually become the popular jubilee-style gospel singer (and influence on Elvis) Martha Carson, while Opal-Mattie would reemerge in the '50s as the blonde bombshell rockabilly Jean Chapel. So it would have been very interesting to hear what the unladylike singer of "Whiskey Took My Daddy Away," "Ain't Gonna Wash My Face for a Month," and "Welcome to the Club" would do with banjo-backed Jimmie Rodgers songs.

Meeting Jimmie Rodgers

A truly obscure but tremendously talented pair billed as "Harold and Hazel" featured an unidentified, gifted female singer and fiddle player whose attack on Jimmie Rodgers material pointed the way to the more aggressive recordings by women that showed up more than a decade later, after World War II. This duo recorded a remarkable pair of Rodgers songs for Bluebird in December 1933, "Texas" (a version of "T for," of course) and "Pack My Things," which proves to be Jimmie's "Never No Mo' Blues." Harold's intricate, sophisticated version of Rodgers-style guitar picking runs all around and right through Hazel's highly syncopated, laid-back, sometimes black-inflected, and often dynamically phrased vocals. What sounds like a musical saw joins in, but there is too much note control for it to be that; it is likely a fiddle trick pulled off by Hazel. You can hear when she pulls her head away from the fiddle chin rest to sing. In "Texas," instead of simply ignoring poor old Thelma, Hazel sings of shooting a guy named "Teddy." In "Pack My Things," she is still leaving her mama and sister, Nell, saddened that she (not the usual man) is leaving them behind. This country girl rambles! On both sides, Hazel's high, hard, athletic but still Rodgers-based yodel seems a direct precursor of Bill Monroe's. These are recordings that ought to be reissued. "Harold" also recorded as "Harold Maus" on some finely picked guitar instrumentals built around Emmett Miller's "I Ain't Got Nobody" ("Guitar Medley") and John Philip Sousa's "Stars and Stripes Forever" ("Guitar March")—apt material for an instrumentalist who could extend Rodgers-style picking as he did.

As in so many other musical and social ways, after World War II, this whole situation changed. Methods of taking on Rodgers music that the mysterious Hazel had dared to experiment with were now adopted and employed with punch. Texas Ruby (Ruby Agnes Owens), sister of Tex Owens, the author of the yodeling classic "Cattle Call," was billed in the '30s as the "Sophie Tucker of the Feminine Folk Singers"—the red-hot mama of '20s white vaudeville blues being about the only point of reference anyone could think of for a comparison, though Ruby bore some facial resemblance to Mae West.

Ruby was not a long-suffering lady who played at being a cowgirl on the radio just because that was the trend; she was a rough, rowdy, physically imposing western woman who owned that southwestern musical spirit Jimmie Rodgers had helped to define. She had been there to take in the brassy, modernizing developments in the swing music of her native state; she drank, often too much, and cussed, apparently artfully. She would have to wait for the era of electric, small-group, saloon-based honky tonk to find an environment ready for her particular gifts, notably her rich, male-deep voice.

Radio stints in St. Louis, Des Moines, and elsewhere through the '30s did not bring Texas Ruby stardom, but her 1937 version of "T for Texas," recorded while she was still paired with her first performing partner, radio cowpoke Zeke Clements, is the first great record of a Rodgers tune by a woman that many people actually heard. It starts out conventionally enough with a jaunty acoustic guitar strum, but then off of this record, out of the jukeboxes, comes this aggressive, cutting, near-operatic but deeply bluesy, Bessie Smith–like voice. Rougher and rowdier sounding than most male singers around at the time, and many since, Texas Ruby, sight unseen, has often been mistaken for a man. Her vocal attack is as gender-bending and musically liberating as the male crooners' falsettos. When this big-voiced woman chooses to keep the original lyric about "Thelma, who made a fool out of me," a listener may be led to wonder exactly how personal this particular woman's relationship with Thelma might have been that she now wants to watch her jump and crawl. After World War II, teamed with her fiddle-playing husband Curly Fox and reaching her heyday as a recording and Grand Ole Opry star, Ruby delivered an even better Rodgers take in her swinging 1946 "Travelin' Blues." When she says she's "gonna find that man, bring him home if I can," you cannot imagine what could possibly stop her.

The first truly wondrous, no-holds-barred female version of "Mule Skinner Blues" followed in short order—not by Texas Ruby, but by an eventual icon of California country music, Rose Maddox. The saga of the Maddox Brothers and Rose is straightforwardly epic, from their trek with their parents from Alabama to California as, essentially, a hitching, hoboing boxcar family of Depression refugees to success performing everything from Woody Guthrie songs to Bill Monroe numbers, hard honky tonk and early rockabilly. The youngest sibling, the only girl in a band of boys, the feisty Rose would always be the downhome vocal focus of the act. "The World's Most Colorful Hillbilly Band" were among the first to don fully spangled costumes that Elvis envied when he met them at the Louisiana Hayride in the early '50s. By then they had met Woody Guthrie, Hank Williams, Bill Monroe—and Jimmie Rodgers.

The Maddoxes' dad, Foncy, had had a brief musical career as a blackface entertainer back in the Southeast, with a singing style that apparently bore some resemblance to that of Emmett Miller. The first of his sons, Cliff, was a Jimmie Rodgers devotee from the moment the first Rodgers record appeared and, according to the Maddoxes' domineering mom, Alta, Cliff and Foncy went backstage to meet Jimmie at a performance in Gadsden, Alabama. With that pedigree and their Southeast-to-Southwest itinerary, blue yodels were a natural part of the family's developing act before they even knew they really had one. And when they began their exodus west, they started out from Meridian, Mississippi.

By the time they got around to recording "New Mule Skinner Blues," the Maddoxes had a road-tested, raucous, exciting, often hilarious, yet sometimes touching act, able to leap from "Gathering Flowers for the Master's Bouquet" to "Whoa Sailor!" and carry a crowd with them. The show was built on instrumental ability and Rose's knife-edge-sharp vocals, but at its core were family interaction, wisecracks, and a smart-alecky impudence that was half vaudeville, half rockabilly. That combination effectively linked the past and future of Jimmie Rodgers music. It is very easy to imagine Jimmie loving this aggregation's high-energy variety, had he lived to see them at work.

The Maddoxes' celebrated January 1949 version of "Mule Skinner" would be highly influential ever after. Rose is up front with her wicked, yipping yodel, a model of unladylike conduct, and the brothers' crazed laughs and cracks crash in from behind. The side's hot rhythm is propelled by Fred's jackhammer slap bass, then pushed even hotter and faster when Don takes a fiddle solo. This crazed version of the Rodgers song had clearly been derived from Bill Monroe's, but here Jimmie's original pint of booze and John B. Stetson hat make a comeback, appropriately, given the riot-in-progress quality of the ensemble's performance. The Maddox Brothers and Rose showed that a workable way to add to Monroe's bluegrass propulsion of Jimmie's blue yodel was to add still more propulsion.

Rose handles the gender issue uniquely, asking the "captain" about some work for her man; some might even say that she is pimping him. When she gets a yes, she lets loose with a "That's my Mule Skinner!" that lets us know, clearly, how very well she knows the laborer in question. Aggressive, but at a slight remove, Rose cleverly exploits Jimmie Rodgers' trick of having it both ways. She did not record many Rodgers songs after that, with her brothers or on her own, but her singing on that track would impact female and male acts forever. Some of those acts would be in bluegrass, some well outside of it; later on, she was often asked to do the song at rockabilly revival shows.

While the Maddox Brothers and Rose were at the height of their popularity in the early '50s, their national fan club had the idea, to which the family consented, to dedicate an issue of their mimeographed club fanzine to Jimmie Rodgers and to making Carrie Rodgers an honorary member. In 1960, Fred Maddox made some joint appearances with the Fendermen as their own electrified, propulsive "Mule Skinner" rode up the rock charts. The musical link might not have been direct, but the teaming was precisely right.

After that, you might expect a subgenre of female rockabilly versions of Rodgers' music to follow—but that was not the mood of the time, and throughout the '50s, you would be hard pressed to find a cut like that, let alone a trend. There was still more resistance to women performing in that aggressive style than support for it.

Indeed, a Rodgers' interpretation like that of Rose's contemporary Molly O'Day, the 1949 "Fifteen Years Ago"—a version of "Years Ago," the last song Jimmie ever recorded—seems to be a southeastern rejection, Roy Acuff–style, of such brazen cowgirl adventures. The song was not a particularly good or characteristic piece of Rodgers material to begin with; it was a Tin Pan Alley concoction that recalled roamin,' leaving old daddy in the Mississippi "gloamin,'" principally, it seems, because the words had been rhymed in song before. A city slicker leads the country boy who is singing the song astray, to a long term in jail and lonely regret. In her version, Molly is not incarcerated, but she is all alone and regrets her "wrongs." And what were these? The city slicker stole her heart, enticed her away, misled her, then left her alone for another. The unspecified wrongs she is paying for, in sharp contrast to the illegal money schemes or botched theft that led the boy of Rodgers' original to jail, are intended to be understood not as her own terminal naïveté, but her brief sexual escapade with a bounder.

Whatever Appalachian community standards might have inflicted on the singer for being foolish, self-flagellation is no small part of Molly's mix there. She was occasionally referred to at the time as "the female Hank Williams," but it was the hearth and Bible aspect of Hank Williams' repertoire, the Acuff- rather than Ernest Tubb-derived side, that Molly would feature in her very early recordings of his songs. Inevitably perhaps, she left secular singing altogether, determined to sing all gospel, all the time, so we are fortunate to have that Rodgers song done by that talented, plaintive hillbilly singer at all. On radio, she even ventured, as had Roy Acuff, into an assertive, hard-yodeling "Mule Skinner." A transcription survives as a tantalizing artifact from the road not taken; it would be twenty years before another hillbilly mountain girl took that idea further.

Over in the emerging commercial folk field of the early '50s, Molly might have been welcome if she could just have turned down the twang and presented herself as an Anglo-Appalachian museum piece like Jean Ritchie. In that world, the notion of a pristine mountain madonna, at once romanticized and backward-looking in the worst sense, still held sway, and would for years to come. Onto that unpromising scene came Odetta and her Woody Guthriesque version of "Mule Skinner," her singing style earthy, assertive, and very African-American, pulling few punches. She had left classical music for folk, with a mission.

"I was singing prison songs and work songs," she recalled in 2007, "and so up comes 'Mule Skinner Blues' as a song in the work area. That's what I was interested in. With the anger that I felt, the frustrations, the questions

Meeting Jimmie Rodgers

that I had, in the day of the colored fountain and the white fountain, with the prison songs and work songs, I could get my rocks off! Even if you couldn't stand up and fight with somebody, I could expose something I was feeling. And those were the songs, that helped *me* to heal—because with that sort of song, I could holler my head off."

Odetta's deliberate, dramatic, intense way of hollering "Mule Skinner" was not accidental; she knew perfectly well that it was unusual for a woman to present this song to the folk world and even to broader pop and country music audiences, as when she performed it years later in March 1960 on the Tennessee Ernie Ford TV show, accompanied by a jazz bass player.

"Mine *is* slower than other people's," she admitted with a laugh. "I think there was an interest in fast, tied to intensity, that the guys would get into, fast for the sake of *that*. But I've always been a slowpoke. Really, for me, presenting a work song like 'Mule Skinner' had nothing to do with whether it was a male singing the song or a female singing the song—except in my dress. I wouldn't show my legs, because I couldn't then *be* that person [in the song]; I wore long dresses or pants, so I could be whatever character it was that was singing."

In the mid-'50s, women who might have performed hard country honky tonk or rock 'n' roll were more often than not steered toward cute or sultry pop instead. One interesting case was the country singer Bonnie Buckingham, out of Seattle, who came to be known as Bonnie Guitar for her Los Angeles session work and her work as a rock entrepreneur and producer. The label she headed, Dolphin, brought the world the hit-making guitar rockers the Ventures and the pop harmony singers the Fleetwoods. Her own pop hit of 1957, "Dark Moon," had a Hollywood cowgirl-crooner clip-clop pop sound, and Dot Records had her expand the theme into an LP, *Moonlight and Shadows*, full of both. Amongst the moon songs, Bonnie, who was well versed in country and jazz of the '20s, included Jimmie's "Roll Along, Kentucky Moon," in a version that was smooth, lazy, and, despite the presence of typical milquetoast chorus boys of the period, pretty sultry. Somewhat like Jimmy Wakely's crooned version, but with a saxophone break, it was the first significant modern pop version of Rodgers' music by a woman. Bonnie dared to just sing it straight and sexy. There would be more of that sort of thing farther down the road.

Rockabilly queen Wanda Jackson's Jimmie Rodgers recordings, which she only got around to in the mid-'60s on an album saluting the first few inductees into the Country Music Hall of Fame, share some of those pop qualities. The backing, however, would be quality mainstream country, with James Burton on guitar, Earl Ball on piano, and Ralph Mooney on steel. Not that Wanda has anything against anyone rocking out on Rodgers material.

"I think that's very *fitting*," she says. "The man was so far ahead of his time that it's unreal . . . so it doesn't surprise me at all that you can take any Jimmie Rodgers song and jazz it up, you can make it more bluesy, you can make it country or rock—just about anything. And they *have!*"

If Jackson has made a couple of unusual choices of Rodgers numbers to perform, "Blue Yodel No. 6" and "Tuck Away My Lonesome Blues," and has done them in a country rather than rock style, that has much to do with how and when she learned them. "My dad was a big Jimmie Rodgers fan; he was a musician who sang, played guitar, played fiddle, and had a band in Maude, one of the little boom towns around Oklahoma. His family picked cotton or something, but on Saturday, he could go down into town and stand there at the drugstore where they had outdoor speakers—and they played Jimmie Rodgers music. He said he knew he was going to get spanked for it, going down there and standing there through all the music, but it was worth it. And he had some of the 78s. My dad put a guitar in my hand when I was about six and began teaching me some chords, and the first song that I learned the chords to, as he would sing, was 'Blue Yodel No. 6.' That's still just my favorite Jimmie Rodgers song. I've also got the Rodgers songbook, because I play a little bit of piano; I play 'Tuck Away My Lonesome Blues' on it. That chord progression that he uses there is what excited me.

"I was singing those Rodgers songs already when I was a teenager; I sang a lot on the weekends, and had my own radio show, just a little fifteen-minute show, five days a week, but after school I carried my guitar to the station and did my little show—and I was *always* singin' the Jimmie Rodgers songs then. They meant a lot to me in my growing-up years. I still do 'Blue Yodel No. 6' on any show when I do a straight country."

The most famous reimagining of a Rodgers song by a woman came but a few years after Wanda's recordings—the 1970 Dolly Parton version of "Mule Skinner Blues." It may have started out as several people's idea of a joke, but it went on to turn county music's gender reticence inside out while giving Parton her own career outside the context of being Porter Wagoner's girl singer. Dolly not only introduces the notion of an outright "lady mule skinner" who can make any mule listen without any help, thank you, but adds a new verse in which she makes it clear the singer has been a working waitress, and if you think mule driving for hire is tough, waitressing in a greasy spoon is worse!

"I came up with the idea to have a girl verse," Dolly recalls today. "I just remember trying to throw something out to make it a *lady* mule skinner; I thought the little verse that I threw in would make it a little more Dolly-ized and a little more girl-ized."

There has long been speculation about which versions of the song she had known before Porter and Buck Trent suggested she do it. Hearing the whip cracking and aggressive yodeling on her record, you might guess that she had heard Bill Monroe's version, and perhaps Rose Maddox's too, and you would not be wrong. "I knew Bill Monroe's version very well," Dolly explains. "I had sung that song in the past, singing harmony with other people who sang it, back on the old radio shows, but I had never recorded it, nor thought to do so because it was such a boy's song. But every bluegrass band and every country band that I ever worked with, *someone* had done that. Of course, I loved Jimmie Rodgers' version; he was the writer and the original, and I loved Rose Maddox's version. I knew about everything that Rose ever sang or recorded; anything she did was okay by me.

"I have always been able to yodel—well, if you call that yodeling, yeah! I am not a true yodeler like Rose Maddox, Jean Shepherd, and some of the other girls who do yodel really good. I was never able to do that really pure, true yodel, but I can do the Bill Monroe and Jimmie Rodgers kind. To me, Jimmie Rodgers was a great writer and a great singer. He had his own style and was his own person. He loved country music and put a lot of heart, soul, guts, and meaning into it."

Jimmie's "Blue Yodel No. 8" has clearly proven to be one sturdy and *useful* song. Ask Woody Guthrie, Bill Monroe, Odetta, the Fendermen, and Dolly Parton how useful. There was much that could be done with its combination of brazen, boastful aggression, a touch of workingman's contempt, and good-natured cockiness. It was, after all, really a song about a freelance worker primed to take on some extra work right now, with no obstacles about to get in his way, because he needs to rush home to his hot mama with extra cash and a bottle of booze. The words have been played with endlessly, the mule kick of a yodel bucked to the stratosphere, arrangements reimagined. While it might be overstating the case to claim that Jimmie Rodgers' music, by its very nature, has empowered women performers, it certainly has provided them with a high-powered vehicle to ride when they felt ready to head that way. In turn, they have expanded what Rodgers' music can say, and how it says it.

In the expanse of her own career, Dolly Parton herself has arguably risen to the level of roots music pop heroine, in the Rodgers mode—enjoying worldwide stardom, widening musical and audience vistas, and multimedia success, yet always keeping firm ties to the place and people she came from and representing them on the larger stage. By comparison, Loretta Lynn, who came to fame in country music at about the same time, never quite achieved that universal acceptance. She has done TV commercials and been portrayed in the movies but has never really been in them herself nor been able to cross over into pop music, which, to a degree, she wanted to. It is at least an interesting coincidence that Loretta seems never to have been interested in performing Rodgers songs, despite her early working relationships with Ernest Tubb and the Wilburn Brothers, who might have given her many chances to do so. The relatively cosmopolitan Dolly was drawn into the Rodgers music fold almost by gravitational attraction.

The brash attack of Dolly's "Mule Skinner Blues," with its echoes of the Monroe and Maddox versions, almost immediately opened the door for women to sing Jimmie Rodgers in the more tradition-minded bluegrass world—though some spin was still required. Rhonda Vincent was all of nine years old when she recorded her first version, modeled upon Dolly's, just a year later, the first record with her own name on it. She had been hearing the number as a member of her family's band, the Sally Mountain Show, since she was too young to read the songwriter's name on a label—or care who the writer might be. Her childhood take used Parton's "lady mule skinner" but omitted the waitress verse to keep it kid-friendly short—and also because, whatever a mule skinner was, waitressing was not much of a childhood fantasy.

"Yeah; I wouldn't really relate to *that*," she agrees. "When I was three, what we were singing was considered country music. So we were performing at the Ernest Tubb Record Shop on the Midnight Jamboree, and they start the show, after you sing 'Walkin' the Floor Over You,' with the very first song of the night always a Jimmie Rodgers song. I heard *a lot*—Blue Yodel Number however many there are! A lot of times, on Saturday night, we were playing a show, so we'd miss the Grand Ole Opry—but we never missed hearing the Midnight Jamboree afterwards. I'd hear many more Jimmie Rodgers songs just from listening to that.

"I don't care how many times you do 'Mule Skinner,' people love it. That song has a magic about it; people react—and they were doing that when I was nine. My dad said okay, we're going to put this on a single. The motivation was—to sell a record! And it's haunted me, all of my life. That's why I always tell kids to be careful what your parents make you sing—you'll be singing it from now on! It's still our most requested song, an instant encore for my band. It has all of the elements for us; the banjo is hard-driving, the fiddle is doing these shuffles; it's become a real featured song for everyone."

Hazel Dickens grew up in West Virginia near coal mining camps, daughter of a Baptist preacher. She had older brothers who, through the '40s, played and sang songs of Jimmie Rodgers, Bill Monroe, and Roy Acuff in union halls or at home, joined by other musicians, some of them black miners who could play slide guitar blues—when such racial mixing was unusual. She began singing country songs and playing guitar early in life;

her eventual collaboration in the early '60s with Alice Gerrard would produce, among other sounds, unprecedented ways for women to sing lead and harmony in bluegrass. Gerrard, no coal-town girl herself, was the daughter of classical musicians from Oakland, California. As so many did, she turned to traditional folk music performance while at college.

The Dickens-Gerrard gender-bending version of Jimmie's "Mean Mama Blues" proved how far outside the lines they were ready to color. The material had been one of Jimmie's most successful jazz recordings, done with the Bob Sawyer Jazz Band, and very different in sound and structure from typical bluegrass or commercial folk-bag songs. They introduced their 1975 "Mean Papa Blues" along with such Dickens originals as "Ramblin' Woman" and "Working Girl Blues," songs that pointedly illustrated women pushing against social and political limits. Of "Ramblin' Woman," Hazel says, "I got tired of hearing songs about men leavin' women, you know, leavin' her in the smoke along the tracks! I kept trying to find songs like that for a woman, and I finally just sat down and wrote one."

If Rodgers blues, as Charlie Louvin, for instance, has noted, presented challenges for brother acts, they did so even more for two women attempting to harmonize on one, with Alice singing lead and Hazel tenor. "I can still remember us working on that song, and the pleasure and fun we got out of trying to work it out," Dickens recalls. "It was the most unusual thing we'd ever done . . . I had to come up with a tenor, because *Jimmie* wasn't one . . . and then it had to fit what Alice was doing, too. Just finding the keys is hard. The real blue stuff was what we picked out from his repertoire to do. I didn't do the more silly ones; I'd thought that some of his stuff wasn't really that good, didn't have a lot of depth to it or anything, when I started getting into lyrics, to write more serious songs myself. But he wasn't really trying to do that; he had a little genre all on his own."

From the more determinedly frivolous end of the folk boom, out of the jug band revival, had come Maria Muldaur, whose eponymous 1973 LP put Jimmie's "Any Old Time" in the company of Dolly Parton's "Tennessee Mountain Home" on one hand and Wendy Waldman's "Vaudeville Man" on the other. The album is among the key artifacts of the '70s revival of Rodgers music *as* vaudeville, as part of a varied American musical heritage, however pop in origin, worthy of being revived and reused as anything more patently traditional. The Joe Boyd–produced track does not just revive a well-chosen jazzy number in a modern woman's care—it even leaves the horns in. Muldaur's "Any Old Time," recorded forty years after Jimmie's death, seems to be the first Rodgers cover in which a woman brasses it out with horns. Maria's phrasing harks back to the blue yodeler era, her jazzy reading of the phrase "one more chance" reminiscent of Gene Autry's. In sound and intention, it could not be further removed from Webb Pierce's modernized honky tonk version of twenty years earlier.

As mainstream country music came to experience the broadening of outlook and sound that singer-songwriter pop and folk had been through, provocative versions of Jimmie Rodgers songs started arriving from increasingly empowered women performers there, too. Crystal Gayle, Loretta Lynn's folk- and jazz-friendly hit-making younger sister, recorded a poignant, smooth, and highly influential version of "Miss the Mississippi and You," backed by a tinkling piano. It got, and deserved, a good deal of attention as the title track of a 1979 album, especially after she sang it on one of her prime-time network TV specials dressed in ironic southern belle gear, parasol and all, on a boat floating in New York's harbor, with the World Trade Center towers looming in the background.

"I was very lucky to come around at that time," Crystal acknowledges. "Working with Allen Reynolds was great because he let me record all different styles—where other producers would say, 'You're going to do country, and you can't do *that* . . . So it was great that we could do a song like 'Miss the Mississippi' and do it in our own way. We just were gathering together songs; he brought up the song, and when Allen references a song, he *knows* it."

Reynolds, who worked with Gayle regularly and was one of Nashville's most respected, creative producers, had a musical history that went back to assisting Cowboy Jack Clement at Sun Studios, Memphis, in the glory days; he was there when Jerry Lee Lewis began recording Rodgers tunes. He was also the author of such strong songs with themes reminiscent of Jimmie's as the country "Dreaming My Dreams with You" and the pop working-day song "Five O'Clock World." He had heard and admired "a fair amount" of Rodgers music over the years, he reports—and had always found "Miss the Mississippi and You" particularly charming, melodically and lyrically. The number really came to his attention when the soulful singer-songwriter Danny Flowers was singing it around Nashville in the early '70s, though Reynolds was also familiar with Merle Haggard's version.

"I probably wasn't as familiar with Jimmie Rodgers music as some people would have been," Crystal recalls, "but of course, loving folk music and growing up singing all different styles, from the jazz to blues to the bluegrass, I felt that Jimmie loved music like I do. You could tell; that's what I felt from his music. I try to sing all of those styles, but that's still the one and only time I've yodeled—if you can call that yodeling. To me, that song, even if he didn't write it, is *his*. The song has the sentiment of an artist on the road in it, if you think about it: 'I'm growing tired of the big city lights.' It's awfully nice to get home—and that situation has held up! It makes you want to sing it yourself."

A famously, singularly, affectingly earthy country heroine—born, it seems in retrospect, to tackle Jimmie Rodgers songs head-on—took the unmitigated yet, as she proved, still timely sentiment of Jimmie's "Daddy and Home" to the upper reaches of the country charts in 1988, after having fought to make it a single. Tanya Tucker was born in the late '50s but had been raised on Rodgers music. Her daddy, Beau Tucker, from dust bowl Oklahoma, had taught her the music "pure and simple, the way Jimmie played it," as she has described it, when she was still a toddler, along with other tunes from the classic country repertoire. Before "Delta Dawn" made her a country star at twelve, she had already recorded a duet (now lost) on "Mule Skinner Blues" with Merle Haggard. She went on to become such a fixture at the annual Jimmie Rodgers Festival in Meridian through the '90s, belting out the likes of "T for Texas," that she was the only woman whom local residents inducted into the "Blue Yodeler's Hall of Fame" there—right alongside Merle and Ernest Tubb and Hank Snow. The plaque that says so is on display at the Jimmie Rodgers Museum.

As Tucker reports in some detail in her memoir, she recorded "Daddy and Home" with a personal purpose. It was a moment in her often headline-making drama of a life when she was so far estranged from the person she started out to be, because of "booze and drugs" and generally raising hell, that she had managed to become estranged even from her daddy, Beau. The record was a direct expression of reaching back to her father with the sounds he had loved and taught her—and in choosing to do that, in that way, she made the old song that Jimmie had sung on film and Patsy Montana on radio, an immediate, visceral experience all over again, a hit in a very different era. In the music video, she watches Jimmie Rodgers singing the song on a TV, then lies down thinking about her own dad, and sings the song over family home movies. Tanya Tucker was understanding her audience, sharing this moment of outreach with them, elementally, without preaching or judging, transmitting her own style of wit and rhythm, sexuality, ego aggression and love of performing right back into and through the music of Jimmie Rodgers.

From that time on, people have not often asked whether Jimmie Rodgers' songs are "girls' material." Heading into the '90s, if Linda Ronstadt, with Emmylou Harris and Dolly Parton behind her, happened to feel like singing "Hobo's Meditation," nobody questioned it—or even worried very much about whether the hit album *Trio* containing the song was country or pop. The three of them could even kid about their choice of the song as they performed it on Dolly's prime-time television variety show. Ronstadt noted how she "just loved the idea of three grown girl singers singing a song that had a line 'Will there be any freight trains in heaven?'" Parton replied,

"Yeah—the idea of us being hoboes; this is a song about female rights." And Harris, laughing, demanded, "Equal rights for women hoboes!"

If Emmylou, out on her own, wanted to render a gorgeous "Miss the Mississippi," or Alison Krauss to revisit "Any Old Time" on the Dylan salute CD to Jimmie, now there were female precedents. Iris DeMent could trill the story of "Hobo Bill," and her husband Greg Brown's metaphorical "Train Carrying Jimmie Rodgers Home," too. The musical gates were open, and the music of Jimmie Rodgers was as much affected by women as it was available to them.

They could even rock out with it. The Austin-based alternative country rock band the Meat Purveyors, for instance, who sometimes referred to the combustive combination of punk rock and twang they played as "black and bluegrass," began a decade-long exercise in simulated and sometimes genuinely bourbon-fueled abandon with an electrified, head-banging version of Dolly's "Lady Mule Skinner" on their first, 1997 CD. The band's front women, lead singer Jo Walston and bass player Cherilyn DiMond, deliberately exemplified the brazen hussies of at least some of the country music world's worst nightmares, seemingly a long, long way away from the decorum of the Girls of the Golden West. If you squinted a little, though, and were aware of this act's serious musical grounding, then the distance could seem slight.

"We first started doing the song in our earlier band, Joan of Arkansas, a less formal band with about eight people in it, in around 1989," Jo Walston recalls. "But it was always about girl power . . . I heard Dolly's 'Lady Mule Skinner' when I was a teen—on one of those big Time-Life or Reader's Digest sort of country music collections that they mail to you. My grandmother had one of those—and that's where I first heard it. I thought it was just the coolest thing—that *Dukes of Hazard*, made-for-TV sound, but with this *yelling*, a sort of punk rock mentality. It was the perfect song. I wanted to *be* a lady mule skinner—whatever the hell that was. It's perfect in every way, and we always did it, always. We did Hazel Dickens' 'Truck Driving Woman' too."

It somehow seems right that for the Meat Purveyors, the thumping "Mule Skinner" was their regular opening number, after which they would just hit harder and build from there—even as for Rhonda Vincent, in bluegrass, it could be the encore. Jimmie Rodgers music, girl-power style, is not going away.

"I had a girl recently come up to my show," Rhonda notes, "and she said 'Listen to this!' She had her cell phone out, and it had as the ring the line 'If you don't like your boss,' which she pulled from our record of 'Mule Skinner Blues.' She made it her ringtone! It's the warning for when her boss calls."

Select Soundtrack

- **Moonshine Kate:** "Texas Blues" ("T for Texas"), 1930, is on *Fiddlin' John Carson and Moonshine Kate, Volume 6*; "My Man's a Jolly Railroad Man" is on *Volume 7* of the same series (Document, 1998), and on various anthologies.

- **Sara Carter with Jimmie Rodgers:** "T for Texas" (in *The Carter Family and Jimmie Rodgers in Texas*), "Why There's a Tear in My Eye," "Hot Time in the Old Town Tonight" (in *Jimmie Rodgers Visits the Carter Family*), and "The Wonderful City" are all on the complete Jimmie Rodgers and Carter Family sets on Bear Family and JSP, described previously.

- **Bob Dylan and Mavis Staples:** "Gonna Change My Way of Thinking," with the Rodgers-Carters parody, is on *Gotta Serve Somebody: The Gospel Songs of Bob Dylan* (Columbia, 2003).

- **Girls of the Golden West:** "Baby's Yodel" ("Lullaby Yodel") is on their *Roll Along, Prairie Moon* (BACM); "Treasures Untold" is on the 1963 LP *Dolly and Millie Good: Girls of the Golden West, Volume 3* (Bluebonnet).

- **Beverly Long:** Her Champion recording of "The Soldier's Sweetheart" is on the *Let Me Be Your Sidetrack* Rodgers influence box set (Bear Family).

- **Patsy Montana:** "Daddy and Home," the 1941 San Antonio radio transcription, is distributed by American Gramaphone and Wireless; "Treasures Untold," from the same source, is on the *Let Me Be Your Sidetrack* box set. "Roll Along, Kentucky Moon" is on *The Cowboy's Sweetheart* (Flying Fish, 1993).

- **Cackle Sisters (DeZurick Sisters):** "Peach Pickin' Time Down in Georgia" and "Shanghai Rooster" are on *Checkerboard Square Radio Show* transcription discs, early '40s, sometimes available online.

- **Harold and Hazel:** "Texas" ("T for Texas") and "Pack My Things" ("Never No Mo' Blues") were recorded for Bluebird in 1933 and are out of print.

- **Texas Ruby:** "T for Texas" is on *Decca 5000 Series Classic Country* (BACM) and *Let Me Be Your Sidetrack* (Bear Family);

"Travelin' Blues" is on A *Memorial Tribute to Texas Ruby and Curly Fox* (Binge).

- **Maddox Brothers and Rose:** "New Mule Skinner Blues" is on *America's Most Colorful Hillbilly Band, Volume 2* and *Live on the Radio* (both Arhoolie, 1995).

- **Molly O'Day:** "Fifteen Years Ago" is on *Molly O'Day and the Cumberland Mountain Folks* (Bear Family, 1992). "Mule Skinner Blues" appears on the O'Day transcription compilation *Radio Favorites* (Old Homestead, 1990).

- **Odetta:** "Mule Skinner Blues" is on *Odetta* (Tradition Master Series, 2002). She is seen performing the song on the DVD *The Ford Show Starring Tennessee Ernie Ford, Volume 4* (Tennessee Ernie Ford Enterprises).

- **Wanda Jackson:** "Tuck Away My Lonesome Blues" and "Blue Yodel No. 6" are both on her 1966 LP *Country Music Hall of Fame* and the box set *Tears Will Be the Chaser for Your Wine* (Bear Family, 1997). "Tuck Away" is also on *I Am Sad and Weary: Jimmie Rodgers Revisited* (Bear Family), and "Blue Yodel No. 6" is updated live on *The Wanda Jackson Show: Live and Still Kickin'* (DCN, 2000).

- **Bonnie Guitar:** "Roll Along, Kentucky Moon" is on *Dark Moon* (Bear Family, 1996).

- **Dolly Parton:** "Mule Skinner Blues" (1970) is on various Parton hits packages.

- **Rhonda Vincent:** "Mule Skinner Blues"; the original childhood version is on her compilation CD *Yesterday and Today* (Lighthouse, 1995), and the latter-day encore version is seen on the DVD *Ragin' Live* (Rounder).

- **Hazel Dickens and Alice Gerrard:** "Mean Papa Blues" and "Ramblin' Woman" are on *Hazel Dickens and Alice Gerrard* (Rounder, 1998).

- **Maria Muldaur:** "Any Old Time" is on *Maria Muldaur* (Reprise, 1973).

- **Crystal Gayle:** "Miss the Mississippi and You" is on *Columbia Country Classics, Volume 5: A New Tradition* (1991) and her Columbia LP *Miss the Mississippi* (1979).

- **Tanya Tucker:** "Daddy and Home" is on *Strong Enough to Bend* (Capitol, 1990) and *Greatest Hits* (EMI, 1995). The video is on the DVD *Video Hits and More* (Capitol).

- **Linda Ronstadt:** "Hobo's Meditation" with Emmylou Harris and Dolly Parton is on *Trio* (Warner's, 1990).

- **Emmylou Harris:** "Miss the Mississippi and You" is on *Roses in the Snow* (Warner's, 1980). "My Blue-Eyed Jane," a duet with Bob Dylan, was released on the multimedia CD-ROM *Highway 61 Interactive* and has been available on various Web sites.

- **Alison Krauss and Union Station:** "Any Old Time" is on *The Songs of Jimmie Rodgers: A Tribute* (Columbia/Egyptian, 1996).

- **Iris DeMent:** "Hobo Bill's Last Ride" is on *The Songs of Jimmie Rodgers: A Tribute*; "The Train Carrying Jimmie Rodgers Home" is on *Going Driftless: An Artist's Tribute to Greg Brown* (Red House, 2002).

- **The Meat Purveyors:** "Lady Muleskinner" is on *Sweet in the Pants* (Bloodshot, 1997).

October 29, 1932: The last visit to Meridian. A moustache-sporting Jimmie Rodgers with Carrie and Anita, left, and Elsie McWilliams and her immediate family on their right; the only known photo of the two collaborators together.

fifteen

Down the Old Road to Home

It was a halting waltz, on the face of it just one more "missing home and you, dear" song sung by a wanderer, one that sounded more than a little like "Daddy and Home." It wasn't a big Jimmie Rodgers number, really, and it has not been recorded by many other artists. Jimmie evidently just tossed together "Down the Old Road to Home," written with his friend Carey Harvey, for the eclectic February 1932 sessions in Dallas. Yet this throwaway song offers a peculiarly ambiguous and telling sentiment in its chorus, perhaps accidentally, maybe just because — well, a rhyme is a rhyme and songs, like books, draw to a close:

> I'm lonesome and blue for some place to roam . . .
> And I wish it could be down the old road to home.

"Roam" would not be the word choice of someone interested in the fastest, most direct way back, let alone a permanent return — even if he really were heading home to the "dear" he claims to long for in the song. As the next line makes clear, he is not actually coming, waylaid or even drawn elsewhere for reasons apparently not worth going into. If there really were just one place he would choose to be lonesome for, Jimmie Rodgers sings, home would be right at the top of his list. In effect, he tells us, with a straight face, "You know, if I wasn't wild, I'd be domestic."

So there he is, half drawn to the comforts of his roots but still out there on the road and roaming, aware of what he is supposed to be feeling under the circumstances, full of contradictions and able to spell them out with a little help from his friend—quite a complex, modern situation to fit into a simple little throwaway song. In his direst moments, we know, he did call out to be taken home, and with no ambiguity. It is evident even from the way he consistently pronounces the word "wishing" on this record as "wurshing," that the home he refers to is still Meridian, Mississippi, the place where they would lay him to rest.

Jimmie Rodgers visited that hometown, his starting place, for the last time in late October 1932, for his in-laws' golden wedding anniversary. The Williamson clan photo taken on that occasion resulted in the only known image of Jimmie and his immediate nuclear family alongside Elsie McWilliams and hers. Today, the quiet churchyard family plot at Oak Grove Cemetery where Jimmie was buried holds others close to him, too, family who have had parts to play in the story of his legacy: Carrie Rodgers, their daughter Anita Rodgers Court, and Jimmie's main songwriting collaborator, Elsie.

Across town, the Jimmie Rodgers Museum at Meridian's Highland Park, home of the Jimmie Rodgers monument as well, opened on May 27, 1976. In the years since then, Anita Court, and then the Rodgers estate, have filled the museum with Jimmie Rodgers memorabilia, from personal items and his railway work effects to the most important of his guitars—the Martin with "Thanks!" on the back. It is the same guitar Ernest Tubb borrowed and used for years. It is all worth seeing. There is some talk, at this writing, of relocating the museum to downtown Meridian, nearer to the railway station museum and Singing Brakeman Park.

Edward and Jean Bishop, the knowledgeable managers of the museum for most of its thirty-plus years, have now retired. They showed visitors from virtually every continent the Rodgers keepsakes there. "People from thirty-nine states and eight foreign counties have come in here," Jean recalled. "It was unreal—the governor, movie stars, artists. The artists come in to look and feel and to honor . . . and some of them are crying." Ed, who has been a historian and collector of things Rodgers for decades, added, "We've had a lot of entertainers come in here—incognito, in street clothes, and people from Germany, England, Australia, Japan, the Netherlands." When the Jimmie Rodgers commemorative U.S. postage stamp was issued in 1978, after years of efforts by supporters such as the Rodgers Society's Henry Young to make it happen, the event was celebrated there at the museum and elsewhere in Meridian.

Those early efforts to install his cousin Jesse Rodgers as a sort of successor reminds us that, unlike some legends, Jimmie Rodgers did not have children who would carry on his legacy as a performer. As an adult, his daughter Anita Rodgers Court could by all accounts be quite theatrical with people who crossed her or threatened, as she saw it, to reduce the Jimmie Rodgers legend in any way, but she never was interested in performing. Her son Jimmie Dale Court, however, seemed a born entertainer. "When I was in Nashville," he told a television interviewer, "I stayed in this log cabin for a while, and . . . it seemed like every song I wrote, playing the guitar, just learning a G chord and a C chord, would be like a Jimmie Rodgers song. I couldn't get away from that."

In fact, he could. While often pressed to sing in something approaching his grandfather's style, Jimmie Dale, named after his grandfather and Ernest Dale Tubb, admirably, and very much in Jimmie Rodgers' truest tradition, attacked Rodgers songs and others in his own personable, contemporary '70s style — influenced by Memphis rhythm and blues and '60s rock. He seems to have associated Memphis soul with Jimmie Rodgers' legacy. "I've got to go my own way," he told the Kerrville Folk Festival's Kathleen Hudson in 1987. "There's lots I don't know about Jimmie; he died before I was born. But I lived with my mother and grandmother until I was about nineteen. They embedded me with a certain soulful feeling."

Having been raised in San Antonio, he became quite well known across Texas, especially for fine, energetic, contemporary shows. He had such first-rate musicians on his recordings as Jimmy Day on steel, Floyd Domino on keyboards, and Alvin Crow on fiddle. He had his own long-time touring band, which backed him at appearances such as a nationally televised Farm Aid benefit show in which Willie Nelson played right along. He was a fixture at the Jimmie Rodgers Festivals in Meridian, and as a family spokesman.

"We get calls and letters from all over the world about Jimmie Rodgers being the one who inspired this one and that one," he told his one-time manager, the disc jockey and radio interviewer Ken Berryhill. "He had no enemies. I can't do enough for the man." Court's love for his grandfather's music and legacy was serious; he spent years researching the first Jimmie's life, along with actor/singer Billy Ray Reynolds, for a Hollywood screenplay that did not materialize into a movie during Court's too-brief lifetime. In 1996, not long after headlining a big Jimmie Rodgers salute show at Austin's Broken Spoke honky tonk, he died suddenly, at the age of forty-five. It was characteristic of Jimmie Dale Court's self-deprecating charm that his best-known self-penned song was "I'm the Son of the Daughter of the Father of Country Music."

For a short while toward the end of the twentieth century, another Rodgers relative, cousin Conrad "Sonny" Rodgers, made a name performing Jimmie Rodgers songs and hosting "Yodelers' Paradise" blue yodeling competitions at the Old Time Country Music Festival at Avoca, Iowa. Sonny's grandfather, S. G. Rodgers, was one of Jimmie's dad Aaron's brothers; his father was the brother of performer Jesse Rodgers. Sonny's branch of the family was raised and still lives near Crystal Springs, in the heart of Mississippi blues country, but he spent most of his life as a pharmaceutical salesman in Columbia, South Carolina. On retiring at sixty-two, he began to perform, promulgating Jimmie Rodgers' music during the last decade of his life.

He appeared occasionally with Rick McWilliams, Elsie's grandson, a smooth, affecting singer and songwriter who still calls Meridian, Mississippi, home. A more laid-back, Deep South sort of balladeer than his cousin Jimmie Dale Court (with whom Rick also appeared from time to time), McWilliams performs, solo or with his string band Swing Shift, across the South and as far away as the Thomas Fraser Festivals in the Shetlands. Bookers tend to describe him as Jimmie Rodgers' nephew; his earliest performances were in tandem with grandma Elsie herself.

"When I was seven or eight," Rick recalls, "we had a big wind-up Victrola, and we had Jimmie Rodgers 78s, of course, and I would play them . . . I got interested at about that time, and we'd go to the festivals, meet the artists. Grandma Elsie's daughter Jean, my Dad's sister, was married to Prince Wheeler [an officer in the Jimmie Rodgers Society]; I remember him playing that music in the parlor, with a guitar; he was real close with Jim Evans . . . Later in life, Grandmother and I got to do some programs together. She would come out and talk and talk and talk, then play some piano a little bit, and then she'd introduce me, and build me up higher than I needed to be. I'd play the guitar and sing. Some people who would say 'Why, you've got your own unique sound,' and some who would say, 'You sound just like Jimmie Rodgers!' I had an electric guitar, and I would play the Beatles songs and all that stuff, but in 1972 I bought a Martin and started to learn Jimmie Rodgers songs." Hank Snow introduced Rick to the crowd at the Rodgers Festival two years later.

The qualities in Jimmie Rodgers and in his music that were most rooted in Mississippi life have endured, and you do not have to be from his family to spot that. As we have seen, B. B. King, who started out a dirt-poor kid in Indianola, Mississippi, and rose to worldwide fame beyond the supposed limits of race, nationality, and musical genre, finds significant, heady Mississippi experiences in common with Jimmie Rodgers, who started out from similar economic circumstances and a similar place. He was not alone.

Cary Hudson, the Mississippi-raised modern rocker who chose to put blues back in his band Blue Mountain's music when most performers working the same circuits did not, notes: "The thing about Mississippi is, it was very segregated, and it still is, but we were all around each other a lot, and musicians tend to be less socially constricted than most folks. And that was so even back in Jimmie Rodgers' time. When I started looking into earlier music, most of the stuff that I got into was either blues—Robert Johnson or Skip James, those cats—or it was Dock Boggs or Clarence Ashley, that stuff. But with Jimmie Rodgers, you kind of hear them come together. For maybe the first time, you had the whole 'black culture meets white culture' there— and *that*, to me, is why he sounds like he's from Mississippi. And it's why I think of him as a compadre."

Marty Stuart, a Grand Ole Opry star who freely and adeptly jumps from honky tonk to gospel, bluegrass, or hillbilly rock as the mood strikes, says, "As a country musician, and as a Mississippian, I claim my rightful owner- ship of the fact that I can go do and find *variety*. It's the eclectic nature of the state. It's easy to understand why Jimmie Rodgers' music was so diverse; Mississippi was so culturally rich, but I do hear Mississippi in his records most when I hear the blues. Townes Van Zandt, the singer-songwriter, said, 'There's only two kinds of music; there's blues and there's zippity-doo dah,' but even when Jimmie Rodgers sang things that were zippity doo-dah, he had a bluesy streak in there. That's the most common thread in Mississippi, the soul of all that."

Steve Forbert, raised in Meridian itself, a genre-jumping singer- songwriter with a vaudevillian streak, sees the local tie a little bit differently: "Jimmie Rodgers was so *indivisible*, so real, that losing touch with Missis- sippi wasn't going to happen to him. For me, really, it's not that I hear a lot of my hometown in Jimmie Rodgers—it's that I find a lot of Jimmie Rodgers in my hometown. That's what happens with a genius-level artist. Someone who lives in the Delta—or in Oxford—and has read Faulkner starts to become a little more like his creations, too."

Everyone finds a personal limit, somewhere, to geographical connec- tion. Sid Selvidge, who has relocated from Mississippi to Memphis, as he has moved on occasion from sensitive, interpretive folk singing and scholar- ship to head-banging garage rock, remarks, "Jimmie's from the other *side* of the state, see; Meridian is so far out of my consciousness that I almost think of it as Alabama. When I found out he was from Meridian, I didn't find any special cultural identity with him for that. I just thought that he was a very cool guy!"

Nevertheless, to suggest, as this book does, that Jimmie Rodgers was the original model of a heroic exponent of rooted American pop is to imply the importance of his starting place. Jimmie Rodgers was very much of Mis- sissippi and let us all know it; yet he transcended geography. He was of his time; yet he continues to transcend that. This book-length adventure in pop- lore has been an attempt to show how.

The long journey—eighty years and counting—and continuous mutations of the music Jimmie Rodgers brought us, and of the sorts of music-making he helped make possible, have taken place on the record, often literally so, in the first century when such a process could be so public and traceable. That timing has made it possible to detail the moments and situations where Jimmie Rodgers touched people, and they touched back.

If this is the story of how the man changed the pop sounds of a century, it has inevitably turned out to be, also, the story of how the trends of a century have led us to change our conception of Jimmie Rodgers. Of all the stories and individual legacies of those who have developed his contributions and the hundreds of performances of songs created or influenced by him that have accumulated over time, any one might be the strongest, "right" point of entry for a given listener—for you—to get further inside this music. The individual readings of Jimmie Rodgers' music and image that have come down to us may, perhaps, have been delineated sharply enough in these pages that the waxy yellow buildup of time can also be more easily recognized, named, and cleared way. Unencumbered by intermediaries' interpretations, you may even be able to experience the music of Jimmie Rodgers more directly, whole, and new.

That suggests that it is time now, in the words of the late Sam Cooke (of Clarksdale, Mississippi), to bring it on home to me. My name is Barry Mazor, and I have voluntarily entered the stream of intermediaries between you and Jimmie Rodgers' music—without pretense that it is otherwise. You may very well want to clear me out of your way, too, and I will briefly provide the necessary tools.

I was born in 1950, raised in various parts of Pennsylvania—towns, rural areas, mining areas, suburbs, the state capital, even the streets of Philadelphia. We moved a lot. My father, Joel, who at this writing has just turned ninety and lives in Nashville, Tennessee, as my wife and I do, was a Benny Goodman and Ella Fitzgerald fan, a lawyer, and a World War II vet who took a while to find his rightful place; it turned out to be as a railway attorney. My late mother, Bettye, and her sister Florence were kids appearing in speakeasies and Northern vaudeville, a singing-dancing sister act billed as the Dancing Dolls, at the very time when Jimmie Rodgers was working. My mother, who at age five was belting songs and dancing with the likes of Cab Calloway and Red Nichols at Atlantic City's Steel Pier, never liked being a performer, or the spotlight, and turned to oil painting instead. Her sister, my aunt, went on in theater and during my childhood founded and ran Ramblerny, a summer school for young performing arts professionals near New Hope, Pennsylvania. I spent summers there in the early-'60s late Beatnik era, in a place peopled by modern dancers, emerging musical comedy stars, Method actors, and jazz musicians, and I was struck by the music that many of the more barefoot among them were playing when out of class, offstage, and off-hours—folk. A banjo player who knew a lot about Pete Seeger and a guitar-strumming actress who knew songs by the scruffy newcomer Bob Dylan added much interest to way too many choruses of "Greenback Dollar."

Something in me had always responded most strongly to the simplest, most rooted American sounds around me. Allowed to buy 45-rpm singles of my choice at age six, I chose the likes of Patti Page singing "Cross Over the Bridge" and Burl Ives records. My first country idol was Molly Bee on the *Tennessee Ernie Ford Show*, which I watched daily, as avidly as I did Little Richard and the Everly Brothers on the locally based *American Bandstand*. It has been suggested that all of this may have had something to do with the poor country girl my folks had taken in while I was an infant; she apparently sang Hank's "Hey Good Lookin,'" and "Good Night, Irene," Ernest Tubb–and Red Foley–style, over my crib. Country and even folk music were weird, rootsy stuff to be taking to in that northern, sometimes show business hip, sometimes quite middle-class environment—and the dislocation could be estranging. The first time I heard what I knew to be Jimmie Rodgers' music was from the Jack Elliott LP of Jimmie Rodgers and Woody Guthrie songs, which I heard at sixteen. I was soon exploring seriously both hardcore blues and undiluted commercial country music. When I heard, really heard, Merle Haggard's horn-laden Rodgers salute a few years later, the blend of the jazzy and the country stunned me. The reconciliation felt deeply personal, a connection between my seemingly idiosyncratic love of simple American roots music and the sounds of those I had grown up among. Jimmie Rodgers was a connector. I began buying up every Rodgers compilation LP I could find. I inscribed little dots next to each of Jimmie's cuts that was not stripped down and solo, that had band accompaniment, for special attention. And I have never stopped listening to Jimmie Rodgers' music in the forty years since. Make of any of that what you will.

But do yourself a favor; do something else, too. This book has been an attempt to let Jimmie Rodgers have once again, in a new century, as he put it, "another chance to prove what he can be." Call up a Jimmie Rodgers recording that suits you. Let those ones and zeroes flow from your database of preference at the bit-rate of your choice. His "Miss the Mississippi and You" might be nice; vaudeville needs a big, beautiful, sentimental ending. And crank it up.

Meet Jimmie Rodgers.

Select Soundtrack

- **Jimmie Dale Court:** *Jimmie Dale Court and Jimmie's Texas Blues*, which includes his studio versions of five songs by his grandfather and his song "Son of the Daughter of the Father of Country Music" is marketed online by his keyboard player, Steve Edwards (Inherited Productions; e-mail address: swe251@yahoo.com). Court's recording of "Peach Pickin' Time," one of the songs on that CD, also appears on the collectors' item *Superstars Salute Jimmie Rodgers* (StepOne, 1988), an LP of Rodgers song covers from over the years by major stars.

- **Rick McWilliams:** *Down the Line*, sold at his shows, includes a selection of Rodgers songs and medleys along with ones he has written.

- **Jimmie Rodgers:** "Down the Old Road to Home," "Any Old Time," and "Miss the Mississippi and You" are on any number of Rodgers compilations.

acknowledgments

I had been listening to the music of Jimmie Rodgers for pure pleasure for some forty years before the possibility arose of delving into its story. Speaking with the performers, producers, scholars, and other interviewees for this book, and tracking down the sometimes obscure documentation of the Rodgers experiences of those who were gone before I could meet them, have added up to one of the fascinating rides of my life—and that would have been so even if this book were not the goal and result.

This book would not exist if I had not had encouragement and help, often extraordinary help, from a great many supportive people, and I want to acknowledge and thank them here.

The whole project began, in one real sense, as my answer to the question "Could a new look at Jimmie Rodgers from a twenty-first-century perspective make him more accessible to more people today?" The question was asked by my literary agent, Paul Bresnick, an agent of the extremely rare sort who tends to be as taken with the stories and themes of the writers he represents as the writers are. His counsel and enthusiasm have been invaluable.

That contemporary perspective, by definition, has the benefit of following decades of scholarship into the musical worlds that Jimmie Rodgers inhabited, in blues, country music, pop, folk, and the life of Rodgers himself. I am indebted especially to a short list of trailblazing scholars: Nolan Porterfield, Tony Russell, Bill C. Malone, David Evans, and the late

Charles K. Wolfe. Building on their work was crucial for a project like this—and virtually inevitable. The counsel and encouragement I have received from Nolan Porterfield has been especially gratifying; the lasting power, authority, and charm of his Jimmie Rodgers biography was a key reason that my immediate answer to Paul Bresnick's question about the possibility of a new look at Jimmie was "Yes—but not as a biography."

I am most thankful, also, that a number of contemporary writers I have admired and come to know added weight, early on, to the notion that I might be the one to take on this task reasonably well, and they have in many instances provided useful comment and directional pointers since then, including Colin Escott, Bill Friskics-Warren, Alan Light, Yuval Taylor, and Diane Pecknold. I have also enjoyed the benefit of source leads and comments on particular topics in this book from Holly George-Warren, Daniel Cooper, Andrew Smith, Paul Garon, Kevin Fontenot, Peter Guralnick, Doug Green, Ronald McConnell, Charles Townsend, Neil Rosenberg, Edward Morris, Roy Kasten, David Cantwell, Jon Weisberger, Jack Palmer, Rick Coleman, Bart Plantenga, Richard (Pete) Peterson, Scott Barretta, Sam Charters, and Kathleen Hudson. My sincere thank-you goes out to them all.

Before this book was finished, the world lost Eddy Arnold, Hank Thompson, Don Helms, Charlie Walker and Odetta, five of those interviewed for these pages, a reminder of the generational loss further limiting our access to so much musical history. Seventy-five years after Jimmie Rodgers' death, the opportunity to gain that vital sense of direct access to Jimmie, the man, is not easily achieved; but it was part of my task, so I am quite grateful for the invaluable aid in that regard provided by his family and friends and their acquaintances and associates.

I found it extraordinary to be able to spend hours listening to the reminiscences of Hoyt "Slim" Bryant, one hundred years old at this writing, who is the last man known to be alive who played and recorded music with Jimmie Rodgers himself. It was a special pleasure to receive so much aid and acceptance from members of Jimmie and Carrie Rodgers' families. Rick and Terri McWilliams, in particular, proved to be extraordinary hosts and friends, as well as keepers of the flame for both Jimmie Rodgers and Elsie McWilliams. Important information, artifacts, and a sense of the man and his family were provided, too, by Rodgers cousins Cara Pollard Herlin, Ann Shine Landrum, Jannea Rogers, and Erma Rodgers Sykes, as well as by Jean and Ed Bishop, Steve Forbert, Jimmy Snow, and Ken Berryhill.

Kevin Lamb, vice president at Peer Music in Nashville, knew about little-known and unknown surviving Rodgers artifacts and memorabilia and helped open doors for me to see them—sometimes, as in the case of Jimmie Rodgers' musician's diary, going literally well out of his way to make them accessible for me. His support of this project, both personally and on behalf of Peer Music, has been singular.

Kevin also introduced me to the Rodgers estate representatives at the Jackson, Walker law firm in San Antonio, Texas. With the help there of Eric Hoffman, Dan Chapman, and Sharon Maule, I found myself going through the personal scrapbooks of Jimmie and Carrie Rodgers, culling important unpublished photographs and (inside a San Antonio bank vault) having the extraordinary privilege of holding and reading the last letters and post-cards Jimmie Rodgers sent to Carrie from the Taft Hotel in New York in his final days.

I could not have described the varied turns on Jimmie's music over the past eighty years if I had not heard or seen them, so I am especially grate-ful to the record collectors, video collectors, and archivists who made rari-ties available to me. My thanks in this regard go to Richard Wieze of Bear Family Records, Kerry Richardson, Dennis Flannigan, Greg Geller, Brad Bechtel, Karla Buhlman of Gene Autry Entertainment, Elijah Wald, Jeffrey Dreves, Steve Reid, Fred Bartenstein, Bobbie Phelps Beard, Joyce Katzberg, Frank Ballinger, Diane Thram, Tim Ausburn, Jerry West, Charles Lochet, Linda Ray, Karl Simpson, and Steve Edwards.

I also want to acknowledge and extend special thanks to the staff at the Country Hall of Fame and Museum here in Nashville for their tireless and remarkably knowledgeable help with access to relevant recordings, oral his-tories, publications, and photos from the museum's vast archive in response to my regular calls for aid. I am particularly indebted in this regard to John Rumble, and also to Alan Stoker, Michael Gray, Jay Orr, and Tim Davis. I want to encourage all who read this volume to support this unique, invalu-able, nonprofit institution.

Others commanding my thanks for aid in connecting me to intervie-wees or important documentary evidence are Jim Henke, Craig Inciard and Warren Zanes with the Rock and Roll Hall of Fame, Darlene Bieber and Brenda Calladay with the Grand Ole Opry, Mary Katharine Aldin, Tex Whitson, Mike Seeger, Rich Kienzle, James Akenson, Michael McCall, Lucinda Cockrell, Phoebe Lewis, Ike Jonson, Brian Mansfield, Pen Bogart, Ed Morris, Jim Nelson, Dick Grant, Teresa Hughes, Clarence Grelle, Mal-colm Rockwell, Gary Anwyl, Thomas Wells, Don Grubbs, Kissy Black, Tresa Redburn, Gaynell Rogers, Nancy Sefton, and Stanley Coutant.

I will always be indebted for the careful attention, guidance, profession-alism, and kindness of my editor at Oxford University Press, Suzanne Ryan, and to the staff members at OUP who have worked on this volume. The book you are holding would not be the book you are holding without their work, care, thought, and enthusiasm.

Finally, I will attempt to express here my unending thankfulness and appreciation, for the life of this project and throughout life, to the genuine, certified historian in this household, my wife, Nina Melechen, Ph.D. (Her surname, incidentally, rhymes with *pelican*, as mine rhymes with *razor*.) It may be that only spouses and partners of other authors of books of this sort can entirely appreciate the patience, fundamental support, and unearthly endurance the process demands. Nina provided me all of these, plus a good deal of discerning historical and editorial judgment. The author is a lucky guy.

Barry Mazor
Nashville, Tennessee
October 2008

notes

Introduction: Meeting Jimmie Rodgers, Halfway

3 Author interview with Cowboy Jack Clement.

4 Author interview with Stan Jacobson.

4 Additional on Cash broadcast: Charles K. Wolfe, "Country Music in Black and White," in the *Oxford American*, Issue 54, Music Issue, 2006.

6 Carnegie Hall: Johnny Cash and Patrick Carr, *Cash*.

6 Johnny Cash letter to Anita Rodgers Court of April 22, 1962: in the files of the Rodgers family estate, reviewed with permission.

6 Tosches on Cash: Nick Tosches, *Country*.

7 Johnny Cash and Louis Armstrong rehearsal: unreleased recording of preparation for *The Johnny Cash Show*, from the archives of Sony-BMG Legacy Recordings, made available to author for audio inspection, courtesy Greg Geller.

7 "George Evans": Lynn Abbott and Doug Seroff, *Out of Sight*.

1. The Man Who Walked into Southern Show Business

12 Jimmie Rodgers' early life: Nolan Porterfield, *Jimmie Rodgers*, chapters 1 and 2; testimony of Virginia Shine Harvey in the 1986 television documentary *Jimmie Rodgers: The Father of Country Music* (GBN Productions); and author interview with Ann Shine Landrum. In passing, Mike Paris and Chris Comber, *Jimmie the Kid*; Sydona M. Young, "Jimmie Rodgers: America's Blue Yodeler," in *Country Music Who's Who*, 1972; and Richard Johnson, "America's Blue Yodeler," in *Acoustic Guitar* magazine, September 1997.

13 Tent show rep: *Theatre in a Tent*, William Lawrence Stout, chapter 5.

13   Learning instrumentals from coworkers: Virginia Shine Harvey, on *Jimmie Rodgers: The Father of Country Music* (GBN Productions).

15   Elsie McWilliams on Meridian sanitarium: Edward Allen Bishop, *Elsie McWilliams (I Remember Jimmie)*.

16   No "T for Texas" at Bristol: Carrie Rodgers, *My Husband, Jimmie Rodgers*, chapter 23.

18   Greil Marcus on deadpan singing: Greil Marcus, *Invisible Republic*.

18   Henry Pleasants: Pleasants, *The Great American Popular Singers*, chapter 5.

18   Thomas Townsend: Townsend, "On the Vanguard of Change: Jimmie Rodgers and Alfred G. Karnes in Bristol, 1927," in *The Bristol Sessions*, ed. Charles K. Wolfe and Ted Olson.

19   Roy Acuff: transcript of interview with Douglas Green, October 10, 1972, for the Country Music Foundation Oral History Project, in the Frist Archive of the Country Music Hall of Fame and Museum, Nashville, TN.

19   Author interview with Doc Watson.

20   Author interview with Hoyt "Slim" Bryant.

23   The Austin-Rodgers relationship and musical relation: Barry Mazor, "Gene Austin: The Father of Southern Pop," *No Depression* magazine, November 2004.

23   Austin as Rodgers cover story: author interview with Austin's cousin and protégé Tommy Overstreet.

24   Charlie Poole: Hank Sapoznik, in notes for *Charlie Poole and the Roots of Country Music*, Columbia Legacy Records, 2005, and Tony Russell, *Country Music Originals*.

26   Carter Family biographical references, including 1936 divorce: Mark Zwonitzer and Charles Hirshberg, *Will You Miss Me When I'm Gone?*

26   "Frankie and Johnny" before Bible study audience: Porterfield, *Jimmie Rodgers*, chapter 9.

27   Mae West and "Frankie and Johnny": Emily W. Leider, *Becoming Mae West*, chapter 10.

27   Cummings' musical and "Frankie and Johnny": Christopher Sawyer Laucamo, *E. E. Cummings*, and Richard S. Kennedy, *Dreams in the Mirror*.

2. Close to the Ground: The Singing Brakeman

32   Uniformed rail employees as mentors: Max Haymes, *Railroadin' Some*, which is also a source for the changing definition of hotshot.

32   Jimmy Carter comments: Jimmy Carter, *An Hour Before Daylight*.

32   Rodgers' railroad jobs: Nolan Porterfield, *Jimmie Rodgers*. Web sites of the Pacific Southwest Railway Museum (www.sdrm.org/) and Nebraska "Iron Roads" (www.rootsweb.ancestry.com/~nerailrd/job.html) provided further background on brakeman's work.

33   Brakemen songs: Norm Cohen, *Long Steel Rail*.

33   Distinctions between hoboes, tramps, vagrants, and migratory workers: Paul Garon and Gene Tomko, *What's the Use of Walking If There's a Freight Train Going Your Way?* and George Milburn, *The Hobo's Hornbook*.

34   Albert Fullam: Fullam's oral memoir released as part of the Hank Snow LP *The Jimmie Rodgers Story* (RCA Victor, 1972).

34 *Norfolk Ledger-Dispatch* review and performance reports: clippings pasted in Jimmie and Carrie Rodgers' scrapbook, Rodgers estate archive, San Antonio, TX.

35 *Midland Reporter-Telegram, San Angelo Morning Times,* and *Abilene Daily Reporter* accounts, and details of March 1929 Texas tour: Joe W. Specht, "The Blue Yodeler Is Coming to Town: A Week with Jimmie Rodgers in West Texas," in *Journal of Texas Music History,* vol. 1, no. 2, Fall 2001.

35 Young Ernest Tubb: Ronnie Pugh, *Ernest Tubb.*

36 Shows out of Ft. Worth and Dallas: handbill with additional handwritten notes, preserved in Jimmie and Carrie Rodgers' scrapbook, as above.

36 Swain's Hollywood Follies shows: Porterfield, *Jimmie Rodgers.*

36 Jimmie Skinner: interviews with Cecil Whaley (November 1970) and Doug Green (January 1975) for the Country Music Hall of Fame and Museum Oral History Project, Frist Archive, Nashville, TN.

39 Ma and Pa Ferguson campaigns: Porterfield, *Jimmie Rodgers.*

39 The I.W.W. and hoboes: Garon and Tomko, *What's the Use of Walking?*

39 "Underrest dog": Carrie Rodgers, *My Husband, Jimmie Rodgers.*

40 Red Cross Tour with Will Rogers: Will Rogers, *Weekly Articles* and *Daily Telegrams*; Carrie Rodgers, *My Husband, Jimmie Rodgers*; the *San Antonio Light* of January 25, 1931; the documentary short *Distant Son: How Will Rogers and Jimmie Rodgers Saved the South in 1931,* produced in support of a proposed feature film by Austin Signal Productions, and historical background material assembled for it by authors Daniel Kuehm and Andrew Leranth; Alton Delmore, *Truth Is Stranger Than Publicity,* for details on the proposed Rogers and Rodgers Hollywood pairing.

3. America's Blue Yodeler No. 1.: This White Guy Sings Blues, Too

45 Abbe Niles comments: *Bookman* magazine, July 28, 1928.

45 "Bloodthirsty" Victoria Spivey ad: reproduced in Daphne Duval Harrison, *Black Pearls.*

46 Cliff Carlisle on Jimmie: Tony Russell, *Blacks, Whites and Blues.*

47 Albert Murray "nonchalance": Albert Murray, *Stomping the Blues*; and on comedy endings and how blues performers derive material, Murray, *The Hero and the Blues.*

47 Author interview with B. B. King.

48 Howlin' Wolf (Chester Burnett) on Rodgers: backstage interview with Wolf by Topper Carew, seen on the DVD *Howlin' Wolf in Concert 1970* (Vestapol). His earlier musical exposure: James Segrest and Mark Hoffman, *Moanin' at Midnight.*

49 Davis on Smith and Rainey: Angela Davis, *Blues Legacies and Black Feminism.*

49 Bessie Smith and the Klan: Chris Albertson, *Bessie.*

50 Evans' study: David Evans, *Big Road Blues.*

50 Max Haymes: *Railroadin' Some.*

51 Muddy Waters and Autry: John W. Work, Lewis Wade, and Samuel C. Adams, *Lost Delta Found*; also Alan Lomax, *The Land Where Blues Began.*

51 Johnny Shines on Robert Johnson and Rodgers: Mark Humphrey, "Johnny Shines: A Living Legacy of Delta Blues," *Frets* magazine, November 1979.

52 Papa Charlie Jackson background: Chris Smith, notes to Document's Jackson CDs, and comments by Max Haymes in *Ralroadin' Some*.

53 Black and white ballad narrating stances: Tom Freeland and Chris Smith, "That Dry Creek Eaton Clan," in *Nobody Knows Where the Blues Come From*, ed. Robert Springer.

53 Lead Belly and Jimmie Rodgers: John Lomax and Alan Lomax, *Negro Folk Songs as Sung by Lead Belly*, and "Notes on the Songs of Huddie Ledbetter," Library of Congress Archive of Folk Songs.

54 John Jackson: Larry Benicewicz, "Remembering John Jackson," on the Blues world.com Web site.

54 Sam Chatmon: author interview and resulting article, Barry Mazor, "The Surviving Sheik Shoots It at Ya," *Soho Weekly News* (New York), February 26, 1976.

55 David Evans on Bracey et al.: David Evans, "Black Musicians Remember Jimmie Rodgers," in *Old Time Music*, Winter 1972.

55 Houston Stackhouse and Jimmie: Terry Currier, "Houston Stackhouse," in *BluesNotes*, May 1995; Evans, *Big Road Blues*. The quote is from the interview with Jim O'Neal in *Living Blues* magazine, Summer 1974, anthologized and expanded in *The Voice of the Blues*, ed. Jim O'Neal and Amy Van Singel.

55 Hammie Nixon on Jimmie: interview with Kip Lornell, in *Living Blues*, January 1975, anthologized in *The Voice of the Blues*.

56 Earl McDonald/Clifford Hayes background: Brenda Bogert, notes for the CD *Clifford Hayes and the Louisville Jug Bands, Vol. 2* (RST Records), and author correspondence with Pen Bogert. See also Nolan Porterfield, *Jimmie Rodgers*.

58 Jimmie Skinner on Rodgers, whites, and blues: Jimmie Skinner, audio memoir included with the Bear Family box set *Doin' My Time*, and in the November 1970 and January 1975 interviews for the Country Music Hall of Fame and Museum Oral History Project, Frist Archive, Nashville, TN.

4. America's Blue Yodeler No. 2: Instigator of Blue Yodelmania

63 Author interview with Eddy Arnold (also the source for Gene Autry meeting Rodgers via Gene Austin).

63 W. E. Myers and yodels: Barry O'Connell, notes to *Doc Boggs: Country Blues* CD (Revenant Records).

65 Emmett Miller blue yodel theory: Nick Tosches, *Where Dead Voices Gather*.

65 Yodel history: Bart Plantenga, *Yodel-Ay-Ee-Oooo*.

66 Rodgers-Autry telegram: Letter to Autry reminding him of the telegram by Grover T. O'Dell, quoted by Holly George-Warren, *Public Cowboy No. 1*.

66 Abbe Niles quote: in his "Ballads, Songs and Sounds" column, *The Bookman*, September 1928.

67 Vaudeville yodel history: Lynn Abbott and Doug Seroff, "America's 'Blue Yodel,'" in *Musical Traditions*, the U.K. magazine, Fall 1993, and posted for reference on the publication's website: www.mustrad.org.uk/articles/b_yodel.htm.

69 Billy Terrell report: *America's Blue Yodeler*, Jimmie Rodgers fan club journal, no. 2, Spring 1954.

70 Claude Grant to Nolan Porterfield: Nolan Porterfield, *Jimmie Rodgers*, chapter 3.

70 High school auditorium handbill for Rodgers Entertainers: in Jimmie and Carrie's scrapbook, Rodgers estate archive, San Antonio, TX.

72 Cliff Carlisle on blue yodels and Jimmie Rodgers: Carlisle interview with Henry Gilbert and Douglas Green, July 1974, for the Country Music Hall of Fame and Museum Oral History Project, Frist Archive, Nashville, TN. Additional Carlisle comments are from a short self-written bio Carlisle submitted to the Hall project in 1967, a second interview he did there along with brother Bill Carlisle in 1968, and passing comments he made in his 1971 Los Angeles interviews with Eugene Earle and Norm Cohen, which reside in the University of North Carolina Southern Folklife Collection, Wilson Library, Chapel Hill, NC. Carlisle recording names: notes to *Cliff Carlisle: A Country Legacy 1930–1939* (JSP Records).

73 Ernest Tubb on Jimmie's yodeling: expressed many times in various places; this succinct version was from *Billboard*, May 16, 1953, in a piece bylined by Tubb and Hank Snow. The sentiment is unmistakably Tubb's.

74 "The Pullman Porters": the deservedly rare side appears on the *Jimmie Rodgers, The Singing Brakeman* Bear Family set, disc 6. It is not even funny.

77 Jimmie Davis: background and quotes from Tony Russell, *Governor Jimmie Davis* (Bear Family CD set booklet), plus Jimmie Davis interview with Doug Green, July 1976, for the Country Music Hall of Fame and Museum Oral History Project, Frist Archive.

79 Elton Britt and Jimmie: liner notes to Britt's *The Jimmie Rodgers Blues* (RCA Camden LP, 1969) by Vaughan Horton.

80 Grandpa Jones: Louis M. "Grandpa" Jones and Charles K. Wolfe, *Everybody's Grandpa*, and author interview with Ramona Jones.

5. International Multimedia Star

85 *America's Blue Yodeler* album: cover with liner notes in the Frist Archive, Country Music Hall of Fame and Museum, Nashville, TN.

87 Ralph Peer's views of the "hillbilly," "race," and "international" record markets, how Jimmie Rodgers' audience reach was expanded, and sharing songs with cover artists: Peer's extended recorded interview with Lillian Borgeson, 1958, item FT-2774 in the John Edwards Memorial Foundation Collection 1, University of North Carolina Southern Folklife Collection, Wilson Library, Chapel Hill, NC.

88 Jimmie's lyric sheets: Several were published in Nolan Porterfield's *Jimmie Rodgers*; some have been displayed at the Country Music Hall of Fame and Museum in Nashville, TN.

88 Jimmie in the recording studio, New York: author interview with Hoyt "Slim" Bryant.

91 Vaudefilm: John L. Marsh, "Vaudefilm: Its Contribution to a Moviegoing America," in *Journal of Popular Culture*, vol. 18, no. 4, Spring 1985.

91 Hollywood releases appearing on bills with Jimmie Rodgers: newspaper ads and accounts in the scrapbooks of Jimmie and Carrie Rodgers, Rodgers estate archive, San Antonio, TX; ads reprinted in *Jimmie Rodgers* (Bear Family *Singing Brakeman* box set book), and Texas ads and interviews cited by Joe W. Specht in "The Blue Yodeler Is Coming to Town," *Journal of Texas Music History*, vol. 1, no. 2, Fall 2001.

93 The two versions of *The Singing Brakeman* film: author examination of the two versions, correspondence with Grover Crisp of the Columbia Pictures/Sony

archives, and conversations with Sherwin Dunner of Yazoo/Shanachie Entertainment and Nolan Porterfield.

94 Radio: Carrie Rodgers, *My Husband, Jimmie Rodgers*, chapter 17; Porterfield, *Jimmie Rodgers*; clippings and reviews of radio appearances from Jimmie and Carrie Rodgers' scrapbook.

95 Grant Turner recalls Jimmie on Texas radio: from the LP *Grant Turner Remembers the Grand Ole Opry as It Was Then* (CVS, 1980).

96 Jimmie on border radio with Horwitz: Gene Fowler and Bill Crawford, *Border Radio*.

96 Plans for England: author interview with Hoyt "Slim" Bryant.

97 Jack Hylton: www.jackhylton.com.

97 Thomas Fraser: notes to his CDs and author correspondence with Fraser's grandson, Karl Simpson, the producer of the released recordings.

98 Australian country and Rodgers: Andrew Smith, "Comparisons and Contrasts: Recorded Country Music to 1950 in Australia and the USA," and "Tex Morton: A Biographical Note," in *Australian Country Music Volume 2* (ed. P. Hayward and G. Walden) and *Volume 3* (ed. M. Evans and G. Waldem). Volume 2 also includes James Akenson on "Tex Banes." And Tex Morton radio broadcasts.

100 South Africa: "uBungca (Oxford Bags)," on the Web at www.mustrad.org.uk; adapted from an article in the print journal *Musical Traditions*, no. 12, Summer 1994.

101 Cajuns Leo Solieau and Maius LaFleur, and Rodgers: Donald Lee Nelson, "Mama, Where You At? The Chronicle of Maius LaFleur" in *Accordions, Fiddles, Two Step and Swing*, ed. Ryan A. Brasseaux and Kevin S. Fontenot; and Ann Allen Savoy, quoting the 1974 Villa Platte *Gazette* interview with Soileau, in *Cajun Music*.

102 Happy Fats and Rodgers: John Broven, *South to Louisiana*.

102 Iry LeJeune songs: Savoy, *Cajun Music*.

102 Kipsigis' "Chemirocha": folklorist Hugh Tracey's original liner notes for the three recordings in the "Catalogue of the Sound of Africa Series" of LPs on which they appeared, from the International Library of African Music; correspondence with Diane Thram, director of the International Library of African Music, Rhodes University, Grahamstown, South Africa; and details provided by the (U.S.) Smithsonian Global Sound Web site, www.smithsonianglobalsound.org.

103 Sammy Ngako: Elijah Wald, Notes to *Classic Kikuyu Music: Yodelers, Guitars and Accordions* (publishing info to come).

103 S. E. Rogie: Bart Plantenga, *Yodel-Ay-Ee-Oooo*.

103 "Blue Yodel No. 10" in Japan: Ramblin' Sho Suzuki, *The Jimmie Rodgers Data Book*.

104 Author interview with Toshio Hirano.

6. Doomed Singer-Songwriter with Guitar

109 Social and medical aspects of tuberculosis in the United States in the 1920s: Katherine Ott's *Fevered Lives* is the principal source used for the background presented; secondarily, Sheila M. Rothman, *Living in the Shadow of Death*, and Thomas Normandy, *The White Death*.

111 Jimmie, sanatoriums, and lunger camps: Edward Allen Bishop, *Elsie McWilliams*, and author interview with Charles Townsend.

112 O. Henry, "A Fog in Santone," can be read on literaturecollection.com and other public domain literature Web sites.

112 Author interview with Steve Earle.

113 Author interview with Marty Stuart.

113 Yuval Taylor on "personal authenticity": his chapter, "T.B. Blues: The Story of Autobiographical Song," in Hugh Barker and Yuval Taylor's *Faking It*.

114 Author interviews with Steve Forbert.

115 Author interview with Hoyt "Slim" Bryant.

115 Background of "Waiting for a Train": Norm Cohen, *Long Steel Rail*.

116 Ralph Peer on the writing of "Waiting for a Train": Peer's interview with Lillian Borgeson, item FT-2774 in the John Edwards Memorial Foundation Collection 1, University of North Carolina Southern Folklife Collection, Wilson Library, Chapel Hill, NC.

116 Elsie's involvement: author interview with Rick McWilliams.

116 Gene Autry's "T.B. Blues" and "Jimmie the Kid" recordings timing: Holly George-Warren, *Public Cowboy No. 1*, and comments by Peer in the Borgeson interview.

118 Elsie McWilliams collaborations with and recollections of Jimmie Rodgers: uncirculated September 14, 1984, audio interview with Elsie by Steve Forbert; Bishop, *Elsie McWilliams*; "An Oral History with Mrs. Elsie McWilliams," Mike Garvey, interviewer, Mississippi Oral History Program, vol. 543, 1975; and the May 23, 1974, interview with Elsie by Douglas Green for the Country Music Foundation Oral History Project, Country Music Hall of Fame and Museum, Frist Archive, Nashville, TN.

119 Raymond Hall: Nolan Porterfield, *Jimmie Rodgers*; Tom Miller, "Prisoner 60339 Sings the Blues," in *Country Music* magazine, February 1975; and Mark Price, "Bad Luck Haunted Song Writer," *Millington (TN) Star*, February 1, 1984.

119 Waldo O'Neal: Priscilla Venable, "O'Neal Remembers Song Writing for Jimmie Rodgers," Meridian *Star*, May 24, 1978.

120 Jimmie's last moments alive: related by Elsie McWilliams in the Mississippi Oral History Program tape, evidently from descriptions of the scene provided to the family by Mr. Castro.

7. Aftermath: The Late, Great Jimmie Rodgers

121 Homer Jenkins: Testimony by Gladys Hunt in the documentary *Jimmie Rodgers: The Singing Brakeman* (GBN Productions).

121 Obituaries: *New York Times*, May 27, 1933; *Memphis Commercial Appeal*, June 3, 1933; *Time* magazine, August 6, 1934.

123 Jimmie Rodgers' letter and postcard to Carrie of May 21, 1933: from the original documents, consulted with permission of the Rodgers estate.

124 Suggestions that the Carrie-Jimmie Rodgers marriage had been over: such suggestions were made by some Rodgers family members and are reported in Nolan Porterfield's *Jimmie Rodgers* and elsewhere.

124 Ken Berryhill interview with Carrie Rodgers, 1958, rebroadcast on his WRVU-FM radio show with this book in mind, Nashville, 2007.

124 Carrie's second marriage: author interview with Ann Shine Landrum, and remarks in Nolan Porterfield's introduction to the Country Music Foundation edition of Carrie Rodgers' *My Husband, Jimmie Rodgers*. Porterfield's introduction also names Dorothy Hendricks as Carrie's collaborator on the book.

126 Young Ernest Tubb: Norma Barthels, *The Original E.T.*, and Ronnie Pugh, *Ernest Tubb*.

127 Jimmie Rodgers Museum questions: author interviews with Edward Bishop and Jean Bishop.

128 Jesse Rodgers: Jimmie O. Rodgers (Jesse's son), "Jesse Rodgers: A Life Dedicated to Country and Western Music" (pamphlet), courtesy of Erma Rodgers Sykes; correspondence with Jesse's granddaughter Jannea Rogers; and author interview with Erma Rodgers Sykes.

129 Film plans: author interviews with Billy Ray Reynolds and Stan Jacobson.

8. South by Southwest: An Easterner in a Cowboy Hat

131 History of the Rodgers briefcase: author interview with Marty Stuart, and letter from Johnny Cash to Anita Rodgers Court, 1962, in the Rodgers family archive, San Antonio, TX.

133 Author interview with Don Edwards.

133 Elsie McWilliams as author of "Yodeling Cowboy": uncirculated September 1984 audio interview with Elsie by Steve Forbert.

136 Gene Autry downplaying Rodgers' influence: Holly George-Warren, *Public Cowboy No. 1*, chapter 8; Douglas B. Green, *Singing in the Saddle*, chapter 6; and country disc jockey Mike Oatman's broadcast interview with Autry, 1983.

138 Roy Rogers on Jimmie Rodgers: Douglas Green, *Singing in the Saddle*, and Ken Griffis, *Hear My Song*.

138 Bob Nolan on Rodgers: radio interview with Ken Griffis, KLAC radio, Los Angeles, 1972, from the audio collection of Jerry West of Waxahachie, TX.

139 Hank Snow's beginnings: Hank Snow, *The Hank Snow Story*.

139 New York singing cowboy scene: Douglas Green, *Singing in the Saddle*, chapters 10 and 11; Griffis, *Hear My Song*.

139 Whitley's attempted Rodgers visit: Douglas Green interview with Ray Whitley, March 30, 1975, for the Country Music Hall of Fame and Museum Oral History Project, Frist Archive, Nashville, TN.

140 Jimmy Wakely: Douglas Green, *Singing in the Saddle*; Gerald W. Haslam, *Workin' Man Blues*; and liner notes for Wakely recordings cited.

140 Johnny Bond: Douglas Green, *Singing in the Saddle*; Gerald W. Haslam, *Workin' Man Blues*; and *Johnny Bond at Town Hall Party* (Bear Family DVD, 2005).

140 Wesley Tuttle: Douglas Green, *Singing in the Saddle*; Gerald W. Haslam, *Workin' Man Blues*; and unpublished memoir of Tuttle and liner notes cited by Jerry West.

141 Author interview with Don Edwards.

142 Riders in the Sky: author conversation and correspondence with Ranger Doug Green.

143 Wiley and the Wild West Show: author interview with Wiley Gustafson.

144   Bill and Jim Boyd on radio: interview with Jimmie Boyd (Mrs. Jim Boyd, Bill Boyd's sister-in-law), with assistance from Jerry West.

144   Shelly Lee Alley: author interview with Clyde Brewer.

145   Wills and Brown meet Jimmie: Charles Townsend, *San Antonio Rose*, chapter 6.

145   Marvin Montgomery: Montgomery interview with John Rumble, June 1988, for the Country Music Hall of Fame and Museum Oral History Project, Frist Archive.

146   Milton Brown: Cary Ginell, *Milton Brown and the Founding of Western Swing*; Jean Boyd, *"We're the Light Crust Doughboys from Burrus Mills"*; and author interview with Roy Lee Brown.

147   Bob Wills and Tommy Duncan: author interviews with Glynn Duncan, Herb Remington, and Charles Townsend; Townsend's *San Antonio Rose* biography of Wills; and Tommy Duncan's August 7, 1933, letter to Carrie Rodgers, from the Rodgers family estate archives.

149   Rhythm Wreckers and Whitey McPherson: quotes from Bert Whyatt's *Mugsy Spanner*; Joe Klein's *Woody Guthrie*; and comments in Woody's 1939 "On a Slow Train from California" songbook.

150   Hank Thompson: author interview with Hank Thompson.

9. Back East: The Hillbilly Echo, 1933–1947

155   Jimmie in Nashville: Rodgers' own ledger/notebook, examined with permission of the Rodgers estate, San Antonio, TX; the Nashville *Banner*, July 12, 1932, plus additional *Banner* reports on the preceding Sundays; also, Philip Graham, *Showboats*.

157   Opry 1933 and thereafter: Charles K. Wolfe, *A Good-Natured Riot*, and his notes for the album *Fiddlin' Arthur Smith and His Dixieliners* (County Records).

158   Sam and Kirk McGee: Charles Wolfe, "Sam McGee," in *Traditional Tennessee Singers*, ed. Thomas G. Burton; and in Wolfe's notes to the CD *Sam and Kirk McGee, Live, 1955–1967* (Springfed Records).

159   Delmore Brothers: Alton Delmore, *Truth Is Stranger Than Publicity*.

160   Fleming and Townsend: Tony Russell, *Country Music Originals*.

160   Callahan Brothers: interview with Bill Callahan by Ronnie Pugh and David Hayes, January 1979, for the Country Music Hall of Fame and Museum Oral History Project, Frist Archive, Nashville, TN; also, Russell, *Country Music Originals*.

161   Bill Cox: notes to the two CDs listed on the chapter soundtrack, and Russell, *Country Music Originals*.

162   Rex Griffin: Kevin Coffey, *The Last Letter* (book with Bear Family box set). Tubb comment: notes to Ernest Tubb's 1963 Griffin salute LP *Just Call Me Lonesome* (Decca).

162   Roy Acuff and Rodgers: Roy Acuff and William Neely, *Roy Acuff's Nashville*; Douglas Green interviews with Roy Acuff of October 1972 and June 1977, for the Country Music Hall of Fame and Museum Oral History Project, Frist Archive; Ralph Emery, *More Memories*; and author interviews with Ralph Emery, Rick McWilliams, and Ann Shine Landrum.

165　Bill Monroe and Rodgers: Jim Rooney, *Bossmen*; Neil V. Rosenberg and Charles K. Wolfe, *The Music of Bill Monroe*; Richard D. Smith, *Can't You Hear Me Callin'*; Tom Ewing, *The Bill Monroe Reader* (particularly the interviews with Monroe by Doug Benson, Charles Wolfe, and George Gruhn); interview with Bill Monroe by John Rumble, November 1993, and interview with Clyde Moody by Douglas Green, April 1974, both for the Country Music Hall of Fame and Museum Oral History Project, Frist Archive.

10. Some Sort of Folksinger?

173　*Sing Out Sweet Land*: Ethan Mordden, *Beautiful Mornin'*, chapter 5; and original cast LP for *Sing Out Sweet Land* (Decca).

173　John A. Lomax, "Seven Varieties of American Folk Music," in the *Journal of American Folklore*, no. 27, January–March 1915.

174　John Greenway, "Jimmie Rodgers—A Folksong Catalyst," in the *Journal of American Folklore*, no. 70, July–Sept. 1957, and "Folk Song Discography" in *Western Folklore*, January 1962.

175　Evans on folklorists: David Evans, *Big Road Blues*, chapters 1 and 5.

175　Rodgers on traditional singers: Carrie Rodgers, *My Husband, Jimmie Rodgers*, chapters 13 and 16.

175　"Waiting for a Train" variations: Norm Cohen, *Long Steel Rail*, chapter 8.

176　Jimmie Rodgers, Asheville to Bristol: Nolan Porterfield, *Jimmie Rodgers*, chapters 4 and 6.

176　Helton Brothers: Bob Carlin, "Whip the Devil Around the Stump—The Story of the Helton Brothers," in *The Old Time Herald*, November 1989.

176　Lunsford backgrounds: Loyal Jones, *Minstrel of the Appalachians*.

177　Harry Smith motives: John Cohen, "A Rare Interview with Harry Smith, December 1968," parts 1 and 2, published in *Sing Out!* magazine, April and July 1969; Robert Cantwell, *When We Were Good*, chapter 6; and Greil Marcus, *Invisible Republic*, chapter 4.

179　Henry Jones' Rodgers story: Paola Igliori, "Interview with Henry Jones," in *American Magus*.

179　Author interview with Mike Seeger.

179　Todd, Sonkin, and Jack Bryant: "Voices from the Dust Bowl: The Charles L. Todd and Robert Sonkin Migrant Worker Collection, 1940–1941," online at the Library of Congress American Memory Project: http://memory.loc.gov/ammem/afctshtml/tshome.html.

180　Woody Guthrie and Rodgers: author interview with Jack Elliott; also the source for quotes on Elliott's own Rodgers experiences.

181　Woody and Jack Guthrie musical differences: Ed Cray, *Ramblin' Man*, chapter 12.

182　Sons of Pioneers "aristocrats": Ken Griffis, *Hear My Song*.

183　Peekskill riot and "T for Texas": Alec Wilkinson, "The Protest Singer: Pete Seeger and American Folk Music," in the *New Yorker*, April 17, 2006.

183　Author interview with Arlo Guthrie (on Woody's records).

183　Author interview with Odetta.

184　"Mule Skinner" in skiffle: Charles McDevitt, *Skiffle*.

185　Author interview with Jack Elliott.

186 Bob Dylan discovers Rodgers: Bob Dylan, *Chronicles, Volume One*, chapter 2.
187 Author interview with Mike Seeger.
189 Skip James and John Hurt: David Evans, in "Black Musicians Remember Jimmie Rodgers," *Old Time Music*, Winter 1972.
190 Watson on Rodgers: Author interview with Doc Watson.
191 Author interview with John Lilly.
192 Reed on Rodgers: Author interview with Bud Reed.

11. The Father of Country Music

197 Vernon Dalhart as "father": "The Daddy of Hillbilly Music," *Country Song Roundup*, April 1953; Jack Palmer, *Vernon Dalhart, First Star of Country Music* (on Dalhart background, songs, and Peer comment); and Bill C. Malone, *Country Music USA*, chapter 2.
200 Country self-recognition and markets: Diane Pecknold, *The Selling Sound*.
202 Hank Williams and Rodgers: Big Bill Lister on Hank and Jimmie, memoir on his Web site, bigbilllister.com; author interview with Don Helms; T. Tommy Cutrer and Lefty Frizzell, "Music City USA" radio interview transcription disc, January 15, 1975, broadcast, in the Country Music Hall of Fame and Museum's Frist Archive, Nashville, TN; and Colin Escott, *Hank Williams, the Biography*.
203 Ray Price comments: Ronnie Thomas interview with Ray Price, *Decatur (AL) Daily*, June 11, 2006.
204 Author interview with Lycrecia Williams Hoover.
204 Frizzell and Rodgers: Geoff Lane, "The Last of Lefty Frizzell," *Country Music* magazine, November 1975; and Daniel Cooper, *Lefty Frizzell* (on Rodgers LP session and Lefty at Meridian).
206 Jim Evans: "Blue Yodeler's Work Stays Alive Through Efforts of Lubbock Man," by Gerry Burton, *Lubbock Avalanche-Journal*, May 1972, in Jim Evans Clippings Collection of the Country Music Hall of Fame and Museum, Frist Archive, with material that served as a source for "Jim Evans Keeps Rodgers' Memory Alive," *Country Music Who's Who*, 1972; and Henry Young interview with Jim Evans, Lubbock, TX, April 22, 1980, tape in the Henry Young collection, Center for Popular Music, Middle Tennessee State University, Murfreesboro, TN.
208 Victor's original sales figure reports: reproduced in *Jimmie Rodgers* by Nolan Porterfield (Bear Family Records box set booklet), 1992.
208 Stephen H. Sholes November 4, 1954, letter to Stephen Edwin Woodrich: author's collection.
209 Peer Music's Rodgers Memorial Albums radio scripts: in the Country Music Hall of Fame and Museum collection, Frist Archive, Nashville, TN.
212 Ernest Tubb memorial recordings and Meridian plans: Ronnie Pugh, *Ernest Tubb*, chapter 19. Tubb's "extra special favorite": his own liner notes for Hank Snow's *The Jimmie Rodgers Story* LP (RCA Victor, 1972).
215 Frizzell salute recording background: Charles Wolfe, *Lefty Frizzell: Life's Like Poetry* (Bear Family Records box set book), 1992.
216 Monroe salute recording background: Charles Wolfe, "Bill Monroe," in *Journal of the American Academy for the Preservation of Old-Time Country Music*,

no. 16, August 1993; and "Bluegrass Touches—An Interview with Bill Monroe," radio interview as transcribed in *Old Time Music* magazine, no. 16, Spring 1975, both as anthologized in *The Bill Monroe Reader*, ed. Tom Ewing. Also, Richard Smith, *Can't You Hear Me Callin*,'; author interview with Neil Rosenberg; Neil Rosenberg and Charles Wolfe, *The Music of Bill Monroe*; and Bill Monroe interview with John Rumble of the Country Music Hall of Fame and Museum, November 1993, Frist Archive.

219 Snow salute background: author interview with Jimmie (Jimmy) Rodgers Snow; Hank Snow, *The Hank Snow Story*.

221 Jimmie Rodgers Day: Carrie Rodgers, "My Jimmie," *Country Song Roundup*, no. 20, October 1952; "A Tribute to Jimmie Rodgers," *Billboard*, May 16, 1953; RCA Victor *Picture Record Review* cover story (dealer promotional publication), May 1953; "The Jimmie Rodgers Story," *Country Song Roundup*, no. 25, published Spring 1953 (though dated August).

224 Jimmie Rodgers Day news reports: *Nashville Tennessean*: "Yodeling Brakeman of Bygone Honored," May 26, 1953; "Tennessee 'Hillbilly Day' Seen at Rodgers Dedication," May 27, 1953; *Nashville Banner*: "Clement to Unveil Monument Honoring Jimmy [*sic*] Rodgers," May 26, 1953; "Hillbilly Stars, Railroaders Pay Tribute to Jimmy [*sic*] Rodgers," May 27, 1953. "National Hillbilly Day-1953," *Hoedown* magazine, vol. 1, no. 1, September 1953; "100,000 Mountain Music Devotees Fill Meridian," *Birmingham News*, May 27, 1953; "Rodgers Remembered," *Newsweek*, June 8, 1953.

224 Recording of first Jimmie Rodgers Day speeches and Grand Ole Opry remote broadcast highlights and Lefty Frizzell home movies of the day, Country Music Hall of Fame and Museum, Frist Archive.

225 1953 Universal-International newsreel report, "Memorial to Jimmie Rodgers," videotape in Henry Young Archive, Middle Tennessee State University Center for Popular Music, Murfreesboro, TN.

225 Author interview with Hank Thompson.

226 Author interview with Charlie Walker.

226 Author interview with Charlie Lamb.

227 "Country Hall of Fame" groundbreaking: from newspaper clippings preserved in the extensive Jimmie Rodgers Festival scrapbooks of Meridian historian Edward Bishop.

227 Author interviews with Jimmy Snow and Lycrecia Williams Hoover.

227 Oscar Schmidt guitar: identified by George Gruhn; from author interview with Walter Carter, Nashville, TN.

228 Roy Horton as promulgator: Peer Music obituary for Roy Horton, 2003. Online at peermusic.com.

229 Webb Pierce quote: Ralph Emery and Patsi Bale Cox, *Fifty Years Down a Country Road*.

230 Author interview with Charlie Louvin.

230 Author interview with Eddy Arnold.

234 1953 "All Time Greats" ceremony: "Pickin' Singin' Set Cavorts at Grand Ole Opry Party," *Nashville Tennessean*, November 21, 1953; and "Your tickets to the Opry," *Hoedown* magazine, vol. 2, no. 1, January 1954, pp. 11–12.

234 Jimmie Rodgers and the Country Music Association and Hall of Fame: *CMA Close-up*, July 2, 1959; June 1961; September 1961; December 1961.

12. Rough and Rowdy Ways: To the Rock and Roll Hall of Fame

239 Uncredited liner notes, *Elvis* LP (RCA Victor, 1956).

239 Author interview with Jason Ringenberg.

240 Fats Domino comments: answers to author's interview questions by Fats Domino, as forwarded to and from Fats through his biographer, Rick Coleman; plus additional background provided by Coleman.

241 Chuck Berry comment: Carl Perkins and David McGee, *Go Cat Go*.

241 Rodgers as rough and rowdy rounder: Nolan Porterfield, *Jimmie Rodgers*; Elsie McWlliams, unpublished interview with Steve Forbert.

242 Bonnie Parker and Rodgers: Bonnie's sister, Billie Jean Parker, interview with Jud Collins of WSM TV, Nashville, on the 1967 RCA Victor LP *The Truth About Bonnie and Clyde*. Carey Harvey connection: author correspondence with Frank Ballinger.

243 Sam Phillips and Rodgers: author correspondence and conversations with Peter Guralnick. Philips and Harmonica Frank Floyd: Colin Escott, *Good Rockin' Tonight*; Greil Marcus, *Mystery Train*.

244 Elvis Presley and Jimmie Rodgers: author interviews with Ken Berryhill, Jimmy Snow, and Carl Fitzgerald; reports on Elvis at Meridian in 1955 in *Country Song Round-Up*, September 1955, plus preshow reports in the *Meridian Star* and in *Billboard*, May 1955; Charlie Lamb's *The Country Music World of Charlie Lamb* picture book; correspondence with Elvis Presley Enterprises' archive staff. On Gladys Presley: Patricia Pierce, *The Ultimate Elvis*.

247 Jerry Lee Lewis: author interview with Jerry Lee Lewis, with the assistance of his daughter, Phoebe Lewis; author interview with Cowboy Jack Clement. "Reincarnation" quote: reported by Peter Doggett in his book *Are You Ready for the Country* (New York: Penguin, 2001).

249 The Fendermen: author interview with Phil Humphrey.

250 Jody Gibson (Joe D. Gibson): author interviews with Donna Gibson, Joyce Katzberg, Roger Sprung, Aubrey Mayhew, and Jack Clement; Gibson's liner note comments for his self-made compilation, courtesy of Joyce Katzberg, and Gibson's posts to the Web sites rockabillyhall.com and *The Mudcat Café* (www.mudcat.org).

252 Author interviews with Phil Everly, Steve Earle, and Steve Forbert.

254 George Harrison on Rodgers: George Harrison, *I Me Mine*.

257 Waylon Jennings and Rodgers: Waylon Jennings, *Waylon*.

258 Glaser Brothers and Robbins: author interview with Jim Glaser.

258 Author interviews with Hank Williams Jr. and Lycrecia Williams Hoover.

259 Lynyrd Skynyrd: author interview with Ed King.

263 The Blasters: author interview with Dave Alvin.

264 Author interviews with Cary Hudson and Taylor Hollingsworth.

266 Jerry Wexler induction speech: from a video copy, courtesy of the Rock and Roll Hall of Fame, Cleveland, OH.

13. Sentiments in Context: The Return of Vaudeville Jimmie

271 Author interviews with Merle Haggard.

271 Author interview with Arlo Guthrie.

273 Author interview with Leon Redbone.

276 Author interview with Joe Boyd, and Boyd, *White Bicycles*.

277 Author interview with Ken Nelson.

278 Lefty Frizzell on Haggard's Rodgers salute: T. Tommy Cutrer, "Music City USA" radio interview with Lefty, September 15, 1972, Country Music Hall of Fame and Museum, Frist Archive, Nashville, TN.

279 Haggard on Dylan: author interviews with Benford Stanley and Merle Haggard.

283 Hugh Cherry: Cherry's liner notes for *Same Train, A Different Time*; Charles Wolfe's interview with Cherry for the Bear Family reissue of that Haggard album; and author interview with Merle Haggard; John Rumble interview with Hugh Cherry, February 1996, for the Country Music Hall of Fame and Museum Oral History Project, Frist Archive; and the Hugh Cherry 1960s broadcast, "The Jimmie Rodgers Story," two 1968 episodes of his *The Many Faces of Folk Music* program for the U.S. Armed Forces Radio Service, on tape as items FT-3299–3302 in the John Edwards Memorial Foundation Collection, University of North Carolina Southern Folklife Collection, Wilson Library, Chapel Hill, NC.

285 Author correspondence with Chris Comber.

285 Author interview with Nolan Porterfield.

288 Author interview with Jimmy Snow (Jimmie Rodgers Snow).

289 Author interview with Jimmie Dale Gilmore.

290 Author interview with Marty Stuart.

291 Boxcar Willie on Rodgers: his radio interview with Ken Berryhill, rebroadcast WRVU-FM, Nashville, TN, 2007.

293 Author interview with Steve Forbert.

293 Author interview with Sid Selvidge.

294 Dylan on Rodgers: liner notes to *The Songs of Jimmie Rodgers: A Tribute*.

295 Beck on "Odelay" and Rodgers: online archives of KCRW radio, Santa Monica, CA (www.kcrw.com/archive).

296 Author interview with Mark Rubin.

14. High-Powered Mamas: Women and the Music of Jimmie Rodgers

302 Author interview with Odetta.

303 Author interview with Rhonda Vincent.

303 Author interview with Dolly Parton.

303 John Pankake comment: his liner notes for *Hazel Dickens and Alice Gerrard* CD (Rounder Records, 1998).

304 Author interview with Hazel Dickens.

304 On Stella Kelly Rodgers: author interview with Nolan Porterfield, and biographical material on Stella in his book, *Jimmie Rodgers*.

304 Marks, Stern, and Fox background: Kenneth A. Kanter, *The Jews on Tin Pan Alley*.

307 Ralph Peer on Sara Carter: from comments by Peer in the Borgeson interview, University of North Carolina Southern Folklife collection tapes, Wilson Library, Chapel Hill, NC.

307 Sara Carter on Jimmie: interview with Henry Young, May 29, 1971, on KCHG Radio, San Antonio, TX, released as a single record on the Museum label.

308 Patsy Montana and Rodgers: Patsy Montana and Jane Frost, *The Cowboy's Sweetheart*.

310 Little Texas Daisy: Charles Wolfe, *A Good Natured Riot*; and Wade Hall, *Hell-Bent for Music: The Life of Pee Wee King* (Lexington: University Press of Kentucky, 1996).

310 DeZurick/Cackle Sisters: passages in *Finding Her Voice* by Mary Bufwack and Robert Oermann; and John Biguenet, "The DeZurick Sisters," in *Oxford American* magazine, Summer 2005.

310 Mattie O'Neal/Jean Chapel: Dick Grant, "The Jean Chapel Session Discography" (available at this writing from Mr. Grant via e-mail: dickgrant88@yahoo.com); author correspondence with Don Chapel; and passages in Bufwack and Oermann, *Finding Her Voice*.

311 Harold and Hazel Maus: Tony Russell, *Country Music Records*.

311 Texas Ruby: bio by Ronald D. Lankford Jr. in the *All-Music Guide to Country: The Definitive Guide to Country Music* (San Francisco: Backbeat Books); notes to the Binge/Bronco Buster disc *A Memorial Tribute to Texas Ruby and Curly Fox*; and passages in Bufwack and Oermann, *Finding Her Voice*.

312 Rose Maddox: Jonny Whiteside, *Ramblin' Rose*.

314 Author interview with Odetta.

315 Bonnie Guitar: Linda Ray, "Woman's Work," *No Depression* magazine, January 2007.

316 Author interview with Wanda Jackson.

316 Author interview with Dolly Parton.

318 Author interview with Rhonda Vincent.

319 Author interview with Hazel Dickens.

320 Author interviews with Crystal Gayle and Allen Reynolds.

321 Tanya Tucker: Tanya Tucker, *Nickel Dreams*; and author conversation with Tanya Tucker.

321 Ronstadt-Parton-Harris comments: *Dolly* television broadcast, October 11, 1987 (Sandollar productions/ABC-TV).

322 Author interview with Jo Walston.

15. Down the Old Road to Home

328 Author interviews with Jean Bishop and Edward Bishop.

328 Commemorative stamp release events: video news reports on Texas television preserved in the Henry Young Collection, at the Center for Popular Music, Middle Tennessee State University, Murfreesboro, TN.

329 Jimmie Dale Court: author interviews with Billy Ray Reynolds, Steve Edwards, and Ken Berryhill; Kathleen Hudson, *Telling Stories, Writing Songs*; Ken Berryhill radio interview with Court, included in 2007 Jimmie Rodgers Salute radio broadcast, WRVU-FM, Nashville, TN; Court's comments in the TV documentary *Jimmie Rodgers* (GBN Productions), and video performances of Court provided to the author by Steve Edwards.

329 Sonny Rodgers: author interview and correspondence with his sister, Erma Rodgers Sykes; and his obituary in the *Meridian Star*.

330 Author interviews and site visits with Rick McWilliams.

330 Author interview with B. B. King.
330 Author interview with Cary Hudson.
331 Author interview with Marty Stuart.
331 Author interview with Steve Forbert.
331 Author interview with Sid Selvidge.

bibliography

Original Interviews by the Author

Dave Alvin, Eddy Arnold, Ken Berryhill, Edward Bishop, Jean Bishop, Jimmie Boyd, Joe Boyd, Clyde Brewer, Roy Lee Brown, Hoyt "Slim" Bryant, Walter Carter, Sam Chatmon, Cowboy Jack Clement, Chris Comber, Hazel Dickens, Fats Domino, Glynn Duncan, Steve Earle, Don Edwards, Steve Edwards, Ramblin' Jack Elliott, Ralph Emery, Phil Everly, Carl Fitzgerald, Steve Forbert, Crystal Gayle, Greg Geller, Donna Gibson, Jimmie Dale Gilmore. Jim Glaser, Doug Green, Wylie Gustafson, Arlo Guthrie, Merle Haggard, Don Helms, Toshio Hirano, Taylor Hollingsworth, Lycrecia Williams Hoover, Cary Hudson, Phil Humphrey, Wanda Jackson, Stan Jacobson, Ramona Jones, Joyce Katzberg, B. B. King, Ed King, Charlie Lamb, Ann Shine Landrum, Jerry Lee Lewis, John Lilly, Charlie Louvin, Aubrey Mayhew, Rick McWilliams, Ken Nelson, Odetta, Tommy Overstreet, Dolly Parton, Nolan Porterfield, Leon Redbone, Bud Reed, Herb Remington, Allen Reynolds, Billy Ray Reynolds, Jason Ringenberg, Jannea Rogers, Neil Rosenberg, Mark Rubin, Mike Seeger, Sid Selvidge, Jimmie Rodgers Snow (Jimmy Snow), Roger Sprung, Benford Stanley, Marty Stuart, Erma Rodgers Sykes, Hank Thompson, Charles Townsend, Rhonda Vincent, Charlie Walker, Jo Walston, Doc Watson, Hank Williams Jr.

Books and Articles

Abbott, Lynn, and Doug Seroff. *Out of Sight: The Rise of African-American Popular Music 1889–1895*. Jackson: University of Mississippi Press, 2002.
Acuff, Roy, with William Neely. *Roy Acuff's Nashville: The Life and Good Times of Country Music*. New York: Putnam, 1983.

Albertson, Chris. *Bessie* (Bessie Smith biography), rev. ed. New Haven, CT: Yale University Press, 2003.

Barker, Hugh, and Yuval Taylor. *Faking It: The Quest for Authenticity in Popular Music.* New York: Norton, 2007; particularly the chapter "T.B. Blues: The Story of Autobiographical Song" by Yuval Taylor.

Barthel, Norma. *The Original E.T.* (Ernest Tubb). Roland, OK: Country Roads Publications, 1984.

Bishop, Edward Allen. *Elsie McWilliams (I Remember Jimmie).* Meridian, MS: Self-published/Jimmie Rodgers Museum, 1985.

———. *Memorial to Jimmie Rodgers.* Marion, MS: House of Alohas/Jimmie Rodgers Museum, 1978.

Boyd, Jean. *"We're the Light Crust Doughboys from Burrus Mills."* Austin: University of Texas Press, 2003.

Boyd, Joe. *White Bicycles: Making Music in the 1960s.* London: Serpent's Tail Books, 2006.

Brasseaux, Ryan A., and Kevin S. Fontenot. *Accordions, Fiddles, Two Step and Swing: A Cajun Music Reader.* Lafayette: University of Louisiana, 2006; particularly the article "Mama, Where You At?" by Donald Lee Nelson.

Broven, John. *South to Louisiana: The Music of the Cajun Bayous.* Gretna, LA: Pelican, 1983.

Bufwack, Mary A., and Robert K. Oermann. *Finding Her Voice: Women in Country Music 1800–2000.* Nashville, TN: Vanderbilt University Press and Country Music Foundation Press, 2003.

Burton, Thomas G., ed. *Tennessee Traditional Singers.* Knoxville: University of Tennessee Press, 1981; particularly the chapter "Sam McGee" by Charles K. Wolfe.

Cantwell, Robert. *When We Were Good: The Folk Revival.* Cambridge, MA: Harvard University Press, 1996.

Carter, Jimmy. *An Hour Before Daylight: Memories of a Rural Boyhood.* New York: Simon and Schuster, 2001.

Cash, Johnny, and Patrick Carr. *Cash.* San Francisco: Harper, 1997.

Charters, Samuel B. *Country Blues.* Cambridge, MA: Da Capo Press, 1975.

Cohen, Norm. *Long Steel Rail: The Railroad in American Folksong.* Urbana: University of Illinois Press, 2000.

Cooper, Daniel. *Lefty Frizzell: The Honky Tonk Life of Country's Greatest Singer.* New York: Little Brown, 1995.

Cray, Ed. *Ramblin' Man: The Life and Times of Woody Guthrie.* New York: Norton, 2004.

Davis, Angela Y. *Blues Legacies and Black Feminism: Gertrude "Ma" Rainey, Bessie Smith, and Billie Holiday.* New York: Pantheon, 1998.

Davis, Mary E., and Warren Zanes, eds. *Waiting for a Train: Jimmie Rodgers's America.* Burlington, MA: Rounder Books, 2009.

Delmore, Alton. *Truth Is Stranger Than Publicity.* Nashville, TN: Country Music Foundation Press, 1995.

Dundy, Elaine. *Elvis and Gladys*. New York: Macmillan, 1985.

Dylan, Bob. *Chronicles, Volume One*. New York: Simon and Schuster, 2004.

Ellison, Curtis W. *Country Music Culture: From Hard Times to Heaven*. Jackson: University of Mississippi Press, 1995.

Emery, Ralph, with Tom Carter. *More Memories*. New York: Putnam, 1993.

Emery, Ralph, and Patsi Bale Cox. *Fifty Years Down a Country Road*. New York: HarperCollins, 2001.

Escott, Colin. *Hank Williams, The Biography*, rev. ed. Boston: Back Bay Books/Little Brown, 2004.

Escott, Colin, with Martin Hawkins. *Good Rockin' Tonight: Sun Records and the Birth of Rock 'n' Roll*. New York: St. Martin's Press, 1991.

Evans, David. *Big Road Blues: Tradition and Creativity in Folk Blues*. Berkeley: University of California Press, 1982, and Da Capo edition (New York, 1987).

Evans, Mark, and Geoff Walden, eds. *Markets and Margin: Australian Country Music, Volume 3*. Gympie, Queensland, Australia: Australian Institute for Country Music, 2005; particularly "Tex Morton: A Biographical Note" by Andrew Smith.

Ewing, Tom, ed. *The Bill Monroe Reader*. Champaign: University of Illinois Press, 2000; particularly the Monroe interviews and discussions by Doug Benson, Charles Wolfe, and George Gruhn.

Fowler, Gene, and Bill Crawford. *Border Radio*. Austin: Texas Monthly Press, 1987.

Garon, Paul, and Gene Tomko. *What's the Use of Walking If There's a Freight Train Going Your Way?: Black Hoboes and Their Songs*. Chicago: Charles H. Kerr, 2006.

George-Warren, Holly. *Public Cowboy No. 1: The Life and Times of Gene Autry*. New York: Oxford University Press, 2007.

Ginell, Cary. *Milton Brown and the Founding of Western Swing*. Champaign: University of Illinois Press, 1994.

Graham, Philip. *Showboats: The History of an American Institution*. Austin: University of Texas Press, 1951.

Green, Douglas B. *Singing in the Saddle*. Nashville, TN: Country Music Foundation Press, 2002

Griffis, Ken. *Hear My Song: The Story of the Celebrated Sons of the Pioneers*. John Edwards Memorial Foundation special series no. 5. Los Angeles: University of California/John Edwards Memorial Foundation, 1977.

Harrison, Daphne Duval. *Black Pearls: Blues Queens of the 1920s*. New Brunswick, NJ: Rutgers University Press, 1988.

Harrison, George. *I Me Mine*. New York: Simon and Schuster, 1981.

Haslam, Gerald W. *Workin' Man Blues: Country Music in California*. Berkeley: University of California Press, 1999.

Haymes, Max. *Railroadin' Some: Railroads in the Early Blues*. York, UK: Music Mentor Books, 2006.

Hayward, Phil, and Geoff Walden, eds. *Roots and Crossovers: Australian Country Music, Volume 2*. Gympie, Queensland, Australia: Australian Institute for Country Music, 2004; particularly "Comparisons and Contrasts" by Andrew Smith.

Hudson, Kathleen. *Telling Stories, Writing Songs: An Album of Texas Songwriters.* Austin: University of Texas Press, 2001; particularly the interview with Jimmie Dale Court.

Igliori, Paola, ed. *American Magus: Harry Smith, A Modern Alchemist.* New York: In and Out Press, 1996; particularly the articles "A Rare Interview with Harry Smith" by John Cohen, from *Sing Out!* magazine, 1969, and "Interview with Henry Jones," 1995.

Jennings, Waylon, with Lenny Kaye. *Waylon: An Autobiography.* New York: Warner Books, 1996.

Jones, Louis M. "Grandpa," and Charles K. Wolfe. *Everybody's Grandpa: 50 Years Behind the Mike.* Knoxville: University of Tennessee Press, 1984.

Jones, Loyal. *Minstrel of the Appalachians: The Story of Bascom Lamar Lunsford.* Boone, NC: Appalachian Consortium Press, 1984.

Kanter, Kenneth Aaron. *The Jews on Tin Pan Alley: The Jewish Contribution to American Popular Music 1830–1940.* New York: Ktav Publishing, 1982.

Kennedy, Richard S. *Dreams in the Mirror—A Biography of E. E. Cummings.* New York: Liveright Publishing, 1980.

Kienzle, Rich. *Southwest Shuffle: Pioneers of Honky Tonk, Western Swing, and Country Jazz.* New York: Routledge, 2003; particularly chapters on Tommy Duncan and Hank Thompson.

Kingsbury, Paul, ed., and staff of the Country Music Hall of Fame and Museum. *Encyclopedia of Country Music.* New York and Nashville, TN: Oxford University Press/Country Music Foundation, 2004.

Klein, Joe. *Woody Guthrie: A Life.* New York: Alfred Knopf, 1980.

Laucamo, Christopher S. *E. E. Cummings: A Biography.* Naperville, IL: Sourcebooks, 2004.

Leider, Emily Wortis. *Becoming Mae West.* New York: Farrar, Straus, and Giroux, 1997.

Lomax, Alan. *The Land Where Blues Began.* New York: Pantheon, 1993.

Lomax, John A., and Alan Lomax. *Negro Folk Songs as Sung by Lead Belly.* New York: Macmillan Company, 1936.

Malone, Bill C. *Country Music U.S.A.,* rev. ed. Austin: University of Texas Press, 1985.
———. *Singing Cowboys and Musical Mountaineers.* Athens: University of Georgia Press, 1993.

Marcus, Greil. *Invisible Republic: Bob Dylan's Basement Tapes* (later republished as *The Old Weird America*). New York: Henry Holt, 1997.
———. *Mystery Train.* New York: Dutton, 1975.

McDevitt, Charles. *Skiffle: The Definitive Inside Story.* London: Robson Books, 1997.

Milburn, George. *The Hobo's Hornbook: A Repertory for a Gutter Jongleur.* New York: Ives Washburn, 1930.

Montana, Patsy, and Jane Frost. *The Cowboy's Sweetheart.* Jefferson, NC: McFarland, 2002.

Mordden, Ethan. *Beautiful Mornin': The Broadway Musical in the 1940s*. New York: Oxford University Press, 1999.

Murray, Albert. *The Hero and the Blues*. New York: Vintage Books, 1975; Columbia: University of Missouri Press, 1973.

———. *Stomping the Blues*. New York: McGraw-Hill, 1976.

Normandy, Thomas. *The White Death: A History of Tuberculosis*. New York: New York University Press, 2000.

O'Neal, Jim, and Amy Van Singel, eds. *The Voice of the Blues: Classic Interviews from Living Blues Magazine*. New York: Routledge, 2002.

Ott, Katherine. *Fevered Lives: Tuberculosis in American Culture Since 1870*. Cambridge, MA: Harvard University Press, 1996.

Palmer, Jack. *Vernon Dalhart: First Star of Country Music*. Denver, CO: Mainstream Press, 2005.

Paris, Mike, and Chris Comber. *Jimmie the Kid: The Life of Jimmie Rodgers*. New York: Da Capo Press, 1977.

Pecknold, Diane. *The Selling Sound: The Rise of the Country Music Industry*. Durham, NC: Duke University Press, 2007.

Perkins, Carl, and David McGee. *Go Cat Go: The Life and Times of Carl Perkins*. New York: Hyperion, 1996.

Peterson, Richard A. *Creating Country Music: Fabricating Authenticity*. Chicago: University of Chicago Press, 1997.

Pierce, Patricia Jobe. *The Ultimate Elvis: Elvis Presley Day by Day*. New York: Simon and Schuster, 1994.

Plantenga, Bart. *Yodel-Ay-Ee-Oooo: The Secret History of Yodeling Around the World*. New York: Routledge, 2004.

Pleasants, Henry. *The Great American Popular Singers*. New York: Simon and Schuster, 1974.

Pugh, Ronnie. *Ernest Tubb: The Texas Troubadour*. Durham, NC: Duke University Press, 1996.

Porterfield, Nolan. *Jimmie Rodgers: The Life and Times of America's Blue Yodeler*. Jackson: University Press of Mississippi, 2007; Champaign: University of Illinois Press, 1979.

———. *Jimmie Rodgers* (book accompanying *Jimmie Rodgers: The Singing Brakeman* CD box set). Hamburg, Germany: Bear Family Records, 1992.

Robinson, Ray. *American Original: A Life of Will Rogers*. New York: Oxford University Press, 1996.

Rodgers, Carrie. *My Husband, Jimmie Rodgers*. Nashville, TN: Country Music Foundation Press, 1995; San Antonio, TX: San Antonio Southern Library Institute, 1935.

Rogers, Will. *Will Rogers' Daily Telegrams, Vol. 2: The Hoover Years*. Stillwater: Oklahoma State University Press, 1978.

———. *Will Rogers' Weekly Articles, Vol. 4: The Hoover Years*. Stillwater: Oklahoma State University Press, 1981.

Rooney, Jim. *Bossmen: Bill Monroe and Muddy Waters.* New York: Da Capo Books, 1991; Dial Press, 1971.

Rosenberg, Neil V., and Charles K. Wolfe. *The Music of Bill Monroe.* Urbana: University of Illinois Press, 2007.

Rothman, Sheila M. *Living in the Shadow of Death: Tuberculosis and the Social Experience of Illness in American History.* New York: Basic Books, 1994.

Russell, Tony. *Blacks, Whites and Blues.* New York: Stein and Day, 1970; republished with additional commentary in *Yonder Come the Blues* by Paul Oliver, Tony Russell, Robert M. W. Dixon, and John Godrich (Cambridge: Cambridge University Press, 2001).

———. *Country Music Originals: The Legends and the Lost.* New York: Oxford University Press, 2007.

Russell, Tony, with additional research by Bob Pinson. *Country Music Records: A Discography 1921–1942.* New York: Oxford University Press, 2004.

Savoy, Ann Allen. *Cajun Music: A Reflection of a People, Volume 1.* Eunice, LA: Bluebird Press, 1984.

Segrest, James, and Mark Hoffman. *Moanin' at Midnight: The Life and Times of Howlin' Wolf.* New York: Pantheon Books, 2004.

Shelton, Robert, with photos by Burt Goldblatt. *The Country Music Story: A Picture History of Country and Western Music.* Indianapolis, IN: Bobbs-Merrill, 1966.

Smith, Richard D. *Can't You Hear Me Callin': The Life of Bill Monroe, Father of Bluegrass.* New York: Little Brown, 2000.

Snow, Hank (the Singing Ranger), with Jack Ownbey and Bob Burns. *The Hank Snow Story.* Champaign: University of Illinois Press, 1994.

Springer, Robert, ed. *Nobody Knows Where the Blues Come From: Lyrics and History.* Jackson: University of Mississippi Press, 2006; particularly the article "That Dry Creek Eaton Clan" by Tom Freeland and Chris Smith.

Stout, William Lawrence. *Theatre in a Tent: The Development of a Provincial Entertainment.* Bowling Green, OH: Popular Press, 1972.

Suzuki, Ramblin' Sho. *The Jimmie Rodgers Data Book (Me and Jimmie Rodgers).* Tokyo, Japan: Self-published, 2002.

Taft, Michael. *Talkin' to Myself: Blues Lyrics 1921–1942.* New York: Routledge, 2005.

Tosches, Nick. *Country: Living Legends and Dying Metaphors in America's Biggest Music.* New York: Charles Scribner's Sons, 1985.

———. *Where Dead Voices Gather* (on Emmett Miller). New York: Little, Brown, 2001.

Townsend, Charles. *San Antonio Rose.* Urbana: University of Illinois Press, 1976.

Tucker, Tanya, with Patsi Bale Cox. *Nickel Dreams: My Life.* New York: Hyperion, 1997.

Wald, Elijah. *Josh White: Society Blues.* Amherst: University of Massachusetts Press, 2000.

Whiteside, Jonny. *Ramblin' Rose: The Life and Career of Rose Maddox.* Nashville, TN: Country Music Foundation/Vanderbilt University Press, 1997.

Whyatt, Bert. *Mugsy Spanner, The Lonesome Road: A Biography and Discography.* New Orleans: Jazzology Press, 1995.

Wolfe, Charles K. *A Good-Natured Riot: The Birth of the Grand Ole Opry*. Nashville, TN: Country Music Foundation Press, 1999.

Wolfe, Charles K., and Ted Olson, eds. *The Bristol Sessions: Writings about the Big Bang of Country Music*. Jefferson, NC: McFadden, 2005; particularly "Jimmie Rodgers and the Bristol Sessions" by John Lilly, "The Legend That Peer Built" by Charles K. Wolfe, and "On the Vanguard of Change" by Thomas Townsend.

Wondrich, David. *Stomp and Swerve: American Music Gets Hot 1843–1924*. Chicago: Chicago Review Press, 2003.

Work, John W., Lewis Wade, and Samuel C. Adams. *Lost Delta Found: Rediscovering the Fisk University–Library of Congress Coahoma County Study, 1941–1942*. Edited by Robert Gordon and Bruce Nemerov. Nashville, TN: Vanderbilt University Press, 2005.

Yagoda, Ben. *Will Rogers: A Biography*. New York: Alfred A. Knopf, 1993.

Zwonitzer, Mark, and Charles Hirshberg. *Will You Miss Me When I'm Gone?: The Carter Family and Their Legacy in American Music*. New York: Simon and Schuster, 2002.

Select Audio and Video Sources

Borgeson, Lillian. Extensive recorded interview with Ralph Peer, 1958, item FT-2774 in the John Edwards Memorial Foundation Collection, University of North Carolina Southern Folklife Collection, Wilson Library, Chapel Hill, NC.

Forbert, Steve. Uncirculated recorded audio interview with Elsie McWilliams, September, 14, 1984, Meridian, MS.

GBN Video Productions. Produced and directed by Gina Neville. Written by Cary Ginell. *Jimmie Rodgers: The Father of Country Music* (television documentary).

credits

Photos

Introduction: *Les Leverett.*

Chapter 1, photos 1 and 2; Chapter 2, photo 1; Chapter 3; Chapter 5, photo 2 (film set); Chapter 6; Chapter 8; Chapter 13: *Jimmie Rodgers Properties I, L.P.*

Chapter 4: *Bear Family Records.*

Chapter 7: *Courtesy of the Country Music Hall of Fame and Museum.*

Chapter 9: *WSM radio publicity photo.*

Chapter 10: *Douglas R. Gilbert, from* Forever Young: Photographs of Bob Dylan (*Da Capo Press, 2005*), *with permission of the author.*

Chapter 11: *Courtesy of Ramona Jones and Mary Dean Wolfe.*

Chapter 12, photo 2: *From the Jimmie Rodgers Festival file, photo #P-1170, Southern Folklife Collection, Wilson Library, University of North Carolina at Chapel Hill.*

Chapter 14: *Rosamond Norbury.*

Chapter 2, photo 2 (with dogs); Chapter 5, photo 1 (with car); Chapter 12, photo 1 (beside train); Chapter 15: *Courtesy of Cara P. Herlin, daughter of Mildred Williamson Pollar and niece of Carrie and Jimmie Rodgers.*

Song Lyric Credits

"Moonlight and Skies" by Jimmie Rodgers and Raymond E. Hall
Copyright 1931 by Peer International Corporation
Copyright Renewed
International Copyright secured. Used by permission. All rights reserved.

"My Carolina Sunshine Girl" by Jimmie Rodgers
Copyright 1929 by Peer International Corporation
Copyright Renewed
International Copyright secured. Used by permission. All rights reserved.

"My Good Gal's Gone Blues" by Jimmie Rodgers
Copyright 1935 by Peer International Corporation
Copyright Renewed
International Copyright secured. Used by permission. All rights reserved.

"(The) Mystery of Number Five" by Jimmie Rodgers
Copyright 1931 by Peer International Corporation
Copyright Renewed
International Copyright secured. Used by permission. All rights reserved.

"Never No Mo' Blues" by Jimmie Rodgers and Elsie McWilliams
Copyright 1928 by Peer International Corporation
Copyright Renewed
International Copyright secured. Used by permission. All rights reserved.

"(The) Passing of Jimmie Rodgers" by Elsie McWilliams
Copyright 1936 by Peer International Corporation
Copyright Renewed
International Copyright secured. Used by permission. All rights reserved.

"T.B. Blues" by Jimmie Rodgers and Raymond E. Hall
Copyright 1931 by Peer International Corporation
Copyright Renewed
International Copyright secured. Used by permission. All rights reserved.

"Train Whistle Blues" by Jimmie Rodgers and Elsie McWilliams
Copyright 1930 by Peer International Corporation
Copyright Renewed
International Copyright secured. Used by permission. All rights reserved.

"Travelin' Blues" by Jimmie Rodgers and Shelly Lee Alley
Copyright 1931, 1943 by Peer International Corporation
Copyright Renewed
International Copyright secured. Used by permission. All rights reserved.

"Waiting for a Train" by Jimmie Rodgers
Copyright 1929 by Peer International Corporation
Copyright Renewed
International Copyright secured. Used by permission. All rights reserved.

Credits

"Prairie Lullaby" by Billy Hill
Copyright 1934 by Peer International Corporation
Copyright Renewed
International Copyright secured. Used by permission. All rights reserved.

"What's It" by Jimmie Rodgers and Jack Neville
Copyright 1930 by Peer International Corporation
Copyright Renewed
International Copyright secured. Used by permission. All rights reserved.

"When Jimmie Rodgers Said Goodbye" by Dwight Butcher and Louis Herscher
Copyright 1933 by Southern Music Publishing Co., Inc.
Copyright Renewed
Used by permission. All rights reserved.
Southern Music Publishing Co., Inc. only controls in the USA.

"When the Cactus is in Bloom" by Jimmie Rodgers
Copyright 1931 by Peer International Corporation
Copyright Renewed
International Copyright secured. Used by permission. All rights reserved.

"Why Did You Give Me Your Love?" by Jimmie Rodgers
Copyright 1935 by Peer International Corporation
Copyright Renewed
International Copyright secured. Used by permission. All rights reserved.

"Why Should I Be Lonely?" by Jimmie Rodgers and Estelle Lovell
Copyright 1932 by Peer International Corporation
Copyright Renewed
International Copyright secured. Used by permission. All rights reserved.

"Yodeling Cowboy" by Jimmie Rodgers and Elsie McWilliams
Copyright 1930 by Peer International Corporation
Copyright Renewed
International Copyright secured. Used by permission. All rights reserved.

index

Note: *Songs with as-recorded title variations in the text appear under the original title here, unless noted; pages with photos appear in italics.*

Abbott, Lynn, and Doug Seroff, 7, 67
Ackerman, Paul, 234
Acuff, Roy, 19, 162–65, 170, 181, 199, 223, 226, 234, 314
Africa's responses to Rodgers: Zulu, 100; Kipsigis' "Chemirocha" songs, 102–3, 107; Kiyuku cowboys, 103, 107; Sierra Leone, 102–3, 107
Alexander, Texas, 53, 60
Alley, Shelly Lee, 144–45
Allman Brothers, 129, 253, 255–56, 289, 299
Almanac Singers, 182, 193
Alvin, Dave, 262–63
Americana and alternative country music, 203, 232, 264–65, 296, 321–22
Anderson, Charles, 67, 82–83
Anthology of American Folk Music and Rodgers, 177–79, 190, 209
"Any Old Time," 71, 157, 168, 190, 208, 213, 229, 232, 240, 276, 293, 304, 319, 322, 333
"Anytime," 71, 230
Arnold, Eddy, 63, 71, 230, 234

Armstrong, Louis, 2, 3–5, 7–9, 56, 61, 186, 283
Atkins, Chet, 221, 231, 256, 275, 287
Austin, Gene, 15, 23–24, 30, 38, 68, 97, 150, 175, 210, 273, 277
Australia's response to Rodgers, 98–100, 224
Autry, Gene, 53, 123, 128, 136, 212, 293, 308; as blue yodeler, 64, 66, 78–79, 83, 116–17, 160, 319; as singing cowboy 136–137, 141, 152, 309
"Away Out on the Mountain," 174, 209

Bad Livers, The, 296, 301
Baker, Willie, 61
Band, The (rock group) 73, 290
Banes, Tex, 99, 224
Bare, Bobby, 129
Barner, Wylie, 60
Beatles, The, 25, 162, 252, 253, 254, 289, 330
Beck (Hansen), 295–96, 301
Beckett, Barry, 289
Belafonte, Harry, 183, 194